iRPP

Founded in 1972, the Institute for Research on Public Policy is an independent, national, non-profit organization. Its mission is to improve public policy in Canada by promoting and contributing to a policy process that is more broadly based, informed and effective.

In pursuit of this mission, the IRPP

- identifies significant public policy questions that will confront Canada in the longer term future and undertakes independent research into these questions;

- promotes wide dissemination of key results from its own and other research activities;

- encourages non-partisan discussion and criticism of public policy issues in a manner which elicits broad participation from all sectors and regions of Canadian society and links research with processes of social learning and policy formation.

The IRPP's independence is assured by an endowment fund, to which federal and provincial governments and the private sector have contributed.

Créé en 1972, l'Institut de recherche en politiques publiques est un organisme national et indépendant à but non lucratif.

L'IRPP a pour mission de favoriser le développement de la pensée politique au Canada par son appui et son apport à un processus élargi, plus éclairé et plus efficace d'élaboration et d'expression des politiques publiques.

Dans le cadre de cette mission, l'IRPP a pour mandat:

- d'identifier les questions politiques auxquelles le Canada sera confronté dans l'avenir et d'entreprendre des recherches indépendantes à leur sujet;

- de favoriser une large diffusion des résultats les plus importants de ses propres recherches et de celles des autres sur ces questions;

- de promouvoir une analyse et une discussion objectives des questions politiques de manière à faire participer activement au débat public tous les secteurs de la société canadienne et toutes les régions du pays, et à rattacher la recherche à l'évolution sociale et à l'élaboration de politiques.

L'indépendance de l'IRPP est assurée par les revenus d'un fonds de dotation auquel ont souscrit les gouvernements fédéral et provinciaux, ainsi que le secteur privé.

INSTITUTE FOR RESEARCH ON PUBLIC POLICY

INSTITUT DE RECHERCHE EN POLITIQUES PUBLIQUES

adapting public policy
to a labour market in transition

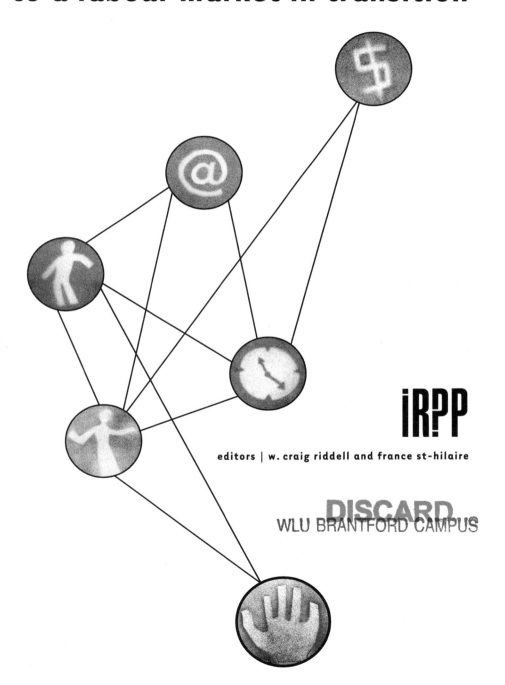

iR?P

editors | w. craig riddell and france st-hilaire

Printed in Canada
Dépôt légal 2000

Bibliothèque nationale du Québec
National Library of Canada

Canadian Cataloguing in Publication Data

Adapting public policy to a labour market in transition

Includes bibliographical references.
ISBN 0-88645-186-8

1. Manpower policy – Canada. I Riddell, W. Craig
(William Craig), 1946- II. St-Hilaire, France   III. Institute for
Research on Public Policy

HD5728.A318 2000 331.12'042'0971 C00-901743-7

Suzanne Ostiguy McIntyre
Vice President, Operations

Copy Editor
Francesca Worrall

Design and Production
Studio Duotone inc.

Cover Illustration
Rossitza Ribarova

Published by
The Institute for Research on Public Policy (IRPP)
l'Institut de recherche en politiques publiques (IRPP)
1470 Peel Street, Suite 200
Montreal, Quebec H3A 1T1

Contents

Acknowledgements i

Introduction and Overview iii
W. Craig Riddell and France St-Hilaire

Chapter 1   The Changing Nature of Work: Implications for Public Policy
Morley Gunderson and W. Craig Riddell

Introduction 1
Establishment of Canadian Labour Laws and Policies 2
Forces Affecting the Changing Nature of Work 4
Employer Responses 10
Employee and Union Responses 18
Policy Responses 20
Emerging Challenges 22

Chapter 2   Employment Outcomes in Canada: A Cohort Analysis
Paul Beaudry and David A. Green

Introduction 39
Data 41
Overall Trends in Employment Outcomes 44
Cohort Analysis of Employment Trends 56
Statistical Analysis 61
Discussion and Conclusions 74

Chapter 3   Human Capital Formation in a Period of Rapid Change
W. Craig Riddell and Arthur Sweetman

Introduction 85
Human Capital Investment: Canada from an International Perspective . . .87
Trends and Developments in Human Capital Formation 93
University Enrolment Rates 111

Labour Market Developments in the 1980s and 1990s 126

Education and Work 128

Summary and Conclusions 134

Chapter 4   Regional Disparities, Mobility and Labour Markets in Canada
Jean-Michel Cousineau and François Vaillancourt

Introduction 143

Theoretical Framework 145

Internal Migration 149

Trends and Changes in Regional Disparities 158

Results 165

Conclusion 168

Chapter 5   Canada and the OECD Hypothesis: Does Labour Market
Inflexibility Explain Canada's High Level of Unemployment?
Peter Kuhn

Introduction 177

One Hypothesis or (at Least) Two? 178

Employment Protection: Cause of Canadian Unemployment? 179

Inflexible Wages: Cause of Canadian Unemployment? 194

Then Why Is Canadian Unemployment So High? 202

Conclusions 202

Chapter 6   Income Redistribution in Canada: Minimum Wages Versus
Other Policy Instruments
Nicole M. Fortin and Thomas Lemieux

Introduction 211

Minimum Wages and the Distribution of Wages 213

The Impact of Minimum Wages and Other Redistributive Programs
on the Distribution of Family Income 223

Conclusion 240

Chapter 7   Reforming the Welfare System: In Search of the Optimal
Policy Mix
Guy Lacroix

Introduction 249

Time Series Evidence on Caseloads and Program Costs 251

The Dynamics of Welfare Participation 257

Incentive Effects of Welfare Programs 266

The Impact of Government-Sponsored Training Programs 271

Conclusion 276

Chapter 8   Public Pension Programs and Labour Force Attachment
Michael Baker and Dwayne Benjamin

Introduction 285

Public Pensions in Canada 287

The Effects of the CPP/QPP on Retirement Behaviour 297

The Effects of Private Pensions 306

Other Linkages with the Labour Market 309

Conclusions 310

Notes on Contributors 314

List of Tables and Figures

Chapter 1

Figure 1   Indicators of Non-Standard Employment in Canada, 1976-1998 23

Figure 2   Non-Standard Employment as a Percentage of Total Employment,
1976-1998 24

Figure 3   Non-Standard Employment as a Percentage of Total Employment, 1998 ..25

Chapter 2

Table 1   Employment-to-Population Rate Differences Between University
and High-School Educated Individuals, 1971-1993 44

Table A1   Employment-to-Population Rate Regressions: Women 78

Table A2   Employment-to-Population Rate Regressions: Men 78

Table A3   Full-Year, Full-Time Employment Rate Regressions: Women 79

Table A4   Full-Year, Full-Time Employment Rate Regressions: Men................79

Table A5   Average (Interrupted) Job Tenure Regressions: Women...................80

Table A6   Average (Interrupted) Job Tenure Regressions: Men 80

Figure 1   Employment-to-Population Ratios by Age, Gender and Education,
               1971-1993 46

Figure 2   Proportion of FYFT Workers by Age, Gender and Education,
               1971-1993 50

Figure 3   Average (Interrupted) Job Tenure by Age, Gender and Education,
               1981-1993 54

Figure 4   Trends of Smoothed Employment-to-Population Rates by Cohort,
               Age, Education and Gender 58

Figure 5   Trends of Smoothed FYFT Employment Rates by Cohort, Age,
               Education and Gender 62

Figure 6   Trends of Smoothed Average (Interrupted) Job Tenure by Cohort,
               Age, Education and Gender 64

Figure 7   Fitted Age-Employment Rate Profiles by Cohort,
               Education and Gender 68

Figure 8   Fitted Age-FYFT Employment Rate Profiles by Cohort,
               Education and Gender 70

Figure 9   Fitted Age-Average Job Tenure Profiles by Cohort,
               Education and Gender 72

Chapter 3

Table 1   Educational Expenditure and Attainment in Canada
               and Selected OECD Countries 88

Table 2   Literacy Skills in Canada and Selected OECD Countries 91

Table 3   Education, Unemployment and Wages by Age and Gender,
               Canada, 1998 92

Table 4   Educational Attainment by Age, Cohort and Gender, Canada,
               1971, 1981 and 1991....................................100

Table 5   Unemployment Rate by Age, Cohort, Education and Gender,
               Canada, 1971, 1981 and 1991 102

Table 6   Weeks Worked by Age, Cohort, Education and Gender, Canada,
               1971, 1981 and 1991....................................104

Table 7   Annual Employment Earnings of Full-Time Employed
               Workers by Age, Cohort, Education and Gender, Canada,
               1971,1981 and 1991 109

Table 8   Annual Employment Earnings of All Workers by Age, Cohort,
               Education and Gender, Canada, 1971,1981 and 1991 110

Table 9   Employment Changes by Educational Attainment, 1980-1995 127

Table 10   Relationship Between Education and Current Job, 1994 129

Table 11   Wage Regression Coefficients for Closeness of Education to Job 130

Table 12   1994 Survey Results on Technological Change
               and Current Employment 132

Table 13	1989 Survey Results on Technological Change and Current Employment	133
Table A1	Educational Attainment by Age, Cohort and Gender for Non-Immigrant Canadians, 1971, 1981 and 1991	138
Table A2	Proportion of the Population Working Full Time/Full Year by Age, Cohort, Education and Gender, Canada, 1971, 1981 and 1991	139
Figure 1	Relative Labour Market Outcomes by Age, Education and Gender, Canada, 1998	96
Figure 2	Educational Attendance by Age and Gender, Canada, 1971, 1981 and 1991	105
Figure 3	Relative Wages by Age, Cohort and Gender, 1970, 1980 and 1990	112
Figure 4	Undergraduate and Graduate Enrolment, Canada, 1971-1995	116
Figure 5	Female Undergraduate Enrolment Rates by Province, 1971-1995	118
Figure 6	Male Undergraduate Enrolment Rates by Province, 1971-1995	120
Figure 7	Female Graduate Enrolment Rates by Province, 1971-1995	122
Figure 8	Male Graduate Enrolment Rates by Province, 1971-1995	124

Chapter 4

Table 1	Summary of Predictions	149
Table 2a	Net Interprovincial Migration by Province/Territory and Gross Flows for Canada, 1970-1995	150
Table 2b	Net Interprovincial Migration Rates by Province/Territory and Gross Migration Rates for Canada, 1970-1995	152
Table 3	Declared Region of Settlement, International Immigrants, Canada, 1981-1995	154
Table 4	Provincial Destination of Interprovincial Migrants, Men, 1991	155
Table 5	The Incidence of Interprovincial Migration by Age and Level of Education, Canada, 1986-1991	156
Table 6	Expected Wage Gains or Losses Associated with Internal Migration Flows by Gender, Canada, 1991	157
Table 7	Results of Model Estimates, Canada, 1972-1994	166
Table A1	Probit Analysis of Internal Migration, Canada, 1986-1991	170
Table A2	Regression Coefficients for Six Canadian Regions	171
Table A3	Testing for Stationarity	172
Figure 1	Personal Income Per Capita by Province Relative to the National Average, Canada, 1972-1995	144
Figure 2	Incidence of Federal Transfer Payments in a Low-Wage, Low-Employment Region	146
Figure 3	Labour Migration from Region A to Region B	147
Figure 4	The Effects of Technological Catch-Up	148

Figure 5   The Coefficient of Variation of Personal Income Per Capita
            by Province (CVPI), Canada, 1972-1994 159

Figure 6   The Coefficient of Variation of the Employment/Population
            Ratio by Province (CVEP), Canada, 1972-1994 160

Figure 7   The Coefficient of Variation of the Participation Rate
            by Province (CVPR), Canada, 1972-1994 161

Figure 8   The Coefficient of Variation of the Unemployment Rate
            by Province (CVUR), Canada, 1972-1994 162

Figure 9   Internal Migration Rate (MR), Canada, 1972-1994 163

Chapter 5

Table 1   Notice Requirements for Termination of Employment in
            Canadian Jurisdictions, 1996 180

Table 2   Changes in Notice Requirements for Termination of Employment
            in Canadian Jurisdictions, 1970-1996 182

Table 3   Permanent Wage Increases Equivalent in Cost to Selected
            Notice Requirements 189

Table 4   Productivity Level of a Redundant Worker Equivalent to a 1 Percent
            Permanent Wage Increase, under Selected Notice Requirements 191

Table 5   Decomposition of the Growth in Mean Weekly Male Earnings,
            Canada, 1981-1992 198

Table 6   Decomposition of the Growth in Mean Weekly Male Earnings,
            US, 1981-1992 199

Figure 1   Real Minimum Wages, Canada and the US, 1981-1996 195

Figure 2   Ratios of Minimum Wages to Average Male Wages, Canada and
            the US, 1981-1992 196

Chapter 6

Table 1   Minimum Wage Relative to the Average Industrial Wage by Province,
            1988, 1993 and 1995 215

Table 2   Characteristics of Low-Wage Workers, Canada, 1988 and 1995 221

Table 3   Percentage of Workers, Hours of Work, and Earnings at the Minimum
            Wage, Canada, 1993 225

Table 4   Distribution of Male Wage-and-Salary Workers and Male Minimum-
            Wage Workers by Age, Education and Family Status, 1993 226

Table 5   Distribution of Female Wage-and-Salary Workers and Female
            Minimum-Wage Workers by Age, Education and Family Status, 1993 ...227

Table 6   Distribution of Minimum-Wage Workers and Earnings by Decile
            of Adjusted Family Income, Canada, 1993 229

Table 7   Average Minimum-Wage Earnings and Government Transfers
            by Decile of Adjusted Family Income, Canada, 1993 232

| Table 8 | Average Minimum-Wage Earnings and Government Transfers by Predicted Decile of Adjusted Family Income, Canada, 1993 | 236 |

Table 8   Average Minimum-Wage Earnings and Government Transfers
           by Predicted Decile of Adjusted Family Income, Canada, 1993.........236

Table 9   Average Wages, Hours of Work and Earnings by Decile of Adjusted
           Family Income, Canada, 1993 238

Table 10   Distribution of Simulated Minimum-Wage Earnings When the Hours Gap
           is Eliminated, by Decile of Adjusted Family Income, Canada, 1993 239

Figure 1   The Impact of Minimum Wages on the Distribution of Hourly Wages
           by Gender, Canada, 1988 and 1995 216

Figure 2   The Impact of Minimum Wages on the Distribution of Male Hourly
           Wages by Region, Canada, 1988 and 1995................................218

Figure 3   The Impact of Minimum Wages on the Distribution of Female Hourly
           Wages by Region, Canada, 1988 and 1995 219

Figure 4   The Impact of Minimum Wages on the Distribution of Hourly
           Wages of Unionized/Nonunionized Workers by Gender, Canada,
           1988 and 1995 220

Figure 5   The Impact of Minimum Wages on the Distribution of Hourly Wages
           of Young Workers by Gender, Canada, 1988 and 1995 222

Figure 6   Minimum-Wage Earnings and Government Transfers as a Proportion
           of Total Income, by Decile of Adjusted Family Income, Canada, 1993 ..234

Figure A1 Density Estimates of Original and Rounded Wages, 1988 243

Chapter 7

Table 1   Social Assistance Program Expenditures and Caseloads,
            Selected Provinces, 1981-1995...251

Table 2   Composition of Welfare Caseloads, Quebec and British Columbia,
            1981-1995 256

Table 3(a) Distribution of Welfare Spells and Exit Rates by Spell Duration,
            Quebec, 1979-1993 260

Table 3(b) Distribution of Welfare Spells and Exit Rates by Spell Duration,
            British Columbia, 1980-1992 261

Table 4(a) Distribution of Off-Welfare Spells and Exit Rates by Spell Duration,
            Quebec, 1979-1993 262

Table 4(b) Distribution of Off-Welfare Spells and Exit Rates by Spell Duration,
            British Columbia, 1980-1992 263

Table 5   Welfare Dependency Index by Household Type, Quebec
            and British Columbia 265

Table 6   Impact of Selected Policy Variables on Welfare Spell Duration
            by Age, Gender and Family Status...270

Figure 1   Welfare Dependency and Unemployment Rates for Adult Males,
            Selected Provinces, 1981-1995...253

Figure 2   Average Welfare Benefits and Dependency Rates,
            Selected Provinces, 1981-1995...254

Chapter 8

Table 1   Old Age Security in Canada and the United States, 1999 288

Figure 1   CPP/QPP Benefits and Contributions per Capita, Canada, 1971-1998 ..290

Figure 2   CPP/QPP Contributions and Benefits per Contributor
and Beneficiary, Canada, 1971-1996 291

Figure 3   Number of CPP/QPP Beneficiaries and Contributors per Capita,
Canada, 1971-1996 292

Figure 4   Population Distribution by Age and Gender, Canada, 1997 294

Figure 5   Male Employment/Nonemployment Transition Hazards
by Age, 1970, 1980 and 1990 295

Figure 6   Female Employment/Nonemployment Transition Hazards
by Age, 1970, 1980 and 1990 296

Figure 7   Employment/Population Ratios by Age and Gender,
Canada, 1971-1995 298

Acknowledgements

We wish to express our appreciation to the contributors to this book for their outstanding work and important contribution to research on labour market issues and the role of public policy. We would also like to thank Francesca Worrall for her help in making fairly technical material accessible to a wider public and Rossitza Ribarova for her meticulous work on the page layout and the numerous charts. For her creativity and innovative design, special thanks to Barbara Rosenstein of Studio Duotone. At IRPP, we benefited from the invaluable production support provided by Chantal Létourneau and Suzanne Ostiguy McIntyre and research assistance from Carlos Del Castillo and Nikolas Bjerre.

W. Craig Riddell and France St-Hilaire

i

Introduction and Overview

W. Craig Riddell and France St-Hilaire

Change is the feature of the Canadian labour market that is most emphasized in current research and policy analysis. Many observers have noted that the economy and labour market are undergoing fundamental structural changes – "deep structural adjustments" in Lipsey's[1] terminology – driven by such factors as technological change associated with information and computer technologies and related phenomena such as the globalization of economic activity. These changes affecting the demand side of the labour market alter not only the skills required by employers and the distribution of economic rewards to workers, but also the nature of work itself. Equally profound developments are taking place on the supply side of the labour market. The gender, age and ethnic composition of the labour force has changed dramatically over the past few decades, as has the industrial and occupational composition of employment. With the population aging and much of the future labour force growth expected to come from net immigration, demographic changes during the next several decades are likely to be just as significant.

In addition to the impact of these powerful forces on the economy and labour market, the experience of the past two decades continues to haunt many Canadians. Simply put, the 1980s and 1990s were the worst two decades of the postwar period in terms of Canada's economic performance. Both periods began with sharp recessions, the effects of which lasted several years. The 1990-92 downturn was especially protracted, and the recovery from this "Great Canadian Slump"[2] was extremely slow. With each recession, unemployment rose

iii

dramatically, and it was not until the end of each decade that the unemployment rate returned to (approximately) its pre-recession level. Since the early 1980s a substantial Canada-US unemployment rate gap has opened up, with the Canadian rate generally being two to four percentage points higher than that of the US.

The 1980s and 1990s were characterized by two other developments. The first was the slowing of real income growth after three decades of substantial increases in living standards. This development was particularly evident in the 1990s, a decade in which the living standards of the average Canadian stagnated or declined and only recovered to 1989 levels by the end of the decade. Also, real income growth in Canada (which had substantially exceeded that in the US during the 1970s) was much lower than that in the US during this period. As a consequence, by 1998 Canadian living standards, relative to those of the US, had fallen to approximately 65 percent (the 1970 level) from about 78 percent in 1980.[3]

The second salient development was the increase in the inequality of market earnings among Canadian workers. As summarized in a recent paper by Riddell,[4] real earnings for Canadian men became less equally distributed around an approximately constant mean, so that those at the bottom of the earnings distribution (generally the less-skilled) suffered declines in real earnings. For women, earnings inequality increased around a rising average, so that those at the bottom of the earnings distribution suffered modest declines in real income while those at the top achieved substantial growth in real earnings. The combined increase in earnings inequality for men and women was much more modest than for each gender separately because the more rapid growth in women's mean real earnings contributed to a significant narrowing of the gender earnings gap and thus to a more equal distribution of earnings overall. Nonetheless, some increase in income inequality is evident for the labour force as a whole.

After two decades of rapid technological and structural change and an overall record of poor economic performance, Canadians need to take stock of this ongoing transformation of the labour market and its implications for public policy. It has been evident for some time that labour and other social policies established decades ago may no longer be adequate or appropriate given the changes that have taken place. However, making the necessary adjustments requires making the distinction between long-term trends and short-run responses to cyclical factors. In many ways, it is only now that we have moved beyond some of the turmoil that we are in a position to make this assessment. For instance, it is becoming apparent that some of the common perceptions about the "new" labour market may not coincide with reality, at least as evidenced by the data. The IRPP asked several leading labour market specialists to examine specific areas of public policy that have generated considerable attention and debate in recent years. The studies in this volume are the result of their work. They provide new evidence on issues of central concern to the well-being of Canadians and a solid assessment of the challenges and avenues for policy reform.

The first chapter, "The Changing Nature of Work: Implications for Public Policy," by Morley Gunderson and Craig Riddell, summarizes evidence on the changing nature of work. It describes the forces leading to these changes, how employers, employees and institutions have responded and the policy implications. A central theme is the need to reassess many current employment policies in order to better address the needs and circumstances arising as a result of a rapidly changing workplace. As the authors point out, the present labour policy framework was essentially established at a time when work could be characterized as stable, male-dominated, blue-collar, manufacturing-oriented and extensively influenced by unionization. It is therefore not surprising that labour legislation and policies relevant then are less than optimal for today's workplace.

The demand side of the labour market has been dramatically affected by the pressures faced by firms in their markets for goods, services and capital. These interrelated pressures include global competition, trade liberalization, technological change, industrial restructuring, greater capital mobility and the prolonged recessions of the early 1980s and 1990s. The responses of employers to these important changes have been significant, both in scope and intensity. As part of their adjustment strategy, organizations have often restructured and engaged in various forms of downsizing, including mass layoffs, plant closings and early retirement programs. Much of the new hiring has been in the form of contractually limited employment, in an effort to put in place a contingent workforce that is flexible and adaptable to rapidly changing needs. More broadly speaking, restructuring has meant that employment is increasingly concentrated in smaller and nonunionized firms. It has also translated into increases in non-standard forms of employment such as multiple-job holding, part-time employment and own-account self-employment.

As Gunderson and Riddell indicate, the adjustment pressures on the Canadian labour market have had significant consequences at an aggregate level. Average real wages have been relatively stagnant since the mid-1970s, and earnings inequality has increased as a result of greater labour market polarization of wages and weeks and hours worked. As the authors point out, the implications of these changes for public policy are significant and wide-ranging. For instance, coverage and enforcement of employment standards legislation and eligibility for various employment-related social benefits are likely to be inadequate among the growing number of workers in small, nonunionized firms and non-standard forms of employment. In addition, even after several years of sustained economic growth, governments continue to struggle with the broader and more difficult consequences of adjustment such as permanent job losses, long-term unemployment, underemployment, wage stagnation and growing wage inequality.

A powerful set of forces has also been at work on the supply side of the labour market as a result of the increased labour force participation of women (especially married women with children), the aging workforce and greater ethnic diversity. As Gunderson and Riddell indicate, these changes have sparked demands for new policy approaches related to childcare, leave and working time arrangements, pensions and retirement, pay and employment equity and antidiscrimination provisions. For instance, they point to the trend toward alternative work-time arrangements such as flextime, compressed workweeks, jobsharing, unpaid leave and permanent part-time jobs as labour market responses to changing needs and diverse preferences. Yet, they argue, it is not clear that the current policy framework is well suited (or flexible enough) to respond or adapt to these new realities. A further challenge for policy makers is to reconcile the (often) diverging needs of employers and employees.

In addition to the policy issues raised as a result of demand- and supply-side pressures in the labour market, the authors also examine the effects of these forces on the institutional environment. Globalization, particularly the increased mobility of capital, has clearly had an impact on governments' ability to intervene effectively and the choice of instruments at their disposal. The deunionization trend in the US and other competitiveness issues have also increased the pressure for a less regulated, more flexible business environment. In addition, real constraints remain on the fiscal side. As a result, governments have been looking to play more of a facilitating role in the adjustment process. There has also been a tendency to transfer responsibility for certain functions to lower levels of government or the private sector. As for actual policy changes in response to new circumstances, Gunderson and Riddell describe these as "tinkering at the margin" and conclude that fundamental rethinking about a variety of emerging challenges is still required. They point to the need for more systematic evidence about the myths and realities of the "new" labour market and emphasize the role of government in addressing market failures related to training and information externalities, in fostering workplace innovations and, most importantly, in dealing with equity and distributional issues. The authors also stress the importance of designing policies that will work in conjunction with market forces in order to achieve broader social objectives. They conclude by arguing that labour and human resources policies should no longer be viewed only as reactive adjustment measures, but rather as integral parts of a coherent and proactive economic strategy.

The growing concern in recent years over worsening employment outcomes is generally based on the perception that fundamental changes in the Canadian labour market have led to a deterioration of long-term prospects for youth entering the job market. In chapter 2, "Employment Outcomes in Canada: A Cohort Analysis," Paul Beaudry and David Green examine the access to and quality of employment in different cohorts of Canadian youths as they enter and work their way through the labour market.[5] By examining how different birth cohorts fare in the labour market over time, the authors are able to differentiate aging effects from more permanent differences among older and younger workers. They also control for cyclical variations in economic activity in order to focus on the long-term trends in the labour market.

Beaudry and Green investigate the outcomes of two skill groups: the high-school educated and the university educated. Their analysis is based on three separate employment outcome measures: employment-to-population ratios, the proportion of workers employed full-year, full-time (FYFT) and average job tenure. Looking at the trends by age group and gender over the 1971-93 period, the authors find that according to all indicators there has been a significant deterioration in the employment situation of less-educated men. The decline is evident in all age groups, but those between the ages 25 and 34 have fared worst. The data also suggest somewhat negative trends for university educated men, especially in comparison with women's employment outcomes over the same period. Less-educated women have benefited from rapid increases in both employment and FYFT employment and have made generally positive gains in job tenure. University educated women have also made impressive gains in employment rates and have done well in securing stable jobs. But for both groups of women, there appears to have been a slowdown (or even a reversal in some cases) in the rate of progress in the early 1990s.

The evidence also suggests increasing differences between age groups over time, with younger, less-educated individuals falling behind older individuals with the same level of education. As the authors point out, such observations raise important concerns about the prospects for recent labour market entrants. For instance, can it be assumed that young, less-educated workers will eventually catch up with the somewhat better performance of their older counterparts? Are the poor employment outcomes for many groups in the 1990s a consequence of the prolonged recession or are they a long-term trend? Are younger workers likely to be scarred by these labour market conditions?

The cohort-based analysis provides important evidence on these issues. For women in both skill groups, the broad pattern in terms of all three outcome measures is one of substantial improvements up to the 1980s, followed by stagnation. Generally, the results show improved employment outcomes and increased stability for women over time. Also, once the cyclical effects are netted out, the data indicate a leveling off rather than actual declines in outcomes for younger women. The results for high-school educated men, however, are more alarming. The overall trend is one of reduced access to employment and, for those who are employed, of reduced access to FYFT work. Moreover, the data reveal both poorer outcomes for more recent cohorts of labour market entrants at all ages and worsening outcomes for older cohorts. According to Beaudry and Green, the worsening employment prospects of high-school educated men of all ages should be an object of considerable policy concern. In 1993, this group represented 52 percent of men over the age of 15 and this does not even include the least skilled individuals (i.e., those with only an elementary-school education). Their results suggest that a substantial portion of Canada's youth could face a future of uncertain and unstable employment.

As for university educated men, the results are mixed. The employment-rate profiles show declines for all cohorts in recent years, although not nearly as large as those experienced by less-educated men. On the other hand, once cyclical effects are removed there is little evidence of a substantial worsening of FYFT employment outcomes for university educated men. Also, the current perception that younger generations take longer to move into a stable working pattern appears unfounded: Beaudry and Green's results reveal the same pattern of gradual entry into the FYFT track across all cohorts.

The growth in non-standard employment and contract work is often cited as evidence of increased instability in the labour market. But Beaudry and Green's analysis of job tenure data reveals no evidence to that effect. Their results indicate that average job tenure outcomes across successive cohorts have either been improving or quite stable for all cohort, gender and education groups. They point out, however, that job tenure data would not reflect trends such as increases in the number of workers on short-term contracts in cases where these contracts are repeatedly renewed. Similarly, the effects of increased layoffs on job tenure data may be offset by fewer quits by dissatisfied workers during periods of high unemployment. Yet both sets of circumstances would likely contribute to greater perceived instability. More generally, workers may feel less secure in an environment where income support programs are less generous or less accessible, average unemployment spells longer and jobs harder to find.

Beaudry and Green thus consider their results to be a starting point in the evaluation of job instability rather than the last word. Overall, they find only limited evidence of secular increases in instability among women and more-educated individuals. For these groups of workers, they argue, one needs to look at factors other than employment outcomes for the source of perceptions of increased instability. The employment prospects for high-school educated men, on the other hand, are quite worrisome and should be the focus of greater attention on the part of policy makers.

The link between skills, education and labour market outcomes is also at issue in chapter 3, "Human Capital Formation in a Period of Rapid Change," by Craig Riddell and Arthur Sweetman. Although the development of human capital is increasingly viewed as a source of comparative advantage in the new economy, there is still considerable debate over the causal aspects of recent labour market trends and the appropriate policy response and direction for our education and training systems. For instance, there are two contrasting explanations for the substantial increase in the educational attainment of the Canadian population over the past several decades. Many consider this increase to be related to technological change and increased globalization, which generate greater demand for highly skilled workers and reduce opportunities for those with lower levels of education. This is the "relative-demand shift" theory. The other explanation, the "overeducation and underemployment" theory, focuses on the recessions, downsizing and restructuring of the 1980s and 1990s and the resulting deterioration of labour market prospects for young adults. According to this theory, young Canadians have been investing heavily in education not only because job opportunities are lacking, but also because employers facing an excess supply of labour are inflating skill requirements and, in the process, upgrading their workforces. Riddell and Sweetman document some of the key trends and developments in human capital formation in Canada over the past three decades and assess which of these two views is more consistent with the Canadian experience.

Several conclusions emerge from their comprehensive analysis. The data show that based on international comparisons Canada devotes considerable resources to education. As a result, its population is among the most highly educated of all the OECD countries. Canada also ranks highly in terms of literacy skills, particularly among young adults and the well-educated. An examination of decennial censuses shows rapid and substantial improvements over the 20-year period. For instance, almost 40 percent of men and women who were in their 40s in 1971 had less than a grade-eight education compared with only three to four percent of those who were in their 20s in 1991. The proportion of university graduates has doubled, and the proportional increase in college and trades certification has been almost as large. As a result, the proportion of Canada's adult population with postsecondary education reached almost one-half in 1995, the highest rate among OECD countries and substantially above that of the US. Also, the educational attainment of women has been increasing much more rapidly than that of men, and this trend, combined with women's higher rate of return on education, has contributed to narrowing the earnings gap between the genders.

Looking at various indicators of labour market outcomes by level of educational attainment is also revealing. The data show that throughout the 1980s and 1990s those with postsecondary education experienced high rates of employment growth, while employment generally declined for those with elementary and secondary schooling. As Riddell and Sweetman point out, these employment differentials do not just reflect education-level differences between younger and older cohorts, they are also observed within the younger cohorts. The unemployment rate among highly educated workers also remained below that of less-educated workers, so even though unemployment increased for the labour force as a whole during this period, the gap between the groups widened. This unemployment-rate differential is all the more important given the massive increase in the availability of more-educated workers, which was compounded by the demographics of the baby boom and the increased labour force participation of women during this period. The data also indicate a decline in the number of weeks worked by less-educated men and more generally a growing gap in the amount of labour (weeks of work) provided by more- and less-educated workers.

Riddell and Sweetman consider the overall behaviour of the Canadian labour market during the period under study to be consistent with a situation of steadily increasing demand for skilled labour, along with decreasing demand for less-skilled workers. The data also suggest that during the 1970s the growth in the supply of more-educated workers exceeded the growth in demand, whereas in the 1980s the supply and the demand grew at similar rates. The authors conclude that overall the evidence seems to support the "relative-demand shift" theory. In addition, they point out that because the supply response was sufficiently large to offset the substantial growth in demand for skilled labour, there was only a modest increase in the earnings differential between more- and less-educated individuals. The labour-supply shift not only increased the number of more-educated workers, it also decreased the supply of less-educated workers, thus reducing the effects of downward pressures on their wages and employment prospects. This, the authors suggest, explains why earnings inequality between the more- and less-educated did not increase as much in Canada as it did in the United States.

Finally, Riddell and Sweetman find little evidence to support the "overeducation or underemployment" theory. Based on trends in university enrolment rates, there is no indication that students remain in or return to school because of poor labour market opportunities. Survey results indicate that highly educated Canadians generally don't consider themselves to be underemployed, and they tend to see their work and education as closely related. There is also evidence of a large wage premium associated with a close education-work relationship. Moreover, the authors find that the earnings of university graduates are typically 35 to 60 percent greater than those of high-school graduates, whereas the earnings premium of nonuniversity postsecondary graduates is in the range of 10 to 20 percent.

In chapter 4, "Regional Disparities, Mobility and Labour Markets in Canada," Jean-Michel Cousineau and François Vaillancourt examine the relative impact of migration, technology and federal transfers on the evolution of regional disparities in Canada. There was a significant degree of convergence in personal income per capita by province between 1972 and 1995, and in theory a number of factors may have contributed to this convergence. For instance, the appropriate level of labour mobility from low-wage and low-employment regions to high-wage and high-employment regions has the potential to reduce provincial income disparities. Technological catch-up and the redistributive effects of federal transfers may also be part of the explanation. Determining the relative importance of these factors would of course help improve the role of public policy in this process. Moreover, the appropriate policy mix may differ depending on whether the objective is to reduce income disparities or other forms of regional inequality such as employment and unemployment disparities.   xi

Cousineau and Vaillancourt begin their analysis with an examination of internal migration trends between 1970 and 1995. As the data show, interprovincial migration has played and continues to play a significant role in the geographic allocation and reallocation of the labour force in Canada. For instance, over the 25-year period British Columbia gained half a million people while Quebec lost more than 450,000 through interprovincial migration. However, there has also been a substantial reduction in the gross migration rate from 19.4 to 11.2 migrants per thousand. The labour force flows are mostly as expected, from Eastern Canada to Ontario and from Ontario and the Prairies to Alberta and British Columbia. The authors find a higher propensity to move among the younger and more educated members of the labour force. Individuals who are bilingual or single also tend to be more mobile. Their estimates of the returns to migration are for the most part consistent with observed patterns of mobility. For instance, they find that moving from Atlantic Canada or Quebec to Ontario as well as from Manitoba and Saskatchewan to Alberta and British Columbia increases gross expected wages. On the other hand, moving from Ontario to

Alberta or British Columbia decreases gross expected wages, which suggests these moves may be motivated by other reasons. While the overall pattern of internal migration in Canada is consistent with the standard predictions of economic theory, questions remain about the extent to which labour mobility has contributed to the reduction of regional income disparities relative to other factors and whether the decline in migration rates is due to reduced incentives or some other change.

Based on an empirical model, Cousineau and Vaillancourt further analyze the determinants of migration and estimate the relative impact of migration, transfers and technology on the evolution of employment, unemployment and income disparities. They find that while the aging of the Canadian population is a significant factor in explaining the downward trend in the internal migration rate, as much as 40 percent of the variation is attributable to the decrease in regional income inequalities. At the same time, they find that migration has also had a positive and significant effect in reducing disparities in personal income per capita. On the other hand, more migration tends to increase both employment- and participation-rate differentials and has little effect on unemployment disparities among provinces. Their estimates also indicate that federal government transfers have contributed both directly and indirectly to reducing regional income disparities. However, the results show that overall these two factors played a relatively modest role and that technological catch-up is by far the most important factor, explaining as much as two-thirds of the observed convergence in personal income per capita by province.

According to Cousineau and Vaillancourt, these results confirm the relative importance of technological diffusion (along with the accumulation of physical and human capital) as an instrument for achieving growth objectives and further reducing regional income inequalities in Canada. In their view, there is a need for greater emphasis on policies to facilitate the diffusion of the best technologies throughout the country and to ensure the necessary adjustments in education and training policies.

In chapter 5, "Canada and the OECD Hypothesis: Does Labour Market Inflexibility Explain Canada's High Level of Unemployment?" Peter Kuhn addresses the issue of policy-induced rigidities in the labour market. The paper provides a critical review and assessment of the well-known hypothesis put forward by the OECD that rigid labour markets are more prone to unemployment and may be the source of the current unemployment differential between the US and other countries, including Canada. As Kuhn usefully points out at the outset, the labour-market-inflexibility hypothesis refers to two distinct and unrelated sources of rigidity and the policies and institutions associated with each.[6] One concerns restrictions on firms' ability to adjust the quantity of labour they employ as a result of employment protection laws (EPLs). The other concerns the lack of flexibility in real wages due to restrictions on the price of labour imposed by minimum-wage laws and unions. The author examines each potential source of rigidity in turn, reviewing both the theoretical issues and empirical evidence to determine their relevance in explaining high Canadian unemployment.

Based on comparisons of US and Canadian unemployment trends during the 1980s and 1990s and the greater level of employment protection provided in Canada, the quantity version of the labour-market-rigidity hypothesis would appear to have some validity. As Kuhn's analysis shows, however, there are theoretically as many reasons to expect EPLs to raise employment in the long term as to lower it. The intuition behind the expected negative employment effects of EPLs is that in raising the cost of dismissal, they raise the expected cost of hiring workers and cause employers to be more reluctant to hire in uncertain circumstances. But in a period of downturn, by making layoffs more expensive, EPLs are likely to raise employment levels relative to what they would have been otherwise. Since these direct and indirect effects can offset one another, the net effect on average employment levels will depend on the state of demand and a variety of other factors. In addition, Kuhn argues, standard labour demand models have several important limitations that should be taken into account when analyzing the effects of EPLs. For instance, the fact that employers may pass costs associated with EPLs on to workers in the form of lower wages or compensatory adjustments in employment-related benefits (e.g., private pension plans or severance-pay provisions) would tend to reduce the expected negative effects on employment and unemployment. Moreover, to the extent that they provide workers with benefits of value, EPLs may increase workers' willingness to work at any given wage.

As Kuhn argues, it is also important to recognize that mandatory advance notices, the most common form of EPL, operate very differently from a cash tax on layoffs, as implied by various models. For instance, in cases where firms possess private information about their closure or layoff plans that they would not otherwise share with workers, mandatory-notice laws can be seen to partially correct a pre-existing labour market distortion, namely asymmetric information, and may even accelerate the economic adjustment process. Evidence also indicates that advance-notice laws directly reduce unemployment by providing workers with a predisplacement job search period that makes it possible for them to find new jobs prior to becoming unemployed. Kuhn also produces estimates of the costs to firms of EPLs and concludes that the economic costs of Canadian advance-notice requirements are quite trivial relative to any policy that raises wages across the board. Moreover, firms can easily avoid these costs through alternative means of adjustments. Finally, stringent EPLs in Canada do not appear to have had inhibiting effects on the reallocation of labour across firms and industries, as this process occurs at about the same pace in Canada as in the US.

The second source of labour market inflexibility examined in this chapter is wage rigidity associated with minimum-wage laws and unions. It is well known that union membership and coverage are greater in Canada than the US. As for minimum wages, in the US there was a markedly more pronounced deterioration in the real minimum wage between 1981 and 1996 than there was in Canada, where the losses experienced during the 1980s were largely recovered by 1996. According to the wage-rigidity hypothesis, countries with centralized collective-bargaining systems or high and binding minimum-wage laws are less able to adjust to technology- or trade-based decreases in the demand for unskilled workers by reducing their wages. As a result, these countries are more likely to face high and persistent unemployment. According to Kuhn, the relevant issue in this case is not whether the high wages associated with unions and/or minimum-wage laws result in a higher level of unemployment, but whether and to what extent these institutionally determined wages respond to negative demand shocks. The author presents tentative evidence that Canada has exhibited a non-negligible amount of real wage flexibility in its unskilled labour market since the early 1980s. For instance, between 1981 and 1992 the real weekly earnings of men in the bottom quintile fell more in Canada than they did in the US. While this partly reflects a decrease in hours worked, the data also indicate that hourly wages declined by about 15 percent in both countries over the same period. As Kuhn points out, since much of the decrease occurred at wage levels that are well above the minimum wage, it is unlikely that it could have moderated much of this decline.

Based on his detailed analysis of Canadian labour markets, Kuhn finds little evidence of the constraining effects of either quantity or price rigidities. He concludes that neither are likely to explain a large part of the unemployment gap between the US and Canada. Rather, the source of the disparity probably resides in factors other than differences in employment protection, unionization levels and minimum wages. He points to differences in the types of demand shock faced by the two countries, tighter monetary policy in Canada in the late 1980s and early 1990s and elements of the Canadian social safety net such as the incentive effects of the employment insurance program as more satisfactory explanations.[7]

adapting public policy to a labour market in transition

In chapter 6, "Income Redistribution in Canada: Minimum Wages Versus Other Policy Instruments," Nicole Fortin and Thomas Lemieux investigate the contribution of minimum-wage legislation to the reduction of inequality in Canada and compare its redistributive impact to that of other policy instruments such as social assistance (SA) and unemployment insurance (UI). The potentially adverse effects on employment that have long been the basis of arguments against minimum wages are the subject of much research and debate. In Lemieux and Fortin's view, these negative efficiency effects should also be assessed relative to the potentially beneficial redistributive impact of minimum wages. The authors present new evidence on two fronts: (1) the incidence of the minimum wage on the distribution of wages and (2) the effects of the minimum wage on the distribution of family income in Canada.

Fortin and Lemieux provide striking graphical evidence that the minimum wage has a significant impact on the shape of the bottom end of the wage distribution. This impact appears to have been more important in 1995 than in 1988, because both the value of minimum wages relative to average manufacturing wages and the proportion of hours worked at low wages increased during this period. The change is particularly important for young workers, who witnessed a dramatic decline in their labour market opportunities. According to the authors, in the mid-1990s minimum wages played an important role as a wage floor for women and for young men, and as such may have helped reduce the wage gap between men and women and between the young and old. It could even be argued, notwithstanding any disemployment effects, that minimum wages to some extent counteracted the effects of increases in low-wage jobs on wage inequality.

In measuring the importance of minimum wages as a transfer program, Fortin and Lemieux point out that only six percent of wage-and-salary workers in Canada earn the minimum wage. The proportions of hours worked at the minimum wage (3.6 percent) and of wages earned by minimum-wage workers (1.5 percent) are even less significant. The reason for this is that minimum-wage workers work fewer hours and have much lower wages than the rest of the workforce. The minimum wage can thus be considered a small program. However, as the authors argue, this small program could still have a sizable effect on specific groups of low-wage workers. In particular, they find that minimum-wage employment and earnings are disproportionately concentrated among young workers, women and the less educated.

By exploring the link between the incidence of the minimum wage and adjusted family income (a measure of economic well-being based on individual family income-to-needs ratios), Fortin and Lemieux are able to compare the redistributive impact of the minimum wage with that of major transfer programs.

They find that more than 67 percent of minimum-wage workers are concentrated in the first five deciles of family income. It is also interesting to note that there are more minimum-wage workers in the second (13.9 percent) and third (16.7 percent) deciles than in the first (12.5 percent). Evidence suggests that the poorest families tend to be poor because individuals in these families tend to work very little, if at all. Indeed, according to the authors, the number of hours worked plays a greater role than wage levels in explaining low family income.

The comparisons with various transfer programs are quite revealing. With 68 percent of minimum-wage earnings in the lower half of the income distribution, the minimum wage is found to be almost as progressive as all government transfer programs considered together and more progressive than UI. Social assistance, on the other hand, is more clearly targeted at individuals in the two lowest deciles. Nevertheless, as the authors point out, aggregate minimum-wage earnings are three times lower than SA and five times smaller than UI. In their view, it is the small size of the minimum wage program that explains its modest redistributive impact compared with other government transfer programs. This perspective differs sharply from the argument made by some that it is because minimum-wage earners are drawn from all levels of family income that the link between the two is relatively weak.

Fortin and Lemieux see an even greater role for minimum wages as a redistributive policy instrument in the future, particularly given the significant cutbacks in income transfer programs since 1993 and the increase in low-wage jobs. In addition, the continuing emphasis on training and employability measures as part of welfare reforms in most provinces is likely to translate into substantial increases in the hours worked by individuals at the bottom end of the income distribution. Since many of these individuals are likely to work at the minimum wage, they argue, the redistributive impact of minimum wages could become more pronounced in the years to come.

Chapter 7, "Reforming the Welfare System: In Search of the Optimal Policy Mix," by Guy Lacroix, addresses some of the more controversial issues associated with welfare reform. As is the case in many countries, welfare programs in Canada have come under more scrutiny over the past decade as a result of unprecedented increases in caseloads and the resulting demands on the public purse. In Canada, the situation has been exacerbated by the tug-of-war between federal and provincial governments over funding and jurisdictional responsibilities for social assistance and the interaction and cost shifting between welfare and unemployment insurance programs. Trends such as the growing proportion of able-bodied individuals among welfare claimants and the dramatic increase in the average length of time spent on welfare (welfare spells) have added to these concerns. Mounting pressures for welfare reform have stemmed from the need to control escalating program costs and also a growing concern that the increase in caseloads may in part be a function of the system itself.

Lacroix provides a comprehensive overview of the evolution of and changes in the composition of caseloads over time in two provinces, Quebec and British Columbia. Looking at data for 1981-95, he finds a strong correlation between unemployment and welfare dependency in Quebec and BC, but finds little evidence of a link between dependency rates and welfare benefit levels. In both provinces the most striking change in the composition of caseloads over time is in the proportion of employable beneficiaries. In BC, the proportion increased from 38 to 56 percent between 1981 and 1985 and was up to 64 percent in 1995, while in Quebec, where the increase was even greater (from 41 to 72 percent between 1975 and 1979), 78 percent of claimants were classified as employable by 1995.

In comparing the dynamics of welfare participation by able-bodied recipients in Quebec and BC, Lacroix finds common patterns as well as puzzling differences. For instance, even though the two provinces fall under the same UI program and have similar welfare programs, the data show that the average spell duration is much longer in Quebec than in BC. On the other hand, return rates are much lower in Quebec, and time spent off welfare is much shorter in BC. In both provinces, however, there is evidence of negative duration dependence, that is, the probability of individuals leaving welfare decreases the longer the period of time they spend on it, and similarly, the longer individuals remain off welfare, the less likely they are to return. Overall, the data show significant flows into and out of welfare, with most individuals experiencing relatively short spells. In these cases, Lacroix argues, the welfare system can be viewed as fulfilling its intended role of providing temporary relief to needy individuals. But the results also show that over time an increasing proportion of those on welfare experience longer spells and account for a disproportionate share of program expenditures. Although long-term recipients can be found in all household categories, they are more likely to be single parents. The dependency index for this group is twice as large as that for any other household category in both provinces, largely because these individuals have both longer welfare spells and shorter stays off welfare. In Lacroix's view, the policy implications of these results are quite clear: welfare services and interventions should target entrants who return to the program within a year or so of leaving, to encourage them to make another attempt at economic independence. It would also appear that in order to reduce recidivism, the crucial period to intervene with postprogram assistance is in the first six months.

xvii

Lacroix also surveys the literature on the incentive effects of welfare programs and the impact of training programs in Canada and elsewhere. Recent evidence indicates that individuals are sensitive to program parameters in their decisions to participate in and remain on welfare. However, while it is clear that parameters such as benefit levels and UI availability do matter, he concludes that too little is known about incentive effects in the Canadian context to make any strong statements about the extent to which they directly affect caseloads. As for training programs, the consensus emerging in the US is that few programs have a significant impact on the outcomes of participants, although it does appear that well-targeted programs usually perform much better and can make a difference. The results of European studies are generally consistent with those of US studies. As for the situation in Canada, Lacroix points out that there are still too few studies available to draw any conclusions.

The final chapter is "Public Pensions and Labour Force Attachment," by Michael Baker and Dwayne Benjamin. Of particular relevance in the present context is whether policy makers can, through changes in the parameters of the CPP/QPP, influence the labour market participation and retirement decisions of older Canadians. The authors begin with an overview of basic trends in working patterns and the financial state of public pension programs. As a pay-as-you-go system, the balance sheet of the CPP/QPP has been dramatically affected by the aging population, increased labour force participation of women and the trend toward early retirement. These demographic factors and changes in the structure of the labour market have caused significant shifts in the ratio of pension plan contributors to beneficiaries. Since 1982 there has been a growing gap between annual benefits and contributions,[8] a pattern that has only recently begun to subside as a result of significant increases in contribution rates.

The figures presented in the paper are quite striking. In both the CPP and QPP jurisdictions, the number of retirees per capita has gone up by a factor of six since 1971. A related measure, the number of contributors per retirement beneficiary, has fallen from over 30 in 1971 to four today. According to the authors, demographic trends also point to continuing increases in the number of retirees per capita for the next 25 to 30 years. Moreover, these age-structure effects are being compounded by the long-term trend toward early retirement. While in 1970 roughly 70 percent of men aged 60 to 64 worked in an average week, by 1995 the proportion had fallen to 40 percent. The trend for women is less dramatic. However, looking at retirement hazards for men and women in 1970, 1980 and 1990, there is evidence that the probability of retiring after age 65 is falling slightly over time, while the probability of retiring before age 65 appears to be rising. The data also show that the introduction of early retirement provisions in the CPP/QPP in the mid-1980s had a significant impact on the number of beneficiaries. This leads to the broader issue of whether the pressure on public pensions can be reduced by setting the parameters of pension plans to compensate for the effects of demographic shifts or influence labour market participation trends.

Drawing on the recent literature on the impact of changes in public pensions in Canada and the US, Baker and Benjamin analyze the links between public pension parameters such as age of retirement, early retirement provisions, retirement tests and labour force behaviour. They conclude that retirement behaviour largely depends on factors other than public pension plans. For instance, the early retirement trend appears to be largely driven by changing preferences and the accumulation of private wealth. Factors like health and labour market opportunities (which may be quite poor for some older workers) also play a significant role in individuals' retirement decisions. According to the authors, there is little consistent evidence that changing the official retirement age or the initial age of retirement strongly influences people's employment decisions, at least within the short time span needed to have a positive impact on pension plan deficits. They point out that increasing the age of retirement could still improve the bottom line, but it would do so mainly by reducing the volume of benefits paid. Evidence shows that when retired Canadians are offered the opportunity to initiate early retirement benefits, they tend to take it. Delaying their benefits will not affect the retirement decision, but it will reduce the amount of benefits collected. A delayed retirement age might also help, to the extent that those who initiate retirement benefits early are advantaged by existing actuarial adjustments.

Based on Baker and Benjamin's analysis, the prospects of policy makers influencing retirement rates through pension-program measures appear rather limited. Recent attempts to address unsustainable budget imbalances in public pension plans have focused primarily on large increases in contribution rates. However, as the authors remind us, we know relatively little about the labour market effects of these types of policy changes. Given their magnitude, they are unlikely to be entirely neutral. In Baker and Benjamin's view, this further highlights the need to learn more about the two-way linkages between pension policy – both public and private – and the labour market, especially in the context of an aging population.

Notes

1. Richard G. Lipsey, "Economic Growth, Technological Change, and Canadian Economic Policy," *C.D. Howe Institute Benefactors Lecture*, 1996 (Toronto: C.D. Howe Institute, 1996).

2. Pierre Fortin, "The Great Canadian Slump," *Canadian Journal of Economics*, Vol. 29 (November 1996), pp. 761-87.

3. Pierre Fortin, "The Canadian Standard of Living: Is There a Way Up?" *C.D. Howe Institute Benefactors Lecture*, 1999 (Toronto: C.D. Howe Institute, 1999).

4. W. Craig Riddell, "Canadian Labour Market Performance in International Perspective," *Canadian Journal of Economics*, Vol. 32 (November 1999), pp. 1097-1134.

5. This paper is a companion study to their analysis of cohort patterns in Canadian earnings. See Paul Beaudry and David A. Green, "Cohort Patterns in Canadian Earnings and the Skill-Biased Technical Change Hypothesis," *Canadian Journal of Economics*, forthcoming.

6. Note that Kuhn's assessment does not include the possible role of income-support programs such as EI/UI and welfare/social assistance, which some analysts have suggested may contribute to labour market inflexibility and it is often argued, play a role in differences between the labour market performance of Canada, the US and Europe.

7. The contribution of these factors is examined in more detail in W. Craig Riddell and Andrew Sharpe (eds.), "The Canada-US Unemployment Rate Gap," *Canadian Public Policy*, Vol. 24, Supplement 1 (February 1998), and Riddell, "Canadian Labour Market Performance in International Perspective."

8. Of course, earlier CPP/QPP contribution and benefit rate policies have also played a role.

xx

The Changing Nature of Work: Implications for Public Policy

Morley Gunderson and W. Craig Riddell

Introduction

Current labour policies were often established in eras when the nature of work was quite different from what it is today. It would therefore be surprising if the labour legislation and policies that were relevant then are the most appropriate for the workplace of today. As we stated in a previous publication:

> "The changing nature of the labour market means that new strategies and directions must be entertained. What was appropriate for a work-force dominated by males working '9 to 5' in a tariff-protected job in a fixed work site with a reasonable degree of job continuity may be less appropriate for today's workforce. Rapid change gives rise to obsolescence not only of plant, equipment and skills, but also of policies."[1]

The dramatic nature of the changes in the world of work are illustrated by the phrases used to describe that change: the transformation of industrial relations; re-engineering the workplace; reinventing government. To the extent that these are accurate descriptors, they would imply the need for transforming, re-engineering and reinventing the labour policies that govern the changing nature of work.

There is general recognition that in today's competitive, global environment, it is necessary to develop strategic responses to survive. This is certainly true of employers as they develop niche markets and try to ensure that their human resource policies are consistent with their competitive strategies. It is also true of employees and their unions, whose very survival may depend upon strategic responses to the changing conditions they face. If active strategic responses to the changing conditions are crucial for employers and employees, they are probably also appropriate for governments in adjusting the legislative and regulatory framework within which labour and management interact.

New problems require new solutions, and this applies as much to labour policy as to other policy areas. The purpose of this paper is to analyze the changes in the nature of work and the implications of these changes for public policy. The paper begins with a discussion of the conditions surrounding various aspects of Canadian labour laws and policies when they were established. The emphasis is on whether those conditions are likely to prevail today. Forces contributing to the changes in the nature of work are then described, paying particular attention to those changes that have important implications for public policy. The paper then highlights the responses to these pressures by the three main actors – employers, employees and their unions, and governments. It concludes with a discussion of the emerging challenges in the area of workplace change and policy responses.

Establishment of Canadian Labour Laws and Policies

The labour policies[2] in place today were generally established at a time when work could be characterized as stable, male dominated, blue collar, manufacturing oriented and extensively influenced by unionization. Collective bargaining legislation in Canada, for example, had its origins around the turn of the century and focused mainly on craft unions. Its current form, which focuses more on industrial unions, was heavily influenced by the 1935 US Wagner Act and consolidated in Canada in 1944 under the Wartime Labour Relations Regulations (PC 1003) and the Industrial Relations and Disputes Investigations Act of 1948. These were subsequently emulated by the various provincial jurisdictions. That legislation was adopted in wartime and under the shadow of the Depression. It was designed to ensure the orderly conduct of collective bargaining in its various phases such as certification, administering the collective agreement and dispute resolution.

Collective bargaining legislation[3] applying to the public sector was formalized in the 1960s, largely under the impetus of the federal Public Service Staff Relations Act of 1967. That legislation followed a period of rapid growth in the public sector. It was, in part, a response to the growing militancy of public sector employees.

Labour standards legislation had its origin in the Factory Acts of the 1880s, and was intended mainly to protect the wages and hours of women and children.

These were consolidated for the general industrial workforce in the early 1900s and dealt with such areas as minimum wages, hours of work and overtime, wage protection, vacations and holidays (introduced in the 1940s) and termination of employment (introduced in the 1970s). The intent was to set minimum standards that would be appropriate for an increasingly industrialized workforce. In fact, the special protective legislation that often applied to females in the earlier years is often viewed as an attempt to protect male jobs by making female workers more costly. As well, the original intent of the labour standards legislation itself may have had as much to do with providing an alternative to unions: if the state could provide certain standards, then workers might be less likely to turn to unions for them.

Human rights and antidiscrimination legislation was generally enacted in the 1950s and 1960s in Canada. It was largely in response to growing labour force participation by women and minorities who wanted to benefit from the expansion that was occurring throughout most of that period.

Occupational health and safety legislation had its origins[4] around the turn of the century, usually with separate statutes for different industries such as mining, construction, logging and manufacturing. In the 1970s in most Canadian jurisdictions they were consolidated into single omnibus statutes, often with separate and detailed regulations for special industries like mining, construction and manufacturing. While the consolidations are recent, the statutes generally deal with the hazards facing workers in conventional industrial work sites and in mining and construction. Whether they are able to deal with the new hazards and occupational diseases associated with information-age technology and non-fixed work sites remains to be seen. Such diseases often have long latency periods and are difficult to attribute to workplace sources.

Workers' compensation legislation was also established early in the 1900s. It largely involved a social tradeoff whereby workers essentially were to receive no-fault insurance in the form of compensation benefits in return for giving up the right to sue their employers.

These are obviously important areas, and the laws and policies certainly have been modified over time. Yet adjustments to them have generally been marginal and often offsetting in nature, as reforms made by pro-labour governments were subsequently revoked by pro-business governments, and so forth. This may be appropriate, since marginal changes are usually less disruptive, and there is the legitimate concern that major changes will simply elicit subsequent offsetting pendulum swings.

Yet it is also possible that these marginal adjustments simply reflect inertia. Governments are not under the same competitive pressure to change in order to

3

survive as are businesses and unions. The security of bureaucrats who administer the legislation and who are therefore most knowledgeable about its interpretation may in fact be enhanced by marginal changes. Interest groups may also want the status quo preserved because they have adjusted to the current situation. Even if the legislation and regulations are costly, they may serve the interests of the incumbent players to the extent that they deter the entry of new competitors.

Even if the status quo did not simply reflect government inertia or the influence of bureaucrats or interest groups, it could be that we are at a local optimum and not a global optimum[5] if the external environment has changed dramatically. It is possible, for example, that the collective bargaining legislation that was developed under the adversarial Wagner Act model is less appropriate for today's workplace, where cooperation between labour and management is favoured to facilitate the survival of both. The public-sector labour laws that were designed to deal with dispute resolution under conditions of expansion may be inadequate to deal with the current downsizing and restructuring in this sector.[6] Labour standards legislation that was largely designed for a male-dominated industrial workforce working nine to five, often in fixed work sites, may simply be unsuited to today's multiple-earner families with flexible work arrangements. The health and safety legislation that was largely designed for that same workforce may be inadequate to deal with the new issues of work-related stress and longer-term diseases that have their origins in both the workplace and other environments.

Furthermore, the existing array of workplace laws and regulations, which were for the most part designed to deal with one specific set of issues, may interfere with each other and with other elements of social policy. Changes in workers' compensation, for example, can have important implications for unemployment insurance and for pension disability programs, and vice versa. Furthermore, labour laws and policies may be inadequately coordinated with other elements of industrial policy, and this may be inhibiting competitiveness. It is generally recognized that firms must coordinate their labour and human resource policies with their competitive product market strategy. Governments also should coordinate their human resource development strategies with policies that influence capital and product markets to ensure that human resource strategies and competitive industrial strategies are mutually consistent.

Forces Affecting the Changing Nature of Work

The forces affecting the changing nature of work are now well known, even though their relative importance in explaining the changes that have occurred is still being debated. (They may continue to be debated, since it is very difficult to disentangle the separate effects given that the pressures are often interrelated.) For ease of exposition, those changing forces can be categorized as those affecting the demand or the supply side of labour markets, and the institutions and laws that affect the interaction of supply and demand. These forces generally affect both the external labour market (e.g., through wages and unemployment) as well as the workplace or internal labour markets of firms (e.g., through restructuring, turnover, retirements and layoffs).

Demand Side Forces
Since the demand for labour is derived from the demand for the products and services of firms, the demand side of the labour market is affected by the pressures that firms face in their markets for goods, services and capital. These interrelated pressures include global competition, trade liberalization, technological change, industrial restructuring, greater capital mobility and prolonged recessions.

For countries such as Canada, competition has generally come from lower-wage countries that assemble and produce manufactured goods. Trade liberalization has been pervasive and associated with reductions in tariff and nontariff barriers to trade, but it has also been accentuated by specific regional trade arrangements such as the FTA with the United States, and NAFTA, which included Mexico. Technological change has been dramatic, especially in the areas of information and computer technologies. The mobility of financial capital has increased as financial markets have become more sophisticated and global and are able to react instantaneously to take advantage of arbitrage opportunities. The same applies to physical capital (both inward and outward direct foreign investment), as multinationals and even small employers make their plant location and investment decisions on a global basis. The prolonged recessions of the early 1980s and 1990s have also had an impact. Recovery has been slow (especially in the 1990s), unemployment has ratcheted upwards and it has only recently fallen back to its prerecession levels.

The public sector has not been immune from demand side pressures. Concern with public debt and deficits has meant pressure to either curb public expenditures or raise taxes in order to achieve balanced budgets. Further tax increases do not seem to be in the political cards leaving curbing expenditures as the only avenue available. Curbing expenditures at one level of government leads to ripple effects at other levels, as transfer payments are reduced and responsibilities are shifted to other levels of government and, in many cases, to the general public in the form of reduced services, diminished public infrastructures and increased user charges.

Supply Side Forces

An equally powerful set of forces, associated with changes in the composition of the workforce, has been at work on the supply side of the labour market. These changes have important implications, not only for external and internal labour markets, but also in terms of labour policy requirements.

There has been a continuous increase in the labour force participation of women, especially married women with children.[7] As a result, two-earner families have increased from a minority of 14 percent in 1961 to a majority of 52 percent in 1985; concomitantly, the proportion of families where the husband is the single earner decreased from a majority of 65 percent in 1961 to a distinct minority of only 12 percent in 1985.[8] More recent data indicates that the trend is continuing, although it appears to have levelled off since the late 1980s. Specifically, dual-earner families increased from 33 percent of husband-wife families in 1967 to 60 percent in 1994 (peaking at 63 percent in 1989), while the proportion of husband-wife families where the husband was the sole earner decreased from 58 percent in 1967 to 18 percent in 1994.[9]

At the same time, there has been a slow decline in the labour force participation of men, much of it due to early retirement. In addition, the workforce has continued to age, with the baby-boom population now well into middle age and approaching early retirement. Much of the new growth in the labour force has come from women and visible minorities, resulting in greater diversity.[10]

These changes emanating from the supply side of the labour market have important implications for the workplace and labour policies. To the extent that many of our labour laws and regulations were geared toward a male-dominated workforce and male breadwinners, they may be outmoded and not suited to the new circumstances. For instance, there has been increased pressure for antidiscrimination policies and for childcare and working time arrangements that meet the new and diverse needs of families. As a result, there is a need not only for new policies, but also for flexible policies: "one size fits all" policies are no longer appropriate.

This diversity of needs can be illustrated by survey data on preferences for alternative working time arrangements. A number of surveys have asked respondents about their preferred work hours relative to their current arrangements.[11] The most recent such survey, the 1995 Survey of Work Arrangements by Statistics Canada, indicated that only about two-thirds of the workforce were content with their working time arrangements. Approximately 27 percent of the labour force wanted more work for a proportionate increase in pay, and about six percent wanted less work (and the associated reduction in pay). This highlights the fact that a substantial proportion of the workforce would like changes in their working time arrangements (and policies that would accommodate those changes), but those preferences are diverse, with some wanting more working time and others wanting less. Again, a "one size fits all" solution would not be suitable.

The diversity of needs is also illustrated by the fact that working hours have become more polarized over the last two decades. Sheridan, Sunter and Diverty examine trends in working hours from 1976 to 1995.[12] They find that the proportion of employees working 35-40 hours has declined, while the proportions working both more and less have increased. This trend toward increased polarization of hours of work has continued in the late 1990s.[13]

The policy challenge, of course, is to facilitate the mutually beneficial trades between the underemployed, who want more working time, and the overemployed, who want less. The underemployed obviously prefer the additional income, while the overemployed are willing to give up income to get more time for family or other activities. Yet current labour policies appear not only to be unable to facilitate such trades but also to discourage them. For example, regulations on hours of work and overtime are geared to individuals and not families, even though family hours are relevant given the growing importance of two-earner families and the time crunch they face.[14] As such, maximum work hours legislation that restricts or regulates working time beyond say 48 hours per week could have a substantial impact on restricting additional hours in a family where a single earner was already working 48 hours, and yet have no impact on an otherwise similar dual-earner family that worked 80 hours, with each party working 40 hours. If the purpose of the maximum hours regulations is to encourage work sharing, it is certainly not obvious that the family working 80 hours should not be under more pressure to share the hours. If the purpose is to restrict long hours for health reasons and to encourage family time, it is also not obvious that the stress and time crunch is not greater in the 80-hour family, even though both parties work a normal work week. The same dilemma would arise with respect to overtime premiums that may be designed to discourage long hours of work. Such premiums would not affect the 80-hour family, but they could discourage employers from providing 48 hours to the 48-hour family.

In this way our legislation may not be conducive to facilitating reductions in the working hours of the overemployed to expand the working hours of the underemployed. In fact, some aspects of our labour legislation may actually discourage such trades. For example, many of our payroll taxes are capped when earnings reach a certain level. This means that once the ceiling is reached, no further taxes are paid if these individuals work longer hours, while additional payroll taxes would be incurred for new hires. As well, legislation that increases the expected costs associated with layoffs or terminations may result in employers anticipating these costs at the hiring stage. In essence, payroll tax ceilings and expected termination costs become quasi-fixed costs at the hiring stage, thereby discouraging employers from hiring new workers and encouraging them to impose longer working hours on the existing workforce. Thus, mutually beneficial trades are not only not facilitated but actually discouraged by these unintended side effects of our labour policies.

In such circumstances, it may be important to re-examine the fundamental purpose of hours of work legislation, for instance, to see if the original purpose is still relevant to today's circumstances. Even if it is, it is also important to ask if this is the best way to achieve those objectives, given the diverse preferences and changing needs of the workforce.

Workers' more diverse preferences with respect to working time arrangements (on the supply side of the labour market) may also coincide with a greater diversity of needs for alternative work time arrangements on the part of employers (on the demand side of the labour market). In essence, employers facing increased market uncertainty may prefer to have their core and expensively trained workforce work long hours and use part-time and subcontracted workers for other tasks. Advances in information and computer technologies have reduced the cost of scheduling and monitoring the activities of part-time and contract workers, thereby making this option less expensive. While this may coincide with the increasingly diverse preferences of the workforce, such matches may be inhibited by working hours and overtime regulations. Moreover, employers' needs may not coincide with workers' preferences. For instance, those asked to work longer (shorter) hours may prefer to work shorter (longer) hours. In such circumstances, the policy issue is whether legislation and regulation is the best way to facilitate matching employers' needs and employees' preferences. In either case, the legislation merits reassessment in light of changing and more diverse circumstances.

Institutional Change

The labour market is being affected not only by demand- and supply-side changes, but also by changes in the institutional environment. Among these is the deunionization trend in the US, our major trading partner. Historically, levels of unionization have been fairly similar in Canada and the United States. However, in the mid-1960s they began to diverge from a common rate of around 30 percent to increase slightly in Canada to approximately 35 percent and decrease steadily in the US to around 15 percent.[15]

This change has potentially important implications for labour policy in Canada. Canadian employers are likely to put more pressure on governments to reduce costly labour regulations, given that they are competing with the less regulated, less unionized United States. They may also be more inclined to resist unionization for the same reasons. If unionization does decline or becomes a less powerful force in Canada it is likely that there will be less pressure for labour policies. Unions have traditionally been a driving force behind such policy. However, it may also give rise to pressure for labour policies to fill the vacuum created by a decline in the influence of unions. This void may also occur in the enforcement of legislation. Unions have often played an important role in that area also, especially in informing workers of the policies and protecting individual workers from reprisals if they file complaints under the legislation.

Perhaps the most important institutional change that is likely to occur is as a result of increased pressure on labour law and policy in general. Because of advances in information and computer technologies, and increased trade liberalization, it is now easier for employers to locate their plants in countries with lower labour costs (including those imposed by laws and regulations) and to export back into countries that have higher labour costs. In essence, it is no longer as necessary for them to have branch plants in various countries as a way to leap the tariff walls by producing from within. Employers can more easily produce in the lowest cost countries and export throughout the world as tariffs and nontariff barriers to trade are reduced. This not only reduces the demand for low-wage labour in countries like Canada, but it also allows employers to exert real pressure on governments to reduce costly legislation and regulations by threatening to relocate plants and investment, and the jobs associated with that investment. In essence, governments are under increasing pressure to compete for investment and jobs, and one way to do so is to reduce costly legislation and regulations. That pressure was always there; it is simply enhanced by trade liberalization and greater international economic integration. 9

Legislation and regulations that impose costs on employers without any offsetting benefits are likely to be put under the most pressure. In contrast, laws like health and safety regulations may be less vulnerable, at least to the extent that they have some offsetting benefits such as fewer costly accidents. Similarly, the cost of workers' compensation is an alternative to the expensive tort liability system, since workers gave up their right to sue employers under the no-fault system. As well, at least part of the costs of labour regulations may be shifted back to workers in the form of lower wages in return for benefits resulting from the regulations.[16]

The labour policies that are most at risk in this more competitive environment are those that only have a distributive or equity rationale and serve no efficiency or competitiveness-enhancing purposes. This is because governments that pursue such policies risk losing business investment and the associated jobs. There is also the possibility that their jurisdiction may become more attractive to individuals in need, especially if public assistance is reduced elsewhere. Unfortunately, the pressure to reduce these redistributive policies is coming just at a time when they may be most needed – as the market forces associated with global competition, trade liberalization, technological change and industrial restructuring are having a disproportionately adverse effect on the least skilled and most disadvantaged.

Employer Responses

Mass Layoffs and Plant Closings

Mass layoffs and plant closings have been widespread, and they have had particularly severe implications for smaller communities where alternative jobs are not available and employees' income loss may be compounded by decreases in the value of their homes and other assets that may be tied to the well-being of the community.

Permanent displacement or job loss has been common,[17] with workers in such circumstances often experiencing large income losses of 10 to 30 percent or more. This raises the question of why presumably risk-averse workers appear willing to risk having a number of workers experiencing job loss rather than engaging in smaller wage concessions spread over a larger number of workers as an alternative. The answers often have interesting implications for public policy. For example, Employment Insurance (EI) may discourage wage concessions because it compensates for some of the loss of earnings that results from unemployment, but not from wage concessions. The exception is the work sharing component of EI, which is given to employees in an approved program whereby employees collectively reduce their workweek by, let's say, 20 percent to avoid 20 percent of the workforce being laid off. Employees may also be reluctant to engage in wage concessions because they are uncertain whether the firm may simply be bluffing about its inability to pay. In such circumstances, employees may rationally compel the employer to engage in costly layoffs as a way to deter such bluffing. Policies that increase the information available to employees (e.g., disclosure requirements) may reduce the need for employees to only give employers the option of layoffs rather than wage concessions in the face of downward demand shocks.

Another reason for the frequent use of layoffs rather than wage concessions as an adjustment mechanism may be that unionized employees with a degree of seniority feel protected from layoffs, and thus exert pressure for that option.

To the extent that union policies are dictated by the median union voter who likely has seniority protection, such insiders are likely to vote for downward adjustment in the form of layoffs rather than wage concessions. Of course, if the risk of layoff encroaches on the median union voter (e.g., a plant closing), then even these insiders may be more willing to engage in wage concessions to avoid the possibility of layoffs. Alternatively, they could be bought out by early-retirement packages if the firm felt it was important not to lay off younger workers who have the requisite new skills and can be paid lower wages.

Even employers may prefer layoffs to wage concessions as a way of adjusting to downward demand shocks if they have followed a high-wage strategy as part of their human resource policy. In general, we think of layoffs as being costly to the firm because of the potential loss of human capital, and of wage reductions as not being costly to the firm. However, some firms may rationally pay an efficiency wage premium above the market rate in order to elicit positive work behaviour such as loyalty, commitment, a queue of applicants, and reduced shirking and turnover.

Clearly, there are a variety of reasons for downward demand shocks to be absorbed through layoffs rather than wage concessions, in spite of the fact that small wage concessions spread over the larger workforce would seem to be less disruptive than a number of workers being laid off and receiving no wages. These reasons include public policy and labour market institutions such as unemployment insurance, disclosure requirements and unions.

Organizational Restructuring

Employers' responses to the changing nature of work have essentially been dictated by their responses to changes in the product and service markets in which they operate. That market has been dramatically affected in recent years by changes on the demand side resulting from increased global competition, trade liberalization, technological change, severe recessions, and restructuring, especially the shift from manufacturing to high-end services (e.g., business, financial, legal, research and development) and low-end services (e.g., consumer services and business maintenance). Since the firm's demand for labour is derived from the demand for the goods and services it produces, the forces affecting the demand for their products and services (and how firms respond to those forces) will also affect their demand for labour.

For example, the shift to just-in-time delivery has led to a demand for a just-in-time workforce that is flexible and adaptable to rapidly shifting needs. The establishment within large organizations of separate profit-centres whose survival within the organization depends upon their ability to meet the bottom line has had similar implications for the workforces in those profit centres. Mergers and acquisitions to reduce redundancy and establish the economies of scale necessary for a global market have often led to workforce reductions, and the associated policy issues of terminations and successor rights that ensue.

Many organizations have essentially become virtual organizations with a small core of employees whose primary function is to organize and monitor the activities of subcontractors. As well, joint ventures and alliances are often formed around a particular project, such as the design of the Boeing 777 aircraft, which was completed by numerous development teams in several countries. The resulting workforce alliances are thus dependent upon the current project and the ability to put together subsequent projects. Employees' loyalty to the organization has often been replaced by efforts to develop and maintain a network of contacts. Clearly, this new work environment requires employees who are not only flexible and adaptable to the changing circumstances but also have the skills required for monitoring, coordinating and interacting tasks.

Employers' emphasis on customer satisfaction and quality control (in part as a response to Japanese success in these areas) has also led to a need for employees who can relate to both customers and suppliers. As well, quality circles and team production require greater employee involvement. Attempts are also often made to establish more secure and quasi-permanent relationships with suppliers and subcontractors to facilitate a continuity of quality inputs. Nevertheless, the organization can easily sever that supplier-subcontractor relationship if demand conditions dictate it or if the service is unacceptable, which, of course, has implications for the job security of employees in those subcontracting organizations. Furthermore, subcontracting and supplier organizations are constantly competing for contracts, and this puts strong competitive pressure on them to constrain costs, including direct and indirect labour costs related to labour laws and regulations. These organizations are often relatively small and nonunionized and thus ones in which labour laws and regulations are more difficult to enforce.

As part of the restructuring that has occurred, organizations have often engaged in various forms of downsizing including mass layoffs, plant closings and early retirements. Much of their new hiring has been in the form of contractually limited appointments that are often geared to a particular project, but that may also be regarded as long probationary periods for both parties to become better informed about the viability of a job match should a more permanent position come available. Delayering has also become more prominent as organizational structures have become flatter, reducing the hierarchies of command that were once prevalent. This has meant workforce reductions, often of large layers of middle management. It has also resulted in the breaking down of narrowly defined job classifications so that employees can do a wider range of tasks, often under minimal supervision. This in turn has put a premium on multi-skilled training as well as broader-based generic skills that can be built upon through subsequent retraining and lifelong learning.

Deregulation and privatization has also become much more prominent in quasi-public-sector organizations. Often this has led such organizations to shed some of their more peripheral activities and to focus on their core competencies, which in turn has resulted in a dramatic downsizing of their workforces. Although there are often expanding employment opportunities in the new firms entering the industry, these jobs may be subject to considerably more competitive pressures and may not be protected by the regulations that previously protected the monopoly and jobs in quasi-public sector organizations. The new jobs are often nonunionized and in small firms that are carving out a market niche in a more competitive industry. It is often more difficult to enforce labour regulations in these types of organizations, especially if neither the employer nor the employees are interested in enforcement (as is sometimes the case with overtime regulations, for example).

As part of the restructuring that has occurred, employment is increasingly concentrated in smaller firms, and while the job creation rate has been highest in small firms, so has the job destruction rate. Because of their high turnover rates, the rate of net job creation (job gains less job losses) is only slightly higher in small firms.[18]

Large multinational organizations have also responded to the changing market conditions by diversifying their plant location decisions, not only to take advantage of new market opportunities, but also to use as a lever in collective bargaining with unions and political bargaining with governments over regulations and possible subsidies. With improved international communication and transportation, flexible factories can more easily be set up in greenfield sites and offshore in response to even small cost and market advantages.

Changing Workplace and Internal Labour Market Practices
The previous sections described how, in response to the changing pressures they face in their product markets, organizations have engaged in restructuring that has had important implications for employees as well as for labour policies. Many of those implications were illustrated and tied to the particular response of employers. In this section, the implications for workplace or internal labour market practices are discussed in more detail[19] and ordered in the sequence of how an employee typically progresses through an organization.

13

In their recruiting decisions, employers are increasingly looking for employees with the skills that will equip them for the new world of work. This often includes a solid base of broad, generic training that is the foundation for more specialized retraining and lifelong learning. There is also more emphasis on people skills such as the ability to work in teams and to relate to customers and suppliers. Broad-based training is important as well for the wide range of tasks (multitasking) often associated with broader job classifications. Job rotation is also more widespread, as employees are rotated through different job assignments, in part to prepare them for a wider range of tasks, and in part to give them a better understanding of the full production process. The training of employees has been geared to these new requirements.

Compensation practices have also changed: pay is often tied to the performance of the individual, the workteam or the organization. Wage patterns such as a common wage structure within each firm in a heavily unionized industry have often broken down, as different organizations' ability to pay becomes an important factor in the joint survival of the organization and its jobs. Pay for knowledge (i.e., for general training and the ability to do a variety of tasks) has become more prominent relative to pay for a specific task, since in an environment of rapid technological and economic change the nature of the required tasks may change dramatically. Co-payment for medical, health and disability benefits is becoming more widespread, in part to demonstrate the costs of these programs and to discourage abuse. Features of occupational pension plans, such as subsidized early-retirement schemes and penalties for postponed retirement, are sometimes part of strategic human resource planning. In essence, compensation has generally become more flexible and geared to market conditions.

Internal employee transfers have become more prevalent, sometimes involving lateral and even downward moves. As organizations have become flatter, and as the baby-boom population exceeds the promotion opportunities, constant upward mobility within the organization is no longer guaranteed, even for good performers.

Alternative work time arrangements are being increasingly adopted to provide the flexibility needed by employers and the growing number of two-earner families. Such arrangements include flexitime (different starting and ending times with a common core working time), compressed workweeks (e.g., four 10-hour days), job sharing (e.g., two employees sharing the same job), unpaid leaves, and permanent part-time jobs. This has given rise to pressures on legislators to accommodate such changes and to deal with associated issues such as coverage and prorated benefits for part-time workers.

Employee involvement programs have become more important, in part to increase commitment and facilitate quality control, and in part to garner information from those responsible for the everyday operations of the organization. In nonunionized firms, these programs may constitute a form of collective representation that provides an alternative to a union, while in unionized firms, such representation may be a supplementary and competing element. As a result, this has raised concerns that these employee involvement programs might be designed mainly to discourage unions or to challenge their exclusive right to represent the bargaining unit when unions exist.

Contingent or non-standard, precarious employment has also become more prominent in various forms including subcontracts, limited term contracts, temporary help agencies and part-time employment. Data from the Labour Force Survey indicates that in 1998 a substantial proportion of jobs in Canada held by individuals aged 15-64 were non-standard: 19 percent were part time, 10 percent were temporary, 5 percent were in multiple employment, and 12 percent were in own-account self-employment.[20] These are not mutually exclusive categories. For example, many part-time workers are in temporary jobs. When we remove this overlap, 34 percent of the workforce is in at least one of the four types of non-standard work. Multiple employment, part-time employment, and own-account self-employment have increased considerably since the mid-1970s.

Obviously, this provides employers greater flexibility to meet their contingency needs, given the uncertainty of their own product-market conditions. It may also meet the needs of some employees who want flexibility in balancing work and family responsibilities. But non-standard employment also creates policy challenges in areas such as coverage and enforcement of legislation. In particular, those in part-time, temporary and contract work and the self-employed are often not covered by employment standards legislation and social programs such as EI. When they are covered, there may be little enforcement of the regulations. This pattern of lower coverage and enforcement also raises the larger question of whether these contingent work arrangements arose in part as responses to the legislation. For example, if it becomes costly to terminate employees, firms may incorporate these costs into their hiring decision and become reluctant to hire new employees. If their demand conditions are uncertain (which increasingly seems to be the case), organizations may prefer to use contingent workers whose termination is easier. As well, they may prefer to use a small core of existing workers and have them work longer hours (to amortize the fixed hiring and training costs) rather than hire new employees. The minimal coverage or enforcement of legislation for the contingent workforce contributes to the lower cost of employing these workers.

15

morley gunderson and w. craig riddell

Pension and retirement policies have also become increasingly important instruments of strategic human resource planning. Pensions are no longer simply regarded as a form of savings up to a normal retirement age of 65, as was the case when the workforce could generally be characterized as being male-dominated and blue-collar and having considerable job security. Now, pension plans often have early and special retirement features that subsidize early retirement as a way to induce voluntary workforce reductions. Furthermore, early-retirement windows are often announced on an *ad hoc* basis.

These issues are creating policy challenges in various areas, including the regulation of pensions. For example, the regulation of defined-benefit plans may cause employers to simply shift to defined-contribution plans where the regulations are minimal, and this can create greater uncertainty among employees about their pension benefits. The issues pertaining to occupational pension plans also have ramifications for reforms to the employment-based Canada/Quebec Pension Plan, since occupational pension plans can provide an alternative source of retirement income. Mandatory retirement is also an issue. Allowing mandatory retirement implies that the human rights legislation in most jurisdictions does not apply to persons 65 years of age and over. In effect, this means that these workers are not covered by legislation that prohibits discrimination on the basis of age. There have recently been constitutional challenges to mandatory retirement provisions.

Clearly, employers' responses to product market conditions have important implications for workplace and internal labour market practices. These, in turn, have important implications for legislation and social policy.

External Labour Market Manifestations
It is a feature of North American labour markets that many of the adjustments occur through the external labour markets in the form of layoffs, unemployed job search and exit from the labour market itself (e.g., early retirement). These adjustments can be observed in aggregate through changes in the unemployment and labour force participation rates. This is in contrast to countries like Japan, where more adjustment occurs within the internal labour market of the firm through internal transfers and relocations, for instance. As well, in Japan the informal sector and subcontracting serve to insulate the core of workers in the larger firms from consequences of adjustment.

As a result of the adjustment pressures on the Canadian labour market, average real wages have been relatively stagnant since the mid-1970s. Earnings inequality has increased, reflecting an increase in the inequality of wages and of hours and weeks worked, and greater polarization of the economy into good jobs and bad jobs.[21] Several interrelated forces have contributed to this polarization including skill-based technological change; import competition that has adverse effects on less skilled workers; export expansion that favours more skilled workers; industrial restructuring that is shifting employment from middle-wage manufacturing to the polar ends of the wage distribution; and institutional forces such as stagnant minimum wages and reduced union power. While earnings inequality in Canada has increased, the increase has not been as great as that in the United States. This is in part because there has been a greater increase in the supply of more educated workers in Canada, which has dampened the wage increases that otherwise would have occurred at the higher end of the wage distribution, and reduced the supply of less educated workers, thus putting less downward pressure on their wages.[22] As well, unionization has remained more prominent in Canada, and unions tend to reduce wage inequality.[23] Furthermore, during the 1980s (when increases in inequality were especially pronounced), minimum wages declined less in real terms in Canada than in the United States.[24]

As an adjustment mechanism, permanent layoffs have been more widespread and often associated with plant closings. This in turn has led to an increase in the proportion of unemployed who are long-term unemployed and permanently displaced from their jobs.[25] These displaced workers, if they remain in the labour force, tend to have long periods of unemployment, and they often take substantial wage losses in their new jobs. The wage losses can reflect various attributes of their previous job that are lost: firm- or industry-specific human capital; union or regulatory rents; efficiency wage premiums; *ex ante* wage premiums designed to compensate for the risk of unemployment (a risk that has now come to fruition); and deferred wage premiums whereby their previous employer overpaid them when they were older in return for underpaying them when they were younger, with the deferral intended to encourage positive aspects of work behaviour.

These external labour market adjustments have manifested themselves in an unemployment rate that has consistently ratcheted upwards since the mid-1960s. Another, more recent concern is that the Canadian unemployment rate has diverged upwards from the US rate compared with earlier periods when rates were almost identical[26], beginning in the late 1970s and accelerating in the early 1980s.

Hours of work have also become more polarized, with a substantial portion of the workforce now working part time and a substantial portion working very long hours.[27] Part-time workers include those doing so voluntarily to combine labour market work with other activities including family and schooling, as well as those doing so involuntarily who would prefer a full-time job.[28] Long hours are often worked by highly paid professionals, but also by people in single-earner families.

17

morley gunderson and w. craig riddell

While the adjustment pressures on labour markets have implications for prices (i.e., wages) and quantities (i.e., unemployment, hours) they also have an impact on the quality of work, especially its intensity. When layoffs occur, the remaining workforce is often called upon to do the work of those who have left. The call is usually heeded, given the threat of additional layoffs. This increased intensity of work combined with the time crunch that many two-earner families face as they try to balance labour market work and household and family activities can result in stress and other negative impacts on workers' welfare.

These manifestations of the changing nature of work have important policy implications. For example, growing earnings inequality has added a new dimension to the traditional policy dilemma involving the tradeoff between inflation and unemployment. The old dilemma becomes all the more complex when earnings inequality is added to the picture, and when a preoccupation with the deficit and the tax burden make it difficult to use tax or spending increases to deal with the problem. The concern over earnings inequality relates to a number of issues: the social tensions between the haves and the have-nots, the fact that working full time does not necessarily yield an income above the poverty line, and the problems associated with a growing underclass and the lack of upward mobility. Declining wages among those at the bottom of the earnings distribution have also put additional pressure on income support programs as social assistance becomes increasingly attractive relative to work.[29]

The persistence of unemployment, the fact that much of the growing earnings inequality in Canada reflects a growing disparity in hours of work, and the fact that many persons are overemployed while others are underemployed or unemployed have brought renewed attention to the issue of work redistribution. As well, the stress associated with unemployment, the increased intensity of work, and the time crunch experienced by individuals attempting to balance work and family life have led to increased policy emphasis on work and health issues.

Employee and Union Responses

Employee and union responses to the changing pressures and their manifestations in the internal and external labour markets have generally been reactive, often designed to cope with the consequences of adjustment. Nevertheless, employees and unions are increasingly confronted with a wide range of strategic choices that can affect their survival in the labour market.

Chief amongst these strategic choices is whether to foster labour-management cooperation or to maintain the conventional adversarial approach. Cooperative strategies emphasize mutual-gains bargaining, win-win solutions, quality teams, profit-sharing and dispute resolution as alternatives to grievances and strikes. The adversarial approach tends to emphasize conventional distributive bargaining: the formal collective agreement and grievances, with the strike as the ultimate weapon.

Unions in Canada are often divided on this issue.[30] Some, like the Canadian Auto Workers, are concerned that cooperation is really just co-option, and that it will be a slippery slope leading to the decimation of unions as has occurred in the United States. Others, like the United Steelworkers and the Communication Workers, have been more open to cooperative strategies, perhaps under pressure that their own survival may be inextricably linked to that of their employers. The differences within the labour movement can be exaggerated, however, since cooperative practices are often followed at the local level even if the official policy is the contrary. As well, unions that do espouse an officially cooperative policy often do so with the veiled threat that they may return to a more conventional adversarial approach. Aspects of cooperation are often negotiated (e.g., wage moderation or allowing subcontracting in return for job guarantees).

A number of high-profile employee buyouts have occurred where employees have ultimately owned much of the organization, although this is still not common. This strategy can facilitate aligning the goals of the organization with those of the employees, and it can induce cooperative and productivity-enhancing behaviour on the part of employees. It can be risky for employees, however, since their earnings, savings, human capital and the value of their homes may all be tied up in the success of a single organization.

Union organizing strategies have also often been modified to adapt to the new realities. More attention has been paid to organizing the service sector, although this is made difficult by the large number of small employers, the part-time nature of much of the employment and the fiercely competitive nature of the industry. Unions have often diversified their organizing across different industries so that their survival does not depend on a single one.

Unions also face strategic choices with respect to the services they will provide. If their ability to garner wage premiums is constrained by competitive market forces, then they may gain popular support by providing other services such as credit unions and financial planning.

Conventionally, unions have tried to organize up to the level of the product market in which they operate. By organizing the majority of firms in a particular product market, they are less threatened by nonunionized firms that could undercut the unionized firms. If the product market has become international, then international organizing strategies are appropriate. Such strategies are extremely difficult, however, given that labour laws and institutions may be different in other countries. Some international cooperative efforts have occurred in the union movement, but even this is difficult given the limited resources available to most unions.

Unions have also focused on the political environment, recognizing that their ability to organize and sustain unions is very dependent upon the legislative environment governing collective bargaining. As well, they have emphasized the importance of labour standards and other regulations affecting the nonunionized sector, in part reflecting a concern for nonunionized workers, and in part to minimize competition from firms that would otherwise employ low-cost, nonunionized labour.

Collective agreements have often been modified in response to the changing pressures. Job classifications are often broader with fewer restrictions on the nature of the work that can be done. Subcontracting and the use of part-time workers have often been allowed in return for job guarantees for the existing workforce.

Policy Responses

Clearly, the various forces affecting the demand side of the labour market have increased the pressure for labour market policies, especially ones that deal with the consequences of adjustment such as job loss, long-term unemployment, stagnant wage growth and growing wage inequality. Changes emanating from the supply side of the labour market, including the increased labour force participation of women, the aging workforce and greater ethnic diversity, have also increased the demand for policy initiatives in such areas as childcare, leave policies, working time arrangements, pensions and retirement policies, pay and employment equity, and antidiscrimination initiatives.

Ironically, while demand- and supply-side pressures are increasing the demand for policy initiatives, there is also increased pressure on governments not to add costly initiatives, and to deregulate where possible. This pressure emanates from the credible threat of capital mobility and plant relocation, and from the lack of support for new expenditures or taxes that would contribute to the deficit.

In the face of increased demand for new initiatives and pressure to constrain costs, governments are increasingly compelled to do more with less. Increased emphasis has been placed on active labour market adjustment strategies[31] (e.g., training and mobility) to facilitate the reallocation of labour from declining to expanding sectors, rather than on passive income maintenance programs (like EI) that might discourage such adjustment by providing income support for people who remain in declining sectors. There has also been some decentralization of programs, an example being the recent decision by the federal government to devolve more training functions to the provinces. Stakeholder involvement in the design and delivery of policies is also being encouraged, in part to garner information from those who are closest to the implementation of the policies, and in part to get the support of those who have to live with the policies.

Sector councils have also been formed in many industries, with government support.[32] Their intent is to provide a forum for labour-management cooperation in order to deal with issues such as adjustment, training and standards. Again, the emphasis is on bottom-up solutions that are geared to the particular problems of each industry, rather than one-size-fits-all remedies.

In the health and safety area, Canadian policy has favoured the internal responsibility system, whereby the workplace parties themselves have extensive responsibility for administering the policies.[33] This is accomplished with employee involvement and empowerment fostered by the three basic rights: the right to be informed about workplace risks and hazards, the right to representation through a workplace health and safety committee and the right to refuse hazardous work in defined circumstances. This internal responsibility system has been adopted as an alternative to the regulatory model of the United States, where health and safety policy is enforced through a myriad of detailed regulations. The internal responsibility system in Canada is facilitated by the higher degree of unionization, since unions are generally regarded as an important ingredient in ensuring the observance of the three basic rights that underpin that system.

The recent federal government decision to transfer responsibility for most of the training functions to the provinces is another strategic response to new pressures for decentralization, as well as a possible solution to the endless jurisdictional battles in this area. In the past, divided responsibility in this area appeared to lead to no responsibility, with each jurisdiction always having a scapegoat onto which to shift blame. The federal government will focus on pan-Canadian issues such as mobility and common standards.

The recent reform of employment insurance has also involved a shift from passive income maintenance toward more active adjustment assistance. This has been done in various ways: reducing the benefit rate; imposing stricter qualification requirements and shorter maximum benefit durations; reducing eligibility for repeat users; and reallocating funds toward training, mobility, job creation and self-employment assistance. As well, the reforms recognize the changing nature of the workforce, as evidenced by eligibility based on hours and not weeks worked (so that part-timers are eligible), and assistance for claimants to establish their own businesses.

Clearly, many of the policy changes have been in response to new and changing conditions. Yet they can generally be described as tinkering at the margin, leaving the basic structures intact. While workplace changes are often regarded as transformations, the policy changes are better described as transitions. This may be appropriate if it minimizes policy pendulum swings that give rise to considerable uncertainty and adjustment costs. Nevertheless, the slowness of the policy responses could also reflect the inertia of vested interests and the fact that initial conditions matter – we tend to stay with what we have.

Emerging Challenges

Evidence on the Myths and Realities

One of the main challenges in assessing the ongoing changes in the labour market is to separate the myths from the realities. Stereotypes and futurist statements abound, yet systematic evidence is not available on a number of key points, and controversy surrounds others. This can be illustrated by a number of examples.

The evidence indicates that a growing portion of the workforce is in non-standard, often precarious, jobs; however, the increase in atypical work arrangements has been gradual rather than dramatic. This point is illustrated in figures 1 and 2, which show several indicators of atypical work arrangements over the period 1976-98: multiple job holding, own-account self-employment, part-time employment and short-tenure employment.[34] Steady upward trends are evident for multiple job holding, own-account self-employment and part-time employment. Short-tenure employment increased in importance between the mid-1970s and the late 1990s, but subsequently declined to below the 1976 level. As shown in figure 2, the proportion of total Canadian employment accounted for by part-time, short-tenure and own-account self-employment – a commonly used measure of non-standard employment – increased from about 24 percent in 1976 to 31 percent in 1998 (see figure 3). In 1998, one-third of employed individuals had part-time work, temporary jobs, own-account self-employment, or multiple jobs.[35] This is a substantial proportion of the workforce, but is probably much smaller than many popular accounts of fundamental changes in work arrangements would suggest.

Despite substantial workforce restructuring and much speculation about rising employment instability, average job tenure does not appear to have changed much. For example, Farber finds that in the US there was no systematic change in the overall distribution of job durations from 1973 to 1993, although the duration did decrease for less educated males and increase for more educated females.[36] This led him to conclude, paraphrasing Mark Twain, that "reports

Figure 1
Indicators of Non-Standard Employment in Canada, 1976-1998

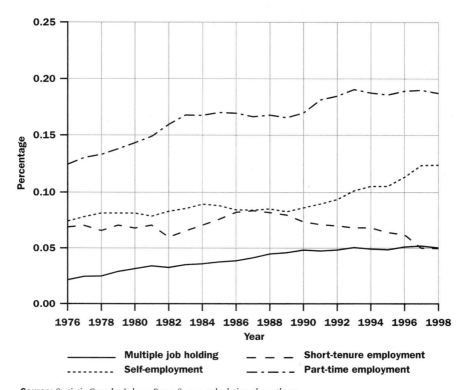

Source: Statistic Canada, Labour Force Survey, calculations by authors.

of the death of the Great American Job are greatly exaggerated."[37] Similar evidence that there has not been a substantial decline in employment stability in the US is provided by Diebold, Neumark and Polsky.[38]

Green and Riddell find average job duration in Canada to have been remarkably stable over time between 1979 and 1992.[39] There were, however, some important differences around that average. Job durations increased for females, especially educated females, and they declined for males, especially less educated and younger males. Furthermore, while average duration was fairly constant, there was increased polarization around that average, with a growing proportion of both short-duration jobs (less than 2 years) and long-duration jobs (greater than 10 years). Similar results are reported by Heitz for the period 1981-94.[40] Additional work is merited in this area, however, especially to determine the extent to which the constancy of the average job duration reflects

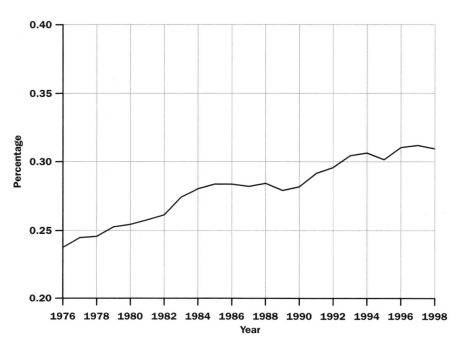

Figure 2
Non-Standard Employment as a Percentage
of Total Employment, 1976-1998

Source: Statistic Canada, Labour Force Survey, calculations by authors.

24

compositional effects (as older people with long tenure and women with their increasing tenure become a larger portion of the workforce) as opposed to average tenure being constant for workers in each age group and of each gender.

Substantial restructuring in the Canadian economy during the late 1980s (associated with such forces as the FTA) and early 1990s (associated with the severe recession of 1990-92) has contributed to a perception of growing employment instability. However, the available evidence on permanent layoffs contradicts this view. Once one has controlled for other influences, there has not been an increase in the permanent layoff rate in the late 1980s and 1990s compared with earlier periods at a similar stage of the business cycle.[41]

Real wages have been stagnant for much of the workforce since the mid-1970s, and individual wage inequality has risen over the same period. Yet there are only a few studies[42] that link wage stagnation and inequality to family earnings and inequality, an important issue given that two-earner families are now the norm and the family is generally regarded as an important unit for the determination

Figure 3
Non-Standard Employment as a Percentage of Total Employment, 1998

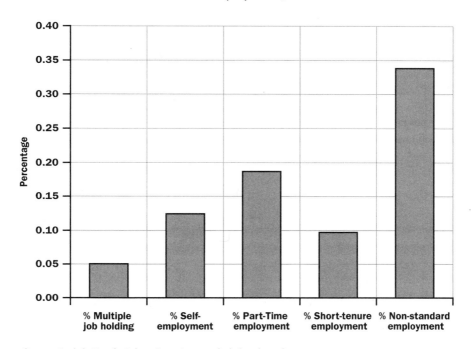

Source: Statistic Canada, Labour Force Survey, calculations by authors.

of well-being. A two-earner family with one high earner and one low earner may well contribute to the rise in earnings inequality and the stagnation of real earnings on an individual basis, but the family's earnings might have increased substantially relative to an earlier period when there was only one earner in that family. As well, the security of family income may have increased, with more than one earner to buffer income fluctuations.

The extent to which there may be a mismatch between the desires of Canadians for alternative work arrangements and their current arrangements also needs further assessment. For example, in the case of hours of work, the 1995 Survey of Work Arrangements concluded that two-thirds of the workforce are content with their current working hours. Among the remaining one-third, the majority (27 percent of the total) wanted more work hours and a proportionate increase in pay and the remainder (6 percent of the total) wanted less work and a proportionate reduction in pay. However, a previous survey (the 1985 Survey of Work Reduction) indicated a much greater desire for reductions in working time, the workforce being approximately evenly split into one-third wanting more work for more pay, one-third wanting less work for less pay and one-third satisfied with their current arrangements. This survey led a number of analysts to conclude that there is substantial mismatch between actual and desired hours as well as considerable scope for work sharing policies.[43] The differences between the two surveys appears to be associated with weaknesses in the design of the Survey of Work Reduction, especially the way the questionnaire treated the desire for more hours and for less hours asymmetrically.[44] Nonetheless, eliciting individuals' preferences for changes in work arrangements and the price they are willing to pay for the desired changes is sufficiently complex that further investigation of these questions appears warranted.

It is frequently claimed that businesses are increasingly willing to locate in countries that have low labour costs, including the costs induced by legislative and policy regulations. Yet we have little systematic evidence of any, let alone all, of the links that are involved: the extent to which regulations are actually enforced; how much they increase labour costs; whether any of those costs are offset in part at least by possible benefits of the regulations; if the regulatory component of labour costs affects plant location and investment decisions;[45] and how such decisions affect net job creation, wages and employment. Labour regulations tend to be seen as increasing labour costs. This is often the case. However, they can also give rise to benefits that may offset at least part of the costs. Workers' compensation reduces the legal costs that would otherwise arise if employees could sue their employers under the tort liability system. Unemployment insurance may enable employees to search for a more lasting job match. Advanced warning and termination protection may facilitate efficient job search. Social safety nets in general may reduce resistance to otherwise efficient changes. Unfortunately, we do not have sufficient empirical evidence about the potential benefits of labour regulations to be able to determine their net contribution to labour costs.

In a related vein, there is growing evidence that workplace issues are related to overall health and well-being. Although cause and effect are difficult to separate in this area, job loss and unemployment, for example, have been associated with stress, health deterioration, child abuse, spouse abuse, suicide, accidents and increased demand for social services.[46] Work-related stress, especially that which the individual has little control over, can lead to health problems. Empirical evidence on the underlying causal relationships and their magnitude would be useful to determine the extent to which the cost of policy initiatives in this area can be offset, at least in part, by reductions in other costs related to health, community and social services.

Equity and Distributional Objectives

Perhaps the most serious emerging policy challenge is that equity and distributional objectives are likely to be most at risk in a competitive global environment where jurisdictions are under pressure to compete for business investment and jobs by reducing costly regulations. Regulations that do not have an efficiency rationale and only serve distributional or equity objectives may not survive in that bidding war. A jurisdiction that does preserve distributional or equity objectives runs the risk of losing its tax base to pay for the programs and serving as a magnet to the most disadvantaged, further increasing costs. Central governments can reduce that risk by providing the programs nationally and taxing accordingly. Yet pressure is mounting for decentralization. As well, competition from other countries can inhibit even central governments from following equity-oriented policies. Furthermore, national redistributive policies can hamper market adjustments from declining to expanding sectors or regions and inhibit overall competitiveness. The fact that the market adjustments caused by such factors as technological change and trade liberalization appear to fall disproportionately on the already disadvantaged also raises important equity issues. In essence, the market forces that are giving rise to adverse distributional consequences are also inhibiting governments from dealing with those consequences. This will be a key policy challenge if we are to maintain the legitimate social objective of distributive equity. The importance of this task is highlighted by the fact that policies that enhance the social safety net do seem to be able to substantially reduce (post-transfer) income inequality, as evidenced by Canada-US comparisons.[47]

Innovation and the Diffusion of Innovations

The changing nature of work will also give rise to new policy challenges with respect to innovations in workplace practices and human resource policies. Such innovations have characteristics of public goods in that the benefits are equally available to all, and the market cannot exclude nonpayers who simply free-ride and adopt successful innovations.[48] In such circumstances, individual organizations do not have the incentive to bear the full cost of innovating because their competitors will simply emulate any successful innovation and not share in the cost of the unsuccessful ones. The only advantage the innovating firm would have is an early start on the successful innovation, but this is not likely to be a lasting advantage in the dynamic world of intense competition, open communication and information dissemination.

In product markets, of course, this problem is dealt with by providing patents whereby the innovators have exclusive right to the innovation for a period of time and can charge others for the use of the innovation. This is not feasible with respect to innovations in workplace practices and human resource policies. As such, the market may fail to yield a socially optimal number of innovations, and firms may be extremely reluctant to engage in innovative workplace practices. Collectively, they may be caught in a conservative, low-innovation equilibrium until shocked out of it by the success of other systems (as perhaps was the case with Japanese workplace practices).

The policy challenge is to design mechanisms that facilitate the socially optimal amount of such workplace innovations. The solution is not obvious. Patents do not seem feasible in this area. Recognition awards are laudatory, but might not pay the bills. Governments could try to introduce such innovations in the public sector, perhaps by making them part of the mandate of crown corporations, but this might be fraught with problems since the social costs and benefits of the innovations would have to be assessed, and the risk of wasteful experimentation could be high. Government support for organizations that analyze and study workplace innovation and its dissemination may be warranted, but again, the social costs and benefits would have to be assessed. While the solution is not obvious, the issue is likely to be increasingly important given the changes in the nature of work brought about by smaller organizations competing in a world of more open communication and information.

Training and Information Externalities

Concerns that the private sector does not provide sufficient training have been voiced for a long time – this is a continuing and not an emerging challenge.[49] The problem arises because firms have little incentive to train their workers in generally usable skills, since other firms could simply poach the trained workers away by offering them higher wages. To keep their trained workers, the firms providing the training have to match the higher wages, which means they double-pay: for the training as well as for keeping their trained workforce.

The obvious solution to internalize this externality is for the worker to pay for the training, to the extent that they reap the benefits in the form of higher wages and more employment opportunities. This may well occur in the form of lower wages during the training period or deferred compensation schemes. However, there may be institutional constraints that prevent paying such lower wages (e.g., minimum wage regulations and union contracts). Furthermore, workers may be subject to liquidity constraints that inhibit them from paying for the training and are exacerbated by the fact that they cannot use their human capital from such training as collateral for a loan.

The same market failures may exist with respect to the provision of labour market information (e.g., new job opportunities). Such information has public good characteristics: the benefits of the information are equally available to all once it is provided, and it is often difficult for the market to exclude nonpayers. Thus, it is often publicly provided, although a social cost-benefit calculation still has to be made as to how much information to provide.

While these problems have long been with us, they take on greater urgency in the current environment. Training and labour market information are becoming more important ways of dealing with the downside and the upside adjustment problems, and could facilitate the reallocation of labour from declining to expanding sectors. Facilitating this reallocation process could reduce all aspects of the emerging trilemma: unemployment would be reduced by reallocating labour to where the employment opportunities are; inflation would be reduced by filling the structural bottlenecks or unfilled vacancies that otherwise may give rise to inflationary wage adjustments; and wage inequality would be reduced by reallocating labour from the low-wage to the high-wage sectors.

The changing nature of work might also further reduce the incentive for the private sector to pay for training. To the extent that there is more rapid turnover of the workforce, there is less incentive for firms to pay for training that requires a stable employment period to amortize the costs of training. To the extent that the new workplace is characterized by more uncertainty, it may be riskier to invest in training.

Importance of Market Mechanisms

As indicated previously, market mechanisms may fail to deal adequately with a number of increasingly important issues: redistribution and earnings inequality; the public good nature of workplace and human resource innovations; and the problem of poaching associated with training. While these market failures provide a theoretical rationale for public intervention, the practical rationale hinges on whether an imperfect market solution will be worse than what is also likely to be an imperfect public sector solution. Market failure is a necessary but not sufficient rationale for government intervention.

Policy makers have to make strategic choices as to how to deal with market mechanisms in pursuing social objectives. Policy initiatives often are designed to blunt market mechanisms, in part because markets tend to impose adjustment costs as they encourage the reallocation of resources from declining to expanding sectors. When faced with a policy problem, it is often tempting to design a policy response that deals with the symptom rather than the cause of the problem. Moreover, for policy makers and politicians who are often legally trained, legislated and regulatory solutions naturally appear to be the appropriate responses. Little attention is paid to the incentive structures that give rise to the problem in the first place, and thus how policy might alter those incentive structures to yield more socially acceptable outcomes. Furthermore, by ignoring market mechanisms, one runs the risk that policy initiatives may be undone by private responses as the parties adjust to these policies.

To the extent that market mechanisms are becoming a more important force under globalization, the policy challenge may be to try to harness or work with (rather than blunt) those market forces to achieve broader social objectives. Moving toward full employment, for example, would reduce the need for income support for the unemployed. Employment equity policies might increase the demand for target groups and hence increase both their wages and employability, in contrast with pay equity policies, which can reduce the employability of people whose wages are artificially increased by the legislation. For unions, the growing difficulty of extracting a wage premium under global competition means that there may be more value in focusing their efforts on ensuring due process and an employee voice in the workplace – functions that can be less costly to employers but nevertheless provide important benefits to union members.

Niche Strategies

Just as firms are having to develop market niches in order to survive, governments may also have to develop niche strategies with respect to their policy initiatives. High-cost firms have often successfully pursued a high-road strategy focusing on specialized activities (e.g., research and development, managerial and financial tasks) at least for their high-cost core workforce. Others have followed a high-performance strategy, investing extensively in their employees as a source of competitive advantage and not just a cost to be minimized.[50] Government policy makers may face similar strategic choices. The high-road, high-performance strategy may well involve accepting the fact that Canada is a high-cost nation, and the best response is to provide the physical infrastructure (e.g., transportation) and the human resource infrastructure (e.g., education) that will ensure the level of productivity and performance required to cover those costs. The policy challenge, of course, is to ensure that the public infrastructure is cost effective and not simply rent generating and wasteful.

Coordinating Strategies

Governments will increasingly face the challenge of coordinating their policy responses in different areas. Restrictions in one area, especially with respect to income maintenance, can lead to potential recipients seeking support through other programs. For example, reductions in the generosity of unemployment insurance can lead to increases in workers' compensation claims and social assistance caseloads, and vice versa.[51] Restrictions to workers' compensation can lead to workers seeking support through the disability component of the Canada Pension Plan. The problem is compounded when different government departments or jurisdictions are involved in that there may be an incentive to simply shift costs to others. Like the perennial leaf blower, the problems simply get recycled elsewhere.

Cost shifting can also occur as a result of governments transferring responsibility to the private sector – an increasingly tempting option when there is political pressure to reduce government spending. Governments shift costs in various ways including imposing user fees and simply not providing the service (in which case the private party foregoes the service or purchases it elsewhere). In many cases, these can be sensible ways to ensure that there is a real demand for services backed by a willingness to pay, and that governments focus on providing services that the private market will not provide and for which the social benefits exceed the social costs.

Another form of cost shifting takes place when governments use their regulatory and legislative power to download responsibility for programs (that otherwise would involve government expenditures) to the private sector.[52] The incentive to do so is enhanced by the fact that the cost of regulatory policies does not go in the books as a cost to the government, but the savings from any reductions in government programs do show up as a reduction in government spending. Again, in times of fiscal restraint, this becomes a politically attractive option. For example, regulations on employer-sponsored occupational pension plans can ultimately reduce the pressure on government pensions. Health and safety regulations (especially when the responsibilities are put on the workplace parties through the internal responsibility system) can reduce the burden on public workers' compensation programs. Sector councils, where training, labour adjustment and standards are handled by joint labour-management councils, can reduce the government burden in these areas. Restrictions on layoffs and terminations can prevent government spending on those who would otherwise be unemployed.

In each of these circumstances, the regulation of the private parties serves other legitimate social objectives, and it may very well be an attempt to place responsibility where it is best handled. Certainly, it is part of the current thrust to involve all the workplace parties in the design and implementation of policies they have to live with. Nevertheless, there is a danger that at least part of the motivation is to shift costs from the public to the private sector. That is, if the private sector is required by legislation or regulation to provide the program, then certainly there is less pressure on governments to achieve the same

31

objectives through public programs. Clearly, there is an increasing need to coordinate policy across government departments and jurisdictions, and to ensure that regulations and legislation are not simply a veiled attempt to transfer the cost of social programs to the private parties.

This challenge applies not only to the coordination of employment and human resource policies, but also to government policies in other areas such as trade and industrial development. While there is general recognition that policies affecting product and capital markets (e.g., trade liberalization, regulations on foreign direct investment and industrial policies) have an important impact on labour adjustment and human resources practices,[53] there is less recognition that policies that affect labour markets and workplaces can have important effects on competitiveness. Just as firms are increasingly integrating their human resource strategy into their broader competitiveness strategy, so should governments be integrating their labour policies as part of their strategies in other areas such as industrial and trade policies. Labour and human resources policies should not just be viewed as adjustment mechanisms in response to the fallout of other policy initiatives. They should be an integral part of a coherent, proactive strategy designed in part to reduce the need for defensive or reactive adjustment measures.

Design and Implementation
The tendency to deal with the symptoms rather than the causes of social problems often produces policy responses designed to provide maximum visibility and give the appearance of a solution. Often only the general policy thrust is set out in the legislation, with the details to be provided in subsequent regulations and perhaps worked out through judicial and quasi-judicial interpretations by the courts or administrative tribunals.

Unfortunately, it is often the case that the devil is in the detail, and well-intended policy initiatives can be gutted by design and implementation problems that are not worked out in advance. Leaving the details to the judicial arena can be expensive and time-consuming, involving lawyers, consultants and expert witnesses. These are real resource costs that are used up in the process; they are not transfer costs where one group's loss is another's gain. Furthermore, this approach can cause extensive delays, and justice delayed is often justice denied. The policy challenge is to design initiatives that minimize this risk and to anticipate the implementation details at the time the legislation is formulated. This is especially important since the new workplace is less likely to be dominated by large organizations with extensive legal and human resources departments that can interpret and deal with complicated legislative initiatives.

Furthermore, government departments are less likely to have extensive enforcement bureaucracies, given the cutbacks that have occurred. The policy challenge is to design policies that are simple, transparent and easily implemented.

Concluding Observations on Emerging Challenges

Clearly, the changing nature of work is giving rise to a new set of policy challenges that may require fundamental rethinking of what is the appropriate role for public policy. It is distinctly possible that the array of workplace policies that were established in earlier eras are not the most appropriate for the new world of work. It is true that the marginal adjustments that have been made to many of these policies may have been sufficient to keep pace with the changes. Yet if changes in the workplace are aptly described as transformation, reengineering and reinvention, the same descriptions do not apply to the policy responses.

Fundamental rethinking about a variety of emerging challenges is required. This will involve gathering evidence on the myths and realities of workplace change; addressing equity and distributional issues, especially the new dimension of earnings inequality; researching workplace innovations and patterns of diffusion; dealing with training and information externalities; understanding the role of market mechanisms; developing niche strategies for policies; coordinating labour policies with other policies; and paying attention to design and implementation details.

It is important that there be a proactive, equitable and efficient response to changing demand, supply and institutional forces that are giving rise to the new challenges. This is all the more important because labour market and workplace adjustments have important feedback effects on the product and capital markets that are giving rise to the pressures in the first place. The changing nature of work has important implications for public policy. The policy responses, however, have important implications not only for the nature of work but also for broader economic and social issues.

33

Notes

1. M. Gunderson and W. C. Riddell, "Jobs, Labour Standards and Promoting Competitive Advantage: Canada's Policy Challenge," *Labour* (Special Issue 1995), pp. S125-S48.

2. The origins of many of the policies are discussed in D. Carter, "Collective Bargaining Legislation," in M. Gunderson and A. Ponak (eds.), *Union-Management Relations in Canada*, 3rd ed. (Toronto: Addison-Wesley, 1995), pp. 53-71; and P. Malles, *Canadian Labour Standards in Law, Agreement and Practice* (Ottawa: Economic Council of Canada, 1976).

3. See M. Gunderson and D. Hyatt, "Canadian Public Sector Employment Relations in Transition," in D. Belman, M. Gunderson and D. Hyatt (eds.), *Public Sector Employment in a Time of Transition* (Madison, WI: Industrial Relations Research Association, 1996), pp. 243-281.

4. C. Digby and W.C. Riddell, "Occupational Health and Safety in Canada," in W.C. Riddell (ed.), *Canadian Labour Relations* (Toronto: University of Toronto Press, 1986), pp. 285-320; and M. Nash, *Canadian Occupational Health and Safety Law Handbook* (Toronto: CCH Canadian Limited, 1983).

5. A global optimum provides the best social outcomes over the entire range of potential policy configurations, while a local optimum provides the best outcomes in the limited neighbourhood of a particular policy regime. All local optima, except one, are therefore dominated by the global optimum, in the same way that all peaks in a mountain are dominated by the highest one.

6. P. Warrian, *The End of Public Sector "Industrial" Relations in Canada?* (Toronto: KPMG Centre for Government Foundation, 1995).

7. The participation of women in the labour force increased slowly from 16 percent in 1901 to 29 percent by 1961, but thereafter it increased rapidly to 40 percent in 1971, 52 percent in 1981, and 60 percent in 1991 (D. Benjamin, M. Gunderson and W.C. Riddell, *Labour Market Economics: Theory, Evidence and Policy in Canada* [Toronto: McGraw-Hill Ryerson, 1998], p. 31.)

8. M. Gunderson and L. Muszynski, *Women and Labour Market Poverty* (Ottawa: Advisory Council on the Status of Women, 1990).

9. Statistics Canada, *Characteristics of Dual Earner Families* (Ottawa: Statistics Canada, 1994, cat. no. 13-215).

10. H. C. Jain and A. Verma, "Managing Workforce Diversity for Competitiveness," *International Journal of Manpower*, Vol. 17, no. 4/5 (1996), pp. 14-29; W. Johnston and A. Packer, *Workforce 2000: Work and Workers for the Twenty-First Century* (Indianapolis, Indiana: Hudson Institute, 1987); C. L. Taylor, *Dimensions of Diversity in Canadian Business: Building a Business Case for Valuing Ethnocultural Diversity* (Ottawa: Conference Board of Canada, 1995).

11. See K. Lang and S. Kahn, "Hours Constraints: Theory, Evidence and Policy Implications," *Conference on Working Time in Canada and the United States* (Ottawa: Statistics Canada, 1996) for a discussion of Canadian and comparable US surveys. In both countries, the general finding is that preferences are stronger for increased work time than for reduced work time.

12. M. Sheridan, D. Sunter and B. Diverty, "The Changing Work Week: Trends in Weekly Hours of Work in Canada, 1976-1995," *The Labour Force*, Vol. 52 (June 1995), pp. C2-C31.

13. K. Hall, "Hours Polarization at the End of the 1990s," *Perspectives on Labour and Income*, Vol. 11 (Summer 1999), pp. 29-37.

14. This time crunch is emphasized in the recent report of the Advisory Group on Working Time and the Distribution of Work (chaired by A. Donner). See Human Resources Development Canada, *Report of the Advisory Group on Working Time and the Distribution of Work* (Ottawa: HRDC, 1994). See also L.O. Stone, *Dimensions of Job-Family Tension* (Ottawa: Statistics Canada, 1994, cat. no. 85-5406).

15. See W. C. Riddell, "Unionization in Canada and the United States," in D. Card and R. Freeman (eds.), *Small Differences That Matter: Labor Markets and Income Maintenance in Canada and the United States* (Chicago: University of Chicago Press, 1993), pp. 109-48 and OECD, *Employment Outlook* (Paris: OECD, July 1997).

16. There is evidence, for example, that approximately 80 percent of payroll taxes are shifted back to workers in the form of lower wages in return for benefits associated with the programs financed by these taxes (see B. Dahlby, "Payroll Taxes," in A. Maslove (ed.), *Business Taxation in Ontario* (Toronto: University of Toronto Press, 1993). There is also evidence that a substantial part of the cost of accommodating the injured workers returning to work is shifted back when workers return to an employer other than the one

where the accident occurred (M. Gunderson and D. Hyatt, "Do Injured Workers Pay for Reasonable Accommodation?" *Industrial and Labor Relations Review*, Vol. 50 [October 1996], pp. 92-104.)

17. J. T. Addison (ed.), *Job Displacement* (Detroit: Wayne State Press, 1991); L. Jacobson, R. Lalonde and D. Sullivan, *The Cost of Worker Dislocation* (Kalamazoo: Upjohn Institute for Employment Research, 1993); L. Jacobson, R. Lalonde and D. Sullivan, "Earnings Losses of Displaced Workers," *American Economic Review*, Vol. 83 (September 1993), pp. 685-709; G. Picot, Z. Lin and W. Pyper, "Permanent Layoffs in Canada: Overview and Longitudinal Analysis," *Canadian Journal of Economics*, Vol. 31 (November 1998), pp. 1154-78.

18. As indicated in G. Picot, J. Baldwin and R. Dupuy, "Have Small Firms Created a Disproportionate Share of New Jobs in Canada?: A Reassessment of the Facts", (Ottawa: Statistics Canada, Analytical Studies Branch, 1994), the average annual net job creation rate was 3.3 percent for firms with 0-19 employees, 1.7 percent for those with 20-29, 1.4 percent for those with 50-99, 1.0 percent for those with 100-499, and 0.1 percent for those with 500 and over.

19. Many of these are outlined in E. Applebaum and R. Batt, *The New American Workplace* (Ithaca: ILR Press, 1994) for the United States, and G. Betcherman et al., *The Canadian Workplace in Transition* (Kingston: IRC Press, 1994) for Canada.

20. Author's calculations using public use microdata from Statistics Canada's Labour Force Survey. Own-account self-employment is self-employed workers without paid employees.

21. G. Picot and A. Heisz, "Canadian Labour Market Performance in Historical Context," *CSLS Conference on the Structural Aspects of Unemployment in Canada* (Ottawa: Centre for the Study of Living Standards, 1999) cites the growing Canadian literature on this topic, and also includes references to the US literature. Canadian studies include Economic Council of Canada, *Good Jobs, Bad Jobs* (Ottawa: Supply and Services Canada, 1990); Economic Council of Canada, *Employment in the Service Economy* (Ottawa: Supply and Services Canada,1991); R. Freeman and K. Needels, "Skill Differentials in Canada in an Era of Rising Labor Market Inequality," in Card and Freeman (eds.), *Small Differences That Matter*, pp. 45-68; R. Morissette, J. Myles and G. Picot, "Earnings Polarization in Canada, 1969-1991," in K. Banting and C. Beach (eds.), *Labour Market Polarization and Social Policy Reform* (Kingston: Queen's

University School of Policy Studies, 1995), pp. 23-50; C.M. Beach and G.A. Slotsve, *Are We Becoming Two Societies?* (Toronto: CD Howe Institute, 1996); and K.M. Murphy, W. C. Riddell and P.M. Romer, "Wages, Skills and Technology in the United States and Canada," in E. Helpman (ed.), *General Purpose Technologies and Economic Growth* (Cambridge: MIT Press, 1998).

22. Freeman and Needels, "Skill Differentials in Canada in an Era of Rising Labor Market Inequality," in Card and Freeman (eds.), *Small Differences That Matter*, pp. 45-68; and Murphy, Riddell and Romer, "Wages, Skills and Technology in the United States and Canada," in Helpman (ed.), *General Purpose Technologies and Economic Growth*, pp. 283-309.

23. R. Chaykowski, "Union Influences on Labour Market Outcomes and Earnings Inequality," in Banting and Beach (eds.), *Labour Market Polarization and Social Policy Reform*, pp. 95-118; T. Lemieux, "Unions and Wage Inequality in Canada and the United States," in Card and Freeman (eds.), *Small Differences That Matter*, pp. 69-108; J. Dinardo and T. Lemieux, "Diverging Male Wage Inequality in the United States and Canada: Do Institutions Explain the Difference?" *Industrial and Labor Relations Review*, Vol. 50 (July 1997), pp. 629-51.

24. For example, the real minimum wage declined by 23 percent in the US over the period 1981-88, while in Canada it fell by only 12 percent (Dinardo and Lemieux, "Diverging Male Wage Inequality in the United States and Canada.")

25. For evidence on permanent layoffs, see M. Gunderson, "Alternative Mechanisms for Dealing with Permanent Layoffs, Dismissals and Plant Closings," in W.C. Riddell (ed.), *Adapting to Change: Labour Market Adjustment in Canada* (Toronto: University of Toronto Press, 1986), pp. 111-62; and Picot, Lin and Pyper, "Permanent Layoffs in Canada." During the 1980s and 1990s, there was an increase in the proportion of unemployment that was associated with permanent job loss as opposed to other sources of increase such as new entrants, re-entrants, quits and temporary layoffs. However, Picot, Lin and Pyper ("Permanent Layoffs in Canada") find that the probability of permanent layoff was no higher in the late 1980s and early 1990s than previously once one controls for the state of the business cycle and individual characteristics of workers.

26. D. Card and W.C. Riddell, "A Comparative Analysis of Unemployment in Canada and the United States," in Card and Freeman (eds.), *Small Differences That Matter*, pp. 149-90. For

35

an overview of research on this topic see W.C. Riddell and A. Sharpe, "The Canada-US Unemployment Rate Gap: An Introduction and Overview," *Canadian Public Policy*, Vol. 24 (special issue, February 1998), pp. S1-S37.

27. HRDC, *Report of the Advisory Group on Working Time and the Distribution of Work.*

28. As of 1993, about 17 percent of the workforce worked part time (about twice the rate in the mid-1970s) and about one-third of them preferred to work full time. Approximately 23 percent of jobs (as opposed to workers) were part time, reflecting the fact that some workers hold more than one part-time job (HRDC, *Report of the Advisory Group on Working Time and the Distribution of Work* [Ottawa: HRDC, 1994], p. 31).

29. Most of the recent growth in the fraction of the working age population on social assistance has taken place among those classified as "employable," especially families and single individuals without children (G. Barrett and M. Cragg, "An Untold Story: The Characteristics of Welfare Use in British Columbia," *Canadian Journal of Economics*, Vol. 31 (February 1998), pp. 165-88.)

30. A. Verma and D. G. Toras, "Employee Involvement in the Workplace," in M. Gunderson, A. Ponak and D. G. Taras (eds.), *Union-Management Relations in Canada*, 4th ed. (Toronto: Pearson Education Canada, 2001) pp. 25-57.

31. OECD, *Employment Outlook* (Paris: OECD, 1993); OECD, *The OECD Jobs Study: Labour Market Trends and Underlying Forms of Change* (Paris: OECD, 1994); OECD, *The OECD Jobs Study: Adjustment Potential of the Labour Market* (Paris: OECD, 1994); and W. C. Riddell, "Human Capital Formation in Canada: Recent Developments and Policy Responses," in Banting and Beach (eds.), *Labour Market Polarization and Social Policy Reform*, pp. 125-72.

32. M. Gunderson and A. Sharpe (eds.), *Forging Business-Labour Partnerships: The Emergence of Sectoral Councils in Canada* (Toronto: University of Toronto Press, 1998).

33. Digby and Riddell, "Occupational Health and Safety in Canada," in Riddell (ed.), *Canadian Labour Relations.*

34. The source of the data is Statistics Canada's Labour Force Survey, which provides the longest consistent time series on the extent of non-standard employment in Canada. Calculations by the authors.

35. The source of the data is the new Labour Force Survey which, since January 1997, includes information on whether an individual's job is permanent. Non-permanent employment includes seasonal, temporary, term and casual work.

36. H.S. Farber, "Are Lifetime Jobs Disappearing? Job Duration in the United States: 1973-1993," in J. Haltiwanger, M.E. Manser and R. Topel (eds.), *Labor Statistics Measurement Issues* (Chicago: University of Chicago Press, 1998), pp. 157-203.

37. Farber, "Are Lifetime Jobs Disappearing?" p. 192.

38. F. Diebold, D. Neumark and D. Polsky, "Is Job Stability Declining in the US Economy?: Comment," *Industrial and Labor Relations Review*, Vol. 49 (January 1996), pp. 348-55.

39. D. A. Green and W. C. Riddell, "Job Duration in Canada: Is Long-Term Employment in Canada Declining?" in M. Abbott, C. Beach and R. Chaykowski (eds.), *Transitional and Structural Change in the North American Labour Market* (Kingston: IRC Press, 1997), pp. 8-40.

40. A. Heitz, "Changes in Job Tenure in Canada," *Canadian Economic Observer*, Vol. 9, no. 1 (January 1996), pp. 81-94.

41. See Picot, Lin and Pyper, "Permanent Layoffs in Canada." The period of their analysis is 1978-93.

42. For example, C. Beach, *Are We Becoming Two Societies?: Income Polarization and the Middle Class in Canada* (Toronto: C.D. Howe Institute, 1995) and S. Phipps, "Poverty and Labour Market Change: Canada in a Comparative Perspective," in Banting and Beach (eds.), *Labour Market Polarization and Social Policy Reform*, pp. 59-88.

43. See P. Benimadhu, *Hours of Work: Trends and Attitudes in Canada* (Ottawa: Conference Board of Canada, 1987); and HRDC, *Report of the Advisory Group on Working Time and the Distribution of Work.*

44. See K. Lang and S. Kahn, "Hours Constraints: Theory, Evidence and Policy Implications" (Boston University, 1996, mimeo); and M. Drolet and R. Morisette, "Working More? Working Less? What Do Canadian Workers Prefer?" research paper no. 104, Statistics Canada, Analytical Studies Branch, Ottawa, 1997.

45. Evidence suggesting labour costs are an important determined of plant location and investment decision is given in D. Carlton, "Why New Firms Locate Where They Do: An Econometric Model," in W. Wheaton (ed.), *Interregional Movements and Regional Growth* (Washington, DC: The Urban Institute, 1979), pp. 13-50; M. Kieschnick, "Taxes and Growth: Business Incentives and Economic Development," in M. Barker (ed.), *State Taxation Policy* (NC: Duke University Press, 1983), pp. 155-280; I. Litvak and C. Maule, *The Canadian Multinationals* (Toronto: Butterworths, 1981); S. Williams and W. Brinker, "A Survey of Foreign Firms Recently Locating in Tennessee," *Journal of Public, Urban and Regional Policy*, Vol. 16 (July 1985), pp. 54-63; and A. Rugman, *Outward Bound: Canadian Direct Investment in the United States* (Toronto: C.D. Howe Institute, 1987), while contrary evidence is given in C. E. Forget and D. Denis, "Canadian Foreign Direct Investment in the United States: Reasons and Consequences," in Rugman (ed.), *Outward Bound*; P. Ghandhi, "The Free Trade Agreement and Canadian Investment in Northern New York," *Canadian Journal of Regional Science*, Vol. 13 (Summer/Autumn, 1990), pp. 205-19; and J. Knubley, W. Krause and Z. Sadeque, "Canadian Acquisitions Abroad: Patterns and Motivations," in L. Waverman (ed.), *Corporate Globalization Through Mergers and Acquisitions* (Calgary: University of Calgary Press, 1991), pp. 23-58.

46. R. Catalono, "The Health Effects of Economic Insecurity," *American Journal of Public Health*, Vol. 81, no. 9 (1991), pp. 1148-52; C. D'Arcy, "Unemployment and Health," *Canadian Journal of Public Health*, Vol. 77 (May/June 1986), pp. 124-31; C. D'Arcy and C.M. Sidduque, "Unemployment and Health: An Analysis of the Canadian Health Survey," *International Journal of Health Services*, Vol. 15, no. 4 (1985), pp. 609-35; R. Jin, C. Shaw and T. Svoboda, "The Impact of Unemployment on Health: A Review of the Evidence," *Canadian Medical Association Journal*, Vol. 153 (September 1995); J. P. Grayson, "The Closure of a Factory and its Impact on Health," *International Journal of*

Health Services, Vol. 15, no. 1 (1985), pp. 69-93; J. P. Grayson, "Reported Illness from the CGE Closure," *Canadian Journal of Public Health*, Vol. 80, no. 1 (Jan./Feb. 1989), pp. 16-19; and K. Pauler and J. Lewko, "Children's Worries and Exposure to Unemployment," *Canada's Mental Health* (September 1984), pp. 14-18.

47. R. Blank and M. Hanratty, "Responding to Need: A Comparison of Social Safety Nets in Canada and the United States," in Card and Freeman (eds.), *Small Differences That Matter*.

48. M. Gunderson, "Alternative Mechanisms for Dealing with Permanent Layoffs, Dismissals and Plant Closings," in Riddell (ed.), *Adapting to Change*, pp. 111-162.

49. W. C. Riddell, "Human Capital Formation in Canada."

50. L. Kaden and L. Smith, *The Cuomo Commission Report: A New American Formula For A Strong Economy* (New York: Simon & Schuster Inc., 1988); Ontario Premier's Council, *Competing in the New Global Economy* (Toronto: Queen's Printer, 1988); Ontario Premier's Council, *People and Skills in the New Global Economy* (Toronto: Queen's Printer, 1990); and J. Pfeffer, *Competitive Advantage Through People* (Cambridge: Harvard Business School Press, 1994).

51. B. Fortin and P. Lanoie, "Substitution Between Unemployment Insurance and Workers' Compensation," *Journal of Public Economics*, Vol. 49, no. 3 (1992), pp. 287-312.

52. The growing regulatory aspect of labour market policy in Canada is emphasized in M. Gunderson, *Efficient Instruments for Labour Market Regulation* (Kingston: Queen's University School of Policy Studies, 1993).

53. M. Gunderson and S. Verma, "Labour Market Implications of Outward Foreign Direct Investment," in S. Globerman (ed.), *Canadian Based Multinationals* (Calgary: University of Calgary Press, 1994), pp. 179-213.

37

Employment Outcomes in Canada: A Cohort Analysis

Paul Beaudry and David A. Green

Introduction

In recent years there has been considerable concern over worsening labour market outcomes, particularly for youth. The concern has centred on three main outcomes: earnings, access to employment, and quality of employment. Concern over earnings has arisen in part because of increases in earnings inequality among men in Canada over the last 15 years. Direct concern about younger workers has arisen out of the observation that earnings differentials by age have increased dramatically over this period and are a significant contributing factor to the overall increase in male earnings inequality. Questions of access to employment are raised by persistent high unemployment rates, much of the burden of which falls on younger workers. In addition, there is concern in many quarters that the employment that does exist is unstable and unlikely to lead to substantial long run attachment to the labour force.[1] A common claim is that young workers (outsiders) are being stuck with no jobs or bad jobs while older workers (insiders) are keeping the good jobs. In this paper, we examine measures of employment outcomes in an attempt to understand the magnitude and location of potential problems in terms of both access to jobs and, more specifically, access to good jobs.[2]

The main obstacle to understanding recent trends in employment outcomes is that it is difficult to untangle the effects of a prolonged recession in the labour market from longer-term trends. Many of the recent claims about the labour market revolve around the argument that there has been a sea change in the Canadian labour market and the economy more generally, brought about by large exogenous forces such as technological change, increased trade flows and increased capital mobility. Furthermore, when one observes differences in employment outcomes across age groups in the 1990s, it is not clear whether they reflect increased returns to experience or just worsening long-term prospects for more recent generations of labour market entrants. If the former is true, then one would expect current poor outcomes for young workers to be reversed as they age. If the latter is true, then a more pessimistic long-term prognosis might be in order. To untangle these competing effects and explanations, we examine employment outcomes over the last 20 years in Canada using a cohort-based analysis. More specifically, we trace the employment outcomes of various cohorts of labour market entrants as they age. We also attempt to remove the main cyclical features from the time patterns of employment outcomes. The result is an analysis that permits differentiation of aging effects from more permanent differences among workers from older and newer generations.

Finally, it is worth noting that much of the concern over rising inequality and worsening employment outcomes stems from examining data on men. In broad terms, female earnings inequality follows similar patterns to that of men if we only focus on full-year, full-time (FYFT) workers, but shows less growth if we examine all workers. In addition, strong movement into the labour force by women in recent decades implies rising rather than falling employment rates. Thus, it is difficult to make broad generalizations about trends in the labour market. For this reason, we investigate trends for men and women separately.

The paper proceeds in five sections. In the second section, we discuss our data sources and describe how we construct various outcomes for each cohort of labour market entrants. The outcomes we examine are employment-to-population ratios, the proportion of the employed who have FYFT employment, and average job tenure. We follow these outcomes for a set of cohorts defined by the year in which individuals enter the mature labour market (i.e., the year in which they turn 25). We carry out the analysis for four different education and gender groups. In the third section, as a precursor to the cohort analysis and to provide a clear description of trends in the economy, we present plots of our outcome measures by year and age group. In the fourth section, we present plots of our outcome measures organized to follow cohorts across time. In the fifth section, we present a statistical analysis of the cohort data. The sixth section contains a discussion and conclusions. Our main finding is that there have been very large increases in employment instability among less-educated men but only limited secular increases in instability among women and more-educated men.

Data

Our empirical approach is to follow the employment experiences of cohorts of workers through time. We do this using data from the Survey of Consumer Finances (SCF) for the years 1971, 1973, 1975, 1977, 1979, 1981, 1982, 1984, 1986, 1988, 1990, 1992, and 1993. The data for the years 1971-79 come from Census Family Files while those for the years 1981-93 come from the Individual Files. In order to create a consistent series over time, we restrict the samples from the Individual Files to include only individuals who are heads or spouses of census households.[3]

We define an entry cohort as a group of individuals who were age 25 or 26 in an even-numbered year. Thus, the cohort entering in 1972 contains individuals who turned 25 or 26 in 1972. We chose 25 as the age of entry into the mature labour market to focus attention on the period after most individuals have finished their education and during which they become more permanently attached to the labour market. We chose this focus in part to simplify measurement, since the greater flexibility exhibited by younger individuals creates potentially substantial selection issues. However, we also believe that this is an interesting age range on which to concentrate since it is the age of transition to stable work patterns, accelerating careers and family formation. If changes in the economy are negatively affecting access to stable employment after this age, this should be a source of major policy concern. Alternatively, if changes in the labour market require more adjustments on the part of the youth themselves, for example increased education, but they still move on to stable career paths after 25, then these labour market changes may not raise as much concern. Results in Card and Lemieux[4] indicate that newer generations are taking longer to settle into stable work and family-formation patterns. In our analysis this would show up as poorer outcomes at age 25.

We follow the cohorts entering in 1962 and after. We do not examine all possible cohorts in all years, in order to avoid trying to make predictions too far out of our sample. In particular, the older cohorts observed at the start of our sample period probably experienced a very different labour market than did those who entered in the 1960s and later. If this is true, then attempts to extrapolate backwards from our data to predict the earliest parts of the age-employment profiles of these workers in order to compare their outcomes with more recent cohorts would be misguided. We restrict our data to individuals who are under the age of 56 in any given sample year to avoid the fluctuations associated with early retirement.

We further divide our entry cohorts into subgroups based on education level. We examine two education groups: (1) those with some or completed high-school education; and (2) those with a university degree or more. The first group includes individuals who have some postsecondary education but have not obtained a postsecondary certificate or degree. A preliminary investigation of the data indicated that their behaviour is very similar to that of those with a high-school education. Note that we do not present results relating either to individuals with less than some high-school education or to those who have completed a postsecondary certificate or a degree other than a university degree. The group with some or completed high-school education is relatively large and important throughout the period under study. Thus, in 1993, 52.3 percent of men and 53.0 percent of women (regardless of their labour force status) fell into this education category. The university educated also make up a substantial group, though not nearly as large as that with some or completed high-school education. The university educated comprise 14.0 percent of men and 11.5 percent of women in 1993.[5]

One potential concern in using this data is that the definitions of educational categories changed in 1990. One key change was the division of the "some or completed high school" category into two categories, the "some high school but not completed" category and the "completed high school" category. This change does not present any difficulty under our data definitions since we group together all individuals with some or completed high-school education. A change which is potentially of more concern is the transfer of those with postsecondary education where a high-school diploma is not required from the "some or completed high school" category to the "postsecondary education" category. To the extent that individuals after 1990 enter but do not complete these programs, they will continue to be grouped with high-school educated individuals under our assignment system. However, individuals who do earn a certificate from a program not requiring a high-school diploma will be categorized as having a high-school education before 1990 and a postsecondary certificate after 1990. This will alter the composition of our high-school educated group while other, smaller changes at the same time will affect our university educated group. Gower[6] investigates the impacts of these changes in definitions and finds that they generate a 9 percent decrease in the size of the some or completed high-school education category and a 7 percent decrease in the size of the university education category. The decreases in both categories are offset by increases in the "postsecondary certificate or diploma" category. The reader should keep these changes in definitions in mind when examining the results that follow.

Our analysis consists of following employment measures for each cohort in each of our sample years. For example, we examine the employment outcomes of all individuals in the 1968 entry cohort in 1971, 1973, 1975, etc. In principle, this provides us with a picture of the employment path followed by this group of individuals over time. Since the SCF does not form a true panel, we are not actually following the same group of individuals over time in this exercise. However, as long as the composition of the group being followed does not change over time, employment measures such as average job tenure in each year for this synthetic cohort will provide an accurate picture of the average experience for individuals in the cohort. The composition of the cohort groups may change over time as individuals acquire more education. We believe that problems of this sort are minimized by the fact that we only examine individuals over the age of 25.[7] Immigration is potentially another source of compositional change, as new members could be added to a cohort over time. To investigate the impact of immigration, we generated all the results in this paper for a separate sample of men which excluded immigrants. The results of that exercise were very similar to those presented below.[8]

Since our goal is to investigate the claim that young workers today are having greater difficulty getting access to employment, particularly stable, long-term employment, we focus on the employment-to-population ratio, the proportion with FYFT jobs and average job tenure as employment outcome measures. To create the employment-to-population-ratio variable, we first create a dummy variable for each individual, which equals one if they are employed in the reference week and zero otherwise.[9] We then calculate the proportion of individuals in a given sex, year, cohort and education group for whom this variable equals one. The proportion who work FYFT is defined as the number of individuals who worked at least 49 weeks in the reference year and who report themselves as "mostly working full time" (i.e., at least 30 hours a week) as a percentage of those individuals who worked at least one week in the reference year. We also examine the average tenure in the current job of individuals working in the reference week. Note that this is tenure in ongoing jobs, not completed jobs. The difficulty with using measures based on ongoing job tenure is that they reflect not only the effects of labour market events in the current year but also the selection mechanism determining which jobs are still ongoing in the current year. The selection mechanism will be based on job entry rates in the past and economic events in all years between job starts and the current year. Thus, one could observe a short average ongoing job tenure in 1984 not because many long-term jobs terminated in that year but because a disproportionate number of long-term jobs were terminated in preceding years, thus decreasing the average in 1984. However, the reported tenure variable in the public version of the SCF is the only available measure of job tenure and we believe that useful information can be extracted from its patterns over time. This is particularly true when one is following specific cohorts over time.[10]

43

paul beaudry and david a. green

Table 1
Employment-to-Population Rate Differences Between University and High-School Educated Individuals, 1971-1993 (selected years)

Age group	25-34	35-44	45-54
FEMALES			
1971	.20	.25	.32
1977	.24	.19	.34
1982	.24	.16	.30
1986	.18	.15	.31
1990	.19	.11	.32
1993	.25	.13	.38
MALES			
1971	.03	.05	.13
1977	.05	.06	.18
1982	.10	.10	.17
1986	.10	.09	.23
1990	.14	.12	.25
1993	.13	.10	.25

Source: Statistics Canada, Survey of Consumer Finances,
"Income of Economic Families, 1971, 1977," microdata tapes
(1972, 1978); Survey of Consumer Finances, "Individuals
With and Without Income, 1982, 1986, 1990, 1993," microdata tapes (1983, 1987, 1991, 1994); calculations by authors.

44

Overall Trends in Employment Outcomes

We begin our examination by looking at long-term trends in employment for various groups defined by gender, age and education. This is a useful place to start because employment is both the goal and the main labour market outcome for most individuals. Further, employment is less subject to measurement error than either unemployment or labour force participation, since it can be defined more objectively. Finally, it allows us to address one of the principal claims about the current labour market: that younger people are having more difficulty gaining access to employment.

Employment-to-Population Ratios
Figures 1a and 1b show the employment-to-population ratios for women in specific age groups with some or completed high-school and university education, respectively, for the period 1971-93. The dominant pattern in these figures

is the substantial rise in the ratio for all age and education groups over the last 20 years. Underlying that common trend, however, are very different patterns for the various subgroups. The less educated experienced much lower employment/population rates at every age, with the difference in employment rates between education groups in any year being as much as 0.40 for the oldest age group. The differences between education groups (shown in table 1) stay relatively constant over time for the youngest and oldest age groups, but there has been substantial convergence in employment rates for the 35-44 age group, whose education differential fell from 0.25 in the early 1970s to 0.13 in the 1990s. The cyclical patterns of employment rates in the two education groups also differ, with the high-school educated showing strong cyclical patterns and the university educated showing almost none. Both education groups appear to have experienced a significant slowdown in the growth rate of the employment ratio after the mid-1980s, though this trend is difficult to separate from cyclical factors. Finally, while the university educated show little differentiation by age, particularly after the 1981/82 recession (figure 1b), there are large differences by age for the less educated. In fact, the employment-rate gap between less-educated women aged 25-34 and 35-44 increased from approximately 0.02 in 1971 to 0.09 in 1993 (figure 1a).

Figures 1c and 1d show the employment/population rates for men broken down by education and age over the period. In contrast to the female rates, male rates decline for every age and education group. For less-educated men, some of these declines are nearly as dramatic as the corresponding increases for less-educated women. For example, for less-educated, older men, the employment rate falls by 0.20, while the corresponding group of women experiences an increase of 0.15. But the declines in the employment rate for university educated men are small, and some of the decline at the end of the period is perhaps due to cyclical rather than long-term factors. It is worth emphasizing, though, that declines occur in all age groups. Thus, claims that declining male employment rates are due primarily to trends toward early retirement cannot be the whole story. The substantial 0.18 drop for less-educated men aged 25-34 in particular indicates that something else is behind these declines. It also raises serious policy concerns.[11]

The combination of patterns in figures 1c and 1d implies strongly increasing education differentials for men. This fits with the very strong trends in employment numbers (as opposed to employment/population rates) by education level documented by Riddell.[12] Riddell shows that between 1980 and 1993 there was a 57 percent drop in the number of employed workers with an elementary education and a 77 percent increase in the number with a university degree. Figures 1c and 1d indicate that part of that growing employment differential is

45

Figure 1
Employment-to-Population Ratios by Age, Gender and Education, 1971-1993

(a) High-School Educated Women

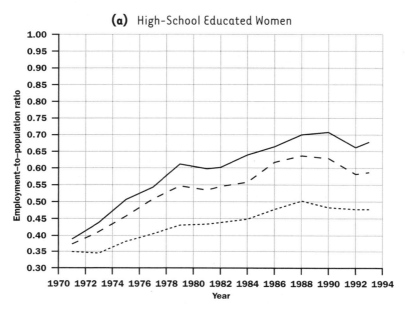

(b) University Educated Women

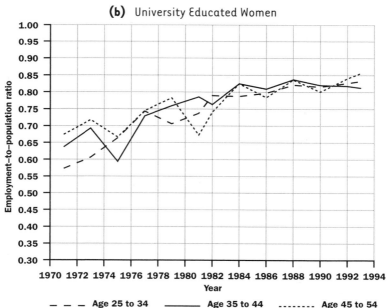

— — — Age 25 to 34 ——— Age 35 to 44 ········· Age 45 to 54

Figure 1 (cont'd)

Employment-to-Population Ratios by Age, Gender and Education, 1971-1993

(c) High-School Educated Men

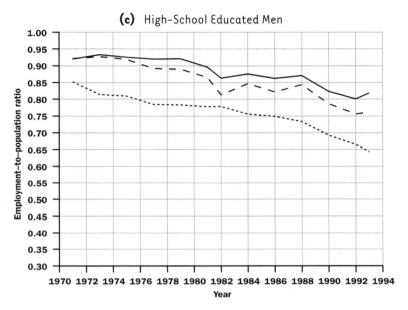

(d) University Educated Men

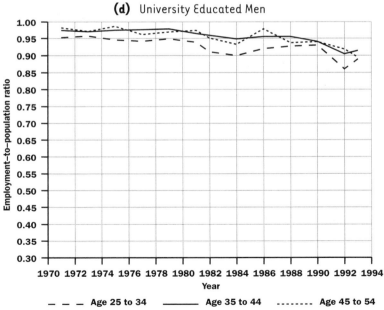

– – – Age 25 to 34 ———— Age 35 to 44 ·········· Age 45 to 54

Source: Survey of Consumer Finances, various years; calculations by authors.

paul beaudry and david a. green

due to declining labour force outcomes for less-educated men. The retirement of the older, less educated cohorts and changing education choices of new cohorts over time are also contributing factors.

Increased cyclicality for younger, less-educated workers is reflected in both male and female employment rate outcomes. Also, for less-educated men and women there has been a trend toward increased differentials between the youngest and the next oldest groups over time. For more-educated men, there appears to be more cyclicality than is directly evident for similar women. Whereas all the age groups among more-educated women have virtually identical employment rates after the 1980s, the youngest group of educated men has employment rates that are persistently below and more cyclical than those of their older counterparts (figure 1d).

Taken together, these trends indicate declines in employment outcomes among men that are more than offset by increases among women. Statements that there has been substantial long-term deterioration of employment appear to be accurate for less-educated men but not for any other group. The increases in education differentials for men in all age groups, as well as the increased age differential for less-educated men and women, may fit with claims that there have been relative shifts in demand in favour of individuals with more skills[13]. The strong increases in employment rates for less-educated women that persisted at least up until the late 1980s, however, do not appear to fit with this claim. It is worth noting that the upward employment trends for women mirror increases in women's labour force participation over time and indicate that there has been some degree of success in integrating a large group of new employment entrants. In recent years there has been a slowdown in the growth of female participation rates and employment rates.

Full-Year, Full-Time Employment Rates

The results in figures 1a-1d suggest that declines in employment are of concern largely among less-educated men, rather than being a pervasive phenomenon throughout the economy. Access to employment and access to good jobs that provide some degree of stability, opportunities for advancement and substantial earnings, however, are two different things. Bad jobs are likely to be defined as those associated with contract work, intermittent work patterns and short hours. To assess whether there has been a substantial increase in these types of jobs, we first examine trends in FYFT work. Figures 2a and 2b plot the proportion of less- and more-educated female workers who work FYFT. Figure 2a indicates that among high-school educated women, the increases in employment rates (figure 1a) have been accompanied by a movement toward more FYFT jobs. For those under the age of 45, the increases are in the order of 0.10 over the sample period. Note that since these figures are expressed in terms of the proportion of all workers, they indicate gains in stable working patterns over and above the gains in employment. The results for university educated female workers are more mixed (figure 2b): the proportion working FYFT among those aged 25 to 34 increases at the same rate as among their less-educated counterparts, while among those over the age of 35 the proportion is essentially stable.

As with the employment rate outcomes, the proportion of men employed FYFT is significantly higher than that of women in comparable age/education categories. The trend among men is also the opposite of that among women over the last 20 years. For less-educated men over 35, the drop in the FYFT employment rate is in the order of 0.10, and it is even greater for those aged 25 to 34 (figure 2c). For this gender/education group, the results display more cyclicality than any other group, however, which makes the overall trend difficult to read. For high-school educated men aged 25-34, for example, a sharp drop in the FYFT employment rate in the 1981/82 recession is nearly erased by 1988, only to re-emerge in the 1990s. University educated men in the 25-34 age group also displayed a strong decline in FYFT employment over the period, but only mild declines are evident for older, more-educated men (figure 2d). The declines in FYFT employment rates for less-educated men fit with the findings of Morissette et al.,[14] that increased polarization in the distribution of hours has played an important role in increased male earnings inequality in Canada in the last 15 years.

As with the employment rate outcomes, it is difficult to claim that there has been a universal worsening of stable work patterns, as measured by the FYFT employment rate, at any time in the last 20 years. The rate of stable work among women of all age and education groups has either increased or remained steady. As with employment outcomes, FYFT employment rates have worsened for men in general, but the trend is more evident among less-educated men and, to a somewhat lesser extent, younger university educated men. Also like the employment outcomes, the FYFT employment rate among less-educated men shows greater cyclicality than it does in other groups and reveals some tendency toward increased age differentials favouring older workers.

Job Tenure
Even within these patterns of employment and FYFT jobs, there may be large increases in the instability of employment. A common claim is that there has been a shift toward more contract and other types of secondary-labour-market jobs. Thus, even if the proportion working FYFT did not change, a smaller portion of the workforce might have access to the types of stable, long-term jobs

49

Figure 2
Proportion of FYFT[1] Workers by Age, Gender and Education, 1971-1993

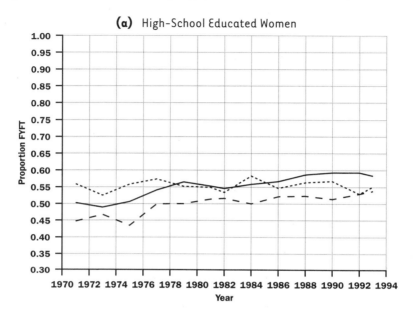

(a) High-School Educated Women

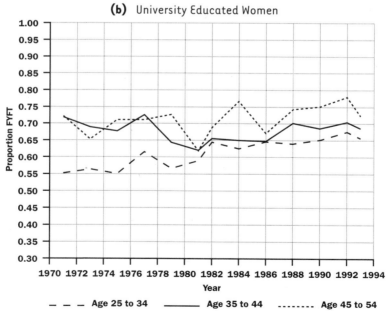

(b) University Educated Women

— — — Age 25 to 34 ———— Age 35 to 44 ········ Age 45 to 54

adapting public policy to a labour market in transition

Figure 2 (cont'd)
Proportion of FYFT[1] Workers by Age, Gender and Education, 1971–1993

(c) High-School Educated Men

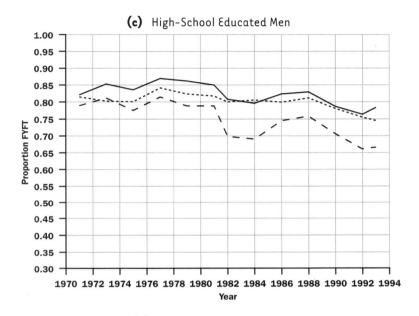

(d) University Educated Men

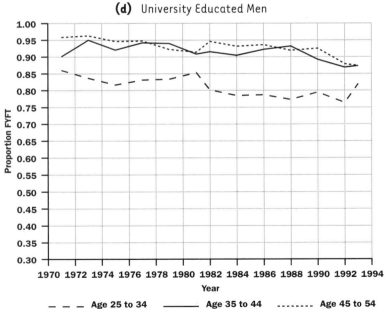

– – – Age 25 to 34 ——— Age 35 to 44 ········ Age 45 to 54

[1] FYFT refers to workers employed on a full-year, full-time basis.
Source: Survey of Consumer Finances, various years; calculations by authors.

paul beaudry and david a. green

that provide both an opportunity for training and greater security for workers. This could be true if there were an increased tendency toward shorter-duration, albeit full-time, jobs.

To assess whether the work relationship has changed dramatically in this respect, we present results pertaining to tenure on the current job.[15] Figures 3a and 3b plot average (interrupted) job tenure for women employed in the survey week for 1981-93.[16] There is a strong increasing pattern of average job tenure among high-school educated women in the 35-44 age group. In the younger group there is very little change, and in the older group there is a somewhat weaker increase (figure 3a). For university educated women (figure 3b), there is a strong trend upward in the oldest age group until the late 1980s, in the middle-aged group there is an increase to 1986 followed by a levelling off, while the pattern for the youngest group is one of stability. The implication is that there are increasing age differentials in average job tenure in both education groups, but that this is caused by apparent increases in job duration among older workers rather than decreases in job duration for the youngest workers.

There are also some slight moves upward among less-educated men in the 35-44 age group (figure 3c). Note, though, that this upward trend could occur if some shorter-tenure workers were laid off and not re-employed. Thus, the trend could reflect the declining employment rates for this group seen earlier. This would not be true of women, since their employment rates were either increasing or stable over this period. Among more-educated men, average job tenure is strikingly stable, with the exception of the oldest age group, whose average job tenure displays relative increases (figure 3d). Overall, the job tenure figures do not provide clear evidence of work becoming more unstable in the sense of being of shorter duration.

How do these results fit with other discussions of increased instability in the labour force? Krahn[17] documents an increase in part-time work from 11 percent to 17 percent of the workforce from 1976 to 1994, which suggests a more substantial weakening in labour market outcomes than we reported above with the FYFT measure for all groups except less educated men. The increase, however, is due almost entirely to increases in part-time work for those aged 15-24. The rate of part-time work among workers over age 25 is relatively stable at approximately 3 percent for men and 20 percent for women over the same period.[18] One wonders whether the strong increase in part-time work in the 15-24 age group is a consequence of the rapid increase in school enrolment over the same period and thus not a major concern. This, of course, points to the fact that part-time work need not be seen as a negative outcome to the extent that workers choose it to accommodate other activities in their lives. The proportion of part-time workers who report themselves to be involuntarily employed part time in 1994 was approximately 25 percent among workers aged 15-24, but 32 percent among women and 42 percent among men over the age of 25. This reflects the fact that older workers, particularly older men, are less likely to be employed part time by choice. All age and gender groups experienced substantial increases in involuntary part-time employment rates in the 1990s, but among older workers there is little evidence of a long-term upward trend before that point. One must also keep in mind that the proportion of all workers aged 25-34 who are involuntarily employed part-time is still small (in the order of 3 percent) even in the 1990s.[19]

Earlier studies of job tenure report mixed results. After controlling for cyclical factors, Green and Riddell[20] find a shortening of job tenure among young and less-educated men and women over the past 20 years. This was offset by increases in job tenure for older women and some groups of more-educated, prime-aged men. These patterns, plus the conclusion that the overall average job tenure has not changed in the last 20 years, are broadly consistent with the results in figures 3a-3d. Krahn[21] examines the proportion of workers who declare that they are working on contract. He finds either no observable trend or a slightly negative trend among women over age 25 in the 1990s, but an increasing trend among men, with the proportion of men aged 25-34 who hold contract jobs increasing from 6 percent in 1989 to 10 percent in 1994.

These results paint a complicated picture. Less educated women have experienced a rapid increase in employment and FYFT employment over the last 20 years. In general, their outcomes in terms of job tenure have also been positive: either increasing or stable job tenure in all the age groups. University educated women have made equally impressive gains in employment rates but generally have more stable FYFT employment patterns, particularly in the 1980s. More-educated women have done particularly well in securing more stable (i.e., longer lasting) jobs. In both education groups there has been some slowdown or even reversal of these positive patterns in the 1990s. Less-educated men have experienced worsening employment outcomes according to all measures, particularly since the 1970s. They have experienced dramatic declines in employment rates, FYFT employment rates and job tenure. The fact that this trend is evident in all age groups, but is particularly pronounced in the 25-34 age group, indicates that the outcomes cannot be accounted for by moves toward earlier retirement. Less-educated men are also by far the most cyclically sensitive group in terms of their employment outcomes. For university educated men, the trends, according to all our measures, are also generally negative, but to a much smaller extent than for high-school educated men. Combining the male and female results,

Figure 3
Average (Interrupted) Job Tenure by Age, Gender and Education, 1981–1993

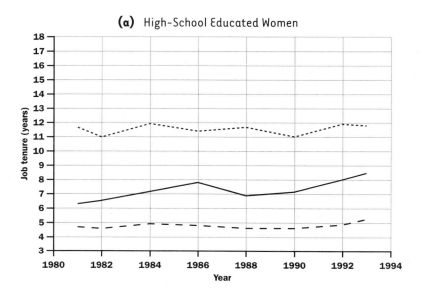

(a) High-School Educated Women

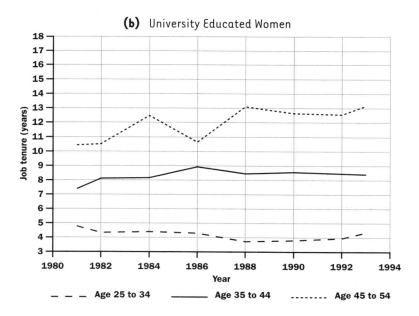

(b) University Educated Women

– – – Age 25 to 34　　—— Age 35 to 44　　‧‧‧‧‧‧‧ Age 45 to 54

Figure 3 (cont'd)
Average (Interrupted) Job Tenure by Age, Gender and Education, 1981-1993

(c) High-School Educated Men

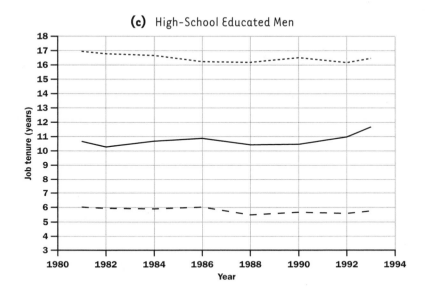

(d) University Educated Men

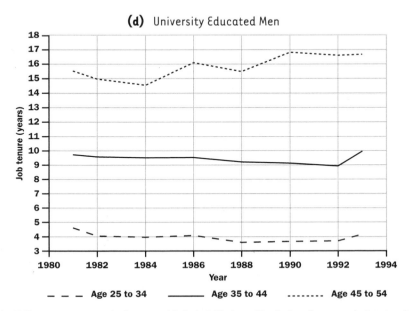

— — — Age 25 to 34   ——— Age 35 to 44   ·········· Age 45 to 54

Note: Refers to average tenure in the current job for individuals working in the reference week. Data is only available from 1981 because that is when the SCF Individual Files, which contain the job tenure data, started.
Source: Survey of Consumer Finances, Individual Files, various years.

paul beaudry and david a. green

the pattern appears to be one of relative stability for university educated workers but a potential displacement of less-educated men by female workers from employment in general, and longer-term, stable employment in particular.

One key question arising from these trends is what they imply in terms of future prospects for current labour market entrants. Should young, less-educated male workers expect to catch up to the (somewhat) better performance of older workers at the same education level? Are the poor outcomes for many groups in the 1990s just a reflection of a prolonged recession in the labour market or should we view them as a long-term trend? Again, this issue seems more pressing for younger workers who might be scarred by current labour market difficulties. One wonders, as well, whether apparent increases in job tenure among older workers over the last 20 years reflects changes in the labour market or just the aging of the baby boom. In the next section, we provide evidence on these issues by presenting the data in a different format: following specific groups of individuals through time.

Cohort Analysis of Employment Trends

We now examine profiles of employment outcomes against age by entry cohort. Our goal is to investigate whether these profiles have different levels across cohorts and whether the slopes of the profiles have been changing as newer cohorts enter the labour market. Thus, a reasonable hypothesis to verify is whether newer-entry cohorts have poorer initial employment outcomes than earlier cohorts, but catch up quickly.

Plots of age profiles of employment-to-population rates, FYFT employment rates and measures of job tenure for selected cohorts are presented in figures 4-6. The plots are shown separately for high-school educated men, high-school educated women, university educated men and university educated women. In each case, we refer to each specific cohort by the year in which it enters our age window, for example, the 1964 cohort is composed of workers who turned 25 or 26 in 1964. The cohort-specific profiles in Figures 4-6 are presented in a "smoothed" format in order to help focus attention on the main trends in the cohort-specific age profiles.[22] In particular, the profiles are constructed in a way that emphasizes trends, removing both distracting sampling variation and business-cycle effects.[23]

Employment-to-Population-Rate Cohort Profiles
Figures 4a and 4b present the smoothed plots of employment-to-population rates for high-school and university educated women, respectively. In both cases,

there is clear evidence of an upward shift in employment rates for recent-entry relative to earlier-entry cohorts at any given age. This upward shift has slowed to a stop since the early 1980s. For the university educated there appears to be a relatively common age pattern resembling a flattened "S" shape, with a somewhat downward-sloping section for those in their late 20s, possibly associated with labour market withdrawal for child-raising purposes. For the high-school educated, a somewhat similar pattern is evident, but with the downward-sloping segment occurring at earlier ages. The fact that most of the profiles of the high-school educated group decline at the end is interesting, given that we have attempted to remove the cyclical effects. That these declines remain after controlling for the business cycle could mean either that the labour market downturn in the 1990s was different from earlier ones, or that longer-term employment trends are turning against less-educated women. Of course, it could also mean that we did not adequately eliminate cyclical fluctuations.[24] Finally, for both education groups, the slopes of the age profiles appear to flatten across successive cohorts. The overall implication is that the increased age differentials over time for high-school educated women (figure 1a) are a result of differences across cohorts rather than changes in returns to experience. If the latter were the source of the age differential changes, one would expect to see steepening age profiles for all cohorts over time. Instead, we witness successively flatter profiles.

Figures 4c and 4d plot the employment rates for high-school and university educated men. Figure 4c reveals a striking pattern of worsening employment outcomes across successive cohorts of high-school educated men. At age 28, the 1990 entry cohort has an employment-to-population ratio that is over 0.20 lower than that of the 1968 entry cohort. This could be due to declining prospects for high-school educated workers. It might also occur if different individuals have different levels of innate ability and the more able individuals get a university education. In that scenario, when the level of education in the economy increases overall, the most able workers leave the high-school educated category and enter the university educated category. Since those increasing their education level are the most able and therefore the most employable among the high-school educated workers, their movement into the university educated group will reduce the observed employment rate of the high-school educated. At the same time, they will be less able than all other university educated workers and therefore their addition to the latter group will generate a decline in the employment rate of the university educated. Whether this mechanism or simple declining labour market outcomes is behind the observed patterns is unclear. The employment rates of all the cohorts show a negative trend over some age range. This is most

Figure 4
Trends of Smoothed[1] Employment-to-Population Rates by Cohort, Age, Education and Gender

(a) Women with Some or Completed High School

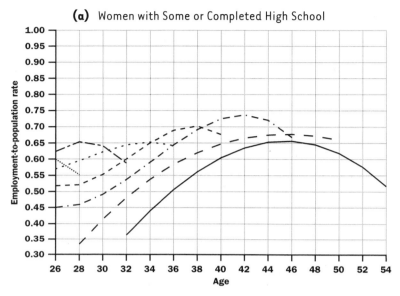

(b) University Educated Women

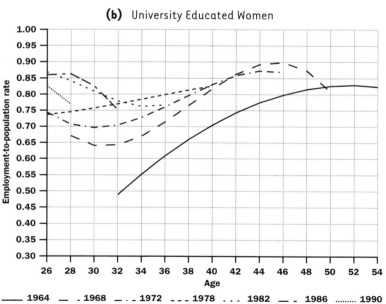

— 1964 — . 1968 — . . 1972 - - - 1978 . . . 1982 — . 1986 1990

Figure 4 (cont'd)
Trends of Smoothed[1] Employment-to-Population Rates by Cohort, Age, Education and Gender

(c) Men with Some or Completed High School

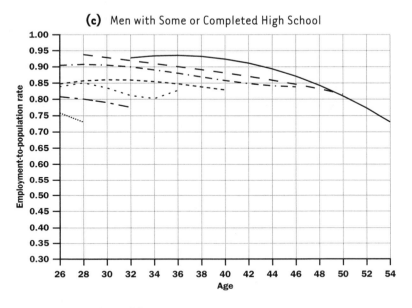

(d) University Educated Men

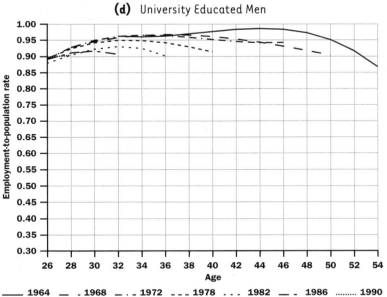

——— 1964   — · 1968   — ·· 1972   — — — 1978   · · · 1982   — — 1986   ········· 1990

[1] Business cycle effects removed.
Source: Survey of Consumer Finances, various years; calculations by authors.

paul beaudry and david a. green

striking after age 40 for the oldest cohort. While some of this decline could be associated with early retirement, the young ages at which it is often observed seems to fit more with the idea that in recent years older blue collar workers have been facing difficulties in the labour market. While the declines are evident in the employment-to-population ratios of high-school educated men (figure 1c), when we follow cohorts over time we see clearly how uncertainty has entered the life-cycle outcomes of all cohorts of less-educated men (figure 4c). For university educated men, there is no evidence of strong cohort patterns at young ages. It does appear, however, that the age profiles are flatter for newer cohorts, leading to lower employment rates at somewhat older ages.

Full-Year, Full-Time Employment Rate Cohort Profiles
Smoothed plots of FYFT employment rates for both female education groups are given in figures 5a and 5b. As with the employment rates, there have been substantial improvements in the FYFT employment rates of more recent entry cohorts relative to those who entered in the 1960s. Unlike the employment rate, however, cross-cohort improvements level off after the cohorts entering in the mid-1970s. After that point, for both education groups, the age profile is relatively flat up to the late 30s, when it begins to slope upward. For less-educated men (figure 5c), there is again evidence of declines in FYFT employment rates across cohorts, with the rates of the most recent entry cohort being particularly low. The profiles are generally flat with a concave shape. In contrast, there is no clear cohort pattern for university educated men. Interestingly, the FYFT rate of every cohort of university educated men shows a very sharp increase from the ages of 26-32, followed by a relatively flat profile thereafter. For the 1978 entry cohort, for example, the FYFT rate increases by nearly 0.15 between the ages of 26 and 32. That pattern suggests that concerns about part-year, part-time employment patterns among recent cohorts of university educated men are not well founded: the pattern of gradual entry into the FYFT track is common across cohorts, and recent cohorts fit right in with that pattern.

Job Tenure Cohort Profiles
Smoothed cohort profiles for average interrupted job tenure are presented in figures 6a and 6b for women and 6c and 6d for men.[25] Among less-educated women (figure 6a), there is some evidence of increases in average tenure at any age across successive cohorts up to the cohorts entering in the early 1980s. Thereafter, the time profiles seem to be quite stable. There is no clear evidence of increases or decreases in the slopes of the profiles across cohorts. Among university educated women, there is a noticeable improvement in average job

tenure between the 1964 entry cohort and all subsequent cohorts (figure 6b). However, the profiles of the post-1964 cohorts are intermingled and show no strong patterns. Looking at high-school educated men (figure 6c), there is slight evidence of increased average job tenure as one moves from the 1964 to the 1978 entry cohort. There is also some evidence of declines in the two most recent cohorts shown relative to their predecessors although these patterns are quite weak. Among university educated men, however, even weak cross-cohort patterns like these are not evident (figure 6d). Notice that the strongest positive slopes in these profiles are those for the most-educated men followed by the less-educated men, the most-educated women and finally the less-educated women. The profiles of university educated men and women actually are quite similar up to the age of 34, with the female profile falling significantly behind after that point. The key point to be made about these figures is that with the possible exception of less-educated men, the cohort plots do not provide any strong evidence of worsening outcomes in terms of job durations among more recent labour market entrants.

Statistical Analysis

Employment-to-Population Ratios

We now attempt to refine our understanding of age profiles and long-run trends by analyzing the cohort profiles using regression analysis. Examining the cohort-specific profiles in figures 4a-d, one can see that the profiles differ for various cohorts. To summarize the movements in the profiles succinctly, we regress the employment-to-population rate on age variables (to capture a common profile shape), the cohort number and its square (to capture long-term patterns in differences across cohorts), and the unemployment rate (to remove cycle effects and focus attention on long-term patterns). Tables A1 and A2 in the appendix present estimated coefficients from regressions of this form for each of the four gender/education groups. The estimation approach is a simple linear probability model with a correction for the well known heteroscedasticity problem.[26] In the specification in the first column corresponding with each gender/education group, the cohort effects are summarized by a variable containing the cohort number, while in the specification in the second column there are separate dummy variables corresponding with each cohort. To better illustrate the results of this analysis, we present fitted plots of the age/employment-rate profiles of selected cohorts in figures 7a-7d. In each case, we generate the plots based on the specification with a continuous cohort variable, cohort squared, a cubic in age, the interaction of age and cohort and the

61

Figure 5
Trends of Smoothed[1] FYFT Employment Rates by Cohort, Age, Education and Gender

(a) Women with Some or Completed High School

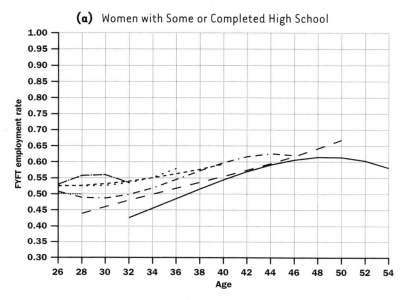

(b) University Educated Women

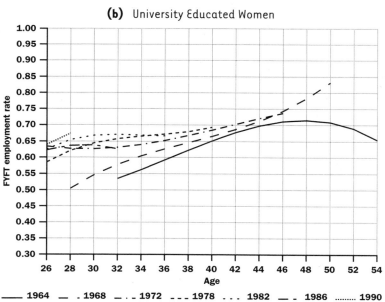

—— 1964 — · 1968 — ·· 1972 - - - 1978 · · · 1982 — · 1986 ········ 1990

adapting public policy to a labour market in transition

Figure 5 (cont'd)
Trends of Smoothed[1] FYFT Employment Rates by Cohort, Age, Education and Gender

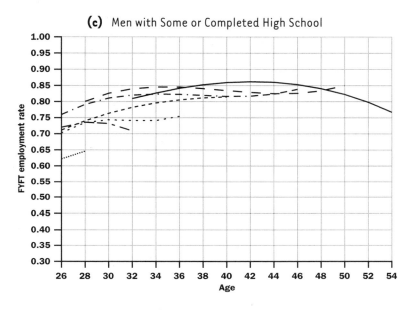

(c) Men with Some or Completed High School

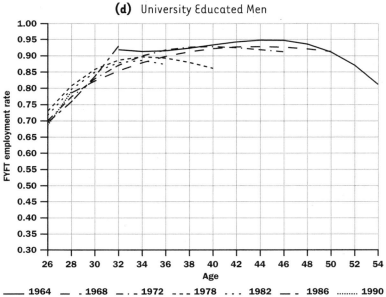

(d) University Educated Men

——— 1964   — . — 1968   — . . — 1972   - - - 1978   . . . 1982   — . — 1986   1990

[1] Business cycle effects removed.
Source: Survey of Consumer Finances, various years; calculations by authors.

Figure 6
Trends of Smoothed[1] Average (Interrupted) Job Tenure by Cohort, Age, Education and Gender

(a) Women with Some or Completed High School

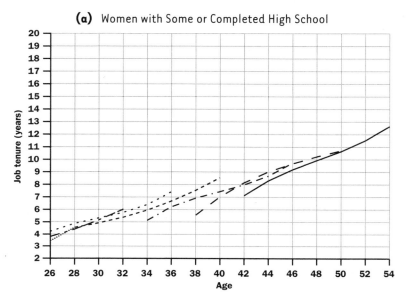

(b) University Educated Women

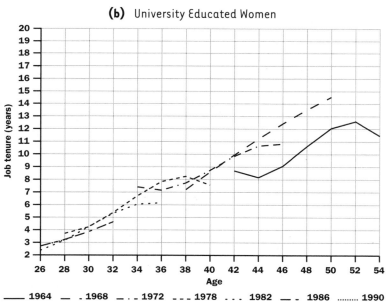

—— 1964 — . 1968 — .. 1972 - - - 1978 . . . 1982 — . 1986 1990

Figure 6 (cont'd)
Trends of Smoothed[1] Average (Interrupted) Job Tenure by Cohort, Age, Education and Gender

(c) Men with Some or Completed High School

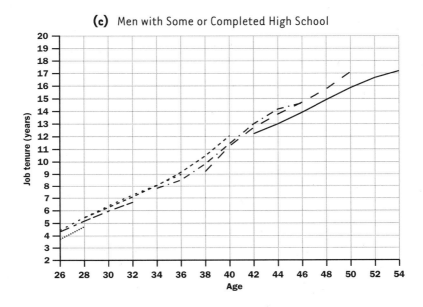

(d) University Educated Men

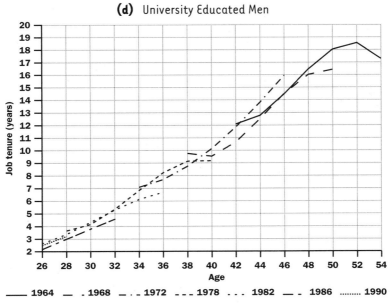

——— 1964 — . 1968 — . . 1972 – – – 1978 . . . 1982 — – 1986 1990

[1] Business cycle effects removed.
Source: Survey of Consumer Finances, various years; calculations by authors.

paul beaudry and david a. green

detrended unemployment rate variable. The extent of the tradeoff between the benefits of greater simplification and the costs of distorting parts of the detailed pattern can be seen clearly by comparing figures 7a-d to figures 4a-d.

The picture for women (figures 7a and 7b) is somewhat complex. For the less-educated group, the earliest cohorts have quite low employment rates at young ages, but show rapid increases with age. In subsequent cohorts, the employment rate at younger ages increases but at a slower rate for each successive cohort. In the cohorts entering since the early 1980s, there has been little cross-cohort difference in entry-level employment rates. At the same time, the age profiles of the most recent entry cohorts have become substantially flatter than those of their earlier counterparts. Though caution should be exercised in examining fitted profiles past about the age of 38 for the most recent cohorts since this is well out of sample, the figure is useful in that it depicts stagnating employment-rate growth across cohorts at young ages and flatter age profiles for more recent cohorts. One way to interpret the figure is to say that there was a general secular increase in employment for women. This would be reflected in higher employment rates in the 1990s for the oldest cohorts and is captured in their steep age/employment rate profiles. It would also be reflected in increased employment rates early in life for successive cohorts entering the labour market between the early 1960s and late 1970s. However, in recent years that increase has stalled, as seen in flatter or declining age profiles and the very similar entry-time employment rates of successive cohorts in the past decade.[27]

66   Interpreting the results for women as reflecting a secular trend that is common across cohorts points out the reduced-form nature of the empirical exercise in this paper. In a more traditional decomposition of trends, one would attempt to break changes over time into age profiles that are common across all cohorts regardless of the economic conditions they experience, year-to-year patterns reflecting cycles and secular trends that affect all cohorts equally and cohort effects reflecting differences across cohorts. We have netted out cyclical effects, but have not attempted to decompose the remaining cohort-specific time profiles into cohort, time and age effects. To do so would require making explicit assumptions about the functioning of the whole economy. We felt that considerable information was contained in the reduced-form plots presented here and that as a first attempt it was better to present the basic patterns without imposing structural restrictions that make basic patterns difficult to discern.

Figure 7b portrays the employment-rate outcomes for university educated women. Again, one sees a pattern of increasing intercepts combined with flatter slopes for the cohort-specific age profiles. Thus, for both education groups the evidence on employment is mixed: there were strong secular increases both across and within cohorts up to at least the early 1980s. That improvement has stalled in the past few years, with employment rate profiles showing no further increases, and some are even projecting within-cohort declines.

For men, the patterns are much simpler. For the less-educated men depicted in figure 7c, the pattern is one of steady decreases in employment rates at any age across cohorts. At the same time, there is little change in the shape of the age/employment rate profiles across cohorts.[28] In contrast, the pattern for university educated men shown in figure 7d is one of very little change in employment rates near the age of 26.[29] However, the age profiles for university educated men become substantially flatter across successive cohorts. By age 36, the employment rate has fallen by 0.10 from the earliest to the latest cohort. This is somewhat smaller than the shifts for less-educated men, who experience a drop of almost 0.20 at age 36. In contrast to the university educated, less-educated men have profiles that shift down evenly across all ages.

Full-Year, Full-Time Employment Rates
Figures 8a and 8b show the simplified age profiles of FYFT employment rates for women. For high-school educated women the pattern is one of large increases across all ages in the 1964-1978 entry cohorts. In the subsequent cohorts FYFT employment rates are very stable. For university educated women the pattern is also one of increases across cohorts, but in this case the size of the increase rises rather than falls across subsequent cohorts.[30] As with employment rates, the increases for women are countered by decreases for men. For high-school educated men, there is an accelerating decline across cohorts at all ages (figure 8c). This generates a drop in the FYFT employment rate of over 0.10 from the first to the last cohorts. For university educated men, there is little change at age 26 and the cohort effects are neither economically substantial nor statistically significant at any conventional level (figure 8d). As with employment rates, there is a flattening of age profiles across successive cohorts that leads to decreasing FYFT employment rates at older ages. It is worth noting, however, that the age-cohort interaction variable is not significantly different from zero at the 10 percent level of significance for this group. Thus, the substantial declines in FYFT employment rates for university educated men apparent in figure 8d must be treated with caution, especially when one compares them with the basic plots in figure 5d, where no such decline across cohorts is evident.

Job Tenure
The results for average job tenure are presented in figures 9a to 9d. For less-educated women there are large improvements in average tenure at age 26 from

Figure 7
Fitted Age-Employment Rate Profiles[1] by Cohort, Education and Gender

(a) High-School Educated Women

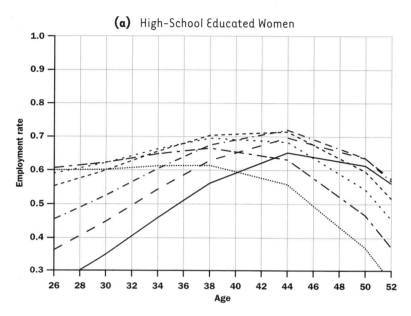

(b) University Educated Women

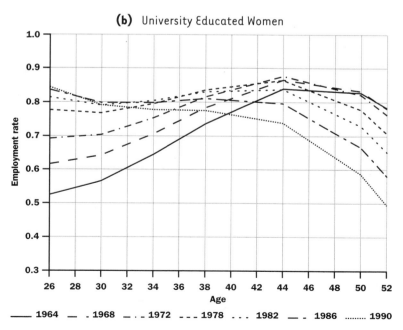

—— 1964   — · 1968   — · · 1972   - - - 1978   · · · 1982   — — 1986   ········· 1990

adapting public policy to a labour market in transition

Figure 7 (cont'd)

Fitted Age-Employment Rate Profiles[1] by Cohort, Education and Gender

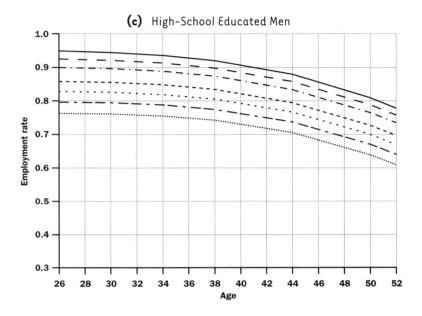

(c) High-School Educated Men

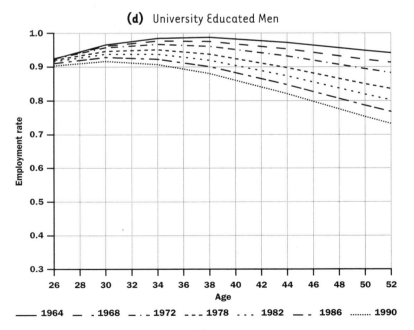

(d) University Educated Men

69

——— 1964 — · 1968 — · · 1972 - - - 1978 · · · 1982 — · 1986 ········· 1990

[1] Allowing differing slopes by cohort and controlling for the unemployment rate.

Figure 8
Fitted Age-FYFT Employment Rate Profiles[1] by Cohort, Education and Gender

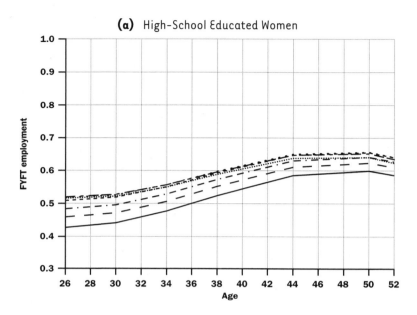

(a) High-School Educated Women

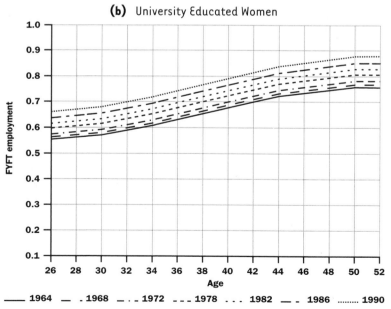

(b) University Educated Women

—— 1964 — · 1968 — · · 1972 - - - 1978 · · · 1982 — — 1986 ·········· 1990

adapting public policy to a labour market in transition

Figure 8 (cont'd)
Fitted Age-FYFT Employment Rate Profiles[1] by Cohort, Education and Gender

(c) High-School Educated Men

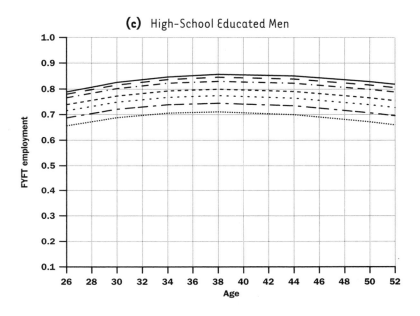

(d) University Educated Men

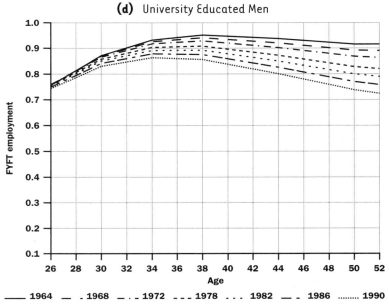

——— 1964　— · 1968　—·· 1972　--- 1978　··· 1982　— · 1986　········ 1990

[1] Allowing differing slopes by cohort and controlling for the unemployment rate.

Figure 9
Fitted Age-Average Job Tenure Profiles[1] by Cohort, Education and Gender

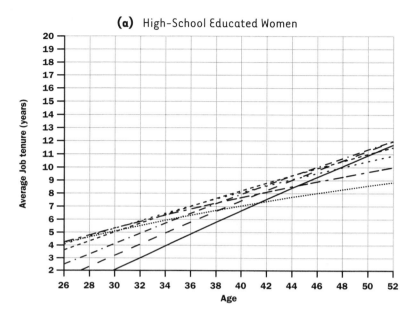

(a) High-School Educated Women

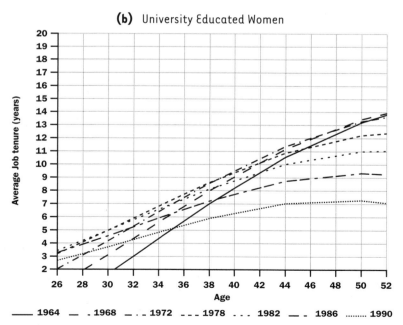

(b) University Educated Women

—— 1964　— · 1968　— ·· 1972　— — 1978　··· 1982　— · 1986　········ 1990

adapting public policy to a labour market in transition

Figure 9 (cont'd)
Fitted Age-Average Job Tenure Profiles[1] by Cohort, Education and Gender

(c) High-School Educated Men

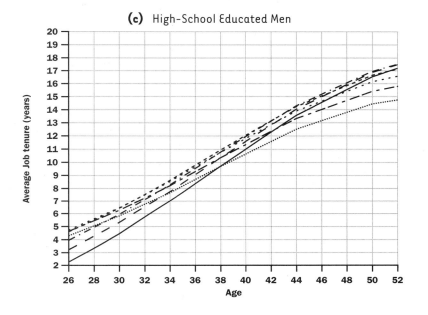

(d) University Educated Men

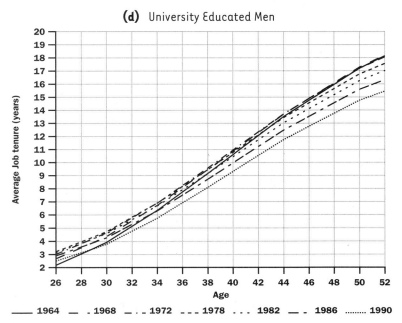

——— 1964 — · 1968 — · · 1972 – – – 1978 · · · 1982 — · 1986 ········ 1990

[1] Allowing differing slopes by cohort and controlling for the unemployment rate.

paul beaudry and david a. green

the earliest entry cohorts up to those entering in the 1980s. At the same time, the quite steep cohort-specific age profiles found in the earliest cohorts become substantially flatter in later cohorts. This fits with a time effect in the form of improved tenure outcomes for women in all age groups in all years through at least the early 1980s. This shows up in increases in average job tenure in earlier cohorts and increased average tenure at younger ages for more recent cohorts. This pattern of improvement appears to have stalled after 1980, however.[31] One should keep in mind in examining these results that they are generated using data for the 1980s only. Thus, plots for young ages in the earlier cohorts and for older ages in the more recent cohorts are well out of sample. The pattern just described, however, is evident even in the parts of the profiles that are within the sample.

For university educated women, the patterns are much the same as those for high-school educated women. Again, there is a pattern of increasing intercepts from the earliest entry cohorts up to those of the early 1980s followed by flatter profiles (figure 9b). There is certainly no evidence that recent cohorts are worse off at the outset and then catch up in subsequent years.

For high-school educated men there is some evidence of a pattern similar to that for women. The cohort-effect estimates (table A6), however, are only marginally significant, so the cohort patterns in figure 9c should be viewed sceptically. This is even more true of university educated men, for whom none of the cohort variables are significant at conventional levels. Together with figures 6c and 6d, these estimates imply that there is very little in the way of an across-cohort pattern in average job tenure, either in the level of the cohort-specific age-tenure profiles or in their slope. Whatever problems have arisen in terms of male employment in recent years, they do not appear to have been manifested in shortened job tenure.

Discussion and Conclusions

The basic plots of the employment outcomes of various sex, age and education groups indicated a number of trends. In broad terms, the figures indicate substantial worsening of employment outcomes for high-school educated men, improvements for both high-school and university educated women and somewhat mixed results for university educated men since the early 1970s. The figures also indicate some increase in differences between age groups at any point in time, with younger, less-educated individuals falling over time behind older individuals with the same levels of education. These trends point to the question of whether recent labour market entrants might expect improved employment outcomes as they age and catch up with the (somewhat) better performance of older workers with the same level of education. The question of whether poorer outcomes in the 1990s are just a reflection of a prolonged labour market downturn or are part of longer-term trends is also important.

Following cohorts of individuals across time provides partial answers to these questions. For women in both education groups the broad pattern in terms of all of the employment outcomes examined here is one of substantial improvements up to the 1980s followed by stagnation. This is reflected in the steep age profiles of employment rates, FYFT employment rates and average job tenure in older cohorts and in the higher intercepts of these profiles in more recent cohorts. The age profiles of these employment outcomes are much flatter for cohorts entering after 1982 than for those entering earlier, and there is substantial stability across cohorts in the levels of the profiles. Generally, the figures reveal improved employment outcomes and increased stability for women over time. While the noncohort plots reveal some declines for women in the 1990s, once cyclical effects are netted out, the cohort plots imply a cessation of improvement rather than significant declines for more recent cohorts of women. Projecting the observed cohort patterns there is no reason to believe that current and future cohorts of women will, in their lifetimes, experience increases in job stability and employment to match those experienced by earlier cohorts. However, there also appears to be little basis for claiming that women have experienced substantial declines in access to employment or in job stability, apart from that associated with cyclical conditions. It is possible that in the longer run female employment outcomes will experience a decline similar to their male counterparts, but there is little in the data to suggest that this will be the case.

The results for high-school educated men are much gloomier. They have experienced reduced access to employment and, if they are employed, they have experienced reduced access to FYFT work. This can be seen in substantial declines in the levels of cohort-specific age profiles of these outcomes across successive cohorts and in the negative slopes of the age profiles of all cohorts. Thus, the figures reflect a combination of poorer outcomes for more recent entry cohorts at all ages and worsening outcomes for older cohorts. The fact that declines in employment and FYFT employment rates start as early as age 40 in older cohorts indicates that these declines cannot be attributed to early retirement. It is worth noting that declines in the age profile levels across successive cohorts could be the result of a selection effect whereby more able individuals who would have had a high-school education in earlier cohorts are staying in school and getting more advanced degrees in later cohorts. If those individuals are also at the bottom end of the ability distribution among postsecondary educated workers, such increased selection into postsecondary education could also imply declines in average outcomes for more-educated workers across successive cohorts.

Whatever their source, these trends indicate that the employment prospects of high-school educated men in all cohorts must be the focus of considerable policy concern. They represent a very sizeable proportion of the population, constituting 52 percent of men over the age of 15 in 1993. Since the least-educated group in our study does not include individuals with only an elementary-school education, the poor outcomes observed are occurring in a group that is not even the least skilled. According to projected age-employment profiles for the most recent cohorts of high-school educated workers, a very substantial portion of Canada's youth may face a future of uncertain and unstable employment. This will necessarily have ramifications both for their personal well-being and for their opinions of the basic justice of their society.

The employment outcomes for university educated men are somewhat mixed. Employment-to-population ratios have changed very little across cohorts at age 26, but flatter age profiles across successive cohorts imply declining employment outcomes for recent cohorts at older ages. The employment rate pattern fits broadly with declines in employment rates in the most recent years in all cohorts. Those declines, however, are not nearly as large as those experienced by high-school educated men. As for the FYFT employment rate, the evidence for university educated men does not indicate any substantial worsening of outcomes once cyclical effects are removed. It is interesting to note that all cohorts of university educated men experienced a pattern of relatively low FYFT employment rates at the age of 26 followed by a rapid rise up to the age of 32 and then a flat profile thereafter. Those who are concerned that "generation Xers" did not move into stable work patterns when they were in their 20s should recall that this pattern is exactly the same as that experienced by their predecessors.

For all cohort, gender and education groups, average job tenure outcomes have either been improving across successive cohorts (for all women and to some extent less-educated men) or have been quite stable. There is no evidence in these numbers of increased instability in the form of shorter job tenure. This is somewhat surprising since those who are concerned about increased instability in the job market often point to the increased use of contract workers by firms as a source of that instability. The fact that this trend does not show up in the average job tenure numbers suggests that such concerns may be more a matter of perception than reality. For instance, increases in the number of workers on short-term contracts will not generate shorter job tenure outcomes if those contracts are repeatedly rolled over but contract workers may still feel that their lives are more insecure than were those of previous generations of workers who were not hired on contract. The stability of the job tenure numbers may also be endogenous: shortened jobs stemming from increased layoffs may be offset by fewer quits as workers who might otherwise want to leave a job decide not to do so when the unemployment rate is high.

To sum up, there have been very large increases in instability in employment among less-educated men but only limited evidence of secular increases in instability among women and more-educated men. It is worth emphasizing, however, that these facts about employment contradict the public perception of a widespread increase in work instability.[32] As Osberg, Erksoy and Phipps[33] point out quite clearly in their simulation of changes in income support programs, the perceived instability may be strongly related to the adequacy of existing insurance against bad outcomes. When transfers to the unemployed become less accessible and/or less generous, those affected may feel more threatened by bad employment outcomes. Card and Lemieux[34] show that recent generations of youth have responded to trends in the labour market by using other forms of insurance, including delaying family formation and living with their parents longer. Similarly, even if employment outcomes such as the percentage of the employed who have full-year, full-time jobs and average job tenure do not change, individuals may become more concerned about employment outcomes if unemployment spells last longer and jobs are harder to find. Thus, our results should be seen as a starting point in evaluating job instability rather than the last word. They indicate that for many groups of workers we need to look to something other than employment outcomes for the source of increases in instability. The big exception to this is high-school educated men who have every reason to be concerned about their employment prospects. There is an immediate need to address their labour market problems.

77

Table A1
Employment-to-Population Rate Regressions: Women

Variable	Education			
	High school		University	
Cohort	0.069 (0.005)*	–	0.055 (0.011)*	–
Cohort squared	-0.003 (0.0003)*	–	-0.002 (0.0005)*	–
1978 cohort	–	0.387 (0.027)*	–	0.339 (0.057)*
1988 cohort	–	0.438 (0.031)*	–	0.449 (0.061)*
1990 cohort	–	0.440 (0.032)*	–	0.386 (0.061)*
1992 cohort	–	0.441 (0.036)*	–	0.454 (0.060)*
Cohort*age	-0.002 (0.0002)*	-0.002 (0.0003)*	-0.002 (0.0005)*	-0.002 (0.0005)*
Age	0.022 (0.003)*	0.022 (0.003)*	0.001 (0.006)	0.002 (0.006)
Age squared	0.001 (0.0002)*	0.001 (0.0002)*	0.002 (0.0003)*	0.002 (0.0003)*
Age cubed/100	-0.005 (0.0005)*	-0.005 (0.0005)*	-0.007 (0.0007)*	-0.006 (0.0008)*
Unemployment rate	-1.150 (0.241)*	-1.142 (0.245)*	-0.056 (0.359)	-0.037 (0.352)
Intercept	0.163 (0.023)	0.153 (0.026)*	0.471 (0.053)*	0.432 (0.056)*
Number of observations	148	148	148	148
Adjusted R^2	0.88	0.88	0.58	0.61

Table A2
Employment-to-Population Rate Regressions: Men

Variable	Education			
	High school		University	
Cohort	-0.011 (0.004)*	–	0.002 (0.005)	–
Cohort squared	-0.0002 (0.0002)	–	-0.0002 (0.0003)	–
1978 cohort	–	-0.097 (0.019)*	–	0.015 (0.027)
1988 cohort	–	-0.179 (0.023)*	–	-0.003 (0.031)
1990 cohort	–	-0.202 (0.026)*	–	0.032 (0.031)
1992 cohort	–	-0.222 (0.032)*	–	-0.022 (0.041)*
Cohort*age	0.0001 (0.0002)*	0.00002 (0.0002)	-0.0006 (0.0002)*	-0.0006 (0.0002)*
Age	-0.0005 (0.002)	-0.0005 (0.002)	0.016 (0.003)*	0.016 (0.003)*
Age squared	-0.0001 (0.0002)	-0.0001 (0.0002)	-0.001 (0.0002)*	-0.001 (0.0002)*
Age cubed/100	-0.0005 (0.0004)	-0.0007 (0.0004)	0.001 (0.0004)*	0.002 (0.0004)*
Unemployment rate	-0.802 (0.191)*	-0.785 (0.195)*	-0.539 (0.191)	-0.605 (0.191)*
Intercept	0.961 (0.016)	0.955 (0.018)*	0.907 (0.023)*	0.888 (0.025)*
Number of observations	148	148	148	148
Adjusted R^2	0.81	0.81	0.52	0.53

Note: Standard errors in parentheses. * indicates significantly different from zero at the 5 percent level. + indicates significantly different from zero at the 10 percent level. All regressions are performed with weighted least squares to address heteroskedasticity inherent in a grouped linear probability model.

Source: Statistics Canada, Survey of Consumer Finances, "Income of Economic Families, 1971, 1973, 1975, 1977, 1979," microdata tapes (1972, 1976, 1978, 1980); Statistics Canada, Survey of Consumer Finances, "Individuals With and Without Income, 1981, 1982, 1984, 1986, 1988, 1990, 1992, 1993," microdata tapes (1982, 1983, 1985, 1987, 1989, 1991, 1993, 1994); calculations by authors.

Table A3
Full-Year, Full-Time Employment Rate Regressions: Women

Variable	Education			
	High school		University	
Cohort	0.019 (0.005)*	–	0.003 (0.013)	–
Cohort squared	-0.0008 (0.0003)*	–	0.0003 (0.0006)	–
1978 cohort	–	0.106 (0.028)*	–	0.041 (0.069)
1988 cohort	–	0.104 (0.031)*	–	0.097 (0.075)
1990 cohort	–	0.090 (0.033)*	–	0.090 (0.075)
1992 cohort	–	0.123 (0.037)*	–	0.111 (0.077)
Cohort*age	-0.0002 (0.0002)	-0.0001 (0.0003)	0.00004 (0.0006)	0.0001 (0.0006)
Age	-0.003 (0.003)	-0.002 (0.003)	-0.001 (0.006)	-0.002 (0.007)
Age squared	0.001 (0.0002)*	0.001 (0.0002)*	0.001 (0.0004)*	0.001 (0.0004)*
Age cubed/100	-0.003 (0.0005)*	-0.003 (0.0005)*	-0.002 (0.0009)*	-0.002 (0.0009)*
Unemployment rate	-0.316 (0.250)	-0.316 (0.253)	0.048 (0.448)	0.011 (0.461)
Intercept	0.410 (0.024)	0.412 (0.026)*	0.551 (0.061)*	0.560 (0.068)*
Number of observations	148	148	148	148
Adjusted R^2	0.66	0.66	0.47	0.45

Table A4
Full-Year, Full-Time Employment Rate Regressions: Men

Variable	Education			
	High school		University	
Cohort	-0.002 (0.004)	–	0.002 (0.007)	–
Cohort squared	-0.0005 (0.0002)*	–	-0.0002 (0.0004)	–
1978 cohort	–	-0.047 (0.022)*	–	0.013 (0.038)
1988 cohort	–	-0.111 (0.025)*	–	-0.003 (0.046)
1990 cohort	–	-0.153 (0.027)*	–	0.002 (0.048)
1992 cohort	–	-0.153 (0.032)*	–	0.026 (0.058)
Cohort*age	-0.0001 (0.0002)	-0.0001 (0.0002)	-0.0005 (0.0003)	-0.0006 (0.0003)
Age	0.012 (0.003)*	0.013 (0.003)*	0.042 (0.004)*	0.043 (0.004)*
Age squared	-0.0006 (0.0002)*	-0.0005 (0.0002)*	-0.002 (0.0002)*	-0.002 (0.0002)*
Age cubed/100	-0.0006 (0.0004)	0.0006 (0.0004)	0.004 (0.0006)*	0.004 (0.0006)*
Unemployment rate	-1.843 (0.198)*	-1.801 (0.199)*	-0.744 (0.275)*	-0.753 (0.278)*
Intercept	0.780 (0.019)*	0.776 (0.020)*	0.715 (0.035)*	0.704 (0.037)*
Number of observations	148	148	148	148
Adjusted R^2	0.85	0.85	0.77	0.76

Note: Standard errors in parentheses. * indicates significantly different from zero at the 5 percent level. + indicates significantly different from zero at the 10 percent level. All regressions are performed with weighted least squares to address heteroskedasticity inherent in a grouped linear probability model.

Source: Statistics Canada, Survey of Consumer Finances, "Income of Economic Families, 1971, 1973, 1975, 1977, 1979," microdata tapes (1972, 1976, 1978, 1980); Statistics Canada, Survey of Consumer Finances, "Individuals With and Without Income, 1981, 1982, 1984, 1986, 1988, 1990, 1992, 1993," microdata tapes (1982, 1983, 1985, 1987, 1989, 1991, 1993, 1994); calculations by authors.

Table A5
Average (Interupted) Job Tenure Regressions: Women

Variable	Education			
	High school		University	
Cohort	9.825 (4.472)*	–	13.23 (8.54)	–
Cohort squared	-0.384 (0.189)*	–	-0.631 (0.358)*	–
1978 cohort	–	44.768 (22.935)*	–	92.76 (42.87)*
1988 cohort	–	52.181 (25.741)*	–	95.11 (48.09)*
1990 cohort	–	46.178 (25.492)*	–	95.44 (47.56)*
1992 cohort	–	43.894 (25.176)*	–	94.54 (46.57)*
Cohort*age	-0.248 (0.184)	-0.202 (0.175)	-0.369 (0.347)	-0.514 (0.321)
Age	6.384 (2.269)*	5.639 (2.173)*	7.893 (4.271)*	10.101 (3.971)*
Age squared	-0.031 (0.065)	0.0227 (0.064)	0.091 (0.120)	-0.039 (0.116)
Age cubed/100	0.014 (0.113)	-0.121 (0.115)	-0.427 (0.216)*	-0.125 (0.216)
Unemployment rate	198.95 (54.54)*	204.13 (51.62)*	56.159 (103.7)	50.982 (95.55)
Intercept	-14.781 (26.18)	-3.516 (25.106)	-32.23 (50.20)	-60.85 (46.90)
Number of observations	148	148	148	148
Adjusted R²	0.95	0.95	0.92	0.94

Table A6
Average (Interupted) Job Tenure Regressions: Men

Variable	Education			
	High school		University	
Cohort	7.349 (4.638)	–	4.139 (7.410)	–
Cohort squared	-0.354 (0.199)*	–	-0.249 (0.313)	–
1978 cohort	–	33.27 (25.70)	–	35.74 (40.50)
1988 cohort	–	28.42 (28.78)	–	33.66 (45.54)
1990 cohort	–	25.50 (28.53)	–	31.41 (45.10)
1992 cohort	–	25.74 (28.23)	–	30.83 (44.58)
Cohort*age	-0.159 (0.193)	-0.129 (0.197)	-0.106 (0.304)	-0.178 (0.309)
Age	5.501 (2.382)*	5.198 (2.443)*	3.366 (3.787)*	4.640 (3.865)*
Age squared	0.240 (0.070)*	0.249 (0.073)*	0.378 (0.112)*	0.304 (0.118)*
Age cubed/100	-0.684 (0.122)*	-0.694 (0.132)*	-0.855 (0.193)*	-0.695 (0.211)*
Unemployment rate	141.48 (57.13)*	138.91 (57.78)*	47.501 (91.127)*	46.027 (92.02)*
Intercept	14.69 (27.27)	20.13 (28.015)	18.619 (43.30)	-0.241 (44.29)
Number of observations	148	148	148	148
Adjusted R²	0.98	0.98	0.97	0.97

Note: Standard errors in parentheses. * indicates significantly different from zero at the 5 percent level. + indicates significantly different from zero at the 10 percent level. All regressions are performed with weighted least squares to address heteroskedasticity inherent in a grouped linear probability model.

Source: Statistics Canada, Survey of Consumer Finances, "Income of Economic Families, 1971, 1973, 1975, 1977, 1979," microdata tapes (1972, 1976, 1978, 1980); Statistics Canada, Survey of Consumer Finances, "Individuals With and Without Income, 1981, 1982, 1984, 1986, 1988, 1990, 1992, 1993," microdata tapes (1982, 1983, 1985, 1987, 1989, 1991, 1993, 1994); calculations by authors.

Notes

1. See G. Betcherman and G. Lowe, *The Future of Work in Canada* (Ottawa: CPRN, February 1997) for a discussion and evaluation of recent arguments about instability in the labour market.

2. In P. Beaudry and D.A. Green, "Cohort Patterns in Canadian Earnings: Assessing the Role of Skill Premia in Inequality Trends," *Canadian Journal of Economics* (forthcoming), earnings differentials patterns are examined using much the same methodology as is employed here to study employment outcomes.

3. The Individual Files do not include a specific variable indicating whether an individual is the head or spouse of a census family. We include males from the Individual files in our sample if they are heads of census households which implies that at least one of the following conditions is true: (1) the individual is listed as the head of a two- parent census family; (2) the individual is listed as the head of an economic family; (3) the individual is a lone parent; (4) the individual lives as a single individual with other unrelated individuals; (5) the individual lives with relatives and is listed as married or divorced. We keep females if they are either heads or spouses of heads of census families, which we define as meeting at least one of the above five conditions plus the condition that the individual is currently married. In earlier work (P. Beaudry and D.A.Green, "Individual Responses to Changes in the Canadian Labour Market," Microeconomic Policy Analysis Branch, Industry Canada, Ottawa, 1998) we followed a smaller set of cohorts through the 1980s using only the Individual Files. The results of that exercise are very similar to those we obtain here for the 1980s following census family heads and spouses.

4. D. Card and T. Lemieux. "Multiple Modes of Adjustment: A Comparative Study of Youth in the US and Canada, 1970-1995," Department of Economics, University of Montreal, May 1996.

5. These numbers are for the total population aged 15 and over. Because older generations are on average less educated, when they retire there should be a larger proportion of individuals in the labour force with a university degree, and that proportion should increase faster.

6. D. Gower, "The Impact of the 1990 Changes to the Education Questions on the Labour Force Survey," Labour and Household Surveys Analysis Division, Statistics Canada, Staff Report, 1993.

7. W. C. Riddell and A. Sweetman, "Human Capital Formation in a Period of Rapid Change," in this volume, show that there is little movement across educational categories within cohorts after age 25.

8. For example, the employment rates among high-school educated males when immigrants are omitted are nearly identical to those when they are included. The rates among the university educated when immigrants are omitted display the same patterns as those presented here, except that they all shift upwards by .02 to .03. We did not generate female samples that exclude immigrants because the immigrant status of spouses was not recorded before 1981. The results from the male sample that excludes immigrants are available upon request.

9. Our definition of employment includes paid and self- employment because we cannot separate the self-employed among spouses in the pre-1980 data. Similarly, our full year/full time employment measure includes self-employment. This is worth keeping in mind given the important role played by self-employment in total employment growth in the 1990s.

10. D.A. Green and W.C. Riddell, "Job Duration in Canada: Is Long-Term Employment in Canada Declining?" in M. Abbot, C. Beach and R. Chayltowski (eds.), *Transition and Structural Change in the North American Labour Market* (Kingston: IRC Press, 1997), pp. 8-40, discuss the shortcomings of the interrupted job-tenure variable and present job length patterns over time. Andrew Heisz, "Changes in Job Duration in Canada," *Industrial Relations*, Vol. 54, no. 2 (Spring 1999), pp. 365-87 uses nonpublic access data to study job length patterns over time using a methodology that overcomes the problems with ongoing job spells. Neither of these studies follows cohorts over time.

11. Since the SCF data is gathered in the spring and our employment measure relates to a reference week, one possible reason for this substantial employment-rate decrease for less-educated men aged 25-34 could be an increase in the seasonality in their jobs. There is no direct way to check this possibility with the SCF. Plots of average annual employment-to-population rates by age group for males also show a substantial decline over time for males aged 25-34 (Beaudry and Green, "Individual Responses to Change in the Canadian labour Market").

81

12. W.C. Riddell, "Human Capital Formation in Canada: Recent Developments and Policy Responses," in H.G. Banting and C.M. Beach (eds.), *Labour Market Polarization and Social Policy Reform* (Kingston: School of Policy Studies, Queen's University, 1995), pp. 125-172.

13. For the US, see for the example, C. Juhn, K. Murphy and B. Pierce, "Wage Inequality and the Rise in Returns to Skill," *Journal of Political Economy*, Vol. 101, no. 3 (1993), pp. 410-42.

14. R. Morissette, J. Myles and G. Picot, "What is Happening to Earnings Inequality in Canada?" research paper no. 60, Analytical Studies Branch, Statistics Canada, Ottawa, ON, 1993.

15. In the SCF, tenure on the current job is based on responses to the question, "How long have you worked for the current employer?" This is then recoded into six tenure categories: 1-6 months, 7-12 months, 1-5 years, 6-10 years, 11-20 years, and more than 20 years.

16. Note that these figures pertain only to the 1980s since only the SCF Individual files contain job tenure information.

17. H. Krahn, "Non-standard Work on the Rise," *Perspectives on Labour and Income*, Vol.7 (Winter 1995), pp. 35-42 (Statistics Canada).

18. H. Krahn, "Non-standard Work on the Rise."

19. H. Krahn, "Non-standard Work on the Rise"; and A. Nakamura, D. Cullen and J. Cragg, "Trends in Part-Time and Part-Year Employment, and in Earnings," in Abbott, Beach and Chaykowski (eds.), *Transition and Structural Change in the North American Labour Market*, pp. 111-25.

20. D. Green and W.C. Riddell, "Job Duration in Canada: Is Long-Term Employment in Canada Declining?" in Abbott, Beach and Chaykowski (eds.), *Transition and Structural Change in the North American Labour Market*, pp. 8-40.

21. H. Krahn, "Non-standard Work on the Rise."

22. Raw data plots corresponding with those in the figures are available upon request from the authors. The raw plots are somewhat erratic because of apparent sampling variability and upward and downward swings that coincide with booms and recessions in the Canadian economy.

23. The smoothed profiles are obtained by estimating up to a cubic age-earnings profile for each cohort, while simultaneously controlling for business cycle conditions. The business cycle indicator is the quadratically detrended unemployment rate for males aged 45-54. The coefficient on this business cycle variable is restricted to be the same across cohorts, but differs across the four gender/education groups. In the regressions, we instrumented for the detrended unemployment rate using the quadratically detrended US male unemployment rate and a dummy variable capturing the post-1982 period when the two countries' unemployment rates jumped apart.

24. In an alternative specification, we attempted to control for the business cycle by including year-specific dummy variables rather than the detrended unemployment rate variable mentioned in the text. In the dummy-variable specification, we restricted the 1981 and 1988 effects to be the same, thus allowing the remaining dummy variables to trace out a cycle relative to a trend line running through the 1981 and 1988 observations. This allows, for example, the 1990s recession to have a much different pattern relative from that of the early 1980s. We restricted the dummy-variable coefficients to be the same across cohorts in a given gender/education group. The smoothed plots generated from this specification for the high-school educated females were extremely similar to those in figure 7a, suggesting that the downturns at the ends of profiles in 7a are not due solely to a poorly specified cyclical variable.

25. Note that average interrupted job tenure is the appropriate measure when following cohorts over time. Average "completed" job tenure figures would require extrapolation over parts of the job tenure distribution that a given cohort could not have experienced at any point (e.g., one would need predictions about the proportion of 26 year olds, in 1993, who will eventually hold jobs for exactly 20 years). Such extrapolations would have to be based on the experiences of other cohorts and would thus blur our attempts to understand differences across cohorts.

26. See G.S. Maddalla, *Limited-Dependent and Qualitative Variables in Econometrics* (Cambridge: Cambridge University Press, 1983) for a description of the weighted least squares estimator used to correct for heteroskedasticity in a linear probability model.

27. The coefficients on the cohort-specific dummy variables in the second column of Table A1 show quite clearly that, relative to the base case of the 1962 entry cohort, there were rapid increases in the age profile intercept up to the 1988 entry cohort and a stall ever since. The intercept increases up to 1982 are statistically significant at the 5 percent significance level, while the intercepts thereafter are not statistically significantly different from one another.

28. That this pattern appears neither to be accelerating or decelerating is reflected in the small size and lack of significance of the cohort squared variable in column 1 of table A2. Similarly, the cohort/age interaction variable is small enough to imply little change in the age slope across cohorts. Column 2 indicates that the differences in intercepts for cohorts more than six years apart are statistically significantly different from zero at the 5 percent level.

29. In fact, neither the cohort nor the cohort-squared coefficients in table A2 are statistically significantly different from zero at conventional levels, and neither are economically large.

30. The rise in profile intercepts from the earliest cohorts to those entering after 1978 is statistically significant at the 5 percent level for high-school educated females, but none of the increases are statistically significant for university educated females (see table A3).

31. This is reflected by the post-1978 intercepts in column 2 of table A5 showing statistically significant increases relative to the base, 1962, cohort but no statistically significant differences relative to each other.

32. Betcherman and Lowe, *The Future of Work in Canada.*

33. L. Osberg, S. Erksoy and S. Phipps, "How to Value the Poorer Prospects of Youth in the Early 1990s?" Department of Economics, Dalhousie University, October 1996.

34. Card and Lemieux, "Multiple Modes of Adjustment."

Human Capital Formation in a Period of Rapid Change

W. Craig Riddell and Arthur Sweetman

Introduction

The issue of human capital formation is at the forefront of current policy debates. This prominence is a result of the increasingly widespread view that the skills and knowledge of the labour force are more important today than they have been in the past because of globalization, technological change, increased international trade, and greater economic integration. Consequently, it is argued, for countries like Canada to achieve high rates of real income growth, more emphasis on human resources and less on physical capital and natural resources in the production process will be required.[1] The development of human capital is thus increasingly viewed as a central ingredient in national economic policy.

85

As a result of the growing emphasis on human capital formation, our education and training system has come under scrutiny. Virtually every part of the system – primary and secondary education, postsecondary education, private-sector training and government-sponsored training – is the subject of public debate and policy development. Yet despite the increased attention being paid to education and training in recent years, there is only a modest amount of Canadian empirical research on the subject. Much of this paper is devoted to documenting some of the key trends and developments in human capital formation in an attempt to partially fill this gap.

As our examination of recent developments will show, the educational attainment of the Canadian population has increased substantially over the past several decades. By commonly employed measures, recent cohorts of young adults are among the most highly educated in the world. There are two sharply contrasting views on this development. One holds that the increased globalization of production and technological change associated with the information and computer revolution have led to an increase in the demand for highly skilled workers and a decrease in the demand for less-skilled workers.[2] The result has been growing employment opportunities for those with high levels of education and declining opportunities for those with lower levels of education. The response of Canadian youths, their parents, and the educational system has been to place greater emphasis on education.

The other view is that rising educational attainment is principally due to the poor labour market conditions facing youth and young adults. During the early 1980s and early 1990s Canada experienced recessions that were severe by both historical and international standards. As is generally the case during downturns in economic activity, young workers were among those most adversely affected. The slow recovery after the 1990-92 recession and downsizing and restructuring in many sectors further limited the labour market prospects of young adults. According to this view, many young Canadians are investing heavily in education because of poor opportunities and because employers, facing a glut of applicants for most jobs, are upgrading their workforces. Proponents of this view argue that there is substantial unemployment and underemployment among the well educated – as demonstrated in anecdotal accounts of university graduates working as waiters and taxi drivers.[3]

The policy implications of these two perspectives differ substantially. According to the "relative-demand shift" theory, there is a need for increased educational attainment in order to meet the growing demand for more-skilled workers, as well as to prevent the increase in unemployment that would otherwise be associated with declining demand for the less-skilled workers. In contrast, the "overeducation/underemployment" theory implies that the rising educational attainment of many Canadians is a waste of society's time and money. According to this thesis, many college and university graduates end up working in jobs that are suitable for high-school graduates. Thus assessing which view is more consistent with the Canadian experience is of considerable importance to policy makers. It is also the focus of our analysis.

A related policy issue is determining the appropriate balance between broad-based educational programs that emphasize generic skills, such as arts and science programs at universities, and more narrowly focused technical and vocational programs that prepare individuals for specific occupations and trades, such as those provided in many community colleges. Again, there are differing views. One is that the widespread use of information and computer technologies in the workplace requires many individuals with highly technical skills. Therefore Canada should invest more heavily in vocational and technical colleges and in programs such as computer science and engineering in universities.[4] The alternative view is that the new economy will increase the need for individuals with broad-based skills and knowledge. Therefore more resources should be devoted to general arts and science programs in universities as well as to the development of generic skills such as literacy, numeracy, analytical and problem-solving skills, and general life skills. Although it is not possible in this paper to examine this debate in detail, we shall contribute to it by comparing the employment and earnings of the graduates of college programs, which are mostly vocational and technical in nature, with the employment and earnings of graduates of university programs, which typically provide general rather than specialized and technical skills.

In the next section we compare the educational attainment of the Canadian population and labour force with that of other countries. We then examine various aspects of the current Canadian situation and analyze Canada's experience over the past several decades.

Human Capital Investment: Canada from an International Perspective

Primary, secondary and postsecondary educational systems vary widely from country to country. For example, some countries stream students into academic and vocational programs at an earlier stage than is the case in Canada. Similarly, there are important differences in the extent to which educational systems provide a "second chance" for those who drop out at some stage, such as in high school. These institutional differences among educational systems must be kept in mind when interpreting comparative statistics such as the ones we are presenting here.

The relative share of resources devoted to formal education varies quite significantly across countries (see table 1). For instance, Canada's educational expenditure of 7.2 percent of GDP in 1994 is the highest among the G7 countries and the fourth highest among OECD countries (exceeded only by Sweden, Denmark and Finland). The (unweighted) OECD average was 6.3 percent. Canada also stands out in the proportion of its educational expenditures that comes from the public sector. At 6.7 percent of GDP, this figure is well above the OECD average of 5.2 percent and compares with levels in other top-ranked countries (Norway, Sweden, Finland and Denmark), whose public expenditures on education range between 6.6 and 6.8 percent of GDP.

Although the proportion of total national income devoted to education is a useful summary measure, it may vary as a result of differences in the quantity and quality of education being provided. The quantity of education depends to an important extent on the age structure of the population, especially the proportion of the population in the 5-25 age range. To obtain some indication of the quality of

Table 1

Educational Expenditure and Attainment in Canada and Selected OECD Countries

a) Expenditure on education, 1994

	Canada	Australia	France	Germany	Sweden	UK	US	OECD Average
Percent of GDP devoted to education								
Public and private	7.2	6.2	6.7	6.0	9.0	n/a	6.8	6.3
Public	6.7	4.8	5.6	4.5	6.6	4.9	4.9	5.2
Post-secondary educational expenditure per student, US$								
	11,471	10,590	6,569	8,897	13,168	7,225	16,262	8,134

Table 1 (cont'd)

Educational Expenditure and Attainment in Canada and Selected OECD Countries

b) Measures of educational attainment, 1995

	Canada	Australia	France	Germany	Sweden	UK	US	OECD average
	Proportion of population with educational attainment							
High school	75	53	68	84	75	76	86	62
Nonuniversity post-secondary	30	10	8	10	14	9	8	9
University	17	14	11	13	14	12	25	13
Post-secondary	47	24	19	23	28	21	33	22
	Average completed years of schooling							
	13.2	11.9	11.2	13.4	12.1	12.1	13.5	11.9

n/a: not available

Source: OECD, Education at a Glance: OECD Indicators 1998 (Paris: OECD, 1998); OECD, Human Capital Investment: An International Comparison (Paris: OECD, 1998).

89

w. craig riddell and arthur sweetman

education, we look first at international differences in expenditures per student. The OECD only provides this information for Canada at the postsecondary level, so it is not possible to provide a complete picture.[5] Nonetheless, the available information does indicate that Canada ranks near the top in expenditure per post-secondary student. It is fourth highest among OECD countries, exceeded only by the US, Sweden and Switzerland. Its level of spending is much higher than the OECD average, albeit substantially below that of the US and Sweden.

The bottom panel of table 1 provides various measures of educational attainment internationally in 1995. In general, they indicate that Canada's substantial investment in education has resulted in a labour force with high levels of measured educational attainment. In 1995, three-quarters of Canadians had completed high school or higher, compared with the OECD average of 62 percent. Canada's rate is similar to that of the UK and Sweden but significantly below that of the US and Germany. However, Canada stands out very clearly in the proportion of the population that has completed postsecondary education. In 1995, 47 percent of Canadians had completed either a university degree or college diploma or certificate, more than double the OECD average and substantially above the rate of the next highest country (the US at 33 percent). This large gap between Canada and other OECD countries in the extent of postsecondary (tertiary) education is principally due to the dramatic growth of (nonuniversity) college diploma and certificate programs in Canada. When the focus is restricted to university graduates, Canada still ranks well above the OECD average but substantially below the US rate.

The average number of completed years of education varies less internationally than does the distribution of the population by the various levels of educational attainment. Nonetheless, here too Canada is among the highest in the OECD, exceeded only by the US and Germany.

In summary, Canada spends a substantial amount on education compared with other industrialized countries. Consequently, according to various measures of educational attainment, its population is among the most highly educated in the OECD countries.

Does Canada's substantial expenditure on education translate into a population with significant skills and competencies? Table 2 sheds some light on this question. The data come from the International Adult Literacy Survey (IALS), an important skills assessment tool that provides internationally comparable measures of document, prose and quantitative literacy.[6]

The top panel of table 2 shows the proportion of the adult population that has low literacy skills in Canada and selected OECD countries. In terms of the adult population as a whole, Canada is in the middle of the pack, below Germany

Table 2
Literacy Skills in Canada and Selected OECD Countries

a) Percent of adults with low literacy skills[1]

AGE	Canada	Australia	Germany	Sweden	UK	US
16-65	42.9	44.9	41.7	25.1	50.4	49.6
16-25	32.6	38.1	34.2	19.7	44.4	55.5
46-55	54.0	51.1	42.4	26.6	52.7	49.6

b) Literacy skills and educational attainment[2]

EDUCATIONAL ATTAINMENT	Canada	Australia	Germany	Sweden	UK	US
Less than high school	227	244	276	281	247	200
High-school graduate	288	288	295	308	286	266
Post-secondary graduate	318	293	315	331	312	303
All adults	279	273	285	306	268	268

[1] With literacy levels 1 or 2 on document literacy. Literacy is measured on a scale from 1 to 5 with levels 1 and 2 being the lowest levels. On a scale of 0 to 500, literacy level 1 corresponds to a score from 0 to 225 and level 2 corresponds to a score from 226 to 275.
[2] Average document literacy scores for persons aged 16-65, on a scale of 0 to 500.
Source: OECD, *Human Capital Investment: An International Comparison* (Paris: OECD, 1998).

and Sweden but above Australia, the UK and the US. However, with respect to the 16-25 age group, Canada does better than all countries except Sweden. In contrast, the literacy skills of Canadians aged 46-55 are the worst of all these countries. Therefore, in Canada, more recent cohorts rank higher compared with other countries than do earlier cohorts. This recent improvement in Canada's relative performance would suggest that the quantity and/or quality of education received by recent cohorts is much higher than that received by previous generations.

Further evidence on this issue is shown in the bottom panel of table 2, which reports average document literacy scores by level of educational attainment. For the adult population as a whole, Canada ranks above Australia, the UK and the US, but below Germany and Sweden. However, the literacy skills of Canada's postsecondary graduates are exceeded only by those of Sweden. This result is especially noteworthy given the fact that the fraction of the population completing

Table 3
Education, Unemployment and Wages
by Age and Gender, Canada, 1998

EDUCATIONAL DISTRIBUTION	20-29 Male	20-29 Female	30-39 Male	30-39 Female	40-49 Male	40-49 Female	50-59 Male	50-59 Female
0-8 years	2.6	2.0	3.5	3.1	5.3	5.9	13.8	14.8
Some HS	12.3	10.6	12.7	11.0	14.2	12.6	16.2	17.0
HS Grad	21.4	18.7	20.6	22.1	19.3	24.0	16.0	20.7
Some PS	18.6	17.1	7.6	8.7	7.0	7.8	5.0	6.1
College	30.1	33.6	35.7	35.6	34.0	32.6	30.1	29.3
Univ Bach	12.2	15.0	13.6	14.4	12.3	11.8	10.4	8.4
Univ Grad	2.8	3.1	6.4	5.1	8.0	5.3	8.6	3.7
Number	7,739	8,040	10,219	10,802	9,984	10,424	7,343	7,437

UNEMPLOYMENT RATES

	20-29 Male	20-29 Female	30-39 Male	30-39 Female	40-49 Male	40-49 Female	50-59 Male	50-59 Female
0-8 years	18.7	29.6	15.3	17.6	10.6	11.0	9.9	13.5
Some HS	16.9	21.2	12.4	11.0	8.4	10.1	6.8	7.4
HS Grad	11.8	12.2	6.5	6.9	6.8	5.5	4.8	5.5
Some PS	11.3	11.6	6.3	9.8	6.7	7.3	6.0	6.4
College	8.4	8.1	5.7	6.3	5.1	5.1	6.7	6.0
Univ Bach	3.1	5.5	3.6	5.2	3.8	4.2	4.9	3.1
Univ Grad	9.6	4.7	1.7	4.8	2.0	2.0	3.2	4.1
Average	10.2	10.0	6.5	7.1	5.8	5.8	6.2	6.4

HOURLY WAGE – ALL WORKERS

92

	20-29 Male	20-29 Female	30-39 Male	30-39 Female	40-49 Male	40-49 Female	50-59 Male	50-59 Female
0-8 years	10.64	8.81	12.80	9.49	14.80	10.01	15.50	10.60
Some HS	10.91	8.56	14.53	10.44	16.49	11.06	17.34	11.84
HS Grad	11.55	9.80	16.20	12.78	18.42	13.98	19.38	14.26
Some PS	10.81	10.06	17.41	14.32	19.32	14.95	19.00	15.25
College	13.32	11.84	18.49	15.27	20.56	16.32	21.37	16.29
Univ Bach	16.85	14.82	21.69	19.36	25.63	22.20	25.41	21.57
Univ Grad	19.79	17.16	25.42	21.99	27.78	24.39	30.25	25.63
Average	12.84	11.68	18.27	15.18	20.48	16.02	20.97	15.79

HOURLY WAGE – FULL-TIME WORKERS

	20-29 Male	20-29 Female	30-39 Male	30-39 Female	40-49 Male	40-49 Female	50-59 Male	50-59 Female
0-8 years	10.88	9.33	12.92	9.48	15.02	9.97	15.60	10.40
Some HS	11.16	8.71	14.75	10.80	16.57	11.30	17.54	12.26
HS Grad	11.79	10.07	16.37	13.20	18.57	14.34	19.58	14.76
Some PS	11.33	10.55	17.57	14.88	19.50	15.48	19.36	16.06
College	13.66	12.19	18.59	15.47	20.69	16.62	21.57	16.99
Univ Bach	17.04	14.99	21.74	19.53	25.96	22.22	25.80	21.55
Univ Grad	20.14	17.39	25.57	22.57	27.90	24.72	30.41	26.71
Average	13.22	12.09	18.40	15.58	20.64	16.37	21.19	16.37

Source: Statistics Canada, Labour Force Survey, June 1998; authors' calculations.

postsecondary education is much higher in Canada than in other OECD countries. In contrast, the literacy skills of Canadians with less than a high-school education rank near the bottom, below all the other countries except the US.

These results suggest that Canada's substantial investment in education is reflected, at least to some extent, in literacy levels that are among the highest of the countries examined here. However, Canadians over 45 years of age and those with low levels of education have particularly low literacy skills by international standards.

This evidence on Canada's performance compared with other countries raises a number of questions. For example, has Canada been an international leader in terms of investment in education and the educational level of its workforce for a long time, or is this a recent development? Given Canada's unique position in terms of the importance of nonuniversity postsecondary educational programs, how do the graduates of these programs fare in the labour market?

Trends and Developments in Human Capital Formation

The Situation Now: A Snap-Shot

We begin by looking at the current distribution of educational attainment and labour market outcomes. Table 3 reports the educational attainment, unemployment rates and average wages by age group for male and female Canadians aged 20-59.[7] The upper panel of table 3 presents the percentage of each age group whose highest level of education falls into each of the seven educational categories listed: elementary (0-8 years), incomplete or some secondary (Some HS), high-school graduate (HS Grad), incomplete or some postsecondary (Some PS), college diploma or certificate (College), university graduate with a bachelor's degree (Univ Bach), and university graduate with a graduate degree (Univ Grad). Note that individuals in some age groups may not have completed their education at the survey date (especially the younger groups). Furthermore, many individuals may return to school later in life, perhaps on a part-time basis, and such increases in educational attainment are not necessarily captured in a survey taken at a point in time. We will return to these issues later.

Successively younger age groups exhibit a clear and substantial decrease in the proportion of both males and females with only elementary education (table 3). The proportion of individuals in their 20s who terminated their education at this level is five to seven times lower than the proportion of those in their 50s. Further, the proportion of the population with incomplete high school also decreases with age. Thus the proportion of individuals with less than completed high school drops quickly with age from about 30 percent of the population for those in their 50s to just under 20 percent for those in their 40s. This share continues to fall, albeit more slowly, across subsequent generations to under 15 percent for those currently in their 20s.

This dramatic increase in basic elementary and high-school education is the largest quantifiable change in educational attainment over the period. Much of the increase in educational attainment occurred in the groups who are now in their 40s and 50s – those born between 1940 and 1960. It is probably associated with the significant educational reforms that occurred in Canada in the 1960s and 1970s[8] and suggests that the elementary and high-school environment has changed considerably over the period as even those with less interest and ability stayed in school longer. Of course, many older individuals may have left school for family and financial reasons rather than a lack of interest or ability. Part of the increase in secondary school enrolment and completion over this period also reflects the fact that relative to previous generations, more individuals with high interest and ability are able to continue in school. Various factors, including the growth in real incomes, declining family size, and the continuing shift in employment and population out of agriculture and rural communities into manufacturing and services and urban communities have contributed to these changes.

The proportion of both men and women graduating with a community college diploma or certificate also rises across age groups from about 30 percent to just over 35 percent. The community college system was established in the 1960s and 1970s and significantly increased postsecondary educational opportunities for those who did not attend university.[9] Those who were in their 50s in 1998 were the first cohort to enroll in community colleges. This unique Canadian feature, which consists of having a substantial proportion of the labour force with completed nonuniversity postsecondary education, dates back several decades.

Similarly, the increased importance of university education across the generations is associated with the expansion of the universities in the late 1960s and early 1970s. In the case of universities, however, the increase in the proportion graduating is greater for females than for males. The proportion of females whose highest level of education is either a graduate or undergraduate degree rises from 12.1 percent of those aged 50-59, to 19.5 percent of those aged 30-39, and 18.1 percent of those aged 20-29. The youngest age group probably includes a considerable number of individuals who have not completed their education. Male educational attainment increases only modestly with age – the fraction of males with a university degree increases from 19 percent for those aged 50-59 to 20 percent for those aged 30-39.

In the lower panels of table 3 we present labour market outcomes according to educational attainment. The unemployment rate, average hourly wage of all workers and average hourly wage of full-time workers are presented in turn. The general pattern emerging from these data is quite clear: as education levels increase, unemployment decreases and wages increase for both genders and for all age groups. The relative unemployment rates and wages of full-time workers aged 30-59 are shown in figure 1. To facilitate comparisons in the bar graphs, the means are normalized by the mean of the group whose highest level of education is a high-school diploma (i.e., the high-school graduate group is set to one and the other groups are measured relative to it). It is clear that there is a greater return to education in terms of wages for females than for males (figures 1a and 1b). However, the unemployment rate profile for females (figure 1d), while steeper than that for males (figure 1c) at low levels of education, is flatter at higher levels. Moreover, within each gender, the educational wage premium is remarkably constant across the age groups; even though there are far fewer (more) younger workers with low (high) levels of education relative to older workers, they obtain the same wage premium. As might be expected, there is a higher variance in unemployment rates across age groups. One notable feature is that for highly educated males aged 50-59, unemployment rates are much higher than those of younger workers with the same education, and there is not a clear pattern of unemployment decreasing as education increases.

The diversity of labour market outcomes among those with a postsecondary education is worth noting. Both males and females with incomplete postsecondary education generally earn a modest amount (5 to 10 percent) more than do high-school graduates who did not pursue postsecondary studies. However, their unemployment rates are typically the same as or higher than those of high-school graduates. Thus it is not clear that their overall labour market outcomes are superior to those of high-school graduates. In contrast, college and university graduates clearly do better in the labour market on all fronts. Both males and females with a college certificate or diploma earn about 10 to 20 percent more per hour than do high-school graduates across all age groups. With the exception of the 50-59 age group, they also have lower unemployment rates. Those with bachelor's degrees earn 35-60 percent more than do high-school graduates and have much lower unemployment rates (with the exception of 50-59 year-old males). Those with graduate degrees earn an even larger wage premium and have substantially lower unemployment.

This evidence suggests that, compared with other options, the time invested in the postsecondary education system generally produces higher returns in terms of higher wages and lower unemployment. For instance, completing college certificate and diploma programs, which represent a relatively large proportion of the educational sector in Canada, does appear to pay off. Most graduates of

Figure 1
Relative Labour Market Outcomes[1] by Age, Education and Gender, Canada, 1998

(a) Relative Wages, Males

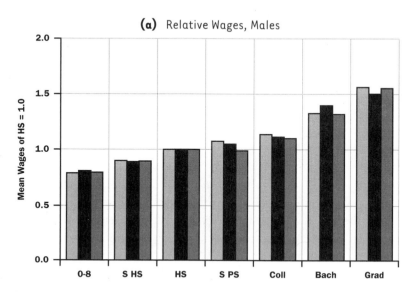

(b) Relative Wages, Females

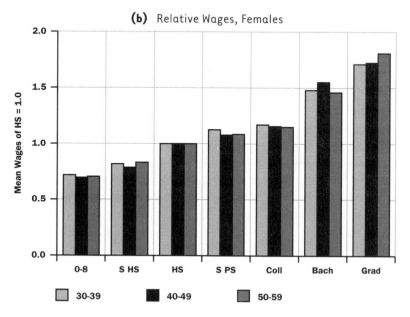

Figure 1 (cont'd)
Relative Labour Market Outcomes[1] by Age, Education and Gender, Canada, 1998

(c) Relative Unemployment, Males

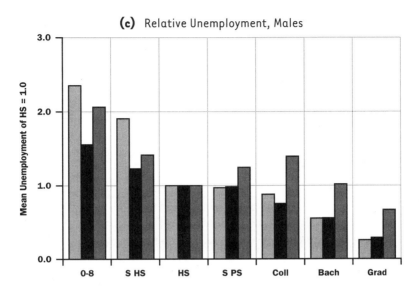

(d) Relative Unemployment, Females

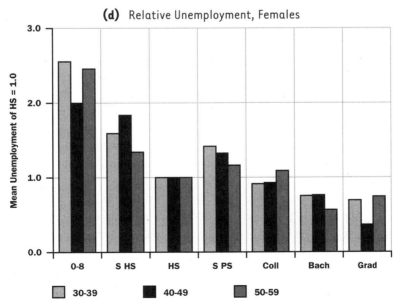

[1] To facilitate comparisons the means are normalized relative to the mean of the group in the high school diploma category.
Source: Table 3 and calculations by the authors.

w. craig riddell and arthur sweetman

these one- to two-year programs earn average hourly wages that are 10-20 percent higher than those of high-school graduates of the same age and gender. For this group education has an intermediate impact on earnings and employability compared with university graduates, who earn substantially more and are more employable but who also spend a longer period of time in school.

Changes in the Past Few Decades

The broad trends in human capital formation in Canada in recent decades can be examined by looking at the evolution of educational attainment as revealed in the 1971, 1981 and 1991 censuses. In the next section, we will turn to annual data from the Labour Force Survey (LFS) and the Survey of Consumer Finances (SCF) to get a more detailed picture of developments in the 1980s and 1990s and to distinguish between trends and cyclical changes.

In tables 4 to 8 (and tables A1 and A2 in the appendix), census information is reported by age group (21-30-year-olds, 31-40-year-olds, 41-50-year-olds and 51-60-year-olds, hereafter referred to as 20- , 30- , 40- and 50-year-olds, respectively), birth cohort and gender. The data can be read in three ways: down a column (age), across a row (birth cohort) and along a diagonal (census year). To facilitate identifying census years, results from the 1971 census are in regular type, those from the 1981 census are in bold type and those from 1991 are italicized. Looking at the distribution of the population by level of education enables us to compare and contrast educational attainment by gender and follow trends over the life cycle and across cohorts (table 4).

To conform with the LFS, we have chosen to report the same seven levels of educational attainment as in table 3. Unfortunately, in the 1971 census it is not possible to distinguish between those with incomplete high school and high-school graduates, so the total for both groups is shown in the "HS Grad" row. The delineation between university undergraduate and graduate degrees is also problematic in the 1971 census. In that year, undergraduate was defined as four or less years of university with a degree, while graduate was defined as five or more years with a degree. Thus the proportion of individuals with graduate degrees is overestimated, and that with undergraduate degrees underestimated. The sum of the two university categories can, however, be reliably compared across censuses. In the later censuses the proportions of those with some postsecondary education that attended university and/or college are disaggregated, and the data show that the majority have some university rather than college education.

Further, although the cohorts do not align perfectly, the education distributions in the 1998 LFS data reported in table 3 and the 1991 census differ somewhat. For example, the 31-40 age group in the 1991 census can be (approximately) compared with the 40-49 age group in the 1998 LFS, and so on in subsequent age groups. While the general pattern of changes across the cohorts is similar, the college certificate and university graduate degree groups are much larger in the LFS. The groups with some postsecondary education are noticeably smaller. Some individuals may have obtained additional education in the seven-year period between the two surveys. More importantly, the classification of those with high-school trades certificates or diplomas, on the one hand, and university degrees and certificates both below and above the bachelor's level, on the other, appears to differ. An important point arises from this comparison: depending on the details of the classification system employed, the education distribution can appear to be substantially different. This is important for comparisons over time and across jurisdictions. The censuses do appear, however, to provide a consistent series for comparisons over time.

Comparing birth cohorts among 30-year-olds, the proportion with an elementary education falls from 30 and 29 percent for males and females, respectively, for the 1931-40 cohort, to 12 and 14 percent for the 1941-50 cohort, and to 5 percent for the 1951-60 cohort. As in the cross-sectional data for 1998 shown in table 3, there is evidence of dramatic declines in the proportion of the population with only elementary education and equally dramatic increases in the proportion with university degrees (undergraduate and graduate). At the extremes, almost 40 percent of those born in the 1920s had less than a grade eight education by the time they reached their 40s. In contrast, only about 3-4 percent of those born in the 1960s had not completed grade eight by age 30. For those with a university education, looking at successive cohorts of 30-year-olds between 1971 and 1991, the proportion with a bachelor's degree increased from 4 percent to 13 percent for men, and 2 percent to 12 percent for women. Further, the gap between men and women with a university degree was essentially eliminated over this period. Among the older cohorts about four times as many men as women hold university degrees, but among more recent cohorts the proportions for males and females are virtually identical.

For each successive cohort, the proportion with only high-school education is affected by two offsetting influences: the decline in the proportion of the population with only elementary education and the growth in the proportion obtaining a postsecondary education. Between the 1981 and 1991 censuses, it appears that increasing proportions were completing high school. The proportion of women with a college certificate almost doubles across cohorts, and the proportion of men increases by about a third. The gender gap in college certificate/diploma programs, like that for university programs, is essentially

99

Table 4
Educational Attainment by Age, Cohort and Gender, Canada, 1971, 1981 and 1991[1]

	YEAR OF BIRTH	21-30		31-40		41-50		51-60	
		Male	Female	Male	Female	Male	Female	Male	Female
0-8 years		—	—	—	—	38.5	37.6	**34.2**	**34.6**
Some HS		—	—	—	—	—	—	**21.0**	**27.1**
HS Grad	1921-30	—	—	—	—	34.6	46.7	**14.3**	**12.2**
Some PS		—	—	—	—	3.7	3.4	**9.8**	**11.2**
College		—	—	—	—	15.7	9.6	**12.1**	**11.3**
Univ Bach		—	—	—	—	3.1	1.6	**5.6**	**2.7**
Univ Grad		—	—	—	—	4.3	1.0	**3.1**	**0.8**
Number		—	—	—	—	12,328	12,187	**23,205**	**24,314**
0-8 years		—	—	30.2	29.1	**24.8**	**25.7**	*24.6*	*24.4*
Some HS		—	—	—	—	**20.8**	**27.7**	*21.0*	*25.4*
HS Grad	1931-40	—	—	38.5	50.9	**15.9**	**14.2**	*17.9*	*17.4*
Some PS		—	—	4.5	4.5	**11.1**	**12.9**	*9.8*	*12.9*
College		—	—	17.4	11.9	**16.1**	**14.3**	*14.7*	*13.6*
Univ Bach		—	—	3.7	2.3	**7.0**	**4.1**	*7.3*	*4.9*
Univ Grad		—	—	5.8	1.3	**4.4**	**1.0**	*4.8*	*1.5*
Number		—	—	12,880	12,682	**25,605**	**25,143**	*36,973*	*37,608*
0-8 years		16.2	16.4	**12.2**	**13.5**	*11.6*	*11.6*	—	—
Some HS		—	—	**18.4**	**22.5**	*17.4*	*20.0*	—	—
HS Grad	1941-50	45.9	55.5	**16.0**	**18.4**	*18.8*	*21.5*	—	—
Some PS		10.1	7.1	**15.4**	**15.8**	*14.1*	*15.9*	—	—
College		16.7	14.4	**19.9**	**19.4**	*19.0*	*18.1*	—	—
Univ Bach		5.5	4.6	**12.5**	**8.6**	*12.5*	*10.1*	—	—
Univ Grad		5.6	2.1	**5.7**	**2.0**	*6.6*	*2.9*	—	—
Number		16,618	16,667	**35,415**	**35,375**	*53,199*	*53,530*	—	—
0-8 years		**5.5**	**5.3**	*5.0*	*4.7*	—	—	—	—
Some HS		**23.9**	**22.7**	*19.7*	*18.5*	—	—	—	—
HS Grad	1951-60	**19.0**	**22.8**	*19.6*	*22.6*	—	—	—	—
Some PS		**20.7**	**18.8**	*16.6*	*18.7*	—	—	—	—
College		**18.5**	**19.4**	*21.7*	*20.3*	—	—	—	—
Univ Bach		**10.4**	**9.9**	*12.9*	*12.4*	—	—	—	—
Univ Grad		**1.9**	**1.1**	*4.5*	*2.9*	—	—	—	—
Number		**44,350**	**44,449**	*68,347*	*70,204*	—	—	—	—
0-8 years		*3.7*	*2.8*	—	—	—	—	—	—
Some HS		*20.1*	*16.7*	—	—	—	—	—	—
HS Grad	1961-70	*20.2*	*19.8*	—	—	—	—	—	—
Some PS		*22.6*	*23.0*	—	—	—	—	—	—
College		*19.9*	*22.7*	—	—	—	—	—	—
Univ Bach		*12.0*	*13.7*	—	—	—	—	—	—
Univ Grad		*1.7*	*1.4*	—	—	—	—	—	—
Number		*64,128*	*64,860*	—	—	—	—	—	—

[1] Results from 1971 Census in regular type, 1981 Census in bold type, 1991 Census in italics.
Source: Census of Canada, 1971, 1981, 1991.

eliminated over the period 1971-91. Further, because of the questionnaire design, the college category in the 1971 census almost certainly includes informal apprenticeship training that the later censuses do not capture, so the increase in formal college training is likely even larger than indicated in these figures.

When we look at the changes over time in the distribution of educational attainment as a birth cohort ages, it is important to note that these distributions are affected to some degree by differential death rates and immigration and emigration across educational categories. Nevertheless, when we look at the same data but exclude immigrants to allow the role of the Canadian education system to be seen more clearly, immigration does not appear to affect the results (see appendix, table A1).

Most people upgrade their education when they are in their 20s; only very modest educational changes are evident in the 30-year-old group, and no significant change is observed among 40-year-olds and 50-year-olds. This reflects the belief that large investments in human capital are best made early in life when the expected remaining time in the labour force, and hence the return on the investment, is greatest. As will be confirmed below, there is little evidence in these data that recent cohorts are participating in lifelong learning in a formal educational setting to a greater extent than did earlier cohorts.

Table 5 reports unemployment rates by educational attainment for these age-gender-birth cohort groups. The most striking trends are those toward higher unemployment rates for labour force participants with less education, and the higher rates of unemployment across successive birth cohorts. In accordance with the expected life cycle phenomena, unemployment is also higher in the youngest and oldest age groups. Further, unemployment is almost universally higher for women than for men.

The increase in unemployment among labour force participants with less education is particularly interesting when one considers the massive changes in supply across cohorts outlined in table 4. Unemployment among those with less than grade eight education increases dramatically across cohorts, despite a massive drop in their supply. One interpretation of this is that the demand for the less skilled is falling faster than their supply. We revisit this issue below when we examine trends in relative wages. Another interpretation is that it has to do with changes in the composition of the less-educated group. Among the early cohorts (for example, those born in the 1920s and 1930s), those with only an elementary education are likely to have included many individuals with high levels of ability and initiative who left school at an early age for family and personal reasons. This group is likely (on average) to have done reasonably well in the labour market. Over time, as financial and other

Table 5
Unemployment Rate by Age, Cohort, Education and Gender, Canada, 1971, 1981 and 1991[1]

	YEAR OF BIRTH	21-30		31-40		41-50		51-60	
		Male	Female	Male	Female	Male	Female	Male	Female
0-8 years		—	—	—	—	6.6	6.2	8.8	9.3
Some HS		—	—	—	—	—	—	5.1	7.4
HS Grad	1921-30	—	—	—	—	3.8	5.5	4.9	6.7
Some PS		—	—	—	—	3.0	4.2	4.1	5.9
College		—	—	—	—	3.7	6.1	4.9	5.1
Univ Bach		—	—	—	—	0.5	3.9	1.7	4.4
Univ Grad		—	—	—	—	1.2	3.1	1.7	4.5
Average		—	—	—	—	4.5	5.6	5.8	7.0
0-8 years		—	—	7.3	7.0	8.4	12.2	11.8	13.9
Some HS		—	—	—	—	5.9	7.9	8.2	8.8
HS Grad	1931-40	—	—	4.3	5.8	4.6	7.6	7.6	8.1
Some PS		—	—	3.1	3.1	3.8	6.0	6.7	6.8
College		—	—	3.7	7.4	3.2	6.1	7.3	6.1
Univ Bach		—	—	2.0	1.3	1.8	3.6	4.0	3.3
Univ Grad		—	—	1.0	4.3	1.0	3.3	2.3	3.5
Average		—	—	4.7	5.9	5.0	7.8	7.9	8.3
0-8 years		10.1	11.7	11.0	12.7	14.7	15.7	—	—
Some HS		—	—	6.5	9.6	9.7	9.8	—	—
HS Grad	1941-50	7.0	8.4	5.3	8.6	6.5	7.3	—	—
Some PS		9.2	7.8	5.0	7.4	6.3	6.1	—	—
College		7.7	7.5	4.8	7.3	6.4	6.5	—	—
Univ Bach		6.0	6.8	2.7	5.1	3.2	3.9	—	—
Univ Grad		5.4	7.9	2.0	5.6	2.4	4.9	—	—
Average		7.7	8.4	5.5	8.3	7.2	7.6	—	—
0-8 years		21.3	19.4	20.7	21.1	—	—	—	—
Some HS		12.7	16.9	12.5	13.4	—	—	—	—
HS Grad	1951-60	9.3	11.3	8.2	9.2	—	—	—	—
Some PS		10.4	12.9	8.0	8.6	—	—	—	—
College		8.3	9.7	7.8	8.8	—	—	—	—
Univ Bach		7.4	9.7	3.7	6.3	—	—	—	—
Univ Grad		5.8	7.8	3.7	6.6	—	—	—	—
Average		10.5	12.3	8.6	9.6	—	—	—	—
0-8 years		27.1	26.5	—	—	—	—	—	—
Some HS		19.1	19.3	—	—	—	—	—	—
HS Grad	1961-70	13.0	11.8	—	—	—	—	—	—
Some PS		13.2	12.5	—	—	—	—	—	—
College		10.4	9.9	—	—	—	—	—	—
Univ Bach		8.5	8.8	—	—	—	—	—	—
Univ Grad		8.5	10.3	—	—	—	—	—	—
Average		13.5	12.2	—	—	—	—	—	—

[1] Results from 1971 Census in regular type, 1981 Census in bold type, 1991 Census in italics.
Source: Census of Canada, 1971, 1981, 1991.

adapting public policy to a labour market in transition

family constraints eased, this type of individual became less likely to leave school early and is therefore no longer in the elementary group. As a result, the elementary education category is increasingly dominated by those with limited ability or aptitude. Thus, on average, the employability of this group is expected to diminish, its unemployment rate to rise and its average wage to decline. Conversely, the unemployment rate of the more educated is much more stable over time than that of the less educated, despite the increase in the proportion of workers with more education. Thus most of the increase in the overall unemployment rate over time is driven by increases in unemployment among the less educated.

The pattern of weeks worked during the census year, shown in table 6, indicates some striking changes over this period. Averages presented in this table are for the entire population, including those who did not work in the census year. Among females there are large increases in the average number of weeks worked from the earliest birth cohort to the most recent, with some evidence of slightly larger increases among those with college and bachelor's degrees relative to those with a high-school education and less. Among males with low levels of education, there is a decline in weeks worked (quite substantial in some cases) from one birth cohort to the next. However, for males with high levels of education, the number of weeks worked is generally stable from earlier to later birth cohorts. There is also some evidence of early retirement becoming more common among those in their 50s. Within cohorts, the expected life-cycle pattern – weeks worked peaking when workers are in their 30s and 40s – is observed. Overall, the total number of weeks of labour supplied in the formal labour market increases over the period. It increases quite substantially among more-educated workers, largely as a result of the increased labour force participation of women, but also because of the declining number of weeks worked among less-educated men and the stable or increasing weeks worked among more-educated males.

When we look at the number of weeks worked in the population as a whole (table 6) and unemployment among those in the labour force (table 5), there are some interesting contrasts. Unemployment rises across cohorts in tandem with labour supply, except among males with less than a grade eight education, whose labour supply drops (this is a small and probably less employable group by 1991). It appears that the amount of work generated by the economy increased substantially between 1971 and 1991, but the supply of labour increased even more. Moreover, the increase in unemployment among the 21-30 age group occurred despite a substantial increase in full-time educational attendance.

w. craig riddell and arthur sweetman

Table 6
Weeks Worked by Age, Cohort, Education and Gender, Canada, 1971, 1981 and 1991[1]

YEAR OF BIRTH	Education	21-30 Male	21-30 Female	31-40 Male	31-40 Female	41-50 Male	41-50 Female	51-60 Male	51-60 Female
1921-30	0-8 years	—	—	—	—	40.9	15.2	**36.0**	**14.0**
	Some HS	—	—	—	—	—	—	**41.9**	**20.7**
	HS Grad	—	—	—	—	45.8	22.1	**43.3**	**22.4**
	Some PS	—	—	—	—	46.9	25.4	**44.0**	**27.3**
	College	—	—	—	—	46.2	25.4	**44.5**	**27.8**
	Univ Bach	—	—	—	—	48.5	23.9	**46.2**	**30.9**
	Univ Grad	—	—	—	—	48.0	32.3	**46.4**	**39.9**
	Average	—	—	—	—	44.2	20.0	**41.0**	**20.5**
1931-40	0-8 years	—	—	41.0	13.1	**39.1**	**19.0**	*31.9*	*16.3*
	Some HS	—	—	—	—	**44.5**	**26.5**	*37.7*	*24.1*
	HS Grad	—	—	45.9	18.9	**46.0**	**28.7**	*39.9*	*27.7*
	Some PS	—	—	46.4	25.5	**46.6**	**32.5**	*40.3*	*30.4*
	College	—	—	46.5	21.9	**46.8**	**32.4**	*41.4*	*32.2*
	Univ Bach	—	—	47.4	23.6	**48.9**	**37.3**	*43.8*	*35.0*
	Univ Grad	—	—	47.0	30.2	**48.8**	**39.7**	*46.1*	*39.9*
	Average	—	—	44.7	18.1	**44.5**	**27.1**	*38.3*	*25.5*
1941-50	0-8 years	36.4	13.4	**37.7**	**17.5**	*34.8*	*22.6*	—	—
	Some HS	—	—	**44.0**	**24.3**	*41.3*	*31.2*	—	—
	HS Grad	41.7	24.6	**45.5**	**26.7**	*45.1*	*36.6*	—	—
	Some PS	32.9	28.2	**46.1**	**30.7**	*44.5*	*38.2*	—	—
	College	41.9	28.9	**46.5**	**29.6**	*45.5*	*38.6*	—	—
	Univ Bach	35.4	28.0	**47.9**	**33.9**	*47.5*	*41.3*	—	—
	Univ Grad	37.1	27.5	**48.0**	**37.2**	*48.1*	*42.7*	—	—
	Average	39.4	23.9	**45.0**	**26.9**	*43.7*	*35.2*	—	—
1951-60	0-8 years	**30.1**	**15.5**	*30.6*	*20.5*	—	—	—	—
	Some HS	**38.9**	**23.0**	*40.0*	*28.9*	—	—	—	—
	HS Grad	**42.5**	**31.5**	*44.0*	*34.3*	—	—	—	—
	Some PS	**37.8**	**31.8**	*43.9*	*35.9*	—	—	—	—
	College	**42.2**	**34.4**	*45.1*	*36.8*	—	—	—	—
	Univ Bach	**39.2**	**34.4**	*47.2*	*38.7*	—	—	—	—
	Univ Grad	**40.4**	**35.9**	*46.9*	*40.5*	—	—	—	—
	Average	**39.5**	**29.7**	*43.3*	*34.2*	—	—	—	—
1961-70	0-8 years	*26.1*	*15.4*	—	—	—	—	—	—
	Some HS	*35.9*	*25.4*	—	—	—	—	—	—
	HS Grad	*40.4*	*33.5*	—	—	—	—	—	—
	Some PS	*36.0*	*33.4*	—	—	—	—	—	—
	College	*41.9*	*37.4*	—	—	—	—	—	—
	Univ Bach	*38.1*	*36.7*	—	—	—	—	—	—
	Univ Grad	*38.1*	*34.9*	—	—	—	—	—	—
	Average	*38.0*	*33.0*	—	—	—	—	—	—

[1] Results from 1971 Census in regular type, 1981 Census in bold type, 1991 Census in italics.
Source: Census of Canada, 1971, 1981, 1991.

Full-time and part-time educational attendance by age and gender is presented in figure 2. Full-time elementary and high-school attendance in 1971 is not plotted because it is not well measured; it appears that many respondents misread the question, which was therefore amended for the 1981 census. There were dramatic increases in full-time school attendance in the period 1981-91. For example, the full-time attendance rate for women aged 20 increased from 25 percent to over 50 percent (figure 2b). The increases for men were not quite as large, but they are nonetheless substantial (figure 2a). Even in 1991, however, full-time educational attendance still drops off rapidly after about age 17 and is quite low by age 25.

Part-time attendance is depicted in the right-hand panels of figure 2 (figures 2c and 2d) for individuals between the ages of 21 and 60. The census question does not intend to capture courses taken for pleasure, but only those in recognized educational institutions that may potentially be used toward a degree, certificate or diploma. Among both men and women, part-time attendance reaches its maximum, at about 12 percent, in their mid-to-late 20s. However, at older ages the behaviour of men and women is quite different. Part-time attendance among women remains high until about the age of 40, and then declines rapidly. For men, part-time attendance declines steadily after it peaks in their mid-20s.

The most remarkable feature of the part-time educational attendance plots is the dramatic increase in women's attendance between the 1971 and 1981 censuses, a testimony to women's continuing human capital accumulation. Men's, in contrast, changed little. In 1971 part-time school attendance for men substantially exceeded that for women. Between 1971 and 1981 women's rate increased relative to that of men and even surpassed it slightly in the 30-40 age group. Thus both the full-time and part-time school attendance data displayed in figure 2 provide further evidence that women have been increasing their human capital at a greater rate than their male counterparts.

Perhaps surprisingly, the relatively high part-time attendance rates of those in their 30s and older observed here does not translate into substantial increases in educational attainment within cohorts over time (see table 4). The reasons for this are unclear. Perhaps older part-time students do not complete their certification courses, or the certification is at a level equal to or below the level of education they already have so it is not observed as an increase in educational attainment in broad categories such as those reported here.

Given that the supply of more-educated workers and the number of weeks of work supplied by those more-educated workers has increased, what has happened to wages over the same period? In tables 7 and 8 we present different measures of monetary income from the censuses in a format similar to table 4,

Figure 2
Educational Attendance by Age and Gender, Canada, 1971, 1981 and 1991

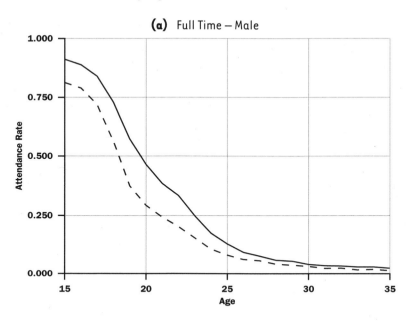

(a) Full Time – Male

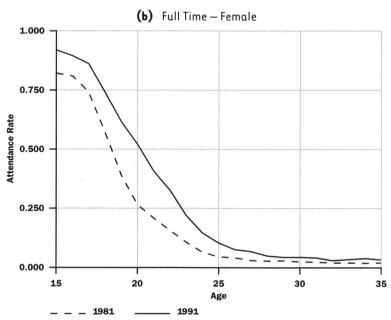

(b) Full Time – Female

Figure 2 (cont'd)
Educational Attendance by Age and Gender, Canada, 1971, 1981 and 1991

(c) Part Time – Male

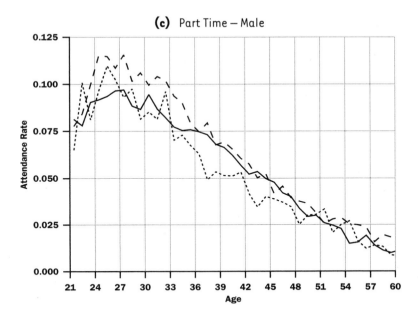

(d) Part Time – Female

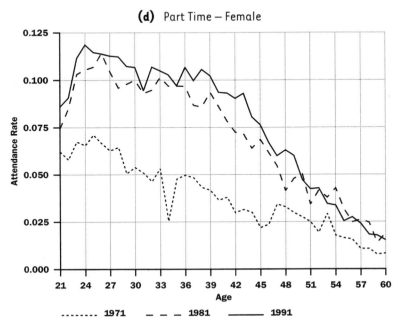

Source: Census of Canada, 1971, 1981, 1991.

w. craig riddell and arthur sweetman

for the calendar years 1970, 1980 and 1990. We focus primarily on the annual employment income of full-time, full-year (FTFY) workers reported in table 7 since this measure provides the closest estimate of the price of time obtainable from census data. Estimates of annual employment income for the entire population are presented in table 8.[10] All monetary values are reported in 1990 dollars using the national consumer price index (CPI).[11]

Several important trends stand out in these figures. First, as is well known from other evidence, females in every category earn less than males. However, this comparison of cohorts allows us to see that while the gender earnings gap declines across cohorts, it does not change much within cohorts over time. It is also evident that in most cases the real wages of men working full-time increased from 1970 to 1980, but then decreased from 1980 to 1990. Those of women working full-time increased throughout both decades, but the increases were larger in the earlier period.

There is also a steep wage profile across educational categories for both sexes. To facilitate observation of this profile, we plotted histograms based on the data reported in table 7 (figure 3). Three educational categories are shown: less than grade eight, high school (incomplete and completed high school are combined to make the data comparable with the 1971 census), and bachelor's degree. Note that by combining the incomplete and completed high-school categories, we have sacrificed comparability with the histograms based on the LFS data. To allow us to focus on the relative differences across groups, all of the group averages are normalized relative to the mean annual earnings of the high-school group.

Figure 3 therefore plots the education premium of each cohort at certain ages. The figure can be read in several ways. Each of the six panels shows the movements in the returns to education across birth cohorts for a given age and gender group. Note here that we are also comparing the data for 1970, 1980 and 1990. The left plot in each panel uses data from the 1971 census, the middle plot the 1981 census and the right plot the 1991 census. Comparing the left-hand and right-hand panels in a given row produces the differences between men and women. Finally, comparing the three panels on each page reveals how the educational premium changes with age for men and women, respectively.

Perhaps the most striking feature of figure 3 is the substantially higher education premium for females than males at all ages and in all cohorts. Focusing first on the two bottom panels (figures 3c and 3f), which depict the premia at ages 41-50 of those born in the 1920s, 1930s and 1940s, for both men and women there is a clear decrease in the returns to a university degree between the 1920s and the 1930s cohorts. This coincides with the large increase in educational attainment across these two groups noted earlier. In the two middle panels

Table 7
Annual Employment Earnings of Full-Time Employed Workers by Age, Cohort, Education and Gender, Canada, 1971, 1981 and 1991[1] (1990 dollars)

	YEAR OF BIRTH	21-30 Male	21-30 Female	31-40 Male	31-40 Female	41-50 Male	41-50 Female	51-60 Male	51-60 Female
0-8 years		—	—	—	—	22,656	12,026	**25,473**	**17,278**
Some HS		—	—	—	—	—	—	**32,633**	**20,096**
HS Grad		—	—	—	—	31,813	16,900	**36,587**	**22,542**
Some PS	1921-30	—	—	—	—	40,135	23,003	**41,875**	**26,699**
College		—	—	—	—	33,491	19,568	**38,655**	**25,069**
Univ Bach		—	—	—	—	53,894	36,233	**57,482**	**38,711**
Univ Grad		—	—	—	—	54,896	43,487	**58,585**	**52,074**
Average		—	—	—	—	31,445	17,170	**35,918**	**23,269**
0-8 years		—	—	23,551	11,758	**27,348**	**16,504**	*25,151*	*15,668*
Some HS		—	—	—	—	**33,183**	**20,606**	*31,876*	*19,640*
HS Grad		—	—	30,062	17,026	**37,851**	**22,383**	*36,823*	*22,642*
Some PS	1931-40	—	—	37,666	23,625	**43,645**	**26,471**	*41,797*	*26,729*
College		—	—	32,663	19,252	**38,990**	**24,882**	*38,172*	*25,427*
Univ Bach		—	—	46,842	35,676	**54,184**	**38,502**	*52,883*	*38,956*
Univ Grad		—	—	46,095	38,537	**57,600**	**45,020**	*58,519*	*43,094*
Average		—	—	31,040	17,843	**38,246**	**23,427**	*37,353*	*23,861*
0-8 years		20,476	12,092	**26,029**	**15,651**	*26,177*	*16,027*	—	—
Some HS		—	—	**31,982**	**19,742**	*31,981*	*20,686*	—	—
HS Grad		25,067	16,592	**35,050**	**22,527**	*37,329*	*23,658*	—	—
Some PS	1941-50	27,290	20,411	**38,026**	**27,358**	*42,083*	*28,951*	—	—
College		27,043	18,610	**37,074**	**24,290**	*39,565*	*25,775*	—	—
Univ Bach		33,231	26,824	**45,883**	**37,875**	*50,804*	*39,306*	—	—
Univ Grad		32,924	29,452	**50,753**	**41,852**	*55,756*	*45,137*	—	—
Average		25,733	17,569	**37,249**	**25,119**	*40,238*	*26,898*	—	—
0-8 years		**21,966**	**14,193**	*22,272*	*14,559*	—	—	—	—
Some HS		**26,306**	**18,772**	*28,883*	*19,578*	—	—	—	—
HS Grad		**28,404**	**20,757**	*32,719*	*22,782*	—	—	—	—
Some PS	1951-60	**28,992**	**22,627**	*36,209*	*26,762*	—	—	—	—
College		**31,002**	**22,781**	*36,320*	*25,195*	—	—	—	—
Univ Bach		**35,304**	**29,007**	*44,692*	*36,172*	—	—	—	—
Univ Grad		**35,421**	**32,324**	*45,909*	*40,356*	—	—	—	—
Average		**29,272**	**22,208**	*35,818*	*26,041*	—	—	—	—
0-8 years		*18,505*	*12,694*	—	—	—	—	—	—
Some HS		*23,204*	*16,880*	—	—	—	—	—	—
HS Grad		*25,192*	*19,046*	—	—	—	—	—	—
Some PS	1961-70	*25,637*	*20,954*	—	—	—	—	—	—
College		*28,849*	*21,708*	—	—	—	—	—	—
Univ Bach		*32,873*	*28,464*	—	—	—	—	—	—
Univ Grad		*33,766*	*31,236*	—	—	—	—	—	—
Average		*26,838*	*21,550*	—	—	—	—	—	—

[1] Results from 1971 Census in regular type, 1981 Census in bold type, 1991 Census in italics.
Source: Census of Canada, 1971, 1981, 1991.

109

w. craig riddell and arthur sweetman

Table 8
Annual Employment Earnings of All Workers by Age, Cohort, Education and Gender, Canada, 1971, 1981 and 1991[1] (1990 dollars)

YEAR OF BIRTH		21-30		31-40		41-50		51-60	
		Male	Female	Male	Female	Male	Female	Male	Female
0-8 years	1921-30	—	—	—	—	19,049	3,453	18,894	4,215
Some HS		—	—	—	—	—	—	26,383	7,107
HS Grad		—	—	—	—	28,470	6,546	30,922	8,572
Some PS		—	—	—	—	30,320	9,027	35,397	12,512
College		—	—	—	—	36,638	10,579	33,517	11,848
Univ Bach		—	—	—	—	50,442	15,018	50,364	21,086
Univ Grad		—	—	—	—	52,009	24,734	50,372	36,700
Average		—	—	—	—	27,146	6,083	28,289	8,057
0-8 years	1931-40	—	—	19,786	3,045	**21,957**	**5,827**	*16,881*	*4,843*
Some HS		—	—	—	—	**29,126**	**9,451**	*23,949*	*8,617*
HS Grad		—	—	27,234	5,700	**34,029**	**11,253**	*28,650*	*11,070*
Some PS		—	—	30,134	7,644	**38,766**	**15,117**	*32,292*	*14,339*
College		—	—	33,471	11,149	**35,633**	**14,062**	*30,797*	*14,419*
Univ Bach		—	—	44,156	14,856	**51,333**	**25,797**	*43,746*	*23,696*
Univ Grad		—	—	42,953	20,130	**52,528**	**31,469**	*50,413*	*31,276*
Average		—	—	27,300	5,804	**32,813**	**11,060**	*27,573*	*10,720*
0-8 years	1941-50	15,250	3,118	**20,622**	**5,238**	*18,870*	*6,803*	—	—
Some HS		—	—	**27,976**	**8,357**	*26,027*	*11,593*	—	—
HS Grad		20,370	7,777	**31,266**	**10,481**	*32,580*	*15,399*	—	—
Some PS		22,442	10,287	**33,741**	**14,961**	*35,159*	*19,523*	—	—
College		16,679	11,002	**33,966**	**12,767**	*34,693*	*17,701*	—	—
Univ Bach		21,294	13,865	**42,021**	**22,739**	*45,820*	*28,980*	—	—
Univ Grad		22,758	15,300	**45,489**	**27,356**	*50,782*	*35,024*	—	—
Average		19,701	8,042	**32,430**	**11,825**	*33,480*	*16,663*	—	—
0-8 years	1951-60	**13,823**	**4,234**	*14,812*	*5,892*	—	—	—	—
Some HS		**20,268**	**7,687**	*22,765*	*10,123*	—	—	—	—
HS Grad		**23,604**	**11,887**	*27,907*	*13,889*	—	—	—	—
Some PS		**20,491**	**12,892**	*29,852*	*16,936*	—	—	—	—
College		**25,291**	**14,467**	*31,322*	*16,533*	—	—	—	—
Univ Bach		**24,961**	**17,590**	*39,667*	*24,689*	—	—	—	—
Univ Grad		**25,585**	**20,958**	*39,520*	*27,995*	—	—	—	—
Average		**22,111**	**11,877**	*29,352*	*15,671*	—	—	—	—
0-8 years	1961-70	*10,192*	*4,059*	—	—	—	—	—	—
Some HS		*16,348*	*7,812*	—	—	—	—	—	—
HS Grad		*19,793*	*11,583*	—	—	—	—	—	—
Some PS		*16,673*	*12,340*	—	—	—	—	—	—
College		*22,854*	*14,949*	—	—	—	—	—	—
Univ Bach		*22,262*	*18,403*	—	—	—	—	—	—
Univ Grad		*23,199*	*18,976*	—	—	—	—	—	—
Average		*19,011*	*12,716*	—	—	—	—	—	—

[1] Results from 1971 Census in regular type, 1981 Census in bold type, 1991 Census in italics.
Source: Census of Canada, 1971, 1981, 1991.

adapting public policy to a labour market in transition

(figures 3b and 3e), when those born in the 1930s were in their 30s, the average female with a bachelor's degree received more than twice the wages of the average high-school graduate, while the ratio for men is only slightly over 1.5. By the time the cohort born in the 1950s reached their 30s, the return had declined somewhat, reflecting the greater supply of graduates. The premium for females was nevertheless higher than that for males, with ratios of university to high-school earnings of 1.7 and 1.4, respectively. At the same point in their life cycle, cohorts born in the 1920s and 1930s had higher returns to university degrees than younger cohorts, reflecting the lower proportion of graduates in the earlier period.

When we look at the earnings of all workers (table 8) the means are, as expected, less than those of FTFY workers. And the profiles, although somewhat similar, are substantially steeper; that is, the returns to education are greater, reflecting the greater number of weeks worked (and also hours per week, which is not shown) by those with higher education. If the education premium includes both wages and employment, comparing the hourly (or weekly) wage of high-school and university graduates understates the economic return to a university education, because university graduates work more hours per week and weeks per year than do high-school graduates. Of course, the time away from work may have a positive value to some individuals that is not captured in the earnings data.

Another approach is to look at the proportion of the population, by cohort and age group, that works FTFY (see appendix, table A2). Males are more likely to work FTFY, and the proportion of male and female FTFY workers increases substantially with education. The pattern is similar to that reflected in the data on number of weeks worked; more recent cohorts of males with low levels of education are much less likely to work FTFY than earlier cohorts, but the proportion is more stable at higher education levels, especially at the university level. Overall, for males there is a decline during the period, especially from 1970 to 1980, whereas for females there is a substantial increase over the entire period.

University Enrolment Rates

University enrolment rates give us some idea of students' (and parents') opinions of the private return to education. In addition, if individuals stay in school simply because they are constrained by poor labour market opportunities, then one might expect enrolment rates to fluctuate with the business cycle and more students to stay in school in times of economic bust than those of economic boom. The motivation to stay in school during the recessions of 1981-82 and

Figure 3
Relative Wages[1] by Age, Cohort and Gender, 1970, 1980 and 1990

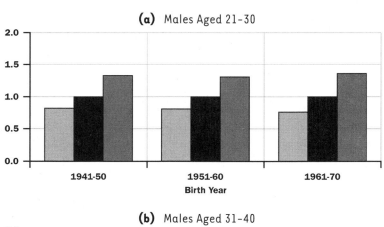

(a) Males Aged 21-30

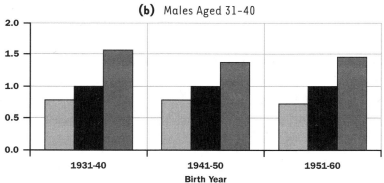

(b) Males Aged 31-40

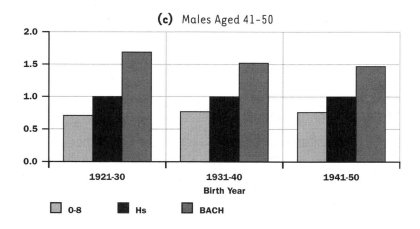

(c) Males Aged 41-50

Figure 3 (cont'd)
Relative Wages[1] by Age, Cohort and Gender, 1970, 1980 and 1990

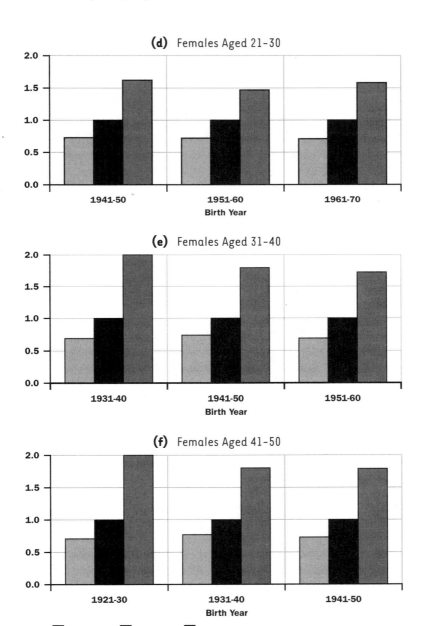

(d) Females Aged 21–30

(e) Females Aged 31–40

(f) Females Aged 41–50

Birth Year

0-8   Hs   BACH

[1] The mean annual earnings of the high-school group is set to 1.0 and the other groups are measured relative to it.

w. craig riddell and arthur sweetman

1991-92 would have been particularly strong in Canada compared with the US, since those recessions were more severe in Canada. To get a general sense of the pattern of university enrolment rates over the last 25 years, we plotted undergraduate and graduate full-time enrolment, by gender, for Canada (figure 4). Rates are calculated by dividing university enrollees by the population aged 18 to 24.

The most striking features are the strong upward trend in both the rate and the level of enrolment for females and the weaker but nonetheless upward trend for men. These results are consistent with those from the census data. In the early 1970s, among undergraduates, the enrolment rate for females was just over half that for males (figure 4a); by 1985 the rates were the same for males and females and by 1995 there was substantially higher university enrolment among females. Given that there is a higher wage premium associated with education among females, this is not unexpected. Graduate enrolment (figures 4c and 4d), although much lower than undergraduate enrolment, displays a similarly strong upward trend for both genders over the period. Female rates were at a lower level in 1971 and increased relative to male rates in the 1970s, but male and female enrolment increased at roughly the same rate over the 1980s and early 1990s. Despite the decline in the male enrolment rate in the last few years of the period under study and the increase in the female rate, female graduate enrolment remains below that of males. While there are some fluctuations in the series, the movements do not coincide with the business cycle. There is some evidence of a modest increase in enrolment associated with the 1980 recession in some of the plots, but no other indication of a business cycle effect.

Overall, the data on university enrolment are consistent with the census data. Recent cohorts are accumulating more human capital than did earlier cohorts, and women are increasing their educational attainment more quickly than are men, but they are starting from a lower level. There is no clear evidence that fluctuations are concurrent with the business cycle. Therefore, while this evidence is far from conclusive, because of the lack of cyclical responses in the educational enrolment series, we find no support for the contention that students today are staying in school simply because of poor job opportunities.

Next we explore the variation in university enrolment rates in 1971-95 across provinces using data taken from the Statistics Canada publication *Education in Canada*.[12] The undergraduate enrolment rates for females are presented in figure 5 and those for males in figure 6. Clearly there are large differences across the provinces. That Nova Scotia has the highest enrolment rate among the provinces also points to the important fact that many students attend university in a

114

province other than their home base. Universities in Nova Scotia, for instance, are reputed to be "destination" universities. Some of the provincial differences can also be attributed to the heterogeneity of provincial educational systems. For example, British Columbia has an integrated university-college system whereby students can attend a college for two years before switching to one of the province's universities for their final two years. However, in the data, university-bound college enrolment is categorized as college rather than university enrolment. Consequently, in the data for BC, unlike that for the other provinces, the number of students in first- and second-year university programs is understated.

Despite the issue of comparability of the provincial data, there are still large differences in university enrolment that can be seen as true provincial effects. There are differences in the patterns of change in undergraduate enrolment rates over time. For example, Saskatchewan's enrolment rate increased dramatically in the mid-to-late-1980s, and Alberta experienced a very significant dip in enrolment, especially among men, in the late 1970s and early 1980s. Also, British Columbia, Quebec and Newfoundland have quite low enrolment rates (especially at the beginning of the period). As pointed out by Card and Lemieux,[13] Quebec has historically had much lower levels of educational attainment than Ontario. Since Canada's regional economies go through quite different business cycles at times, we also looked at these figures to see if they revealed any business cycle effects that might have been masked in the aggregate national numbers. For example, while the 1981-82 recession was more severe in western Canada, the 1990-92 downturn was mostly experienced in central Canada. There is, however, no obvious evidence of cyclical patterns.

Figures 7 and 8 focus on graduate enrolment by province and gender in the period 1971-95. In an age of rapid technological change, graduate enrolment may play a more significant role in economic performance. Graduate enrolment rates increased rapidly in most provinces over the period, but there is also substantial heterogeneity that cannot be attributed to differences in educational systems and does not replicate the patterns in undergraduate enrolment. First, graduate enrolment rates in Quebec and British Columbia relative to other provinces are not as low as the undergraduate rates. Indeed, by 1995 graduate enrolment rates in these two provinces exceeded Ontario's, for both men and women. Second, the rankings for graduate enrolment in some provinces, for example Manitoba and Saskatchewan, are the reverse of those for undergraduate enrolment, perhaps indicating the differential values placed on graduate and undergraduate education in the allocation of educational funding. Again, there are no obvious fluctuations that coincide with the business cycle.

Figure 4
Undergraduate and Graduate Enrolment, Canada, 1971–1995

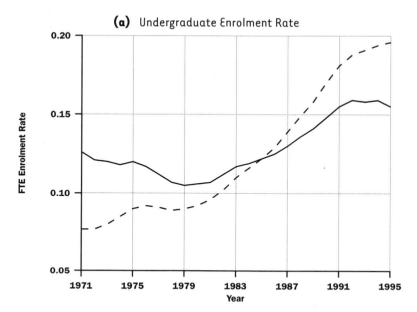

(a) Undergraduate Enrolment Rate

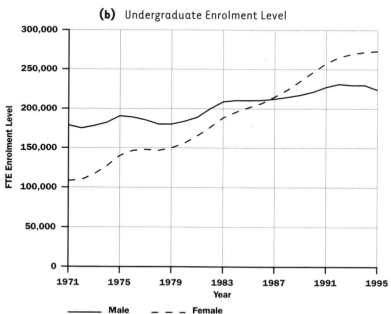

(b) Undergraduate Enrolment Level

——— Male   – – – Female

adapting public policy to a labour market in transition

Figure 4 (cont'd)
Undergraduate and Graduate Enrolment, Canada, 1971–1995

(c) Graduate Enrolment Rate

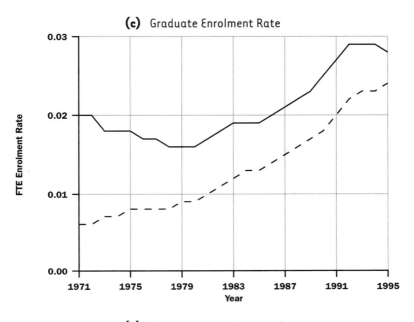

(d) Graduate Enrolment Level

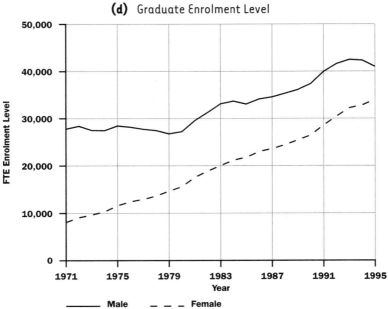

Note: FTE (full-time equivalent).
Source: Statistics Canada, *Education in Canada*, various issues.

Figure 5
Female Undergraduate Enrolment Rates by Province, 1971-1995

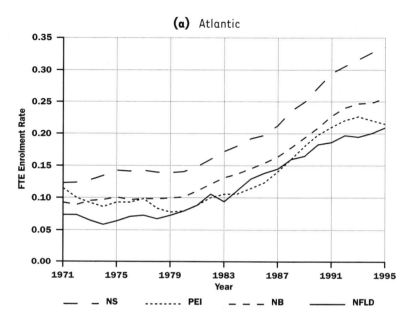

(a) Atlantic

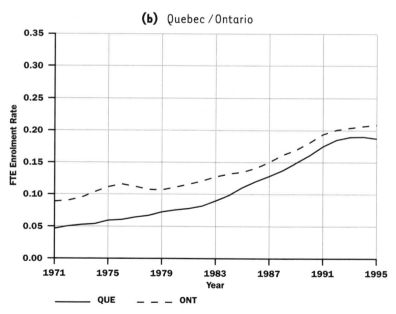

(b) Quebec / Ontario

118

Figure 5 (cont'd)
Female Undergraduate Enrolment Rates by Province, 1971-1995

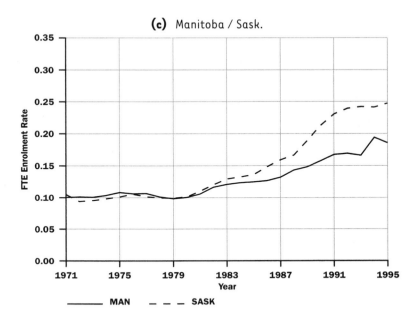

(c) Manitoba / Sask.

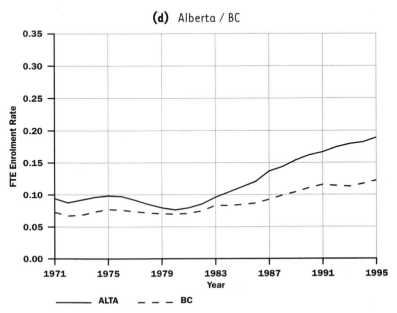

(d) Alberta / BC

119

Note: FTE (full-time equivalent).
Source: Statistics Canada, *Education in Canada*, various issues.

Figure 6
Male Undergraduate Enrolment Rates by Province, 1971-1995

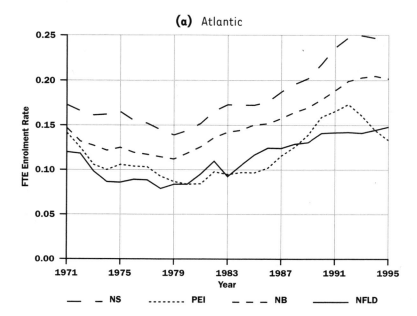

(a) Atlantic

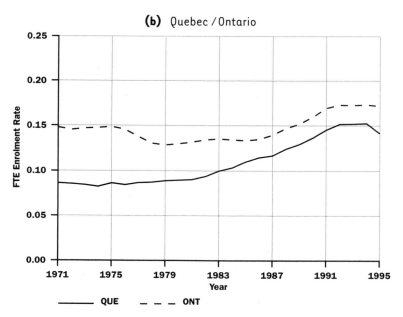

(b) Quebec /Ontario

adapting public policy to a labour market in transition

Figure 6 (cont'd)
Male Undergraduate Enrolment Rates by Province, 1971–1995

(c) Manitoba / Sask.

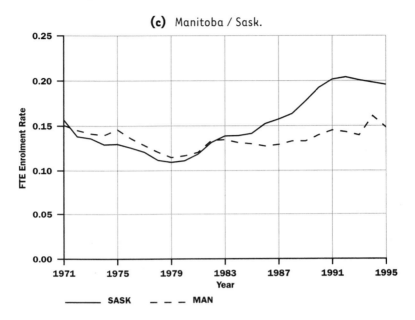

(d) Alberta / BC

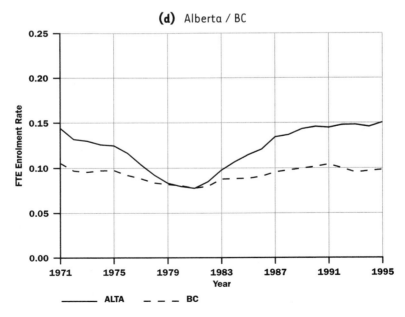

Note: FTE (full-time equivalent).
Source: Statistics Canada, *Education in Canada*, various issues.

Figure 7
Female Graduate Enrolment Rates by Province, 1971-1995

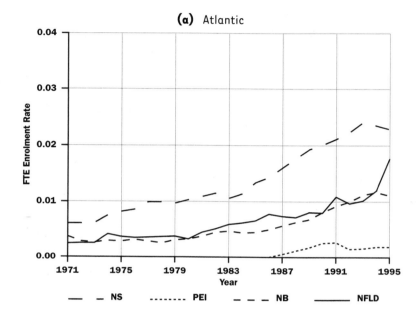

(a) Atlantic

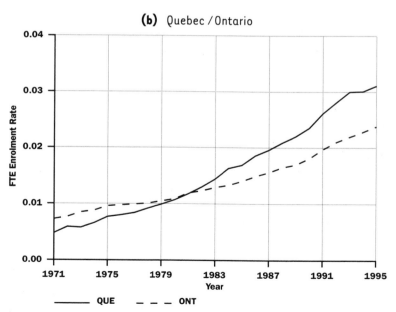

(b) Quebec / Ontario

adapting public policy to a labour market in transition

Figure 7 (cont'd)
Female Graduate Enrolment Rates by Province, 1971-1995

(c) Manitoba / Sask.

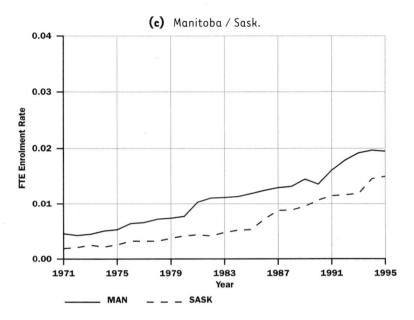

(d) Alberta / BC

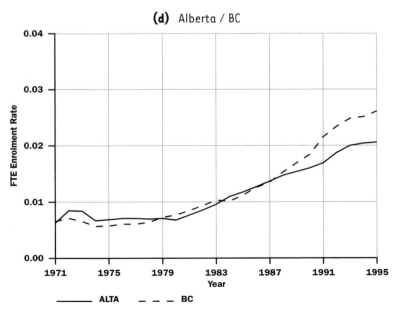

Note: FTE (full-time equivalent).
Source: Statistics Canada, *Education in Canada*, various issues.

w. craig riddell and arthur sweetman

Figure 8
Male Graduate Enrolment Rates by Province, 1971-1995

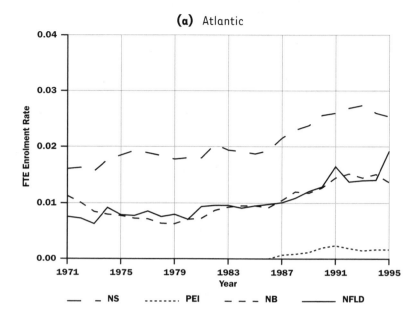

(a) Atlantic

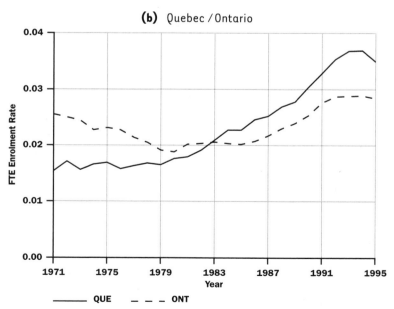

(b) Quebec / Ontario

Figure 8 (cont'd)
Male Graduate Enrolment Rates by Province, 1971-1995

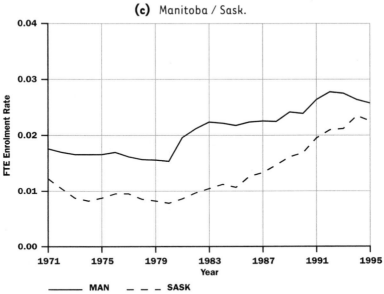

(c) Manitoba / Sask.

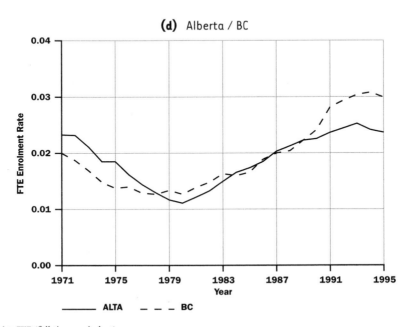

(d) Alberta / BC

Note: FTE (full-time equivalent).
Source: Statistics Canada, *Education in Canada*, various issues.

w. craig riddell and arthur sweetman

Labour Market Developments in the 1980s and 1990s

To examine the situation as it evolved in the 1980s and 1990s, we used information from the LFS. We also used data from the SCF, an annual supplement to the LFS that provides retrospective information on such outcomes as annual earnings and weeks worked during the previous year. The LFS classification of educational attainment is used in this analysis; however, some caution is required in interpreting these data because in 1990 Statistics Canada changed the survey questions relating to education in a manner that makes the pre- and post-1990 measures difficult to compare.[14]

Both decades began with recessions that were the two most severe downturns of the post-war period in Canada. They were also severe by international standards; for example, in each downturn the decrease in employment and output in Canada was substantially greater than that in the US. These downturns in economic activity might have influenced school attendance.

Despite the 1981-82 recession, employment growth in the 1980s was quite robust by international standards, reflecting substantial and protracted expansion during the latter part of the decade. Employment growth in Canada averaged 1.74 percent per year over the 1980-89 period, modestly below the 1.97 percent per year experienced in the US but substantially above growth rates in most OECD countries (particularly European countries). However, underlying this economy-wide average are substantial differences in the rates of employment growth by level of educational attainment. Over the period 1980-89, employment among those with some and those with completed postsecondary education grew by 52.6 and 76.3 percent, respectively, resulting in annual employment growth rates of 4.8 and 6.5 percent (table 9). Employment among those with elementary education declined by 3.8 percent per year, a drop of 30 percent over the same period. Employment among those with some or completed high school increased modestly. These figures apply to all individuals of working age, and are thus affected by differences in the educational attainment of cohorts retiring from and entering the workforce as well as the movement through the labour force of the relatively well-educated baby-boom generation. The lower panel in table 9 shows that substantial differences in employment growth by educational attainment are also evident among those in the 15-24 age group, many of whom are making the transition from school to work.

These differences in employment growth across educational groups were even more pronounced in the 1990s, a period characterized by a lengthy recession and slow recovery, both in terms of output and employment. Indeed, all employment growth during the 1990-95 period was concentrated among those

Table 9
Employment Changes by Educational Attainment, 1980-1995

| | Employment change | | | |
| | 1980-89 | | 1990-95 | |
Education	Compound annual average growth rate	Total change	Compound annual average growth rate	Total change
	(%)			
ALL INDIVIDUALS 15 OR MORE YEARS OF AGE				
Elementary	-3.8	-29.7	-6.7	-29.2
Some high school	+1.1	+10.6	-2.3	-10.8
Incomplete high school	n.a.	n.a.	-4.1	-18.8
High-school graduate	n.a.	n.a.	-0.8	-4.1
Some post-secondary	+4.8	+52.6	+0.2	+0.9
Post-secondary certificate or diploma	+6.5	+76.3	+3.6	+19.6
University degree	+6.1	+69.8	+5.1	+28.4
INDIVIDUALS 15-24 YEARS OF AGE				
Elementary	-3.3	-25.8	-10.2	-41.7
Some high school	-2.4	-19.5	-5.0	-22.6
Incomplete high school	n.a.	n.a.	-5.3	-23.7
High-school graduate	n.a.	n.a.	-4.6	-21.1
Some post-secondary	+3.6	+37.7	+0.2	+0.9
Post-secondary certificate or diploma	+3.6	+37.9	-0.3	-1.4
University degree	+3.1	+31.4	+3.6	+19.6

n.a. not applicable
Source: Statistics Canada, The Labour Force, various issues; Labour Force Annual Averages, various issues; and calculations by the authors.

with postsecondary education. Employment among those with elementary, incomplete high school and completed high school declined during the 1990s for those in the 15-24 age bracket, and in the labour force as a whole. During the same period, employment among university graduates increased by 28 percent and that among college graduates by 20 percent.

Despite the substantial growth in the number of well-educated workers and the decline in the supply of those with low levels of education, the earnings of university and college graduates did not fall relative to those of the less-educated groups.[15] We interpret this evidence to mean that the increase in the demand for more-educated workers was large enough over this period to

w. craig riddell and arthur sweetman

absorb the large increase in their supply, which would otherwise have lowered their relative earnings.

Education and Work

Another way of examining the issue of whether the massive increase in the supply of human capital in the labour market is excessive or whether it is motivated by factors such as skill-biased technological change is to ask workers directly about their jobs and education, and the impact of technology on their labour market prospects. Statistics Canada's 1994 General Social Survey contained a series of questions to that effect. The question "How closely is your job related to your education?" was asked in two contexts: in relation to respondents' first job following the completion of their highest degree, and in relation to their current job. There were three possible responses: "closely related," "somewhat related" and "not at all related."

Table 10 tabulates the responses by level of education and postsecondary field of study, where applicable. Over 70 percent of those with a university degree or college/trades certification replied that their education was closely related to their first job. In contrast, only 20 percent of those with a high-school diploma and 6 percent of those with less than high-school education responded positively to that question. With respect to their current job, the proportion responding positively is somewhat lower among those with university degrees or college/trades graduates. Furthermore, the differences across fields of study suggest some heterogeneity. Among university-educated social science and fine arts/humanities graduates, only about 60 percent reported that their job is closely related to their education. The percentage that stated that their first or current job is "not at all related" is much higher for arts and social science graduates. In contrast, the percentages of positive responses are considerably higher for science, engineering and education graduates. Further stratification by gender and age (25-45 and 46-50 age groups) produces very similar results. It is also interesting to note that the response to the same question posed earlier in the 1989 General Social Survey was almost identical.

Table 11 includes job-related dummy variables in a standard wage regression with economically and statistically significant results. Equation 1, which includes all educational groups, suggests that having a job closely related to one's education is associated with wages that are about 46 percent higher than the wages of those whose jobs are unrelated to their education.[16] A somewhat related job is associated with a 28 percent wage increase. Even larger coefficient estimates are obtained in equations 2 and 3, which exclude individuals without

Table 10
Relationship Between Education and Current Job, 1994[1]

	Closely		Somewhat		Not at all			
	1st job	Current job	1st job	Current job	1st job	Current job	1st job	Current job
EDUCATION	(%)						(N)	
UNIVERSITY	71	69	14	17	15	14	1,135	1,091
Science	77	76	10	12	12	12	257	248
Eng.	77	68	17	25	6	8	108	105
Soc. Sci.	59	58	17	22	24	19	212	200
Business	68	67	21	25	11	8	168	171
Educ.	83	77	8	12	9	11	219	216
Arts/Hum.	60	64	12	12	28	24	171	151
COLLEGE/ TRADES	72	61	12	18	16	21	1,868	1,628
Science	83	73	7	10	10	17	371	338
Eng.	70	63	10	18	19	19	590	545
Soc. Sci.	69	59	13	15	18	26	67	54
Business	67	53	18	24	15	24	558	467
Educ.	82	57	6	20	12	23	93	75
Arts/Hum.	63	53	10	16	27	31	189	149
HIGH SCHOOL	20	22	23	31	57	47	1,653	1,380
LESS HS	6	10	13	24	81	66	1,475	914

[1] This table reports the answers to the question: "How closely is your job related to your education?"
Source: Statistics Canada, General Social Survey, cycle 9, 1994.

postsecondary certification. A high wage premium is associated with all the fields of study, except for fine arts/humanities where it is essentially zero.

While these statistical correlations point to the economic importance of this aspect of the school-to-work transition and raise the issue of the coordination of education and labour market demand, they are very difficult to interpret. Although the point estimates are very large, suggesting that a substantial wage effect might follow from the relationship between the content of one's education and the requirements of one's job, several factors may be at play. First, obtaining a job for which one is well prepared by virtue of having studied closely related material at school increases one's productivity and wage. Second, within each discipline there are individuals who are at the top of their class and are much more likely to obtain a job in their field of study, but the wage premium primarily reflects the fact that they were at the top of their class. Finally, there may be high-paying sub-fields within each broad field that have education-

w. craig riddell and arthur sweetman

Table 11
Wage Regression Coefficients for Closeness of Education to Job

REGRESSION	(1)	(2)	(3)
Closely	0.38 (.026)	0.49 (.036)	—
Somewhat	0.25 (.025)	0.37 (.046)	—
JR*Science	—	—	0.30 (.063)
JR*Eng	—	—	0.22 (.050)
JR*SocSci	—	—	0.30 (.062)
JR*Bus	—	—	0.17 (.061)
JR*Educ	—	—	0.29 (.105)
JR*FineArt/ Hum.	—	—	0.03 (.089)
R²	0.28	0.24	0.23
N	5,887	2,284	2,276

Note: Dependent variable: log of hourly wage. Included in regressions (1),(2) and (3) are the variables: female, age, age2, single, five regional and three educational dummy variables. Further, in regression (1), which includes all educational groups, there are two additional education dummy variables, and in equation (2), which like equation (3) includes only post-secondary graduates, there are five field dummy variables (engineering omitted). All coefficients displayed are significant in excess of the 1 percent level, except for fine arts/humanities, which is not significant at conventional levels. Standard errors are heteroskedasticity consistent. "JR" stands for "Job Related" and is an indicator variable that is set to 1 if the job is "closely related."

Source: Statistics Canada, General Social Survey, cycle 9, 1994.

work connections that are closer than the average. Further research is needed to get a better understanding of the full implications of the education-work relationship and what this implies in terms of the links between educational institutions and the labour market.

Technological change is also an important aspect of the issues under study. Tables 12 and 13 present the responses to several questions in the Canadian General Social Survey about technology and current employment in 1994 and

1989, respectively. The responses are categorized according to the highest level of education achieved. Column 1 reports the percentage of workers who use a computer at work. In 1994, highly educated workers were much more likely to use a computer: the figures range from a high of 82 percent for those with a graduate degree to a low of 18 percent for those with less than a high-school education. As DiNardo and Pischke (1997) point out,[17] this correlation may simply arise from heterogeneity of employment rather than an increase in productivity associated with computerized technologies.

Columns 2 and 3 report the answers to the question: "In the last five years, how much has your work been affected by the introduction of computers or automated technology?" The possible responses were: "greatly," "somewhat," "hardly," and "not at all." Clearly, as was the case with computer use, the jobs of highly educated workers were substantially more affected by technological change than were those of less-educated workers. Of those who answered "greatly" or "somewhat," a third question was asked: "In the last five years has the skill level required to perform your work increased, decreased, or stayed the same as a result of the introduction of computers or automated technology?" Most respondents reported that the skill requirements of their job had increased as a result of new technology, and very few reported that it had decreased (columns 4 and 5).

All those who were employed were asked: "Considering your experience, education and training, do you feel that you are overqualified for your job?" An average of 21 percent reported that they believed they were overqualified. Individuals with less than high-school education were the least likely to answer positively at 15 percent (column 6). Nevertheless, a clear majority responded negatively, reporting that they believed themselves to be either appropriately qualified or underqualified for their jobs.

Finally, all workers were asked: "In the last five years, has job security increased, decreased, or stayed the same as a result of the introduction of computers or automated technology?" Among more highly educated workers, small and approximately equal proportions reported either an increase or decrease in job security as a result of new technology (columns 7 and 8). Of those with less education, a slightly higher proportion reported a decrease in job security. In every educational group, however, the majority answered that their job security was unaffected by new technology. In response to a later question to those who had lost jobs in the last five years, less than 1 percent responded that the loss was attributable to technological change.

Comparing the years 1989 and 1994, it is clear that over the five-year period the proportion of workers who use computers and are affected by technological

Table 12
1994 Survey Results on Technological Change and Current Employment

	(1)	(2)	(3)	(4)	(5)	(6)	(7)	(8)
	Computer at work	Work affected by technological change*		Skill change		Overqualified for job	Change in job security with technological change	
	Yes	Greatly	Somewhat	Increase	Decrease	Yes	Increase	Decrease
				(%)				
Grad.	82	51	25	69	3	27	13	12
Bach.	74	47	26	72	1	24	14	17
College	56	41	20	72	2	22	15	23
Trade/Voc.	47	38	18	76	1	20	14	19
High Sch.	46	35	19	72	2	21	14	20
Less HS	18	15	12	55	5	15	11	17
Average	49	35	19	71	2	21	14	19

* "hardly" and "not at all" are residual groups.
Source: Statistics Canada, General Social Survey, cycle 9, 1994.

Table 13
1989 Survey Results on Technological Change and Current Employment

	(1)	(2)	(3)	(4)	(5)	(6)	(7)	(8)
	Computer at work	Work affected by technological change*		Skill change		Overqualified for job	Change in job security with technological change	
	Yes	Greatly	Somewhat	Increase	Decrease	Yes	Increase	Decrease
				(%)				
Grad.	56	40	25	68	1	20	17	8
Bach.	57	40	22	69	1	24	16	8
College	40	35	15	68	4	24	15	9
Trade/Voc.	40	33	18	71	2	22	23	11
High Sch.	37	31	17	68	2	26	19	11
Less HS	12	13	12	55	4	17	18	19
Average	35	29	17	22	2	22	18	11

* "hardly" and "not at all" are residual groups.
Source: Statistics Canada, General Social Survey, cycle 4, 1989.

133

w. craig riddell and arthur sweetman

change has increased substantially. Computer use has increased by 40 percent, from 35 to 49 percent of workers. In 1994, a slightly higher proportion of workers reported that the level of skill required to do their job had increased (although the difference is not statistically significant at conventional levels). There was also a statistically significant increase in the proportion of workers reporting less job security as a result of technological change.

These figures suggest that technological change is a widespread phenomenon in the workplace, particularly for more highly educated workers. It seems to be generating greater skill requirements, but not massive numbers of layoffs. A vast majority of workers feel that their education is related to their job and that they are not overqualified.

Summary and Conclusions

Several conclusions emerge from this review of the Canadian experience with respect to human capital formation over the period between 1971 and 1998.

1. By international standards, Canada devotes substantial resources to human capital formation. One consequence of this is that its labour force is very well-educated compared with those of other countries. The literacy of well-educated Canadians is also high by international standards.

2. Based on our examination of data from decennial censuses up to 1991, it is clear that more recent cohorts of Canadians are accumulating substantially more human capital, as measured by educational attainment, than did earlier cohorts. For example, almost 40 percent of men and women who were in their 40s in 1971 had less than a grade eight education compared with only 3 to 4 percent of those who were in their 20s in 1991. The proportion of university graduates has doubled, and the proportionate increase in college and trades certification has been almost as large. Full-time school attendance has also become much more common among those in their late teens and early 20s.

3. Underlying aggregate employment trends are employment growth rates that differ markedly by educational attainment. Throughout the 1980s and 1990s, there were high rates of employment growth for those with postsecondary education, while employment has generally declined for those with elementary and secondary schooling. These dramatic differences in employment growth by education do not simply reflect differences in the educational attainment of entering and retiring cohorts. They are also evident among entering cohorts.

4. Despite the massive increase in the availability of more-educated workers, which is compounded by the demographics of the baby boom and the increased labour force participation of women, the unemployment rate among highly

educated workers remains substantially below that of less-educated workers. Indeed, during a period in which unemployment increased for the labour force as a whole, the unemployment rate of the well educated rose less than did that of the less educated, so that the gap between the groups widened.

5. The amount of labour provided (measured by weeks of work during the year) by men with low levels of education declined between 1971 and 1991, but that provided by those with higher levels of education stayed reasonably stable. Women in all educational categories contributed an increasing number of weeks of market work, but the increase was largest among those with higher levels of education. Thus, not only has the number of individuals with high levels of educational attainment increased substantially, but the gap in the amount of labour (weeks of work) that more- and less-educated workers are providing has widened.

6. Perhaps surprisingly, the increased supply of highly educated workers during the 1980s did not result in a drop in their relative wages or earnings. However, there was a decrease in relative earnings, particularly for women, in the 1970s. Although we do not formally test this hypothesis, the overall behaviour of the Canadian labour market during the period examined here appears consistent with a steadily increasing demand for more-skilled labour, together with declining demand for less-skilled labour. The evidence is also consistent with the view that during the 1970s the growth in the supply of more-educated workers outstripped the growth in the demand, whereas during the 1980s demand and supply grew at similar rates. In terms of the policy issues raised in the introduction, we interpret the above evidence as supporting the "relative-demand shift" view and contradicting the "over-education/under-employment" view.

7. According to our interpretation of the Canadian experience, the combined activities of students, their parents, and educational institutions resulted in a substantial increase in the supply of more-skilled labour – a supply response that was sufficiently large to offset the growth in demand for more skilled workers. Because of this substantial supply response, the earnings differential between more- and less-educated individuals changed only modestly. Consequently, earnings inequality did not increase as much in Canada as it did in countries such as the US, where the increasing education premium is an important factor contributing to the growing income inequality. In this context, it is important to emphasize that the supply response not only increased the number of more-educated workers but decreased the supply of less-educated workers, thus reducing what would otherwise have been downward pressure on their earnings and employment opportunities.

8. Looking at trends in university enrolment rates, there is little evidence that periods of buoyant economic activity draw students away from school, nor is

there clear evidence that recessions increase the size of the student body. Though this simple examination of the time-series patterns in the data is not conclusive, it does suggest that students are not going back to or remaining in school in increasing numbers simply because of poor labour market opportunities.

9. When Canadians are asked directly about the relationship between their education and their work, those with high levels of education reply that they are closely related. There also seems to be a large wage premium among those with a close education-work relationship. Finally, the jobs of a large proportion of well-educated workers are being affected by technological change that is increasing the skill requirements of those jobs.

10. The diversity of Canada's educational system produces individuals with histories that are not easily captured in a short series of standard questions. The fact that people who enroll in college and trades programs have quite diverse educational backgrounds ranging from elementary to graduate school is evidence of this. More effort should be devoted to understanding the diversity of this human capital accumulation process, particularly the sequence in which education is obtained, and its impact on labour market outcomes.

11. There is substantial heterogeneity across provinces in university enrolment rates. Nova Scotia's undergraduate enrolment (the highest of all provinces) is two to three times that in BC, the province with the lowest rate. The sources of these differences and their implications need to be better understood.

12. Women have been increasing their educational attainment more rapidly than have men. Indeed, women's participation in postsecondary education went from being below that of men to exceeding it during the period examined here. Women's rising educational levels, together with their higher rates of return to education, have contributed to narrowing the earnings gap between the genders.

13. There is some evidence in the data examined here of an increasing focus on lifelong learning, in that part-time and full-time school attendance has increased substantially at ages beyond usual school completion levels. This tendency is most evident for women, who have high rates of part-time school attendance until the age of 40. However, this apparent increase in lifelong learning has not yet translated into noticeable gains in the broad measures of educational attainment such as those used in census or Labour Force Survey data.

14. An especially noteworthy feature of the Canadian experience is the importance of nonuniversity postsecondary programs delivered by CEGEPs in Quebec and in community colleges in the rest of Canada. This is a long-standing and unique feature of the Canadian system. The proportion of the labour force completing college diploma and certificate programs is much higher in Canada than in other countries – more than triple the OECD average. Consequently,

the proportion of Canada's adult population with postsecondary education (college certificate/diploma or university degree) – almost one-half in 1995 – is the highest among OECD countries and substantially above that in the US, the second highest country (one-third in 1995). Our analysis indicates that, on average, graduates of nonuniversity postsecondary programs earn 10 to 20 percent more per hour than high-school graduates, but much less than university graduates whose hourly earnings are typically 35 to 60 percent above those of high-school graduates. Relative to university degrees, college diploma and certificate programs are an intermediate category, both in terms of the duration of the programs and their impact on earnings and employability.

137

Table A1
Educational Attainment by Age, Cohort and Gender for Non-Immigrant Canadians, 1971, 1981 and 1991[1]

	YEAR OF BIRTH	21-30		31-40		41-50		51-60	
		Male	Female	Male	Female	Male	Female	Male	Female
		(%)							
0-8 years	1921-30	—	—	—	—	40.6	37.8	36.0	34.4
Some HS		—	—	—	—	—	—	22.4	27.6
HS Grad		—	—	—	—	36.1	47.5	14.5	12.5
Some PS		—	—	—	—	3.5	3.3	9.0	11.3
College		—	—	—	—	13.0	8.9	10.0	10.9
Univ Bach		—	—	—	—	3.0	1.7	5.6	2.8
Univ Grad		—	—	—	—	3.9	0.8	2.6	0.6
Number		—	—	—	—	9,447	9,562	17,371	18,448
0-8 years	1931-40	—	—	31.0	27.9	25.4	24.2	25.1	21.9
Some HS		—	—	—	—	23.1	29.5	23.4	27.6
HS Grad		—	—	41.5	53.8	16.8	14.9	18.8	18.0
Some PS		—	—	4.1	4.2	10.8	13.1	9.3	13.2
College		—	—	15.3	10.9	14.1	13.8	12.7	13.4
Univ Bach		—	—	3.5	2.2	6.5	3.7	6.8	4.7
Univ Grad		—	—	4.7	1.0	3.4	0.8	3.8	1.1
Number		—	—	10,009	10,009	19,085	19,215	27,116	28,280
0-8 years	1941-50	16.2	15.50	12.4	12.7	11.8	10.5	—	—
Some HS		—	—	19.8	23.8	19.1	21.5	—	—
HS Grad		47.8	57.7	16.9	19.4	19.9	22.4	—	—
Some PS		9.6	6.7	14.9	15.6	13.6	15.6	—	—
College		16.0	14.1	19.4	19.3	18.4	18.1	—	—
Univ Bach		5.3	4.3	12.0	7.8	11.9	9.6	—	—
Univ Grad		5.0	1.7	4.6	1.4	5.4	2.4	—	—
Number		13,885	13,872	27,618	27,684	40,327	40,739	—	—
0-8 years	1951-60	5.3	4.6	4.5	3.8	—	—	—	—
Some HS		24.7	23.4	20.7	19.2	—	—	—	—
HS Grad		19.7	23.4	20.6	23.6	—	—	—	—
Some PS		20.2	18.5	16.1	18.4	—	—	—	—
College		18.4	19.6	21.9	20.6	—	—	—	—
Univ Bach		10.1	9.7	12.3	12.0	—	—	—	—
Univ Grad		1.7	1.0	3.8	2.5	—	—	—	—
Number		39,003	38,686	56,708	57,848	—	—	—	—
0-8 years	1961-70	3.4	2.4	—	—	—	—	—	—
Some HS		20.6	17.0	—	—	—	—	—	—
HS Grad		20.5	20.0	—	—	—	—	—	—
Some PS		22.0	22.6	—	—	—	—	—	—
College		20.4	23.4	—	—	—	—	—	—
Univ Bach		11.7	13.4	—	—	—	—	—	—
Univ Grad		1.5	1.2	—	—	—	—	—	—
Average		55,399	55,833	—	—	—	—	—	—

[1] Results from 1971 Census in regular type, 1981 Census in bold type, 1991 Census in italics.
Source: Census of Canada, 1971, 1981, 1991.

adapting public policy to a labour market in transition

Table A2
Proportion of the Population Working Full Time/Full Year by Age, Cohort, Education and Gender, Canada, 1971, 1981 and 1991[1]

	YEAR OF BIRTH	21-30 Male	21-30 Female	31-40 Male	31-40 Female	41-50 Male	41-50 Female	51-60 Male	51-60 Female
						(%)			
0-8 years		—	—	—	—	57.3	15.8	**43.1**	**12.2**
Some HS		—	—	—	—	—	—	**57.3**	**19.4**
HS Grad		—	—	—	—	74.7	25.7	**59.8**	**23.9**
Some PS	1921-30	—	—	—	—	79.1	29.8	**65.2**	**29.0**
College		—	—	—	—	75.0	30.2	**64.0**	**29.3**
Univ Bach		—	—	—	—	80.3	30.5	**69.0**	**35.6**
Univ Grad		—	—	—	—	76.8	42.5	**65.3**	**49.5**
Average		—	—	—	—	68.5	22.8	**55.3**	**20.3**
0-8 years		—	—	56.3	12.5	**47.1**	**17.5**	*36.4*	*14.6*
Some HS		—	—	—	—	**62.9**	**26.9**	*49.9*	*23.7*
HS Grad		—	—	74.5	20.6	**67.0**	**31.0**	*54.5*	*28.8*
Some PS	1931-40	—	—	76.8	27.1	**70.2**	**35.4**	*57.5*	*32.6*
College		—	—	74.5	24.0	**69.0**	**33.5**	*57.2*	*34.1*
Univ Bach		—	—	78.4	26.7	**76.9**	**42.0**	*64.8*	*38.5*
Univ Grad		—	—	75.7	32.1	**73.7**	**45.6**	*66.2*	*46.3*
Average		—	—	69.3	19.3	**62.9**	**27.9**	*51.1*	*26.0*
0-8 years		44.3	13.0	**45.2**	**15.1**	*40.5*	*21.1*	—	—
Some HS		—	—	**59.3**	**23.3**	*56.7*	*34.2*	—	—
HS Grad		58.6	29.8	**64.7**	**27.3**	*65.8*	*43.6*	—	—
Some PS	1941-50	39.5	27.2	**67.1**	**31.4**	*66.8*	*44.8*	—	—
College		58.9	33.3	**68.3**	**28.9**	*66.9*	*44.4*	—	—
Univ Bach		43.1	25.6	**74.9**	**37.0**	*75.3*	*51.3*	—	—
Univ Grad		45.9	25.4	**72.5**	**41.8**	*73.0*	*54.8*	—	—
Average		52.8	27.1	**64.1**	**26.8**	*63.3*	*40.6*	—	—
0-8 years		**28.4**	**11.7**	*32.4*	*18.5*	—	—	—	—
Some HS		**44.4**	**20.9**	*51.1*	*29.1*	—	—	—	—
HS Grad		**54.7**	**35.0**	*62.0*	*38.4*	—	—	—	—
Some PS	1951-60	**44.1**	**31.5**	*63.0*	*39.8*	—	—	—	—
College		**54.3**	**35.9**	*64.9*	*40.2*	—	—	—	—
Univ Bach		**49.7**	**33.3**	*75.1*	*44.3*	—	—	—	—
Univ Grad		**50.6**	**36.9**	*70.4*	*45.6*	—	—	—	—
Average		**47.9**	**29.9**	*61.3*	*37.3*	—	—	—	—
0-8 years		*24.6*	*11.4*	—	—	—	—	—	—
Some HS		*38.5*	*22.9*	—	—	—	—	—	—
HS Grad		*48.9*	*34.6*	—	—	—	—	—	—
Some PS	1961-70	*39.2*	*31.5*	—	—	—	—	—	—
College		*54.7*	*40.3*	—	—	—	—	—	—
Univ Bach		*48.3*	*38.3*	—	—	—	—	—	—
Univ Grad		*47.1*	*34.2*	—	—	—	—	—	—
Average		*44.8*	*33.1*	—	—	—	—	—	—

[1] Results from 1971 Census in regular type, 1981 Census in bold type, 1991 Census in italics.
Source: Census of Canada, 1971, 1981, 1991.

w. craig riddell and arthur sweetman

Notes

The authors would like to acknowledge helpful comments from David Green and France St-Hilaire.

1. See, for example, Premier's Council of Ontario, *People and Skills in the New Global Economy* (Toronto: Premier's Council, 1990); Steering Group on Prosperity, *Inventing Our Future: An Action Plan for Canada's Prosperity* (Ottawa: Steering Group on Prosperity, 1992); and OECD, *The OECD Jobs Study* (Paris: OECD, 1994).

2. There is a vast literature on this topic. See, for example, L. Katz and K.M. Murphy, "Changes in Relative Wages, 1963-1987: Supply and Demand Factors," *Quarterly Journal of Economics*, Vol. 107 (February 1992), pp. 35-78; K. M. Murphy *et al.*, "Wages, Skills and Technology in the United States and Canada," in E. Helpman (ed.), *General Purpose Technologies and Economic Growth* (Cambridge: MIT Press, 1998), pp. 283-309; and W.C. Riddell, "Canadian Labour Market Performance in International Perspective," *Canadian Journal of Economics* Vol. 32 (November 1999), pp. 1097-1134.

3. For an example of this perspective in the Canadian context, see D. W. Livingstone, *The Education-Jobs Gap: Underemployment or Economic Democracy* (Boulder, CO: Westview Press, 1997). In the United States, see D.E. Hecker, "Reconciling Conflicting Data on Jobs for College Graduates," *Monthly Labor Review*, Vol. 115, no. 7 (July 1992), pp. 3-12; and J. Tyler *et al.*, "Are Lots of College Graduates Taking High School Jobs: A Reconsideration of the Evidence," NBER working paper no. 5127 (May 1995).

4. See, for example, British Columbia Labour Force Development Board, *Training For What?* (Victoria: British Columbia Labour Force Development Board, 1995) for a policy document that takes this position. This perspective also seems to have substantial public support. For example, a recent poll found that 52 percent of Canadians would advise young people to attend a community college to learn a trade or skill versus only 36 percent who would recommend attending a university for a general education. See "More Prefer College to University: Poll," *Globe and Mail*, June 22, 1999, p. A9.

5. Research by the Economic Council of Canada concluded that Canadian expenditure per student is especially high at the primary and secondary levels, second only to Japan among the G7 countries and among the highest in the OECD (Economic Council of Canada, *Education and Training in Canada* [Ottawa: Minister of Supply and Services, 1992]).

6. See OECD and Statistics Canada, *Literacy, Economy and Society: Results of the First International Adult Literacy Survey* (Paris and Ottawa: OECD and Statistics Canada, 1995).

7. We use the LFS for June 1998 because it corresponds well with the census, which is taken in June of each census year.

8. During the 1950s and 1960s there was substantial government involvement in secondary education, massive reorganization and consolidation. In addition to a major expansion of the high-school system, spending per pupil was increased (R. Manzer, *Public Schools and Political Ideas: Canadian Education Policy in Historical Perspective* (Toronto: University of Toronto Press, 1994).

9. J.D. Dennison (ed.), *Challenge and Opportunity: Canada's Community Colleges at the Crossroads* (Vancouver: UBC Press, 1995).

10. When we examined income from all sources (not reported here) the results were very similar to those reported in table 8.

11. For reasons of confidentiality, there is an upper bound on reported wage and salary income in the public use census data. However, Statistics Canada increases the cap on the released income data each census. Sensitivity analysis suggests that the cap is approximately constant in real terms and its existence is not likely to affect our results.

12. Statistics Canada, *Education in Canada* (Ottawa: Ministry of Supply and Services, various years, 1971-1998).

13. D. Card and T. Lemieux, "Education, Earnings and the Canadian 'G.I. Bill'," NBER working paper no. 6718 (September, 1998).

14. See Statistics Canada, *Guide to the Labour Force Survey* (Ottawa: Statistics Canada, 1998). The principal change was to ask about the highest grade of primary or secondary education completed rather than number of years of primary and secondary education completed. Significant changes were also made to the questions relating to post-secondary education.

15. See K.M. Murphy *et al.*, "Wages, Skills and Technology in the United States and Canada,"

in E. Helpman (ed.), *General Purpose Technologies and Economic Growth*, pp. 283-309.

16. The percentage wage gain is obtained from the estimated coefficient b reported in the table using the transformation: $\exp(b) - 1$. Thus, in column (1), $\exp(.38) - 1 = 0.46$

17. J.E. DiNardo and J-S Pischke, "The Returns to Computer Use Revisited: Have Pencils Changed the Wage Structure Too?" *Quarterly Journal of Economics*, Vol. 112 (February 1997), pp. 291-303.

141

4

Regional Disparities, Mobility and Labour Markets in Canada

Jean-Michel Cousineau and François Vaillancourt

Introduction

The recent literature on regional disparities in Canada focuses mainly on the technological-catch-up hypothesis to explain the convergence of provincial nominal and real per capita incomes.[1] As figure 1 shows, from 1972 to 1995 personal income per capita by province clearly tends to converge toward the national average. Whether the starting point is above or below this average, all provinces, except for Manitoba, come closer to the average by the end of the period.[2]

The technological-catch-up hypothesis is both interesting and helpful for its policy prescriptions. It suggests that in order to reduce income disparities among the Canadian provinces, governments should facilitate the diffusion of high-performance technologies throughout Canada. But other factors such as internal migration or federal transfers may explain this convergence, leading to other policy implications; that is, eliminating the factors that impede internal or inter-provincial labour mobility in the case of internal migration or increasing equalization payments in the case of federal transfers.

Finally, it may be useful to compare the effectiveness of these policies with respect to other forms of regional inequality, such as employment and unemployment disparities, because reducing income disparities and reducing provincial employment or unemployment disparities are different matters. The instruments that serve the purpose of reducing income disparities may differ from the ones that reduce other forms of disparities. For example, Canadian studies of the incidence of migration on regional unemployment disparities and employment income have generally concluded that its impact is greater on the former than

Figure 1

Personal Income Per Capita by Province Relative to the National Average, Canada, 1972–1995

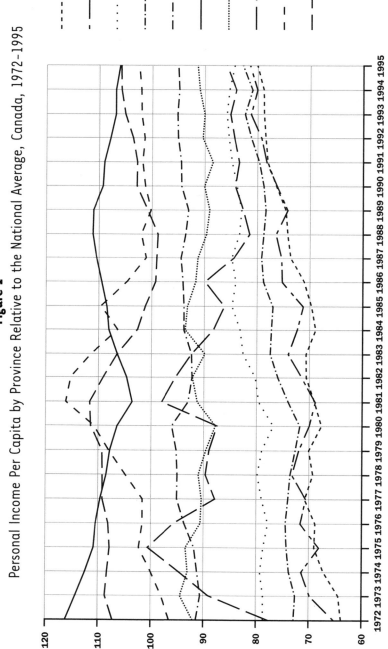

Year

Sources: Department of Finance, *Economic Reference Tables* (August 1995), p. 31; 1995: CANSIM, series D31236 and D31248.

on the latter.[3] While these studies are based on structural equations and simulations[4] or on reduced-form equations on the dynamics of regional wages and unemployment,[5] none has yet provided direct evidence on the statistical links between migration and a set of aggregate measures of regional disparities. This study attempts to provide information about the impact of migration, technology and federal fiscal transfer payments on the evolution of regional disparities in Canada and the implications for labour market adjustment and public policy.

In the first section, we present the main empirical predictions derived from a flexible-wage model. In the second section, we present evidence on internal migration in Canada. In the third section, we describe the evolution of the relevant regional disparities indicators. In the fourth and fifth sections, we test a number of hypotheses that may improve our understanding of the trends in regional disparities in Canada. The conclusion summarizes the main findings and draws policy implications.

Theoretical Framework

Following Boadway,[6] there are two prototypical approaches to examine how migration and labour market conditions interact: the flexible-wage view and the sticky-wage view. We will examine the incidence of federal government transfers, migration and technology through the lens of the flexible-wage view. This approach leads to clear, precise and usually testable hypotheses about their incidence on income, employment and participation rates, while leaving unemployment-rate effects uncertain. The alternative – the sticky-wage approach – produces more precision on the unemployment rate but much less on the other components of the labour market.

Federal Government Transfers

We assume that federal government transfers to individuals and to provinces enter directly into the calculation of personal income per capita by province. And while the interregional redistributive effects of transfers to the provinces are obvious, transfers to individuals may also have interregional redistributive effects to the extent they provide more support to provinces where eligible individuals are concentrated. Furthermore, both types of transfers may be seen as an important way of sustaining regional aggregate demand and thus the demand for local goods and services in low-income and low-employment regions. Such a displacement of the demand for goods and services is expected to create a shift in the labour demand that raises relative employment and labour force participation in the low-income regions. Thus, this framework predicts a

Figure 2
Incidence of Federal Transfer Payments in a Low-Wage, Low-Employment Region

Region A: low employment and low wages

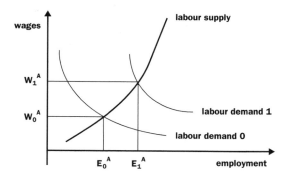

Region B: high employment and high wages

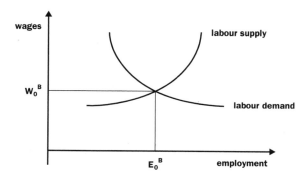

decrease in income, employment and participation-rate disparities because the demand increases in the low-income region (region A) but not in the high-income region (region B) (figure 2).

Migration

Our analysis of the labour migration effect emphasizes the supply side rather than the demand side of the labour market: workers move from the low-wage and low-employment region to the high-wage and high-employment region. And, as expected, this displacement of the labour supply generates opposite movements in the wage/employment combinations. Wages increase but the level of employment decreases in the low-wage and low-employment region,

Figure 3
Labour Migration from Region A to Region B

Region A: low employment and low wages

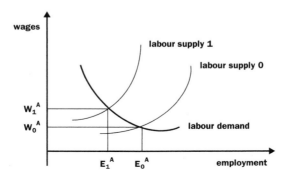

Region B: high employment and high wages

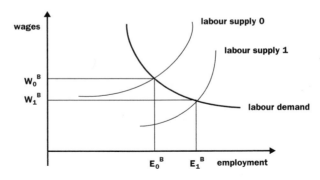

while the opposite is true in the high-wage and high-employment region. It is therefore expected that the convergence of incomes should be accompanied by a divergence of regional employment and participation rates (figure 3).

Technology
In the case of a technological-catch-up process, the impulse essentially comes from the productivity component of the demand for labour. The provinces where the technological gap is larger at the beginning of the period are expected to be the ones that will benefit from larger productivity growth, and income disparities should diminish throughout the period. If the labour supply is assumed to be perfectly inelastic – that is, if in the very long run the labour supply is

jean-michel cousineau and françois vaillancourt

Figure 4
The Effects of Technological Catch-Up

Region A: low employment and low wages

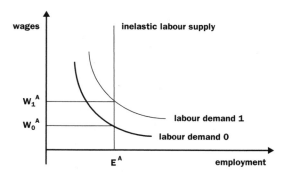

Region B: high employment and high wages

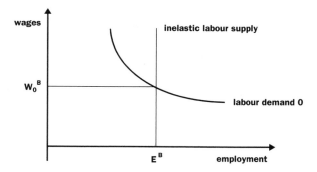

completely inelastic with regard to the wage level, and the economy cannot employ more than its potential labour force – no particular or predictable change is expected to show up in terms of employment, participation-rate or unemployment-rate disparities in the long run. Technological change increases the wages and incomes of workers but not the potential labour supply, which is given by demographic forces. This case is analogous to figure 2, except that the labour supply is considered perfectly inelastic in both markets (figure 4).

Table 1 summarizes our predictions about changes in regional disparities following either an increase in federal government transfers or the migration of labour from low-employment and low-wage regions to high-employment and high-wage regions, or a process of technological catch-up between low-productivity and high-productivity regions.

Table 1
Summary of Predictions

Variable	Trends in the dispersion of		
	Personal income per capita	Employment/ population ratio	Participation rates
Government transfers (demand side)	–	–	–
Labour migration (supply side)	–	+	+
Technological catch-up (inelastic supply)	–	0	0

Internal Migration

Internal migration has an important cumulative impact on total population, particularly in some provinces (table 2a). From 1970 to 1995, Quebec experienced the largest net out-migration (-452,130) and British Columbia the largest net in-migration (+544,196). Net out-migration appears to be an established pattern for Newfoundland, Quebec, Manitoba, Saskatchewan, the Yukon and the Northwest Territories. Inflows and outflows more or less balance out for Nova Scotia and New Brunswick, while the net gainers over this period are PEI (only marginally), Ontario, Alberta and British Columbia. Economic activity has an impact on flows, with the recession of 1982-84 coinciding with positive flows into New Brunswick, Nova Scotia, Manitoba and Saskatchewan. This was probably due to unsuccessful job seekers returning home from Alberta, where out-migration continued until 1989 as a result of the economic slow-down in that province. In recent years, only PEI and British Columbia have gained migrants from the rest of Canada. British Columbia has had the steadiest performance overall (22 positive years out of 26), while Ontario was a gainer mainly in the 1980s.

149

Table 2b allows us to assess the impact of migration flows with respect to total population. The last column of table 2b shows that the total in- or out-migration rate, that is, the total number of persons who moved from one province (territory) to another per 1,000 population in Canada as a whole decreased from 19.4 in 1970 to 11.2 in 1995. Various socio-demographic factors may have contributed to this decrease: the aging of the population which reduces individual mobility; the increase in the prevalence of two-earner families which makes it more difficult for a family to move; and the decrease in family size which reduces the number of movers per family who moves. In addition, government

Table 2a
Net Interprovincial Migration by Province/Territory and Gross Flows for Canada, 1970-1995

YEAR	Newfoundland	Prince Edward Island (PEI)	Nova Scotia	New Brunswick	Quebec	Ontario
1970	-5,950	-29	-3,967	-2,373	-41,156	54,590
1971	733	-129	-755	1,798	-25,005	18,580
1972	-189	858	2,845	241	-19,891	8,227
1973	-2,510	478	2,107	2,841	-14,730	-5,275
1974	-618	1,386	1,576	4,192	-11,852	-22,163
1975	915	814	4,454	7,572	-12,340	-25,057
1976	-2,732	309	361	1,640	-20,801	-10,508
1977	-4,009	614	-1,277	-886	-46,536	8,596
1978	-3,540	25	-109	-1,644	-33,424	415
1979	-4,217	-225	-1,840	-2,219	-30,025	-15,317
1980	-3,082	-1,082	-2,494	-4,165	-24,283	-34,919
1981	-6,238	-783	-2,465	-4,766	-22,549	-19,665
1982	261	-6	1,591	2,183	-28,169	19,614
1983	-1,092	799	3,861	2,296	-19,080	32,825
1984	-3,585	524	2,963	812	-10,943	36,691
1985	-5,019	-13	-234	-1,559	-6,023	33,414
1986	-4,682	-493	-739	-2,897	-3,020	42,916
1987	-4,374	301	-2,183	-1,762	-7,410	40,278
1988	-2,154	424	71	-1,215	-7,003	14,898
1989	-2,606	-102	572	-21	-8,379	-1,205
1990	-1,137	-273	-106	1,014	-9,567	-15,117
1991	-1,086	-416	1,039	-79	-13,047	-9,978
1992	-2,731	482	138	-1,155	-9,501	-13,242
1993	-3,656	588	-1,682	-453	-7,177	-11,920
1994	-6,397	623	-2,625	-465	-9,444	-4,749
1995	-6,580	472	-1,741	-779	-10,775	-2,950
Total	-76,275	5,146	-639	-1,849	-452,130	118,979

policies such as changes in the generosity of the unemployment insurance program – both overall and regionally – and regional development policies partially reduce the incentives to labour mobility. The reduction in internal mobility could also be explained in part by (international) immigration flows acting as a substitute for internal migration flows.

If we look at international immigration over the last 15 years (table 3), we find that it first decreases from 1981 to 1985 then increases until 1993, probably in response to economic cycles. This is similar to the decline observed in internal

Table 2a (continued)

Net Interprovincial Migration by Province/Territory and Gross Flows for Canada, 1970-1995

YEAR	Manitoba	Saskatchewan	Alberta	British Columbia	Yukon and Northwest Territories	Total in- or out-migration
1970	-7,707	-28,358	9,898	22,579	2,473	412,559
1971	-7,251	-17,986	2,408	25,034	2,573	405,301
1972	-7,735	-17,296	6,538	24,927	1,475	375,184
1973	-2,200	-13,261	2,698	30,537	-685	433,992
1974	-5,400	-4,835	14,810	22,655	249	421,336
1975	-4,134	6,555	23,463	-2,864	622	385,330
1976	-3,655	3,819	34,215	-1,490	-1,158	376,970
1977	-3,789	384	32,344	15,507	-948	366,918
1978	-9,557	-3,701	31,987	20,698	-1,150	348,929
1979	-13,806	-3,510	39,212	33,241	-1,294	370,862
1980	-11,342	-4,382	46,933	40,165	-1,349	372,167
1981	-3,621	-520	40,243	21,565	-1,201	380,041
1982	1,498	1,743	3,961	-2,019	-657	322,634
1983	950	2,501	-26,246	4,029	-843	285,599
1984	-49	733	-30,591	3,505	-60	273,323
1985	-1,755	-5,014	-9,568	-3,199	-1,030	281,275
1986	-3,039	-7,020	-20,293	910	-1,643	302,352
1987	-4,751	-9,043	-27,595	17,618	-1,079	318,890
1988	-8,584	-16,338	-5,535	25,865	-429	323,685
1989	-10,004	-18,589	3,366	37,367	-399	347,990
1990	-8,613	-15,928	11,055	38,704	-32	332,637
1991	-7,581	-9,498	5,510	34,572	564	315,419
1992	-6,152	-6,914	-73	39,458	-310	306,382
1993	-4,737	-4,770	-2,738	37,455	-910	276,413
1994	-3,791	-3,568	-2,621	33,354	-317	284,673
1995	-2,577	-2,390	3,192	24,023	105	331,131
Total	-139,382	-177,186	183,381	544,196	-7,433	8,951,992

Source: Statistics Canada, *Report on the Demographic Situation in Canada*, 91-209, and CANSIM: series D31236 to D31248.

migration, where the trough is in 1984, from which it increases until 1990, decreases until 1993 and increases again. The second decrease, linked to the 1990 recession, is not found in international immigration, perhaps because of the increasing importance of family reunification and refugee admission as determinants of immigration. Note also that international immigration is very small in Atlantic Canada and decreasing in Quebec and the Prairies, three regions that are also losing population through internal migration. In contrast, it is

jean-michel cousineau and françois vaillancourt

Table 2b

Net Interprovincial Migration Rates by Province/Territory and Gross Migration Rates for Canada, 1970-1995 (per thousand)

YEAR	Newfoundland	Prince Edward Island (PEI)	Nova Scotia	New Brunswick	Quebec	Ontario
1970	-11.51	-0.26	-5.07	-3.78	-6.84	7.23
1971	1.38	-1.14	-0.94	2.79	-4.06	2.36
1972	0.35	7.53	3.54	0.37	-3.21	1.03
1973	-4.58	4.16	2.59	4.31	-2.36	-0.65
1974	-1.12	11.95	1.92	6.28	-1.88	-2.69
1975	1.64	6.90	5.38	11.15	-1.94	-3.01
1976	-4.84	2.60	0.43	2.37	-3.24	-1.25
1977	-7.07	5.12	-1.52	-1.27	-7.21	1.01
1978	-6.22	0.20	-0.13	-2.34	-5.17	0.05
1979	-7.39	-1.83	-2.16	-3.15	-4.63	-1.76
1980	-5.37	-8.73	-2.92	-5.88	-3.72	-3.98
1981	-10.83	-6.31	-2.88	-6.73	-3.43	-2.22
1982	0.45	-0.05	1.85	3.07	-4.27	2.19
1983	-1.88	6.34	4.43	3.20	-2.88	3.62
1984	-6.16	4.13	3.37	1.12	-1.64	3.99
1985	-8.64	-0.10	-0.26	-2.15	-0.90	3.58
1986	-8.10	-3.82	-0.83	-3.98	-0.45	4.53
1987	-7.58	2.33	-2.44	-2.41	-1.09	4.16
1988	-3.74	3.26	0.08	-1.66	-1.02	1.51
1989	-4.52	-0.78	0.63	-0.03	-1.21	-0.12
1990	-1.96	-2.08	-0.12	1.36	-1.36	-1.46
1991	-1.87	-3.18	11.32	-0.11	-1.84	-0.95
1992	-4.67	3.65	0.15	-1.53	-1.33	-1.24
1993	-6.26	4.42	-1.81	-0.60	-0.99	-1.10
1994	-11.01	4.61	-2.81	-0.61	-1.30	-0.43
1995	-11.44	3.47	-1.86	-1.03	-1.47	-0.27

increasing in Ontario and British Columbia, two regions that are gaining population through internal migration. Thus, the observed pattern of international immigration and internal migration flows in Canada is more consistent with the view that these flows are complementary rather than substitutes.

The typical migration flows, shown in table 4, are from Atlantic Canada and Quebec to Ontario, from Ontario to Alberta and British Columbia, and from Manitoba and Saskatchewan to Alberta and British Columbia, with strong flows between the latter two provinces. Quebec provides and receives few

Table 2b (continued)
Net Interprovincial Migration Rates by Province/Territory and Gross Migration Rates for Canada, 1970-1995 (per thousand)

YEAR	Manitoba	Saskatchewan	Alberta	British Columbia	Yukon and Northwest Territories	Total in- or out-migration rate
1970	-7.84	-30.14	6.21	10.61	49.46	19.37
1971	-7.24	-19.26	1.44	11.13	45.95	18.40
1972	-7.70	-18.74	3.85	10.78	25.00	16.84
1973	-2.18	-14.51	1.56	12.84	-11.05	19.24
1974	-5.29	-5.31	8.41	9.24	4.02	18.42
1975	-4.03	7.13	12.93	-1.14	9.57	16.60
1976	-3.53	4.09	18.26	-0.59	-17.03	16.03
1977	-3.64	0.41	16.55	6.01	-13.94	15.42
1978	-9.16	-3.88	15.76	7.88	-16.43	14.52
1979	-13.29	-3.65	18.63	12.43	-18.49	15.28
1980	-10.94	-4.52	21.32	14.58	-19.00	15.13
1981	-3.49	-0.53	17.47	7.60	-16.68	15.26
1982	1.43	1.76	1.67	-0.70	-8.76	12.80
1983	0.89	2.49	-10.94	1.38	-11.24	11.22
1984	-0.05	0.72	-12.75	1.18	-0.78	10.63
1985	-1.62	-4.87	-3.97	-1.07	-12.88	10.84
1986	-2.78	-6.80	-8.32	0.30	-20.54	11.54
1987	-4.32	-8.73	-11.29	5.75	-13.16	12.01
1988	-7.77	-15.83	-2.25	8.27	-5.17	12.04
1989	-9.05	-18.17	1.34	11.64	-4.75	12.71
1990	-7.77	-15.75	4.33	11.73	-0.37	11.97
1991	-6.81	-9.44	2.12	10.23	6.27	11.23
1992	-5.50	-6.86	-0.03	11.34	-3.33	10.73
1993	-4.21	-4.71	-1.02	10.48	-9.68	9.55
1994	-3.35	-3.53	-0.97	9.09	-3.34	9.73
1995	-2.26	-2.35	1.16	6.38	1.09	11.18

Source: Statistics Canada, *Report on the Demographic Situation in Canada*, 91-209, and CANSIM: series D31236 to D31248.

interprovincial migrants. These results are similar to those of Finnie[7] derived from the Longitudinal Administrative Database.

When we look at another dimension of labour migration in Canada – its composition – we find that the younger and more-educated members of the labour market are also more mobile (table 5). The highest out-migration rate is found in the 25-29 age bracket. In fact, the incidence of migration increases by age from the 15-19 to the 25-29 age group and then decreases. Thus, internal

Table 3

Declared Region of Settlement, International Immigrants,
Canada, 1981-1995

YEAR	Number of immigrants to Canada	Atlantic	Quebec	Ontario	Prairies	British Columbia
		(%)				
1981	128,618	2	16	43	21	17
1982	121,147	2	18	44	21	16
1983	89,157	2	18	45	18	16
1984	88,239	2	17	47	19	15
1985	84,302	2	18	48	17	15
1986	99,219	2	20	50	15	13
1987	152,098	2	18	56	12	12
1988	161,933	2	16	55	13	14
1989	192,001	2	18	55	13	13
1990	214,230	1	19	53	13	13
1991	230,626	1	22	52	11	14
1992	252,598	2	19	55	10	15
1993	255,473	2	18	53	10	18
1994	223,493	2	13	52	11	22
1995	209,216	2	12	55	10	21

Source: Statistics Canada.

154 migration appears to be higher after the completion of post-secondary education. This may be an artifact of the data sources, since the family allowance files and the tax files both probably underestimate the movement of young (15-19 age bracket) single adults. Notice also that the incidence of migration is higher than average among individuals in their early 20s to their late 30s. The rate of migration by level of education, also shown in table 5, increases fivefold between the primary education and university graduate levels.

To further analyze the determinants of migration, we used a probit model that estimates the probability of an individual migrating. The explanatory variables included in the probit analysis are education, marital status, language, age group and occupation. We used the 1991 Canadian census data to compile a sample of 170,479 men and 146,009 women between the ages of 25 and 60 who had positive earnings in 1990. The probit results (see appendix, table A1) confirm that the younger and more educated members of the labour force have a higher propensity to move. The education variable and the 25-29 and 30-34 age brackets have positive and significant coefficients for both males and females, which means that better educated workers are more likely to move than less educated ones.

Table 4

Provincial Destination of Interprovincial Migrants, Men, 1991

	Province / Region of birth						
	Atlantic	Quebec	Ontario	Manitoba	Saskatchewan	Alberta	British Columbia
	(%)						
Emigration by province[1]	26.35	9.34	11.15	36.80	45.58	23.60	12.73
Province of destination							
Atlantic[2]	–	8.9	12.2	–	–	–	–
Quebec	12.0	–	19.7	2.1	0.7	1.7	3.1
Ontario	57.7	64.9	–	24.9	13.1	16.8	34.1
Manitoba	3.1	2.0	6.9	–	8.1	3.9	6.0
Saskatchewan	1.5	0.7	3.7	9.9	–	7.7	6.2
Alberta	13.1	9.9	25.5	26.5	38.7	–	50.7
British Columbia	12.6	13.4	32.0	36.6	39.2	69.9	–

[1] Refers to the percentage of those born in the province who were resident of another province at the time of the 1991 Census.

[2] Data was not available for migrants from Manitoba, Saskatchewan, Alberta and British Columbia whose destination was Atlantic Canada. Overall, less than 10% of western migrants go to Atlantic Canada.

Source: M. Vachon and F. Vaillancourt, "Interprovincial Mobility in Canada, 1961–1996: Importance and Destination," in H. Lazar and T. McIntosh (eds.), *Canada: The State of Federation 1998–99, How Canadians Connect* (Kingston: School of Policy Studies, 1999), pp. 101–22.

jean-michel cousineau and françois vaillancourt

Table 5

(a) The Incidence of Interprovincial Migration by Age, Canada, 1986-1991

Age	Incidence[1] (per thousand)
15-19	33.3
20-24	58.1
25-29	76.2
30-34	61.7
35-39	48.5
40-44	36.5
45-49	28.6
50-54	23.0
55-59	19.5
60-64	17.5
65+	15.6
Average	40.0

(b) The Incidence of Interprovincial Migration by Level of Education, Canada, 1986-1991

Education level	Incidence[1] (per thousand)
Primary	14.9
Secondary	35.1
Post-secondary	46.1
University	
- undergraduate	62.1
- graduate	81.3

[1] For individuals aged 15+ with positive earnings.
Source: 1991 Census micro-data file, calculations by the authors.

The same can also be said of younger workers (25 to 39 years old) relative to older workers. In fact, the upper age brackets have negative and significant coefficients, which means that these workers are less mobile than those aged 35-39. The negative effect associated with being married is explained by the need for both spouses (in most cases) to find new employment following a move.

Table A1 also shows that bilingual anglophones are more mobile and unilingual francophones less mobile than unilingual anglophones. Finnie[8] shows that Quebec anglophones (who are the most bilingual in Canada) are the most

Table 6
Expected Wage Gains or Losses Associated with Internal Migration Flows by Gender, Canada, 1991 (dollars)

Province/Region of origin	Province of destination					
	Ontario		Alberta		British Columbia	
	Male	Female	Male	Female	Male	Female
Atlantic provinces	2,899	2,103	n.c.	n.c	n.c.	n.c.
Quebec	2,777	1,016	n.c.	n.c.	n.c.	n.c.
Ontario	–	–	-1,341	-1,379	-1,280	-1,272
Manitoba and Saskatchewan	n.c.	n.c.	2,835	2,833	3,564	1,280

n.c.: not computed.
Note: Simulation results based on the following equation: log (earnings) = β0 + β1 education +β2 experience + β3 experience² +β4 weeks worked +ε.
Source: Census of Canada, 1991. Calculations by authors, regressions results are reported in Table A2.

mobile group and Quebec francophones the least mobile group in Canada. Individuals working in the service occupations show quite high propensities to move, as do male managers, natural science workers and construction workers.

Table 6 shows the expected wage gains (losses) from moving for the most common origin-destination pairs, based on 1991 Canadian census data. A standard human-capital wage equation was estimated for provinces and regions (see appendix, table A2), and used to calculate the expected wages of the migrants in the destination provinces for those who were between 25 and 60 years old and earned a positive income in 1990. The equations estimated for migrants are not corrected for the sample-selection bias that results from the use of this population subgroup. However, given that our purpose is to capture all of the wage impacts of the migration decision, these are the appropriate equations to use. 157

The results of these calculations show that moving from Atlantic Canada or Quebec to Ontario, and moving from Manitoba and Saskatchewan to Alberta or British Columbia increases expected wages. These results are consistent with observed mobility. Gross wages decrease, however, as a result of moves from Ontario to Alberta or British Columbia. Why people move from Ontario to these provinces is not clear. Perhaps there are more attractive amenities in these two provinces (the Pacific Ocean and the Rockies) or better employment opportunities and chances of promotion. Lower taxes (especially in Alberta) may also be a factor.

In summary, these observations show that internal migration is an important phenomenon in Canada. It changes the regional composition of the population in the medium and long term. British Columbia gained half a million people over the last 25 years due to internal migration, while Quebec lost more than 450,000 during the same period (table 2a). The pattern of internal migration in Canada is consistent with economic theory. The labour force flows from low-wage and low-employment regions to high-wage and high-employment regions, that is, from Eastern Canada to Ontario and from there to Western Canada. It is also the younger, more educated people who move and have a higher propensity to do so. This is in accordance with standard human capital theory, since they have a longer working period over which to recoup the cost of this decision. However, it appears that people do not always move to increase their employment income. The case of migrants from Ontario moving to Alberta and British Columbia seems to indicate that they also move for other reasons or, alternatively, that these individuals have characteristics that are not captured by the model.

Finally, while migration seems to fill an important role in adjusting labour supply to demand regionally, its relative importance, as shown in table 2b (last column), has decreased considerably over time. Whether this decline is a source of concern or whether it reflects a natural adjustment to reduced incentives in the labour market is examined in the next section.

Trends and Changes in Regional Disparities

The four main indicators used in this study to measure the level and evolution of regional disparities in Canada are the coefficients of variation of personal income per capita, employment/population ratios, participation rates and unemployment rates across the 10 provinces. Coefficients of variation (standard deviation/mean) capture differences between regions while accounting for changes in the absolute size of the variables used. Each province is weighted by its share of total Canadian employment. The reference period, which is 1972 to 1994, appears to be relatively homogeneous in terms of the nature of federal government transfer programs[9] (but not necessarily the amounts spent). We briefly comment on the evolution of each of these variables and provide a general assessment of the appropriateness of the predictions in table 1.

The coefficient of variation of personal income per capita (CVPI) ranges from a high of 4.0 in 1972 to a low of 2.5 in 1994 (figure 5). This represents a 38 percent drop over the entire period, indicating a significant decrease in regional income disparities.

In contrast, the coefficients of variation of employment/population ratios (CVEP) and participation rates (CVPR) show no sign of a specific time trend (see figures 6 and 7, respectively) although they both peak in 1982, a year of severe recession. Finally, the coefficient of variation of unemployment rates

Figure 5
The Coefficient of Variation of Personal Income Per Capita by Province (CVPI), Canada, 1972-1994

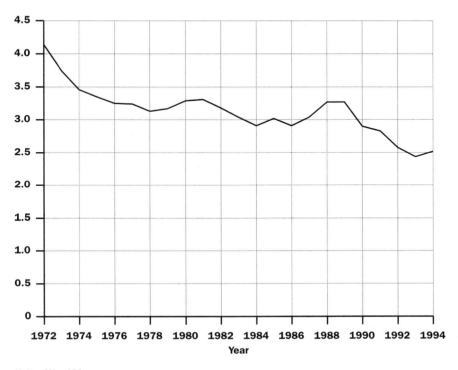

Units: CV x 100.
Source: *Economic Reference Tables*, August 1995, and calculations by the authors.

(CVUR) is quite unstable (see figure 8), with peaks during expansions (1973, 1980 and 1989) and troughs during recessions (1982 and 1992). Overall, no clear trend is discernible, but there is obvious cyclical variability.

The opposite is true for the internal migration rate, where there is a clear downward trend (figure 9). It varies from a high of 18 per 1,000 population in the beginning of the period to a low of 14-15 at the end of the period.

If we examine figures 5, 6 and 7 in light of the predictions presented in table 1, technological catch-up appears to be the most appropriate explanation: personal income per capita differentials decrease, while employment-rate and participation-rate differentials do not change in any significant way.

This suggests that the diffusion of technology and/or the differential rate of accumulation of both (or either) physical and human capital may have been the most powerful instruments in reducing interprovincial income differentials

jean-michel cousineau and françois vaillancourt

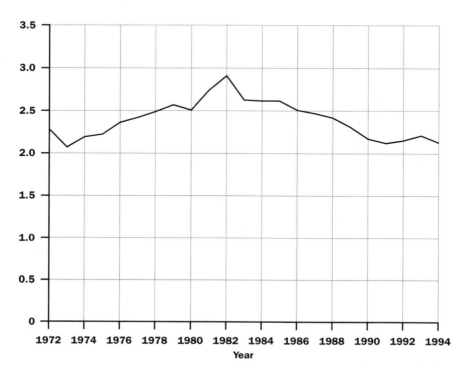

Figure 6

The Coefficient of Variation of the Employment/Population Ratio
by Province (CVEP), Canada, 1972-1994

Units: CV x 100.
Source: *Economic Reference Tables*, August 1995, and calculations by the authors.

in Canada. However, this does not tell us why migration rates declined as they did at the aggregate level or if they contributed to the convergence of per capita incomes. It also fails to tell us if migration rates were the reflection of this convergence; if they had any effects on regional employment and unemployment disparities; and what was the impact, if any, of federal government transfers in reducing regional employment, unemployment and income differentials. To answer these questions and determine their policy implications requires a more sophisticated approach, one that indicates the respective effects of each potential instrumental variable (i.e., migration, transfers and technology) on each relevant target variable (i.e., employment, unemployment and income).

The empirical model that was developed to satisfy these requirements comprises five equations that attempt to capture: 1) the aggregate determinants of the migration rate, 2) the incidence of this migration rate on the regional dispersion

adapting public policy to a labour market in transition

Figure 7
The Coefficient of Variation of the Participation Rate by Province (CVPR), Canada, 1972-1994

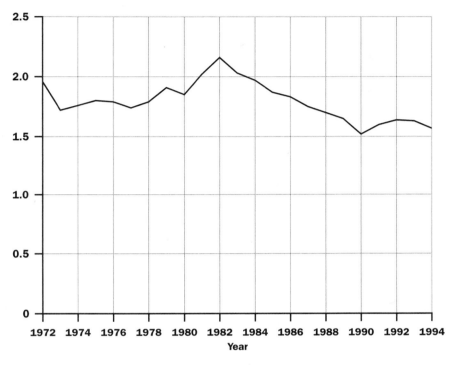

Units: CV x 100.
Source: *Economic Reference Tables*, August 1995, and calculations by the authors.

of employment, participation rates, unemployment and personal income per capita in Canada and 3) the parallel influence of federal government transfers and the diffusion of technology on these same variables. The five equations are:

$$CVEP = a_{10} + a_{11} MR + a_{12} Tr_1 + a_{13} Tr_2 + a_{14} UR + u_1 \tag{1}$$

$$CVPR = a_{20} + a_{21} MR + a_{22} CVEP + a_{23} CVPI + a_{24} UR + u_2 \tag{2}$$

$$CVPI = a_{30} + a_{31} T + a_{32} MR + a_{33} Tr_1 + a_{34} Tr_2 + a_{35} CVEP + a_{36} UR + u_3 \tag{3}$$

$$CVUR = a_{40} + a_{41} CVEP + a_{42} CVPR + a_{43} UR + u_4 \tag{4}$$

$$MR = a_{50} + a_{51} T + a_{52} Tr_1 + a_{53} Tr_2 + a_{54} CVEP + a_{55} CVPI + a_{56} Age + a_{57} UR + u_5 \tag{5}$$

(1) The employment equation (CVEP)

Three types of variables are expected to influence the disparities in the employment ratio by province:

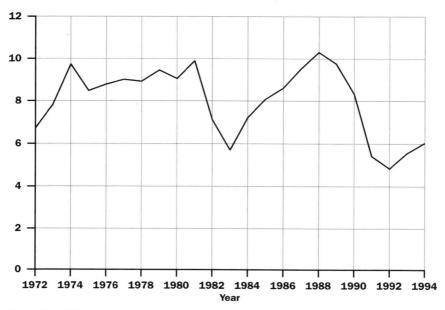

Figure 8

The Coefficient of Variation of the Unemployment Rate
by Province (CVUR), Canada, 1972-1994

Units: CV x 100.
Source: Economic Reference Tables, August 1995 and previous years, and calculations by the authors.

162

a) Migration rate (MR) – As predicted in the first section, the increase (decrease) in geographic mobility from low-employment regions to high-employment regions should increase (decrease) the disparities in employment/population ratios.

b) Transfer payments (Tr_1 and Tr_2) – As predicted in the first section, federal government transfers to individuals (Tr_1) and to other levels of government (Tr_2) should increase labour demand and thus reduce employment/ratio disparities between regions.

c) Unemployment rate (UR) – As figure 6 revealed, there appears to be a certain degree of cyclical sensitivity in the coefficient of variation of employment over time. The unemployment rate was chosen as a proxy for this effect.[10]

(2) The participation-rate equation (CVPR)

The coefficient of variation of participation rates is dependent on the migration rate (MR) and unemployment rate (UR) for the same reasons as described for the coefficient of variation of employment ratios. Two other variables were added:

Figure 9
Internal Migration Rate (MR), Canada, 1972-1994

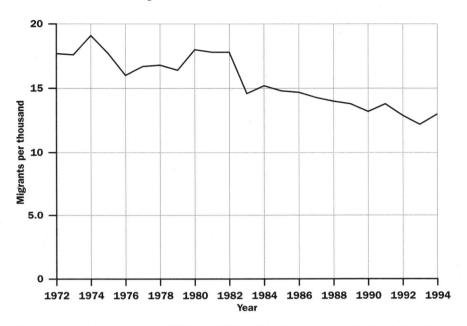

Source: CANSIM series C122874 to C122886; *Economic Reference Tables*, August 1995; and calculations by the authors.

a) The coefficient of variation of employment/population ratios (CVEP) – If a 163
higher employment ratio encourages a higher fraction of the adult population to participate in the labour force, then the participation rate within a
province should increase with that province's employment ratio. Thus, the
coefficient of variation of participation rates should follow the coefficient
of variation of employment/population ratios.

b) The coefficient of variation of personal income per capita (CVPI) – Income
inequality may be linked to participation-rate differentials by province. If
wages (income) are higher in one province, the participation rate should also
be higher and *vice versa*. Thus, the dispersion of participation rates should
follow the dispersion in personal income per capita.

(3) The personal income per capita equation (CVPI)

As predicted by the theoretical model in the first section, changes in regional
income differentials in Canada should mainly depend on the diffusion of
technology, proxied by a time trend (T), federal government transfers (Tr_1
and Tr_2), employment rate differentials (CVEP) and the migration rate (MR).

Thus each of these variables is included in the CVPI equation. Also, because regional income differentials could vary cyclically, the unemployment rate (UR) variable is included as an explanatory variable.

(4) The unemployment rate equation (CVUR)
The unemployment rate (coefficient of variation) equation is considered as a residual of labour force and employment. If it was the level of employment or labour force, this equation would be an identity. However, nonlinearities make it possible to estimate the respective influence of participation and employment rate disparities on the unemployment rate disparities. The unemployment rate variable was also kept in this specification in order to capture its apparent cyclical sensitivity (see figure 8).

(5) The migration rate equation (MR)
MR could be influenced by a wide range of factors:
a) The long-term decline in the growth of GDP generally discourages inter-provincial migration,[11] thus the time trend T should negatively affect the migration rate.
b) Federal government transfers to the "poorer" provinces constitute a signifi-cant disincentive for workers to move to the "richer" provinces: each or both transfer variables should negatively affect the migration rate.[12]
c) Interprovincial employment and/or income differentials stimulate the interprovincial mobility of labour: that is, a reduction in income and/or employment differentials between regions should also reduce the propen-sity to migrate from one province to another.
d) Young workers are more prone to move geographically: the age variable should positively affect the migration rate (age is defined as the percentage of the provincial labour force under 25 years of age).
e) Interprovincial mobility should decrease when UR is high but increase when it is low.

Given this whole set of expectations, several estimates were run and it was found that:
- only a limited set of variables entered significantly into the MR equation;
- simultaneity was present between MR and CVPI;
- the CVUR equation appeared to be insufficiently specified, however, a dichoto-mous variable (D) that coincides with a series of changes in the 1990s to the unemployment insurance program changed the nature of the observed residuals radically;

- only one of the two federal government transfer variables enters into two distinct equations, and it is a different variable that enters (significantly) into each equation;
- tests of cointegration were run on each equation with values that reject their nonstationarity on the whole (see appendix, table A3);
- all but one variable (Tr_2) was found to be nonstationary (See appendix, table A3).

Results

General Comments

Table 7 contains information on the impact of each of the independent variables (columns 1-10) on each of the dependant variables (rows 1-5). The last two columns of this table present the coefficient of determination or R^2 (column 11) and the Durbin-Watson statistics (column 12). The R^2 measures the degree of fitness of the data to the theory, while the Durbin-Watson statistic tests for the presence of nonrandom residuals in which case the quality of the estimates could be questioned. A value close to 1 for R^2 indicates a high degree of fitness. A value close to 2 for the Durbin-Watson statistics generally indicates the absence of specification errors and t-statistics that are reliable.

The R^2 and Durbin-Watson statistics range between 0.88 and 0.96 and 1.86 and 2.26, respectively. Although it may be normal to find such R^2 values in time series analyses, we made every effort to minimize the chances of a specification error (e.g., missing variable) and maximize the reliability of our t-tests.

Second, if we look at the impact of the unemployment rate (UR) variable (column 1), we observe that employment and participation-rate inequalities (CVEP and CVPR) increase when the unemployment rate increases, that is, during recessions. The opposite is true for income and unemployment inequalities (the coefficient of UR is negative).

Third, CVPR (row 2) is positively correlated with CVEP and CVPI, that is, regional inequalities in the participation rates by provinces parallel inequalities in employment and income inequalities.

Fourth, the employment (CVEP) variable (column 2) enters positively and significantly[13] into the income (CVPI) equation (row 3). That is, part of the interprovincial differential in per capita incomes is attributable to differences in provincial employment levels.

Fifth, the employment (CVEP) and labour force (CVPR) variables (columns 2 and 4) play an important role in explaining the unemployment (CVUR) variable (row 4). They have the expected sign and both are highly significant. But, as

Table 7

Results of Model Estimates, Canada, 1972-1994

	UR (1)	CVEP (2)	CVPI (3)	CVPR (4)	Age (5)	MR (6)	T (7)	Tr₁ (8)	Tr₂ (9)	D (10)	R² (11)	D-W¹ (12)
(1) CVEP	0.177 (11.32)	–	–	–	–	0.034 (2.60)	–	-0.385 (-8.29)	–	–	0.882	2.02
(2) CVPR	0.050 (4.66)	0.363 (5.68)	0.220 (4.04)	–	–	0.035 (3.76)	–	–	–	–	0.927	2.26
(3) CVPI	-0.059 (-2.39)	1.108 (4.90)	–	–	–	-0.490 (-4.81)	-0.167 (-6.01)	–	-1.137 (-5.55)	–	0.928	2.18
(4) CVUR	-0.629 (-9.40)	8.58 (10.71)	–	-10.66 (-10.67)	–	–	–	–	–	-1.38 (-3.56)	0.882	1.86
(5) MR	–	–	2.020 (2.58)	–	0.340 (4.81)	–	–	–	–	–	0.956	1.94

¹ Durbin-Watson statistic.

Note: All equations have been estimated with a constant term. "t" statistics appear in parentheses.

previously noted, a dichotomous variable for the 1990s was essential to get somewhat random residuals. This last result may be interpreted as the effect of UI reforms that reduced regional inequalities in the unemployment rate during that period.

Sixth, the evolution of the migration rate (MR) in Canada (row 5) is significantly related to age and changes in income differentials between provinces (CVPI) (using the two-stage-least-squares technique).[14] Thus, while the aging of the Canadian population appears to play an important part in explaining the downward trend in the internal migration rate in Canada, it is estimated that 40 percent of the total calculated variation in this rate between 1972 and 1994 is attributable to the reduction in regional income inequalities. Therefore, the reduction of the migration rate is at least partly the result of the economy achieving a new equilibrium with less income disparities.

Migration, Technology and Federal Government Transfers
Internal migration flows in Canada contribute to the allocation and reallocation of the labour force in the directions predicted by the neoclassical theory (table 7, column 6 [MR]). A positive coefficient for the migration-rate variable indicates that more migration increases employment differentials as well as participation rate differentials by approximately the same order of magnitude (0.034 and 0.035, respectively), leading to a small or marginal effect on unemployment disparities between provinces. However, a coefficient of -0.490 (row 3, column 6) means that an increase of one migrant per 1,000 population (i.e., an increase of about 5 percent in the mean rate over the period) reduces the coefficient of variation of per capita income by close to half a percentage point. This effect is relatively large and it also differs from some of the results of previous research referred to in the introduction. However, these studies did not correct for the simultaneity bias. While it is true that the migration rate may affect employment and income differentials, it is also true that employment and income differentials may affect the migration rate. In this study, we explicitly use the appropriate statistical method (two-stage-least-squares) to correct for this kind of bilateral relationship.

However, as shown in figure 9, the overall internal migration rate in Canada decreased over our sample period and thus cannot alone explain the actual convergence of regional per capita incomes. In fact, we estimate that 2/3 of the total variation of the coefficient of variation of personal income per capita between 1972 and 1994 in Canada is attributable to the time trend (T), that is, our proxy for the technological-catch-up hypothesis.[15]

Federal government transfers also play a role in decreasing regional income disparities in Canada. Federal government transfers to other levels of government (mainly provincial) directly reduce income differentials between provinces (see the coefficient of Tr_2 in the CVPI equation in row 3 of table 7). Federal government transfers to individuals have an indirect effect. They do so by reducing employment (ratio) disparities between provinces (see the coefficient of Tr_1 in the CVEP equation in row 1 of table 7) which then reduces income disparities.

Conclusion

In the introduction, we focused our attention on the issue of internal labour mobility in the general debate about growth and the reduction of regional disparities in Canada. On theoretical grounds, the appropriate pattern of labour mobility from low-wage and low-employment regions to high-wage and high-employment regions has the potential to reduce provincial income disparities.

In the second section we examined internal migration trends in Canada, in particular, how many people migrate, who migrates, and where do they migrate? The data show that internal mobility on the part of young and educated workers is important: it significantly affects the overall distribution of population by province in the long run. But while Canadians have generally moved in the "right" direction, that is, mainly for economic reasons, the overall migration rate has decreased substantially over the past 25 years or so.

When we looked at statistical indicators of regional disparities and migration in Canada, we found that between 1972 and 1994, regional income disparities and the overall migration rate decreased, but that regional employment and unemployment disparities remained more or less unchanged. This suggests that the technological-catch-up/diffusion hypothesis best explains the changes observed in the various indicators of regional disparities, and that the reduction of the overall migration rate in Canada was at least partly the result of a reduction in regional income differentials. Given the growth in the service sector over the period, it is not surprising that this diffusion occurred predominantly through increased investment in human capital, as Coulombe and Tremblay[16] argue.

Finally, results from a more sophisticated empirical analysis suggest that technological-catch-up is the most important instrument (along with the accumulation of physical and human capital) for achieving growth objectives and further reducing regional income inequalities in Canada. We also demonstrated that internal labour mobility still plays a role in the geographic allocation and reallocation of the labour force in Canada.[17] Finally, we showed that by maintaining local demand, federal government transfers to individuals contribute to the reduction of employment and unemployment disparities between provinces.

From a labour market policy perspective, there are two recommendations. First, education and training policies should be oriented toward the implementation of the best technologies throughout the country, in close coordination with policies related to industry, science and technology. A corollary of this would be better targeting of federal transfers for post-secondary education, as argued by Coulombe.[18] Second, the federal and provincial governments should cooperate in removing barriers to interprovincial mobility, focusing in particular on issues of occupational licensing and recognition of qualifications.

Table A1
Probit Analysis of Internal Migration, Canada, 1986-1991

VARIABLES	Men		Women	
Intercept	-1.9604	(0.0375)	-1.9775	(0.0376)
Education (years)	0.0259	(0.0020)	0.0275	(0.0025)
Married	-0.0926	(0.0117)	-0.0869	(0.0125)
Unilingual anglophones	Omitted variable		Omitted variable	
Bilingual anglophones	0.2486	(0.0210)	0.2307	(0.0225)
Unilingual francophones	-1.0879	(0.0397)	-1.0302	(0.0393)
Bilingual francophones	-0.2030	(0.0167)	-0.1368	(0.0189)
Allophones, anglophones	-0.1438	(0.0179)	-0.1559	(0.0206)
Allophones, francophones	-1.2977	(0.3247)	-0.6689	(0.1835)
Bilingual allophones	-0.1198	(0.0384)	-0.0426	(0.0426)
Allophones, other	-0.3057	(0.1219)	-0.1959	(0.1125)
English, French	0.0465	(0.0881)	-0.0620	(0.1059)
Age 25-29	0.1881	(0.0170)	0.2459	(0.0183)
Age 30-34	0.1219	(0.0168)	0.1367	(0.0186)
Age 35-39	Omitted variable		Omitted variable	
Age 40-44	-0.1341	(0.0190)	-0.1188	(0.0211)
Age 45-49	-0.2016	(0.0212)	-0.2240	(0.0245)
Age 50-54	-0.3257	(0.0251)	-0.2631	(0.0285)
Age 55-60	-0.3982	(0.0313)	-0.3394	(0.0368)
Clerical work	Omitted variable		Omitted variable	
Manager	0.1561	(0.0261)	-0.0090	(0.0205)
Natural sciences	0.1527	(0.0297)	0.0438	(0.0406)
Social sciences	0.0998	(0.0440)	0.0020	(0.0340)
Teaching	0.0740	(0.0370)	-0.0299	(0.0257)
Medicine, health	0.1198	(0.0424)	0.0639	(0.0216)
Art	0.2315	(0.0426)	0.1791	(0.0408)
Sales	0.1362	(0.0288)	0.0754	(0.0233)
Service	0.4263	(0.0278)	0.1939	(0.0192)
Farming	-0.0955	(0.0443)	-0.1764	(0.0622)
Other primary	0.1025	(0.0430)	-0.0826	(0.1449)
Processing	-0.0991	(0.0412)	-0.1320	(0.0590)
Machinery, repairing	0.0061	(0.0282)	-0.0632	(0.0423)
Construction	0.1600	(0.0278)	0.1559	(0.0933)
Transportation	0.0841	(0.0320)	0.0254	(0.0661)
Other occupations	0.0805	(0.0314)	-0.0083	(0.0446)
Log likelihood	-31,143.71		-25,191.20	
Number of observations	170,479		146,009	

Note: Standard errors are in parentheses.

Table A2
Regression Coefficients for Six Canadian Regions

	Intercept	Education	Experience	Experience²	Weeks worked	Number of observations	R²
ATLANTIC							
Men	7.3549	0.0718	0.0502	-0.0008	0.0260	14,482	0.3065
	(0.0441)	(0.0023)	(0.0027)	(0.0001)	(0.0004)		
Women	6.6371	0.1085	0.0165	-0.0002	0.0267	11,859	0.2923
	(0.0635)	(0.0034)	(0.0036)	(0.0001)	(0.0005)		
QUEBEC							
Men	7.4438	0.0677	0.0452	-0.0006	0.0262	45,683	0.2378
	(0.0258)	(0.0012)	(0.0014)	(0.00002)	(0.0003)		
Women	6.7744	0.0953	0.0277	-0.0004	0.0274	37,381	0.2607
	(0.0337)	(0.0017)	(0.0017)	(0.00004)	(0.0003)		
ONTARIO							
Men	7.5563	0.0639	0.0414	-0.0006	0.0286	61,347	0.2046
	(0.0226)	(0.0010)	(0.0012)	(0.00003)	(0.0003)		
Women	7.1453	0.0814	0.0138	-0.0002	0.0283	59,325	0.2076
	(0.0287)	(0.0014)	(0.0015)	(0.00003)	(0.0003)		
SASKATCHEWAN & MANITOBA							
Men	7.0904	0.0797	0.0408	-0.0006	0.0305	12,593	0.2358
	(0.0547)	(0.0027)	(0.0031)	(0.0001)	(0.0006)		
Women	6.5302	0.0970	0.0067	-0.0001	0.0348	10,897	0.2792
	(0.0701)	(0.0038)	(0.0038)	(0.0001)	(0.0006)		
ALBERTA							
Men	7.3447	0.0664	0.0421	-0.0007	0.0319	17,451	0.2245
	(0.0465)	(0.0023)	(0.0026)	(0.0001)	(0.0006)		
Women	6.6544	0.0956	0.0142	-0.0002	0.0326	14,694	0.2580
	(0.0610)	(0.0032)	(0.0033)	(0.0001)	(0.0005)		
BRITISH COLUMBIA							
Men	7.7069	0.0411	0.0424	-0.0007	0.0321	21,946	0.2421
	(0.0388)	(0.0019)	(0.0023)	(0.00005)	(0.0004)		
Women	6.9962	0.0781	0.0108	-0.0001	0.0312	18,567	0.2481
	(0.0518)	(0.0028)	(0.0029)	(0.0001)	(0.0004)		

Note: For Oaxaca's calculation purposes; based on 1991 Census. Dependent variable is the natural logarithm of annual employment income of the migrant population. Standard errors are in parentheses.

Table A3
Testing for Stationarity

Variable	t*	t_c
MR	1.05	5.18
CVPI	1.87	5.18
CVEP	1.07	5.18
CVPR	0.52	5.18
CVUR	3.38	5.18
Tr_1	2.79	5.18
Tr_2	5.43	5.18
UR	4.22	5.18

Residuals in each equation	t*	t_c
CVEP	-4.53	-3.67
CVPR	-5.27	-3.67
CVPI	-5.24	-3.67
CVUR	-4.63	-3.67
MR	-4.15	-3.67

The standard test for stationarity (5% level) of each variable is t* < tc (* = estimated t, c = critical t).

The nonstationarity of each variable cannot be rejected for all except the federal government transfer payments to other administrations (Tr₂).

The standard test for the stationarity of residuals (5% level) in each equation is t* < tc for tc = -3.67. The hypothesis of stationarity of the residuals is accepted for each equation.

Notes

We thank FCAR for funding; Kathleen Day, France St-Hilaire, Craig Riddell and Serge Coulombe for helpful comments on the first version of the paper and Marc Vachon and Ariane Brûlé for research assistance.

1. Technological-catch-up means the accumulation of physical and human capital or diffusion of technology in the poorest regions, provinces or countries. See J. Helliwell, "Convergence and Migration Among Provinces," PEAP Policy Study no. 942, Institute of Policy Analysis, University of Toronto, 1994; and S. Coulombe and F.C. Lee, "Regional Economic Disparities in Canada," Discussion Paper no. 9317E, University of Ottawa, 1995.

2. A comparison between 1972 or 1973 and 1989 is also valuable, since these years correspond with peaks in cycles. This process of convergence is, however, judged to be somewhat slow because the estimated speed of adjustment is such that it would take 29 years to fill half of the average gap in the personal income per capita between the "poor" and the "rich" provinces. See Coulombe and Lee "Regional Economic Disparities in Canada," p. 35. For other national and international comparisons, see J. Helliwell and A. Chung, "Are Bigger Countries Better off?" in R. Boadway, T. Courchesne, and D. Purvis (eds.), *Economic Dimensions of Constitutional Change*, Volume 1 (Kingston, Ont.: Queen's University, John Deutsch Institute for the Study of Economic Policy, 1991), pp. 345-67, and R. Barro and X. Sala-i-Martin, "Convergence across States and Regions," *Brookings Papers on Economic Activity, Macroeconomics, Volume 1*, (1991), pp. 107-158.

3. G. Rosenbluth, "Interprovincial Migration and the Efficacy of Provincial Job Creation Policies," *Canadian Business Economics*, Vol. 4, no. 2 (1996), pp. 22-35; J. Vanderkamp, "Regional Disparities: A Model with Some Econometric Results for Canada," in B. Higgens and D.J. Savoie (eds.), *Regional Economic Development: Essays in Honour of François Perroux* (Boston: Unwin Hyman, 1988), pp. 296-396; R. Boadway and A.G. Green, "The Economic Implications of Migration to Newfoundland," discussion paper no. 189, Economic Council of Canada, 1981; and P. Wrage, "The Effects of Migration on Regional Wage and Unemployment Disparities in Canada," *Journal of Regional Science*, Vol. 21, no. 1 (1981), pp. 51-63.

4. See, for example, Vanderkamp, "Regional Disparities."

5. Wrage, "The Effects of Migration on Regional Wage and Unemployment Disparities in Canada."

6. Boadway and Green, "The Economic Implications of Migration to Newfoundland," p. V-1.

7. See R. Finnie, "Interprovincial Mobility in Canada: A Panel Logit Model Analysis," Statistics Canada, mimeographed, 1998, table 1.

8. See R. Finnie, "Interprovincial Mobility in Canada: A Longitudinal Analysis," Statistics Canada, mimeographed, 1998, table 2.

9. The main social security programs that were in place during this period were already set out by the early 1970s (i.e., equalization payments, the Canada Assistance Plan, Old Age Security, Unemployment Insurance, etc.).

10. A referee suggested that we could have used the deviation of the GDP from its trend instead.

11. W.J. Milne, "Macroeconomic Inferences on Migration," *Regional Studies*, Vol. 27, no. 4 (1993), pp. 365-73.

12. T. Courchesne, "Interprovincial Migration and Economic Adjustment," *Canadian Journal of Economics*, Vol. 3 (November 1970), pp. 550-76; K. Day "Interprovincial Migration and Local Public Goods," *Canadian Journal of Economics*, Vol. 25, no.1 (1992), pp. 123-144; and S.L. Winer and D. Gauthier, *Internal Migration and Fiscal Structure* (Ottawa: Economic Council of Canada, 1982) consider the impact of various government policies on interprovincial labour migration.

13. A coefficient is said to be significant when the t statistics appearing under the coefficients are greater than 2.

14. The exogenous variables chosen were T, $Tr_,$, Age and UR, respecting the conditions of identification for this submodel.

15. The calculations were done by adding the absolute value of the product of each coefficient to the decrease in the value of the appropriate independent variable over the sample period and then by dividing each product by the total.

16. S. Coulombe and J.-F. Tremblay, "Capital humain et convergence au Canada" (University of Ottawa, January 1998, mimeograph).

17. International statistics show that the overall actual migration rates in Canada are in between high US rates and the low rates in

173

European Union nations. See L'Étude de l'OCED sur l'emploi, Partie I: Evolution des Marchés du Travail et Facteurs de Changement (Paris: OECD, 1994).

18. S. Coulombe, "Economic Growth and Provincial Disparity: A New View of an Old Canadian Problem," *C.D. Howe Institute Commentary*, Vol. 122 (March 1999).

174

Canada and the OECD Hypothesis: Does Labour Market Inflexibility Explain Canada's High Level of Unemployment?

Peter Kuhn

Introduction

One of the most remarkable features of the global economy in the last decade has been the employment performance of the United States. While unemployment rates in almost all other developed countries remain high by postwar standards, the US unemployment rate has fallen to levels not seen in decades.[1] Even more spectacular than the decline in unemployment is the increase in the proportion of the US population that is employed, which has exceeded that in almost all developed countries.[2]

A phenomenon of such magnitude calls out for an explanation. Probably more than any other single factor, some form of labour market inflexibility has recently been blamed for the high unemployment rates outside the United States. In a number of forums, including the policy recommendations of the Organization for Economic Co-operation and Development (OECD), rigid labour markets, with considerable government and/or union involvement in wage-setting, and considerable restrictions on firms' abilities to adjust the size of their workforces, are commonly seen as more prone to unemployment and less conducive to employment growth than more flexible ones.[3]

The purpose of this paper is to provide a critical assessment of the popular notion that differences in labour market flexibility explain the recent differences between US employment and unemployment rates and those of other developed countries. In addressing this issue I shall focus on comparing two countries, the United States and Canada. On the surface, the recent experience of these two countries appears to support the hypothesis, with the more "rigid" country –

177

Canada, where unions have much more influence on the wage-setting process and employment protection is stronger – experiencing a much worse unemployment performance since the early 1980s. Indeed, because of their proximity and their similarity along other dimensions, these countries may yield an ideal comparison for assessing the labour market flexibility hypothesis.

I proceed as follows. First, I argue that the labour market flexibility hypothesis is not one, but (at the very least) two hypotheses, both of which appear frequently in public discussion, but which have little in common except a notion that governments and/or unions are the source of the problem. Next, I consider each of these hypotheses in turn, considering first some theoretical issues and then the evidence regarding the relevance of each hypothesis to the case of high Canadian unemployment.

One Hypothesis or (at Least) Two?

When one hears talk of labour market flexibility, one can usually be sure that it means less intervention in labour markets by governments and/or unions. But precisely what kind of intervention is seen as problematic differs. According to some discussions, lack of flexibility in firms' ability to hire and fire labour (a "quantity" variable, in economists' parlance) is the main obstacle to full employment; according to others, it is lack of flexibility in real wages (a "price" variable). I outline these two main arguments in turn below.

The quantity version of the labour market flexibility hypothesis[4] is sometimes referred to as the problem of "Eurosclerosis."[5] According to this argument, high levels of employment protection laws (EPLs), or restrictions on firms' abilities to shed workers, are responsible for Europe's poor unemployment performance. While at first glance this may seem paradoxical – if firms can't lay workers off, won't the ranks of the unemployed decrease? – the argument is made that in an uncertain world the inability to reduce the workforce raises firms' expected costs of production, and that this long-term, indirect negative effect on employment outweighs the shorter-term positive effect. If true, this would lead to lower long-term employment rates in countries with stringent firing restrictions and possibly higher involuntary unemployment as well.

According to the price version of the labour market flexibility hypothesis, an important source of the recent increase in unemployment outside the US may be interference in the wage-setting process by minimum-wage laws and unions.[6] According to this hypothesis, all developed countries have been confronted by technology- and/or trade-induced declines in the demand for unskilled labour. In countries with (downward) flexible wages, like the US, this decline in demand has led to a substantial decline in the real wages of unskilled workers, particularly those of young men. In other countries, where unions and/or minimum-wages act to prohibit real-wage declines among the unskilled, the decline in demand for the unskilled manifests itself in an increase in unemployment among these groups.

In what follows I provide critical assessments of the "inflexible quantities" and "inflexible wages" stories in turn, with particular attention to their relevance to unemployment in Canada and how it compares with that in the United States. In discussing each hypothesis, I first outline the relevant institutional differences between Canada and the US, together with some discussion of how the two countries compare with other OECD countries. I then consider a variety of theoretical perspectives on what one might expect the effects of these institutions to be, and conclude by assessing the evidence on whether those institutional differences provide convincing explanations of international unemployment differences, particularly those between the US and Canada.

Employment Protection: Cause of Canadian Unemployment?

(a) Are EPLs Stronger in Canada Than in the US?

EPLs are usually defined to include any legal restrictions on firms' right to reduce their workforces for economic reasons.[7] In Canada, such restrictions are embedded in two main bodies of law. The older of these is the common law, according to which most labour contracts can be discontinued either by letting employees go for cause, or giving them a reasonable amount of notice.[8] Thus in Canada it is possible for individual employees with no specific employment guarantee to sue their former employer for insufficient notice of layoff. In practice, this option is exercised only by relatively highly paid workers.[9]

179

In addition to the common law, Canada also has minimum mandatory-notice statutes for permanent layoffs in all of the 13 jurisdictions that regulate employment contracts.[10] These are summarized in table 1, which shows the state of legislation as of November 1, 1996. In most cases, mandatory notice depends on the duration of employment, ranging from 1 week for relatively new workers to 8 weeks for workers with 10 or more years of experience. Generally, an employee can be given pay in lieu of notice. Interestingly, a number of Canadian jurisdictions require workers to notify their employers of their intent to quit, though it is unclear whether this provision has ever been enforced.

Separate regulations also exist for mass termination in 11 of the 13 jurisdictions. The number of workers necessary to constitute a mass termination is usually 50 or more employees in a period of 4 weeks. The amount of notice

Table 1
Notice Requirements for Termination of Employment in Canadian Jurisdictions, 1996

INDIVIDUAL				MASS	
Jurisdiction	**Length of service**	**Employer notice (wks)**	**Employee notice (wks)**	**Number of employees**	**Notice (wks)**
Federal	3 mos +	2	none	50 +	16
Alberta	3 mos – 2 yrs 2 – 4 yrs 4 – 6 yrs 6 – 8 yrs 8 – 10 yrs 10 yrs +	1 2 4 5 6 8	2 wks	No special provision	
British Columbia	3 mos – 1 yr 1 yr – 3 yrs 3 years 1 additional week for each additional year of employment – max 8 weeks	1 2 3	none	50 – 100 101 – 300 300 +	8 12 16
Manitoba	1 mo +	1 pay period	Same as employer	50 – 100 101 – 300 300+	10 14 18
New Brunswick	6 mos – 5 yrs 5 yrs +	2 4	none	10 or more, if they represent 25% of the employer's workforce	6
Newfoundland	1 mo – 2 yrs 2 yrs +	1 2	Same as employer	50 – 199 200 – 499 500 +	8 12 16
Nova Scotia	3 mos – 2 yrs 2 – 5 yrs 5 – 10 yrs 10 yrs +	1 2 4 8	Same as employer	10 – 99 100 – 299 300 +	8 12 16
Ontario	3 mos – 1 yr 1 – 3 yrs 3 – 4 yrs 4 – 5 yrs 5 – 6 yrs 6 – 7 yrs 7 – 8 yrs 8 yrs +	1 2 3 4 5 6 7 8	If employed less than 2yrs, 1 wk. If employed 2 yrs +, 2 wks	50 – 199 200 – 499 500 +	8 12 16

Table 1 (cont'd)
Notice Requirements for Termination of Employment in Canadian Jurisdictions, 1996

INDIVIDUAL				MASS	
Jurisdiction	Length of service	Employer notice (wks)	Employee notice (wks)	Number of employees	Notice (wks)
Prince Edward Island	6 mos – 5 yrs 5 yrs +	2 4	If employed 6 mos – 5 yrs, 1 wk. If employed 5 yrs +, 2 wks	No special provision	
Quebec	3 mos – 1 yr 1 – 5 yrs 5 – 10 yrs 10 yrs +	1 2 4 8	none	10 – 99 100 – 299 300 +	2 mos 3 mos 4 mos
Saskatchewan	3 mos – 1 yr 1 – 3 yrs 3 – 5 yrs 5 – 10 yrs 10 +	1 2 4 6 8	none	10 – 49 50 – 99 100 +	4 8 12
Northwest Territories	90 days – 3 yrs 1 additional wk for each additional yr of employment – max 8 weeks	2	none	25 – 49 50 – 99 100 – 299 300 +	4 8 12 16
Yukon	6 mos – 1 yr 1–3 yrs 3 – 4 yrs 4 – 5 yrs 5 – 6 yrs 6 – 7 yrs 7 – 8 yrs 8 yrs +	1 2 3 4 5 6 7 8	Same as employer	25 – 49 50 – 99 100 – 299 300 +	4 8 12 16

Source: Labour Canada, Employment Standards Legislation in Canada; the latest figures are now available at http://labour-travail.hrdc-drhc.gc.ca/policy/leg/e/.

that must be given ranges from 8 to 18 weeks depending on the number of workers let go. Exceptions are provided for unforeseeable circumstances such as natural disasters.

In two Canadian jurisdictions employment protection legislation also includes severance pay. Federally, the amount of compensation is not large, consisting of two days wages to be paid per year of service. In Ontario, severance packages only apply to employees with five or more years of service; however the amount of compensation given – 1 week of severance pay for each year of service to a

peter kuhn

Table 2
Changes in Notice Requirements for Termination of Employment in Canadian Jurisdictions, 1970-1996 (in weeks)

	Federal	Alberta	BC	Manitoba	NB	Nfld
Individual terminations	1971-96: 2	1973-87: 2 1988-96: 8	1981-96: 8	1970-96: 1[1]	1985-96: 4	1970-78: 1[1] 1979-96: 2[1]
Mass terminations	1971-96: 16	none	1993-95: 18 1996: 18	1973-91: 16 1993-96: 18	1985-96: 6	1976-96: 16

maximum of 26 weeks – is quite high. An ongoing bone of contention between Ontario and the federal government is that employees are not considered eligible for (federally provided) Employment Insurance (EI, formerly Unemployment Insurance) for periods of unemployment during which they are deemed to be receiving severance payments from their previous employer. Finally, most Canadian jurisdictions with mass termination laws compel employers to establish and finance a manpower adjustment committee, with worker representation, to develop an adjustment program for workers and to help workers to find new employment opportunities. Further, employers must advise and cooperate with local governments regarding the closure procedure.

Unlike the common law, which requires employees to launch a civil suit against their former employer, in most Canadian jurisdictions employee remedies for noncompliance with minimum-notice statutes are relatively fast and costless. In part, this is because mandatory-notice laws are generally administered under the provinces' fair labour standards acts, which assign minimum standards for a wide variety of working conditions and are policed by a set of local offices. For example, in Ontario an employee only has to notify the Employment Standards office, which can be done by telephone. The claim is then investigated, and if the employer is found liable, he or she may be ordered by a judge to reimburse wages for the required notice period.

The current mix of employment protection legislation in Canada is the result of a series of province-by-province increases in legislated notice starting in the 1960s. These changes in legislation related to individual terminations and mass terminations are summarized in table 2. An interesting feature of the evolution of Canadian employment protection laws is that, despite the recent move to the political right in a number of jurisdictions and significant retrenchment in a number of social programs and labour relations legislation, there has not been a single instance of a reduction in employment protection law between 1970

Table 2 (cont'd)
Changes in Notice Requirements for Termination of Employment in Canadian Jurisdictions, 1970-1996 (in weeks)

NS	Ontario	PEI	Quebec	Sask.	NWT	Yukon
1970-72: 1 1973-96: 8	1970-96: 8	1971-91: 1 1993-96: 4	1970-80: 1[1] 1981-96: 8[1]	1970-80: 1 1981-96: 8	1989-96: 8	1986-95: 1 1996: 8
1973-96: 16	1970-96: 16	none	1970-91: 17[2] 1993-96: 16[2]	1995-96: 12	1989-96: 16	1987-96: 16 1996: 8

[1] Prior to 1979 and 1981 respectively, and in Manitoba's case for the entire period, Newfoundland and Quebec's notice requirements were determined by worker's pay period.
[2] After 1970, Quebec's notice requirement is actually 4 months.
Note: Notice is calculated as the number of weeks of notice for a worker with 10 or more years of service, paid weekly.
Source: Labour Canada; *Labour Standards Legislation in Canada*, various years (this publication became biennial in the early 1990's); *Canadian Labour Law Reporter*, CCH Canadian Ltd.

and 1996. This may suggest that current levels of EPL are not perceived as a major obstacle to business, and are sufficiently valued by middle-class voters in a time of greater perceived job insecurity to make any attack on them politically unattractive.

As in Canada, common law and more recent statutes regulate the dissolution of employment contracts in the United States. The US common-law tradition, summarized in the "employment at will" doctrine, differs markedly from the Canadian one in that it views all employment contracts that are not of a fixed, definite duration as subject to immediate cancellation by either party. Thus, there is no notion of reasonable notice for economically motivated layoffs in US common law.

US legislation also imposes no minimum notice or severance requirements on layoffs involving a single worker or relatively small numbers of workers. Plant-closing legislation, the Worker Adjustment and Retraining Notification Act (WARN), came into existence on August 4, 1988 and went into effect six months later.[11] WARN requires firms with 100 or more full-time workers to give 60 days written notice of a plant closing or mass layoff to agents of the affected workers (or the workers themselves if there is no union), the local government and the state dislocated-worker unit. WARN defines a plant closing as the closing of a single location of a firm involving 50 or more employees; a mass layoff is defined as a layoff of more than six months that affects at least one third of the workforce (but not less that 50 employees) at a single location. The one-third rule does not apply if 500 or more workers are laid off, in which case notification must automatically be given.

WARN not only relieves small firms of the responsibility of giving notice; it also includes a number of exemptions, exceptions and exclusions. While some of these are unsurprising and similar to Canadian laws (e.g., destruction of the plant due to a natural disaster), others seem quite open to interpretation and manipulation by the firm. For example, required notice can be reduced or avoided if a company is trying to prevent closure by "actively pursuing capital or business," or because of business conditions that arose unexpectedly at the time notice would have been required.

Unlike the situation in Canada, enforcement of the provisions of WARN is not overseen by any government agency. Instead, the ruling that a firm is in breach of WARN must be established through individual or class-action suits instigated by the wronged parties in federal district court. Penalties for noncompliance are limited to back pay for the notice period plus a single (not per-worker) civil fine of up to $500 for each day of violation.

Overall, it seems clear from the above discussion that employment protection is considerably more substantial in Canada than in the US, both in the level of protection that is provided by law and in the prospects of having those laws enforced. Despite this difference, it is worth noting that while many rankings of the degree of employment protection[12] do not include Canada, those that do[13] tend to rank both it and the US as very low relative to the European countries. This may reflect the failure of those indices to incorporate much of the legislated-notice requirements at the provincial level and the consultative requirements that apply in cases of mass dismissals in Canada.[14] Still, Canadian employment protection levels almost certainly fall short of those in the more stringent European countries, several of which (Greece, Ireland, Italy, Portugal and Spain) have maximum severance-pay requirements of a year or more for long-tenured workers.

(b) Theoretically, What Effects Might We Expect EPL to Have on Employment and Unemployment?

The simple intuition behind the expected negative employment effects of employment protection laws is that because workers hired today might someday have to be terminated, and because EPLs raise the cost of termination, they raise the expected cost of hiring workers in the first place. Essentially, firms will be less likely to take chances on marginal workers or on hiring workers in uncertain times if they know it will be hard to dispose of those workers should the need arise later.[15] The thrust of this argument is, therefore, that employment protection laws are misnamed: what they really mandate is greater job protection (i.e., greater attachment of incumbent workers to their existing jobs), which could have the unintended consequence of reducing employment protection (i.e., the probability that a randomly selected individual can find work). Indeed, one can easily imagine an economy (such as the US) where the labour market is tight, turnover is high and job skills portable, where workers may have very little job security but a high degree of employment security.

What is perhaps most interesting about this very intuitive story is that it tends to be the first one economists think of when they consider the possible effects of EPLs, even though (even in a standard dynamic labour-demand model) it is not the most direct way in which EPLs affect employment. The more direct effect of EPLs on employment is that, by making layoffs more expensive, they raise employment levels during downturns in demand relative to what they would be otherwise. This distinction between direct and indirect effects has been noted and analyzed in the theoretical literature on EPLs. Not surprisingly, due to these opposing direct and indirect effects, EPL in general has an ambiguous overall effect on average employment levels across states of demand at the firm level.[16] More specifically, if firms' discount rates or natural employee attrition are sufficiently high, or if the expected time between hiring and firing periods is fairly long, higher firing costs are likely to raise average labour demand.[17] This is because firms, when hiring, discount the expected costs of having to fire the new employee, but when laying workers off, they pay firing penalties immediately. Thus the direct effects on firing outweigh the indirect ones on hiring. Also, the greater the exogenous attrition rate, the lower the likelihood that a new hire will ever have to be laid off involuntarily. In such situations, then, job-security provisions will improve the long-run employment prospects of all workers, whether they currently have a job or not. The results are more complex when the state of demand is uncertain,[18] but the same intuition applies.[19]

Bertola provides a fair summary of the predictions of standard labour-demand theory about EPL when he says: "[standard dynamic labour demand] theory predicts that job security provisions should have relatively small, functional-form dependent effects on average labour demand."[20] For a number of reasons, however, standard dynamic labour-demand theory, which generally models firms as passive price takers in labour markets and treats EPLs as a fixed cash cost paid by the firm when laying workers off, may not be the most appropriate way to conceptualize the effects of EPLs on firms' uses of labour. One reason is related to the partial-equilibrium nature of these models: in equilibrium, at least some of the burden of these costs will be passed on to workers in the form of lower wages. This is also why (despite the possibility of a large negative effect at fixed wages) payroll taxes may have few, or no, disemployment effects. While this does not mean EPLs are good for workers, it suggests that – especially in the long run – their major effects might be on wages and not on employment or unemployment rates. Further, the literature on the incidence of mandated benefits[21] suggests that the effects of EPLs on employment are likely to be muted because these laws (relative to a pure tax that does not provide an employment-contingent benefit) provide something of value to workers. Essentially, the mandated, employment-contingent benefit raises workers' willingness to work at any given wage, undoing much or all of the disemployment effects of its cost to firms. Overall, then, general equilibrium considerations reduce the expected effects of EPLs on employment and unemployment.

The second limitation of simple labour-demand models in analyzing the effects of EPLs revolves around the central idea of the theory of employment contracts: the possibility that the whole process of hiring and firing is governed not by firms' responses to fixed market prices, but by the rules of explicit or implicit contracts between firms and employees.[22] For example, as pointed out by Lazear,[23] any mandatory transfer between firms and workers, such as severance payments, can easily be undone by changes in private employment contracts. Workers in North America often receive substantial amounts of voluntary severance pay and/or pension adjustments when involuntarily terminated. Adding a legally required amount of severance might have no effect at all on worker or firm behaviour if it is undone by a compensatory change in firms' pension plans or private severance-pay provisions, as would be expected if the original contract had been designed to be Pareto optimal. While Lazear's empirical analysis goes on to dismiss this possibility, it would be very interesting to know whether firms in countries (or jurisdictions within countries) that have high levels of mandatory severance pay tend to offer less generous private early-retirement and severance packages to their laid-off workers. To my knowledge this issue has not been addressed empirically, yet if it is true, mandatory severance-pay laws may not have any effect on labour markets at all.

The third important reason why existing labour demand models may not be the most appropriate way to model the expected effects of EPLs is that not all EPLs are fixed cash taxes that firms must pay when terminating workers. In fact, with the possible exception of mandatory severance pay (though this is paid to workers and not to the receiver general, with the important implications noted above), no EPLs take this form. Indeed, the most common form of EPL, and by far its dominant form in North America, is mandatory advance notice, which could operate very differently from a cash tax on layoffs.[24] For example, to the extent that firms have private information about their closure or layoff plans that they would not otherwise share with workers, mandatory-notice laws are mainly about the sharing of private information, which is very different from a cash tax. Laws mandating the sharing of such information are best analyzed in the context of asymmetric information.[25] Although the results of these models vary depending on the assumptions regarding firms' abilities to precommit to advance notification, they raise the important possibility that rather than simply imposing a tax on otherwise competitive markets, advance-notice laws may correct pre-existing distortions in labour markets. Rather than delaying layoffs or plant closures and hence slowing down the reallocation of labour, notice laws may lead firms to disclose their layoff or closure plans earlier, thus speeding up the economic adjustment process. Much as occupational licensing may increase demand for a service by guaranteeing a minimum level of honesty among suppliers, it is even possible for such laws to reduce the *ex ante* costs of employment, thus raising hiring rates.[26]

The final important difference between mandatory-notice laws and cash taxes is that these laws have an almost mechanical, direct negative effect on measured unemployment that does not arise from cash firing costs: i.e., they provide for a period of predisplacement, employed job search, during which workers can find new jobs without any intervening spell of unemployment. By substituting employed for unemployed search, mandatory notice directly reduces unemployment. This predisplacement search effect is a very robust finding in the large empirical literature on advance notice in both Canada and the US.[27]

Theoretical predictions about the likely effects of EPLs also change when we recognize the fact that EPLs are not the only intervention or distortion in the labour markets. As noted earlier, in a world with no other distortions and no asymmetric information, EPLs raise employment costs and lead to loss of economic efficiency by slowing the redeployment of labour into its most efficient uses. However, other pre-existing distortions in labour markets may be mitigated by EPLs. An example, suggested by Chilton and Addison,[28] is the subsidization of unemployment by the unemployment insurance system. If, as suggested by Feldstein,[29] EI makes firms too willing to lay workers off, then EPL might offset this problem while continuing to maintain income security for unemployed workers.

Another example, suggested by Bertola and Rogerson,[30] is centralized, standardized wage setting, reputedly characteristic of several European economies. Interestingly, in Bertola and Rogerson's model, standardized wage-setting (i.e., a kind of "price rigidity," to go back to the theme introduced earlier in this paper) leads to excessive labour reallocation across firms (i.e., too much quantity flexibility), essentially because firms in contracting industries cannot cut wages to keep workers.[31] EPLs undo this excessive mobility by raising the costs of moving. The two policies work together to allow the right amount of labour reallocation while reducing the amount of unemployment incurred (because workers are less likely to go through an unemployment spell on their way to a new job). Indeed, Bertola and Rogerson use this argument to explain why overall job turnover is similar in Europe and the US, despite stronger EPLs in Europe. Bertola and Rogerson's argument also raises the need to be clear about what kind of rigidity (prices versus quantities) one is worried about, since less of one may in fact cause more of the other.

Finally, and perhaps most importantly given the current interest among policymakers worldwide in labour market training, there is the potential interaction of EPL with the market for employer-provided training, considered by Booth and Zoega.[32] In their model, firms will provide less than the socially optimal amount of training if their employees might leave in the future. If firms find it costly to lay off workers, there is less chance of separation and the benefit to firms of increasing training rises, so they provide more. Thus, one market failure (the underprovision of training) may be partially overcome by another – appropriate EPL. In addition, in the model, the presence of firing costs reduces the loss of specific and general skills (which are assumed to deteriorate during an unemployment spell). Once again, there is a long-term social gain from EPL that outweighs its immediate costs to employers. More generally, the issue of EPL and training is closely related to the employment contracting literature on the tradeoff between separation efficiency and maintaining incentives for investment in specific skills.[33] Contracts that make it hard to separate encourage both firms and workers to make relationship-specific investments, but of course this sometimes means that firms and workers stay together when better matches are available elsewhere. Despite considerable attention from economic theorists, there is no simple solution to this dilemma, and it is in fact not implausible that under parameter values that place sufficient importance on investment incentives, the "Catholic" marriage contract – where voice must take complete precedence over exit – may sometimes be the optimal one.

(c) How Large Are the Costs Imposed by EPLs on Firms?

Despite the large literature on EPLs, it is surprising that very little attention has been paid to estimating the actual costs imposed by these laws on firms. Most analysts seem to assume that, relative to more commonly analyzed policies like (say) payroll taxes, the costs to employers of EPLs are significant. Yet this is not obvious: at the worst, Canadian mandatory-notice laws force firms to keep unprofitable workers on the payroll for two to four months longer than they otherwise would; in Europe this period extends to eight and a half months,[34] though severance payments of slightly more than a year are required for high-tenure employees in a few countries.

Table 3
Permanent Wage Increases Equivalent in Cost
to Selected Notice Requirements

Hourly productivity of redundant worker	Notice required (months)					
	2		**6**		**12**	
$	% of breakeven productivity	Wage increase ($)	% of breakeven productivity	Wage increase ($)	% of breakeven productivity	Wage increase ($)	% of breakeven productivity
13.50	90	0.007	0.05	0.02	0.15	0.04	0.30
7.50	50	0.037	0.25	0.11	0.74	0.22	1.48
0.00	0	0.074	0.50	0.22	1.49	0.44	2.95

Note: The table reports estimates of the permanent wage increase that would reduce the present value of the firm's profits by an amount equivalent to retaining a redundant worker for the notice period. The estimates are based on a real interest rate of 3 percent per annum; worker's productivity and base for all percentages is $15.00 per hour.

One way to get an idea of the costs imposed by EPLs on firms is to do some back-of-the-envelope calculations that convert EPLs into equivalent amounts of a more familiar policy: a uniform percentage payroll tax on labour. In table 3, I consider the following situation: A firm has a wage rate of $15 per hour for all its workers.[35] Some, or all of those workers now have a marginal revenue product (MRP) of less than $15, so the firm would like to lay them off. Both the wage rate and the workers' productivity are expected to stay at their current levels indefinitely.[36] For three different values of a redundant worker's productivity, the table presents the value of the permanent wage increase to a single (presumably profitable) worker, which would result in the same amount of lost profits as retaining a redundant worker for three possible mandatory-notice periods: 2, 6 and 12 months. The most extreme assumption made about the redundant worker's productivity (zero) can be taken to represent either a totally unproductive worker, or a severance-pay requirement whereby the firm is forced to pay the worker his or her regular wage ($15 per hour) even though the worker does not come in to work.

The figures in table 3, which assumes a real discount rate of 3 percent, make the costs of most real-world notice requirements look fairly trivial. Even at the high end of the range of notice for workers laid off individually in Canada (two months), the cost of giving notice to a worker whose productivity is only half the breakeven level is equivalent to a payroll tax of one quarter of 1 percent on a single employed worker. Further, since the notice requirement only has to be met when firms are actually laying off workers, which is far from all the time, and since it only applies to those workers that are actually laid off rather than the whole workforce, it is clear that the economic costs of Canadian advance-notice requirements, relative to any policy that raises wages across the board, are trivial. Notice or severance-pay requirements at the upper end of the European range (6 to 12 months) cost more, but – again given the proviso that they apply only to the small number of workers who are actually laid off – are likely small compared with other policies affecting firms in those countries.

Table 4 presents the results of table 3 in a slightly different way, and it also gives some idea of the sensitivity of these calculations to the assumed real interest rate of 3 percent. In table 4, I show the productivity level a redundant worker would need to have to make a given notice requirement equivalent in cost to a 1 percent, permanent real-wage increase, again to a single "profitable" employee. When the real discount rate is 3 percent, for a two-month notice requirement to be as costly as a 1 percent wage increase, the notified employee would have to be extremely unproductive indeed: his or her hourly productivity would need to equal minus $15 (i.e., he or she would need to cause damage to the firm equal in value to his or her wage).[37] Again, these productivity levels are higher when the discount rate and notice requirements are raised, but even in the extreme case of 12 months notice and a 4 percent discount rate, a firm would need to lose 26 percent (100 percent minus 74 percent) on an employed redundant worker (who, remember, must have been profitable to employ in the recent past – otherwise he/she would not have been there in the first place) to incur a cost equivalent to a 1 percent real wage increase for a single permanent employee.

Of course, these quantitative estimates of the costs of EPLs do not incorporate the possibility that, like consumers faced with price increases, firms may be able to make changes that reduce or minimize these costs. Aside from the possibility (noted by Lazear) that firms may be able to contract their way out of these obligations completely, there are a number of important alternatives to shedding workers in demand downturns. Clearly, one alternative to layoffs, at least for temporary declines in product demand, is a reduction in the hours of all employees, or work sharing. This alternative has been studied by Abraham and Houseman,[38] and Van Audenrode.[39] Abraham and Houseman compare industry-level adjustments in labour utilization in the US and Germany and find that the overall adjustments in total hours worked are similar, but with greater reliance on hours variation in Europe and on layoffs in the US. Houseman reaches similar conclusions[40] in her comparison of labour market adjustments in Europe, Japan and the US. Interestingly, Van Audenrode found that in Belgium, when short-time working was supported by a generous, publicly funded, short-time compensation system, the adjustment in total hours worked to labour-demand shocks was even greater than in the US.

Table 4
Productivity Level of a Redundant Worker Equivalent to a 1 Percent Permanent Wage Increase, under Selected Notice Requirements

Real discount rate (annual)	Notice required (months)					
	2		6		12	
	$	% of breakeven	$	% of breakeven	$	% of breakeven
2%	-30.11	-201	-0.09	-1	7.41	49
3%	-15.11	-101	4.91	33	9.92	66
4%	-7.61	-51	7.41	49	11.16	74

Note: The table reports estimates of the productivity level of an employed redundant worker for a given notice requirement to be equivalent to a 1 percent permanent real-wage increase. The estimates are based on workers' productivity and base for all percentages of $15.00 per hour.

In addition to work sharing, there are other ways firms can minimize the costs of employment protection laws. One of these, especially common in European countries, is to hire workers on temporary employment contracts, under which EPLs are either much weaker or totally inapplicable. While this might have other undesirable consequences, such as the creation of a two-tier workforce, it means that the supposedly costly restrictions of EPLs on firms' abilities to shed labour can be largely undone. Another way is to take advantage of the minimum firm-size threshold for EPLs and stay small (at least on paper). It has been claimed that this explains why there are so many Italian firms with 19 employees.[41] Mass layoffs can sometimes be timed to avoid group-notice requirements by making sure that no more than the threshold number of workers (usually 50) leaves the firm in any given four-week period. Firms can also claim an exemption from the law or simply fail to comply, which seems to have been the response of US firms to the introduction of mandatory notice there.[42] Other potentially very important adjustment mechanisms include relying on natural workforce attrition, such as quits and retirement, and internal transfers of workers.

The final and perhaps most fundamental alternative to layoffs is for firms to change what they produce. It is an old tradition in economics that firms are identified with products, so that when demand or technology changes, workers need to switch firms (or "islands" in another well-known macroeconomic paradigm).[43] But it is worth reminding ourselves that this is only a convention, and that – to the extent that what makes firms work as organizations is not a particular product but the shared knowledge about the characteristics and abilities of its employees[44] – the most efficient way for an economy to adjust to demand and technology

191

changes may be within the nexus of formal and informal contracts that constitutes a firm. This is a practice for which Japanese firms are particularly well known.[45]

In addition to back-of-the-envelope calculations, and taking account of the potentially large number of low-cost substitutes to layoffs, a final source of evidence about the costs of EPLs to firms comes from data on the actual amount of hiring and firing that firms do. If firing costs are truly high, one would expect firms to economize on employee turnover by screening workers carefully when hiring and by avoiding excessive churning of workers. Interestingly, however, a broad consensus in all recent examinations of this issue is that, in some absolute sense, both job and worker turnover are very large in all countries, even those where the EPL is very strict. For example, in a sample of six countries, some of which have quite stringent employment protection, Bertola and Rogerson[46] report annual job turnover rates (the sum of establishment-level employment increases and decreases) of about 10 or more times the level of net employment change in all of them. Even in highly protected countries, a large amount of employment is reallocated across firms each year, making the claim that EPLs substantially inhibit structural adjustment hard to justify. Further, there is no tendency for countries with high levels of employment protection to have lower turnover: strikingly, Italy, France and Canada all have higher turnover rates than the United States according to Bertola and Rogerson's analysis.

Baldwin, Dunne and Haltiwanger[47] find the rates of job destruction and job creation in the US and Canada to be very similar. Examining the same issue in a larger sample of countries, the OECD[48] finds that overall job turnover is negatively correlated with indices of EPL, but that this correlation is confined to the much less stringent EPL regulations that cover temporary workers only. Citing two recent legislative changes in France and one in Germany, they also find no detectable changes in turnover as a result of substantial changes in EPL provisions. Finally, Leonard and Van Audenrode,[49] looking at job turnover in Belgium, where the job protection laws are reputed to be among the strongest in Europe, found that one in five workers separates from their previous employer and about the same number are hired each year.[50] Moreover, in contrast to any existing model of dynamic labour demand with adjustment costs, many firms hire and fire employees at the same time: indeed, the correlation between hiring and firing rates across firms is positive, with 45 percent of all firings occurring in growing firms. Somehow, therefore, even in labour markets with much more stringent EPLs than Canada's, firms do not find it prohibitively expensive to undertake large simultaneous inflows and outflows of workers, and the reallocation of labour across firms and industries occurs at about the same pace as in the US and Canada.

(d) What Evidence Is There That EPLs Explain International Unemployment Differences Generally and Canada-US Differences in Particular?

To my knowledge, the only empirical studies that claim to demonstrate that EPLs have a negative effect on employment or a positive one on unemployment are Lazear[51] and Addison and Grosso.[52] Both are cross-national studies (which is appropriate if one is looking for the general-equilibrium effects of these policies, but of course carries a price in terms of the number of observations). Given the preceding discussion, I believe the interpretation of the correlations found in these studies as causal effects of EPLs needs to be seriously questioned.

Theoretically, there are as many reasons to expect EPLs to raise long-run employment as to lower it, and their effects can be easily offset by other policies. Empirically, the costs imposed by most EPLs on firms' use of labour are likely trivial compared with other policies like payroll taxes, and these costs are easily avoided by using a number of alternative means of adjustment. As well, EPLs do not seem to have had a major inhibiting effect on the reallocation of labour across industries or on the overall level of worker turnover. For all these reasons, it seems highly likely that the cross-national association between unemployment and EPL found by Lazear and Addison and Grosso is driven by other, more economically significant factors, which are correlated with both.[53]

Other factors that might account for the (after all, relatively weak) cross-national correlation between EPL and unemployment are unemployment insurance and short-time compensation systems: do they subsidize layoffs more than they do reductions in hours or vice versa?[54] Other aspects of a country's social safety net, such as the decline in welfare benefits in the US, may also be correlated with EPL and have important effects on unemployment. If any combination of these other factors is the main determinant of cross-national differences in firms' adjustment strategies, then the adoption of policies that (say) reduce EPL with a view to increasing labour market flexibility may have little or no effect on unemployment rates, except perhaps via the direct, mechanical effect of substituting employed for unemployed search during an advance-notice period.

More fundamentally, other factors that predate both EPL and other kinds of legislation or social policy may be the prime causes of international differences in adjustment mechanisms. Lacroix and Huberman[55] argue that the difference between Europe and North America in the use of work sharing predates any unemployment insurance or short-time compensation systems. Instead, a combination of labour market conditions and existing private institutional arrangements made different adjustment modes profitable on these two continents, and when legislation was drafted to assist the unemployed it was designed to accommodate these different practices. The argument that legislated factors are not the primary, exogenous factors determining the dominant mode of adjustment to demand changes is supported by the case of Japan where, despite one of the lowest employee turnover rates in the world, advance notice requirements are minimal.

It is fair to state that the only robust evidence concerning the effects of EPLs on unemployment is that found in the large empirical literature on advance notice. More than a dozen microdata-based studies demonstrate a direct, unemployment-reducing effect of EPLs: unemployment is reduced because workers are given a period of employed, predisplacement search during which to find a new job without ever becoming unemployed. Interestingly, in three quite disparate sources[56] a consensus seems to be emerging on EPL that incorporates both the insights of the micro-level advance-notice literature and the broader cross-national literature. According to this emerging view, because their overall costs are small, and perhaps because of offsetting factors like compressed inter-industry wage differentials (in Europe), EPLs do not have a measurable inhibiting effect on the amount or speed of labour reallocation among firms or industries or even on the overall level of employment. They do, however, have a direct and measurable effect on unemployment, by eliminating the need for some workers to go through an unemployment spell on their way to new jobs. Unfortunately, however, the benefits this confers on workers are limited by the fact that the unemployment spells eliminated by notice requirements tend to be the shortest ones.[57] This selection effect may, however, explain the well-known result that inflows into unemployment are smaller but durations of unemployment are longer in Europe than in North America.[58]

Inflexible Wages: Cause of Canadian Unemployment?

The two institutional sources of wage inflexibility mentioned most often in the flexibility debate are unions and minimum wages.[59] I therefore begin my discussion in this section by briefly describing the state of unions and minimum wages in the US and Canada and discussing some theoretical minimum-wage issues linking unions, minimum wage, and wage flexibility.

(a) Are Unions and Minimum Wages Stronger in Canada Than in the United States?
It is well known that union membership and coverage are greater in Canada than in the US. In 1990, 18 percent of American workers were covered by a collective bargaining agreement, compared with 38 percent of Canadian workers. The number that actually belonged to unions was marginally smaller.[60] The US unionization rate is substantially lower than it was in previous decades, but in

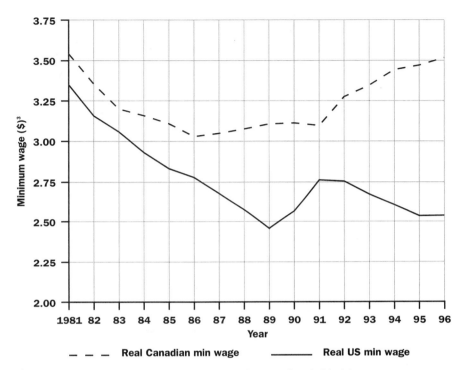

Figure 1

Real Minimum Wages, Canada[1] and the US[2], 1981-1996

Minimum wage ($)[3]

1981 82 83 84 85 86 87 88 89 90 91 92 93 94 95 96

Year

— — — **Real Canadian min wage**　　　————— **Real US min wage**

[1] The Canadian minimum wage is a labour-force-weighted average of provincial minimum wages.
[2] The US minimum wage is the federal minimum wage.
[3] Canadian minimum wages in Canadian dollars; US minimum wages in US dollars.
Note: The series is deflated using the all-items Consumer Price Index.
Source: Survey of Consumer Finances (Canada); Current Population Survey (US).

Canada it has decreased only marginally. Both Canadian and US union coverage rates are low compared with almost all other developed countries – even those where union membership is low, such as France, where mandatory extension of union bargaining agreements means that a large majority of workers are covered by union contracts. I shall take it as given that in Canada, unions have more influence on wage setting than they do in the United States and also that their influence has declined less rapidly in the past decade.

Are minimum wages higher and/or more pervasive in Canada than in the United States? With respect to the segments of the labour force covered by minimum-wage laws, the situations are roughly the same in the two countries, but the issue of wage levels is complicated by the fact that in Canada minimum wages are set by the provinces, while in the US the effective minimum wage in the vast

peter kuhn

Figure 2

Ratios of Minimum Wages to Average Male Wages,
Canada[1] and the US[2], 1981-1992

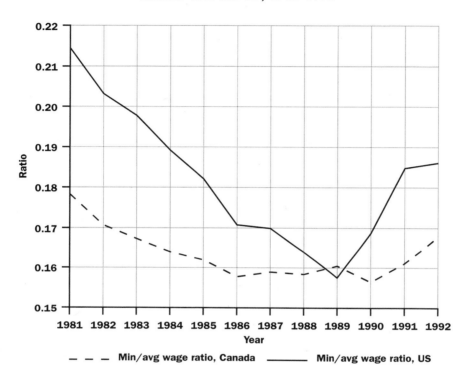

[1] The Canadian minimum wage is a labour-force-weighted average of provincial minimum wages.
[2] The US minimum wage is the federal minimum wage.
Note: Average male wage is measured using average hourly earnings data from the Survey of Consumer Finances and the Current Population Survey.
Source: Survey of Consumer Finances (Canada); Current Population Survey (US).

majority of states is set federally. Figure 1, which compares the US federal minimum wage to a labour-force-weighted annual average of minimum wages in the Canadian provinces, shows that real minimum wages declined in both countries throughout most of the 1980s due to a combination of inflation and the lack of increases in the nominal minimum wage. The decline, however, appears to be smaller and to have been reversed earlier in Canada. In figure 2 the minimum wage is shown relative to a measure of the economy-wide average hourly wage. Interestingly, in this figure the US series now shows an even sharper decline relative to the Canadian one, though much of this is because it starts from a higher base. Still, even relative to the declining average real wage, the Canadian minimum-wage series shows some downward adjustment.

adapting public policy to a labour market in transition

(b) Theoretically, How Do We Expect Unions and Minimum-Wage Laws to Affect Wage Rigidity?

The basic idea behind the wage rigidity and unemployment hypothesis is the following. If a country has a centralized collective bargaining system with the power to maintain a high and compressed distribution of wages, or if it has high and binding minimum-wage laws, then technology- and/or trade-based reductions in the demand for unskilled workers may not be allowed to translate into wage reductions for those groups. An unfortunate by-product of this system is that these groups may then end up being priced out of the labour market, and thus unemployed for sometimes long periods.

Of course, while it is widely accepted that unions raise wages above market levels and increasingly accepted that they compress wage differentials between the skilled and unskilled,[61] the central empirical issue for the wage-rigidity explanation of recent unemployment trends is: how responsive are union wages (and for that matter legislated minimum wages) to labour demand shocks, relative to equilibrium wages in an unregulated market? As there is no empirical consensus (or even much empirical evidence) on this question, it may be worth considering what one might expect, based on some simple theoretical models.[62]

Interestingly, existing theoretical perspectives on this issue embody a number of possibilities that are intuitively likely, with very different predictions regarding the relative responsiveness to demand shocks of union and nonunion wages. For example, Grossman[63] develops a model of the impact of trade on a unionized sector, where the union is characterized by a seniority layoff system and majority rule. His model, like the OECD hypothesis, predicts wage inflexibility. In contrast, Freeman and Katz[64] argue that union wage differentials will act as a buffer, absorbing trade shocks with wage changes and thus reducing employment effects. Essentially, theirs is the partial-equilibrium argument that union wages can adjust to demand declines because unionized workers are earning rents; nonunion firms cannot cut wages because they are already paying market wages. Lawrence and Lawrence[65] present a model of "endgame bargaining." A union, seeing no future for a declining industry, tries to extract as much as possible in the short run. Their model goes beyond union real-wage rigidity to predict increased union wage demands in the face of rising international competition. Finally, Abowd and Lemieux[66] propose that changes in demand or import prices will change the level of quasi-rents available in an industry. Quasi-rents are divided between firms and unions through an efficient bargaining solution. They predict that a decrease in quasi-rents will increase employment. Wage effects will be determined by the change in quasi-rents per worker. In general, we can think of plausible models that generate

Table 5

Decomposition of the Growth in Mean Weekly Male Earnings,
Canada, 1981-1992

Quintile	Change in log weekly earnings	Change in log hourly wage[1]	Change in log hours per week
1	-23.8	-15.2	-8.6
2	-8.7	-8.2	-0.6
3	-3.0	-3.8	0.8
4	-0.1	-2.8	2.7
5	2.8	-1.0	3.7
All workers	-6.6	-6.2	-0.4

[1] The log hourly wage is calculated as the difference between log weekly earnings in the reference year and usual weekly hours in the job held during the survey week.

Note: Includes all males aged 24-60 with positive earnings and weeks worked in the survey year, and positive usual hours worked in the reference week. Self-employed individuals are excluded from the calculations.

Source: Survey of Consumer Finances, various years.

opposite results for the relative responsiveness of union and nonunion wages to negative demand shocks.[67]

Surely, while union wages may in fact respond as much to labour demand shocks as do nonunion wages, it must still be the case that minimum-wage laws limit an economy's ability to cut wages, especially among unskilled workers. While this is the case for a fixed real minimum wage, as figures 1 and 2 show it may not be the case in the real world, where inflation cuts the real value of nominal minimum wages and where governments decide on a regular basis whether the market for unskilled workers is strong enough to support another hike in the nominal minimum wage.

Clearly Canadian governments responded less to declines in the demand for unskilled workers in the 1980s, but this may be a result of political shifts to the left in the three most populous provinces. Holding constant these arguably exogenous changes in the political landscape (thus looking within party regimes rather than between them), it remains an empirical question whether minimum wages are substantially less responsive to labour demand shocks than are equilibrium market wages.

In sum, the relevant issue in the wage-flexibility hypothesis as it is currently posed is not whether the high wages caused by unions and/or minimum-wage laws lead to a higher level of national unemployment.[68] Instead, it is whether these institutionally determined wages respond to negative demand shocks, which we know relatively little about. Evidence suggests that the minimum wage

Table 6
Decomposition of the Growth in Mean Weekly Male Earnings, US, 1981–1992

Quintile	Change in log weekly earnings	Change in log hourly wage[1]	Change in log hours per week
1	-18.2	-14.9	-3.3
2	-13.1	-13.5	0.4
3	-8.0	-10.3	2.3
4	-2.3	-4.9	2.6
5	4.1	0.2	3.9
All workers	-7.5	-8.7	1.2

[1] The log hourly wage is calculated as the difference between log weekly earnings and usual weekly hours in the reference year.
Note: Includes all males aged 24-60 with positive earnings, weeks worked, and usual weekly hours in the survey year. Self-employed individuals are excluded from the calculations.
Source: Current Population Survey, various years.

may, in fact, be quite responsive to demand conditions for unskilled workers, and the same may also be true of union wages.

(c) Is Canada a Rigid-Wage Economy?

Until very recently, there has been considerable consensus regarding trends in the distribution of real wages in Canada since the early 1980s. According to a number of authors and data sources, real wages for men and women became more unequal during this period.[69] Further, since this was a period of declining real wages for men as a group, there were substantial decreases in the real wages for men at the bottom of the wage distribution.[70] Overall, however, most analysts agree that wage inequality has increased less in Canada than in the United States.[71]

Recently, however, this consensus has been challenged in at least two ways. First, data on earnings in the late 1980s and early 1990s show an increase in weekly earnings inequality in Canada, while in the US the increase levelled off. Thus, some recent indicators seem to show increases in inequality in Canada similar to those in the US.[72] In contrast, while most Canadian analysts have been content to treat average weekly earnings as a reasonable measure of the wage rate, Morissette and Picot,[73] using a series of special surveys with information on hourly wage rates, recently painted a picture of a relatively stable wage distribution, with changes in weekly hours of work playing the major role in the weekly earnings decline of unskilled men. Thus the issue of whether Canada is a rigid-wage or a flexible-wage economy, especially relative to the US, is still open.

peter kuhn

In tables 5 and 6, I provide some new and preliminary evidence that may be relevant to this issue for the Canada and the US, respectively. To maximize international comparability, these figures are taken from very similar Canadian and US surveys, and have been constructed from the relevant microdata sources in the most similar way possible. Indeed, the only substantive difference in the calculation of the Canadian and US numbers relates to a well-known shortcoming in the Canadian data: usual hours of work are known only for the job held in the week the survey was conducted, not in the previous calendar year, which is the period for which earnings information is available.

These tables provide relatively up-to-date information on the change in weekly earnings inequality in the US and Canada. Clearly, the message here, as in Kuhn and Robb,[74] is not one of downward inflexibility in Canadian labour markets: real weekly earnings in the bottom quintile fell more in Canada than in the US.[75] I also decompose these changes in weekly earnings into the portions due to changes in hours worked per week and in the average hourly rate of pay. To do this, I rely on the fact that, for each individual:

(1) $\log (E) = \log w + \log h,$

where E is weekly earnings, w is the individual's hourly wage, and h is hours worked per week. I first compute log E, the log of weekly earnings in the calendar year, identically for both countries, and use it to rank individuals into five quintiles. Taking within-quintile means of both sides of equation 1 preserves the identity, as does differencing between 1981 and 1992, the most recent year for which I have comparable data. Finally, note that the hours measures used are different in the two countries (current hours in Canada and usual hours last year in the US), but due to the linearity of the decomposition in equation 1, this should not bias our results as long as current hours are an unbiased estimate of mean hours in the survey year.[76]

Both Canada and the US have seen increased polarization in the weekly hours worked, with unskilled workers reducing, and skilled workers increasing, their weekly hours. However, with the exception of the bottom quintile in Canada, where the decline in hours explains (.086/.238=) 36 percent of the decline in weekly earnings, changes in hours play a very small role in explaining the decline in real weekly earnings among unskilled males. Interestingly, increases in hours worked have played a significant role in maintaining the real earnings of more highly skilled men in both countries. Most importantly from the point of view of the wage-flexibility hypothesis, declines in hourly real wages (or, perhaps more accurately since all we observe directly are weekly earnings and weekly hours, declines in weekly earnings that cannot be explained by the observed declines in weekly hours) among the bottom quintile of Canadian men are comparable with those in the US, at about 15 percent in both countries over this 11-year period.

In further research on this data, I hope to extend the analysis to more recent years to provide more information on intervening years, to understand why these results are so different from Picot's,[77] and to use the US information on average hours in the current job to see whether using current hours makes much difference to these kinds of calculations. If the figures in tables 5 and 6 are substantiated, then they paint a very different picture of the Canadian economy from one in which unions, minimum wages and other institutional forces prevent the downward adjustment of unskilled workers' real wages. Between 1981 and 1992 those wages fell by about the same amount in both countries, despite the higher level of unionization in Canada and the more rapid erosion of real minimum wages in the US.[78]

(d) What Is the Evidence That Differences in Wage Rigidity Explain International Unemployment Differences, Especially Those Between Canada and the US?
Given the considerable amount of recent evidence suggesting that Canadian wages are more rigid than US wages,[79] given the emergence of studies linking a smaller increase in Canadian wage inequality to the relative health of its unions[80] and given the fact that recent increases in Canadian unemployment have been highly concentrated among the unskilled,[81] it may be tempting to draw a link between the maintenance – in the face of declining demand – of high wages for unskilled workers by Canadian unions and governments and the recent increase in Canadian unemployment relative to the US.

The evidence reviewed in this section suggests that such a conclusion would be premature. While real minimum wages did not fall as much in Canada as in the US, it is clear that they were far from static in Canada, certainly allowing some adjustment for declining demand at the very bottom of the wage distribution. Also, much of the decline in the real wages of unskilled workers occurred at wage levels that are well above the minimum, so it is unlikely that minimum wages could have moderated much of this decline. There is no direct evidence that union wages responded to Canadian declines in demand, but it is at least plausible that they did.[82] Most importantly, however, the data presented in this paper suggests that the hourly wages of unskilled Canadian men have not held up any better than those of American men in the 1990s.[83] This of course raises the disturbing possibility that Canadian wages have been as hard hit by technology and demand shocks as US wages, with the tremendous attendant strain on our more generous social programs.[84]

Then Why Is Canadian Unemployment So High?

This is hardly the place to answer one of the central questions facing Canadian economists this decade, but having questioned the role of EPLs, minimum wages and unions, it is important to mention a number of alternative explanations for the well-known Canada-US unemployment rate gap. A substantial number of these were recently summarized in detail by Riddell and Sharpe,[85] so I will limit myself to listing a few key hypotheses. Perhaps most importantly, we should question the assumptions underlying the OECD wage-flexibility hypothesis and other hypotheses on this point: that both countries were subject to the same (trade- and/or technology-induced) demand shocks for unskilled labour. They do not produce the same mix of goods, which makes it unlikely that they would be affected in the same way by either kind of shock.[86] As well, stronger monetary policy shocks may have produced a more severe recession in Canada in the 1990s, and recessions always hurt unskilled workers more than they do skilled workers.

Another key difference is the Canadian social safety net, of which the employment insurance system is a central element. An important factor contributing to the gap, at least in the 1980s, may have been the increasing tendency of non-working Canadians to label themselves as unemployed in order to qualify for benefits.[87] At the same time, sharp cuts in the US social safety net may have simply eliminated any feasible alternatives to very low-wage work in that country.[88] Freeman[89] attributes some of the current low US unemployment to sharply rising incarceration of unskilled young men; Macredie[90] argues that differences in definition (in particular the inclusion of passive job searchers in the Canadian but not the US definition of the unemployed) also account for part of the Canada-US unemployment-rate gap.

Conclusions

In this paper I provide a critical review of some evidence relating to the popular hypothesis that differences in labour market rigidities explain an important part of the current unemployment differential between the US and other countries, including Canada. I began by noting there are two common but quite unrelated conceptions of rigidity in current policy discussions, one concerning restrictions on firms' abilities to adjust quantities of labour (e.g., employment protection laws), the other concerning restrictions on the price of labour (minimum-wage laws and unions). Reviewing the evidence on each of these in turn, I concluded that neither is likely to explain a large part of the current unemployment gap between Canada and the US. Employment protection laws, especially at levels currently prevalent in Canada, are simply not costly enough to have much of an effect. At the same time, I presented new evidence that by 1992, neither unions nor minimum-wage laws prevented Canadian wage inequality from increasing as much as it had in the US. I concluded that other factors, including different shifts in demand in the two countries and aspects of social policy, are more promising explanations of the increase in Canadian relative to US unemployment.

It is important to bear in mind that the current emphasis on emulating the US in labour and macroeconomic policy could be part of a recurring hysteria, common among observers of national economic performance, which attributes long-lasting virtue to the institutional features of those countries whose macroeconomic performance in the current year, or even decade, happens to be above average. Not long ago, the paragon of virtue in this regard was Japan whose very rigid practice of lifetime employment was seen as one to be emulated. More recently, observers of the once-booming South East Asian "tigers" argued that North Americans would do well to adopt the Confucian values of the ethnic Chinese, who figured so prominently in the success of those economies.[91] Currently on the pedestal is the United States, whose hands-off policy and increasing inequality are sometimes seen as necessary prices to pay to get people back to work.

While the features of these successful economies are worth studying as possible ways to improve our own economic performance, I suggested in this paper that concluding that Canada's unemployment situation could be substantially improved by reducing minimum wages, cutting union power or scaling back our relatively weak employment protection laws is premature. Apparently costly regulations on firms' abilities to shed workers may not cost very much at all and may well reduce unemployment. And despite the presence of institutions that are widely seen as impediments to real wage adjustments, unskilled Canadian workers appear to have experienced wage declines that are every bit as dramatic as those in the US. The constraining effects of both quantity and price rigidities are thus very hard to find in a detailed analysis of Canadian labour markets.

203

Notes

I thank Malik Ljutic and Susan Johnson for their careful and timely research assistance.

1. Internationally standardized unemployment rates show a decrease from 9.5 to 5.5 percent in the United States between 1983 and 1995. Over the same period, Canada's unemployment rate decreased from 11.9 to 9.5 percent, while those of Central and Western Europe decreased from 9.8 to 9.2 percent. See Organization for Economic Co-operation and Development (OECD), *Employment Outlook* (Paris: Organization for Economic Co-operation and Development, July 1996), p. 198.

2. Between 1973 and 1995, the US employment-to-population ratio for individuals aged 15 to 64 increased from 65.1 to 73.5 percent. Over the same period, Canada's employment-to-population ratio increased from 63.1 to 67.7 percent, and that of Europe fell from 65.1 to 60.1 percent. See OECD, *Employment Outlook*, p. 186.

3. OECD, *The OECD Jobs Study: Facts, Analysis, Strategies* (Paris: OECD, 1994), and E. Lazear, "Job Security Provisions and Employment," *Quarterly Journal of Economics*, Vol. 105 (August 1990), pp. 699-726.

4. See, for example, Lazear, "Job Security Provisions and Employment."

5. Samuel Bentolila and Giuseppe Bertola, "Firing Costs and Labour Demand: How Bad is Eurosclerosis?" *Review of Economic Studies*, Vol. 57, no. 3 (1990), pp. 381-402.

6. Authors who have made or examined this claim include Adrian Wood, *North-South Trade, Employment, and Inequality* (Oxford, UK: Clarendon Press, 1994); Stephen Nickell and Brian Bell, "The Collapse in Demand for the Unskilled and Unemployment Across the OECD," *Oxford Review of Economic Policy*, Vol. 11 (Spring 1995), pp. 40-62; and L. Katz et al., "A Comparison of Changes in the Structure of Wages in Four OECD Countries," in R. B. Freeman (ed.), *Differences and Changes in Wage Structures*, NBER Labor Market Series (Chicago, IL: University of Chicago Press, 1995), pp. 25-65; and Katherine G. Abraham and Susan N. Houseman, *Job Security in America: Lessons from Germany* (Washington, D.C.: Brookings Institution, 1993).

7. The restrictions on terminations for economic reasons are generally made to distinguish them from unjust dismissal laws, which prevent dismissals for discriminatory reasons or for such activities as union organizing and jury duty. Restrictions on dismissals for cause are contained in provincial labour relations acts, human rights acts, and other legislation. For an analysis of recent US trends in unjust dismissal law, see A. Krueger, "The Evolution of Unjust Dismissal Legislation in the United States," *Industrial and Labor Relations Review*, Vol. 44, no. 4 (July 1991), pp. 644-60.

8. The exception is labour contracts that are made for a specific term. In Quebec, these restrictions are found in the Civil Code. In all cases, what is reasonable is determined by a judge, who is expected to consider such factors as existing practices in the industry and the ease or difficulty with which the employee is likely to find a new job. See H.W. Arthurs, D.D. Carter, and H.J. Glasbeek, *Labour Law and Industrial Relations in Canada* (Scarborough, ON: Butterworths, 1981).

9. Don Downey, "Man Awarded $1 Million in Wrongful Dismissal Suit," *Globe and Mail*, October 31, 1989, pp. B1, B4.

10. In most cases layoffs are classified as temporary and thus not subject to notice requirements if they are for less than 13 weeks, or (in cases of mass layoffs) if the employer advises the director of employment standards that he or she expects to recall the workers within a period of time approved by the director. Some jurisdictions, however, require notice of all large-scale layoffs, whether permanent or not.

11. Before WARN, a handful of states had relatively minimal advance-notice laws. Many unsuccessful attempts were made to pass such laws. From 1975 until 1983, 125 plant-closing bills were introduced in the 30 state legislatures, and over 40 bills have been introduced in Congress since 1979. See Peter Kuhn, "Employment Protection Laws: Policy Issues and Recent Research," *Canadian Public Policy*, Vol. 19 (September 1993), pp. 279-97.

12. See for example, G. Bertola, "Job Security, Employment and Wages," *European Economic Review*, Vol. 34 (June 1990), pp. 851-86; Lazear, "Job Security Provisions and Employment," and D. Grubb and W. Wells, "Employment Regulation and Patterns of Work in EC Countries," *OECD Economic Studies* (Winter 1993), pp. 7-58.

13. OECD, *The OECD Jobs Study: Evidence and Explanations: Part I: Labour Market Trends and Underlying Forces of Change* (Paris: OECD, 1994), p. 73.

14. The OECD's table lists Canada as having a maximum notice period for an individual dismissal of .25 months in the late 1980s. As the OECD reports, taking an average of notice requirements across layoffs for economic and personal reasons, they could have arrived at this number using the federal notice requirement of two weeks, averaged with a zero requirement for personal dismissals.

15. The issue should be familiar to anyone involved in the academic labour market: the ease with which one can deny tenure has important effects on the risks one is willing to take in the initial hiring decision.

16. In the standard model, EPLs do have an unambiguously positive effect on job tenures (preserving high-tenure jobs at the expense of new ones), and causes an unambiguous decline in the (cyclical and/or seasonal) amplitude of employment fluctuations. See Patricia Anderson, "Linear Adjustment Costs and Seasonal Labour Demand: Evidence from Retail Trade Firms," *Quarterly Journal of Economics*, Vol. 108 (November 1993), pp. 1015-42.

17. Giuseppe Bertola, "Labor Turnover Costs and Average Labor Demand," *Journal of Labor Economics*, Vol. 10, no. 4 (October 1992), pp. 389-411.

18. Bentolila and Bertola, "Firing Costs and Labor Demand."

19. Uncertainty matters somewhat more if the EPL is modelled as an advance-notice requirement than the more conventional cash tax formulation. For example, in Giuseppe Bertola's model with no uncertainty, a mandatory-notice law will have no effect at all: firms will just make layoff announcements far enough in advance of each (fully anticipated) layoff date to comply with the legislation. Whether workers benefit from this depends on whether they are as well informed as firms about future demand conditions. See Bertola, "Labor Turnover Costs and Average Labor Demand."

20. Bertola, "Labor Turnover Costs and Average Labor Demand," p. 405.

21. L.H. Summers, "Some Simple Economics of Mandated Benefits," *American Economic Review*, Vol. 79 (May 1989), pp. 177-83.

22. See, for example, Sherwin Rosen, "Implicit Contracts: A Survey," *Journal of Economic Literature*, Vol. 23 (September 1985), pp. 1144-75.

23. Lazear, "Job Security Provisions and Employment."

24. An interesting illustration of the importance of the precise form taken by EPLs is a model by Pietro Garibaldi, "Job Flow Dynamics and Firing Restrictions," Centre for Economic Performance discussion paper 256, London School of Economics, 1995, in which EPLs have no effect unless they are stochastic. Garibaldi justifies this stochastic element by reference to the behaviour of Italian bureaucrats.

25. As has been done by Donald Deere, and Steven N. Wiggins, "Plant Closings, Advance Notice, and Private Contractual Failure," A&M University, Texas, November 1991; Peter Kuhn, "Mandatory Notice," *Journal of Labor Economics*, Vol. 10 (April 1992), pp. 117-37 and "Nonrevelation in Employment Contracts," *International Economic Review*, Vol. 35 (May 1994), pp. 261-82; and most recently J. Chilton and J. Addison, "Nondisclosure as a Contract Remedy: Explaining the Advance-Notice Puzzle," *Journal of Labor Economics*, Vol. 15, no. 1, part 1 (January 1997), pp. 143-64.

26. This is far from a necessary result, however, as asymmetric information models can lead to quite counterintuitive policy implications. For example, in Kuhn's model, mandatory notice can benefit firms while hurting workers (see "Mandatory Notice") and in Chilton and Addison's model it can hurt both parties (see "Nondisclosure as a Contract Remedy.") The main point is that mandatory notice is much more than a simple tax on layoffs, and as such its effects can be quite different from those of the tax.

27. See, for example, John T. Addison and Pedro Portugal, "The Effect of Advance Notification of Plant Closings on Unemployment," *Industrial and Labor Relations Review*, Vol. 41 (October 1987), pp. 3-16; R. Ehrenberg and G. Jakubson, *Advance Notice Provisions in Plant Closing Legislation* (Kalamazoo, MI: W. E. Upjohn Institute, 1988); P. Swaim and M. Podgursky, "Advance Notice and Job Search: The Value of an Early Start," *Journal of Human Resources*, Vol. 25 (Spring 1990), pp. 147-78; C. Ruhm, "Advance Notice and Postdisplacement Joblessness," *Journal of Labor Economics*, Vol. 10 (January 1992), pp. 1-28; S.R.G. Jones and P. Kuhn, "Mandatory Notice and Unemployment," *Journal of Labor Economics*, Vol. 13 (October 1995), pp. 599-622; Jane Friesen, "Mandatory Notice and the Jobless Durations of Displaced Workers," *Industrial and Labor Relations Review*, Vol. 50, no. 4 (July 1997), pp. 652-66; and N. Benos et al., "Advance Notice and Postdisplacement Joblessness: New Evidence," McMaster University, January 1997.

205

28. Chilton and Addison, "Nondisclosure as a Contract Remedy: Explaining the Advance Notice Puzzle."

29. M. Feldstein, "Temporary Layoffs in the Theory of Unemployment," *Journal of Political Economy*, Vol. 84, no. 5 (1976), pp. 937-57.

30. Giuseppe Bertola and Richard Rogerson, "Institutions and Labour Reallocation," *European Economic Review*, Vol. 41, no. 6 (June 1997), pp. 1147-71.

31. It is interesting to note the similarity between this argument and the Rehn-Meidner case for centralized wage setting in postwar Sweden: use standardized wages to shut down inefficient firms and encourage the growth of efficient ones.

32. Alison Booth and Gylfi Zoega, "Quitting Externalities, Employment Cyclicality and Firing Costs," working paper no. 959, ESRC, Research Centre on Micro-Social Change, 1995.

33. See R. Hall and E. Lazear, "The Excess Sensitivity of Layoffs and Quits to Demand," *Journal of Labor Economics*, Vol. 2, no. 2 (April 1984), pp. 233-57.

34. OECD, *The OECD Jobs Study: Evidence and Explanations: Part II: The Adjustment Potential of the Labour Market* (Paris: OECD, 1994).

35. If firms had the power to change wages, the whole notion of mandatory notice would be pointless: firms could just cut wages and induce workers to quit. Most analysts of EPLs therefore assume some kind of wage inflexibility. Note also that the absolute dollar costs of EPLs presented in tables 3 and 4 are independent of the assumption of $15 for a base productivity level. This number is assumed only to derive some representative percentage amounts.

36. Clearly, however, the productivity of the about-to-be-laid-off workers must have been greater than $15 in the recent past, otherwise they would not have been in the firm to begin with.

37. In practice, one would expect employees with negative productivity or those who pose a significant risk of sabotaging the firm's operations to be given severance pay in lieu of notice. The option of severance in lieu thus effectively puts a lower bound on how "unproductive" a redundant worker can be.

38. Abraham and Houseman, *Job Security in America: Lessons From Germany*.

39. Marc Van Audenrode, "Short-Time Compensation: Job Security, and Employment Contracts: Evidence from Selected OECD Countries," *Journal of Political Economy*, Vol. 102 (February 1994), pp. 76-102.

40. Susan N. Houseman, *Labour Market Adjustment in Europe, Japan and the United States* (Kalamazoo, MI: W.E. Upjohn Institute for Employment Research, 1995).

41. Conversation with Pietro Garibaldi, fall 1995.

42. John Addison and McKinley Blackburn, "The Worker Adjustment and Retraining Notification Act: Effects on Notice Provision," *Industrial and Labor Relations Review*, Vol. 47, no. 4 (1994), pp. 650-62.

43. Robert E. Lucas, Jr., "An Equilibrium Model of the Business Cycle," *Journal of Political Economy*, Vol. 83 (December 1975), pp. 1113-44.

44. See, for example, E. Prescott and M. Visscher, "Organization Capital," *Journal of Political Economy*, Vol. 88 (June 1980), pp. 446-61.

45. See for example, H. Lorne Carmichael and W. Bentley MacLeod, "Multiskilling, Technical Change and the Japanese Firm," *Economic Journal*, Vol. 103, no. 416 (January 1993), pp. 142-60.

46. Bertola and Rogerson, "Institutions and Labour Reallocation."

47. John Baldwin, Timothy Dunne and John Haltiwanger, "A Comparison of Job Creation and Job Destruction in Canada and the United States," research paper no. 64, Statistics Canada, Analytical Studies Branch, July 1994.

48. OECD, *Employment Outlook*.

49. Jonathan Leonard and Marc Van Audenrode, "A Difference of Degree: Unemployment Despite Turnover in the Belgian Labour Market," research paper no. 9523, Université Laval, 1995.

50. See also D. Hamermesh, W. Hassink and J. Van Ours, "Job Turnover and Labour Turnover: A Taxonomy of Employment Dynamics," University of Texas, Austin, 1994; and Jonathan S. Leonard and Marc Van Audenrode, "Corporatism Run Amok: Job Stability and Industrial Policy in Belgium and the United States," *Economic Policy: A European Forum*, Vol. 8, no. 17 (October 1993), pp. 355-89, for related evidence on the Netherlands and Belgium.

51. Lazear, "Job Security Provisions and Employment."

52. John T. Addison and Jean-Luc Grosso, "Job Security Provisions and Employment: Revised Estimates," *Industrial Relations*, Vol. 35 (October 1996), pp. 585-603.

53. Another problem with the notion that stringent EPLs cause unemployment to rise or employment to fall is timing: many European countries maintained a combination of low unemployment rates and high EPL until recently, and it is not at all clear that the recent rise in unemployment coincided with an increase in EPLs. This is probably why the differenced estimates in Lazear's paper perform so much worse than do the cross-sectional ones.

54. See, for example, K. Burdett and R. Wright, "Unemployment Insurance and Short-Time Compensation: The Effects on Layoffs, Hours per Worker, and Wages," *Journal of Political Economy*, Vol. 97 (December 1989), pp. 1479-96; and Van Audenrode, "Short-Time Compensation: Job Security, and Employment Contracts: Evidence from Selected OECD Countries." Addison and Grosso, "Job Security Provisions and Employment: Revised Estimates," do include a single variable that summarizes the generosity of a country's unemployment insurance system in their (necessarily short) list of controls.

55. R. Lacroix and M. Huberman, "Work Sharing in Historical Perspective" (Montreal: CIRANO, 1995).

56. Jones and Kuhn, "Mandatory Notice and Unemployment"; Bertola and Rogerson, "Institutions and Labour Reallocation"; OECD, *Employment Outlook*.

57. Jones and Kuhn, "Mandatory Notice and Unemployment."

58. Bertola and Rogerson, "Institutions and Labour Reallocation."

59. Other possible sources of wage rigidities are income support programs, such as employment insurance and welfare. To the extent that these programs provide an income floor that makes low-wage work relatively unattractive, they can be a source of real-wage rigidity at the bottom of the wage distribution. They can, of course, also have direct effects on employment simply by diminishing unemployed workers' incentives to become re-employed. The role of these programs, especially employment insurance, in explaining Canadian unemployment trends has been the subject of a considerable literature. See, for example, D. Card and W.C. Riddell, "A Comparative Analysis of Unemployment in Canada and the United States," in David Card and Richard Freeman (eds.), *Small Differences That Matter: Labour Markets and Income Maintenance in Canada and the United States*, NBER Comparative Labor Markets Series (Chicago and London: University of Chicago Press, 1993), pp. 149-89. While recognizing the potential importance of these programs in unemployment determination – I consider them prime alternatives to those examined in this paper – my focus in this paper is on whether direct restrictions on labour reallocation (EPLs) or direct restrictions on the repricing of labour (unions and minimum wages) can explain Canadian unemployment.

60. OECD, *Employment Outlook* (Paris: OECD, 1994), chart 5.1.

61. See for example, D. Card, "The Effect of Unions on the Structure of Wages: A Longitudinal Analysis," *Econometrica*, Vol. 64 (July 1996), pp. 957-79.

62. The evidence on the countercyclicality of the union-nonunion wage gap (see, for example H. Gregg Lewis, *Unionism and Relative Wages in the United States: An Empirical Inquiry* [Chicago, IL: University of Chicago Press, 1963]), does suggest that union wages show less cyclical sensitivity than nonunion wages. Whether this insensitivity extends to trade- or technology-induced shocks is open to question.

63. G. M. Grossman, "International Competition and the Unionized Sector," *Canadian Journal of Economics*, Vol. 17 (August 1984), pp. 541-56.

64. R. B. Freeman and L.F. Katz, "Industrial Wage and Employment Determination in an Open Economy," in J.M. Abowd and R. B. Freeman (eds.), *Immigration, Trade and the Labor Market* (Chicago, IL: University of Chicago Press, 1991) pp. 235-59.

65. C. Lawrence and R.Z. Lawrence, "Relative Wages in US Manufacturing: An End Game Interpretation," *Brookings Papers on Economic Activity*, Vol. 1 (1985), pp. 47-106.

66. J.M. Abowd and T. Lemieux, "The Effects of International Competition on Collective Bargaining Outcomes: A Comparison of the United States and Canada," in J.M. Abowd and R. B. Freeman (eds.), *Immigration, Trade and the Labor Market*, pp.343-68.

67. Another issue relating to the responsiveness of union wages to shocks that is particularly relevant in the European context is the degree of union centralization. The basic idea is that, if a union is big enough relative to the economy, and if it includes the unemployed in

its membership, then it internalizes all the externalities caused by raising wages and responds to shocks efficiently. This has led some authors (e.g., L. Calmfors and J. Driffil, "Bargaining Structure, Corporatism and Macroeconomic Performance," *Economic Policy*, Vol. 6 (April 1988), pp. 13-61) to propose a U-shaped relationship between national union power and economic performance, with partially unionized countries like Canada performing the worst.

68. This is not to say that that this debate about levels is uninteresting, only that I will not address it here. It is interesting to note that in most of the current literature, the debate over inflexible quantities (EPLs) is phrased in terms of levels (high EPLs cause high unemployment), while that over inflexible wages is phrased in terms of responsiveness to shocks.

69. A source of some confusion is that family income did not become substantially more unequal over this period. This is partly a result of the offsetting increases in male and female earnings but, more importantly, of the increased importance of public transfers to low-income families. See, for example, M. Blackburn and D. Bloom, "The Distribution of Family Income: Measuring and Explaining Changes in the 1980s for Canada and the United States," in Card and Freeman (eds.), *Small Differences that Matter*, pp. 233-66, and C. Beach and G. Slotsve, *Are We Becoming Two Societies? Income Polarization and the Myth of the Declining Middle Class in Canada* (Toronto: C.D. Howe Institute, 1996).

70. See, for example, Peter Kuhn and A. Leslie Robb, "Unemployment, Skill and Labour Supply: Evidence from Canadian Microdata, 1971-1991," in M. Abbott, C. Beach and R. Chaykowski (eds.), *North American Labour Markets in Transition* (Kingston, ON: Industrial Relations Centre and John Deutsch Institute, Queen's University, 1997), pp. 41-85 and Peter Kuhn and A. Leslie Robb, "Shifting Skill Demand and the Canada-US Unemployment Gap," *Canadian Public Policy*, Vol. 24 (Supplement, February 1998), pp. S170-91.

71. See, for example, J. DiNardo and T. Lemieux, "Diverging Male Wage Inequality in the United States and Canada, 1981-1988: Do Institutions Explain the Difference?" *Industrial and Labor Relations Review*, Vol. 50, no. 4 (July 1997), pp. 629-51.

72. See, for example, Kuhn and Robb, "Shifting Skill Demand and the Canada-US Unemployment Gap."

73. René Morisette, "Why has Inequality in Weekly Earnings Increased in Canada?" research paper no. 80, Analytical Studies Branch, Statistics Canada, July 1995; and G. Picot, "Working Time, Wages and Earnings Inequality among Men and Women in Canada: 1981-1993," paper presented at the CILN inaugural conference, Burlington, ON, September 4-7, 1997.

74. Kuhn and Robb, "Shifting Skill Demand and the Canada-US Unemployment Gap."

75. To some extent, Canada's greater decline in real weekly earnings in the bottom quintile was driven by macroeconomic forces such as the greater severity of the 1990s recession. See Pierre Fortin, "The Great Canadian Slump," *Canadian Journal of Economics*, Vol. 29 (November 1996), pp. 761-87. Whatever the source of the shock, the evidence that Canadian real wages fell substantially in response to it is very clear.

76. Suppose that log hours in the current week, log h, equals the "true" measure of hours we are interested in (log h*, or hours last year), plus an error term with mean zero. Then, because our ranking of workers into quintiles is based on a variable that is measured independently of log h (weekly earnings last year), the expected value of log h and log h*, conditional on the weekly earnings quintile, should be the same. In terms more familiar to economists, the expected value of the regression coefficient of log h on weekly earnings quintile should be unaffected by measurement error in the dependent variable, log h.

77. Picot, "Working Time, Wages and Earnings Inequality among Men and Women in Canada: 1981-1993."

78. Recently, the size of the real wage declines shown in tables 5 and 6 has been called into question by the report of the US Advisory Commission to Study the Consumer Price Index (1996), or Boskin Commission. According to the commission, the Consumer Price Index overstates US inflation by 1.1 percent a year, largely due to a failure to adjust adequately for improvements in product quality. For a critical review of the commission's findings, see Jeff Madrick, "The Cost of Living: A New Myth," *New York Review of Books*, March 6, 1997, pp. 19-23. Among other things, Madrick notes that the commission's proposed adjustments for quality changes are highly subjective and that the BLS already makes substantial adjustments for quality improvements, some of which may be excessive. The Boskin Commission's findings, of course, have no impact on our findings regarding the flexibility of the relative wages of skilled *versus* unskilled workers, only on the overall upward or downward trend of wage levels *per se.*

79. Picot, "Working Time, Wages and Earnings Inequality among Men and Women in Canada: 1981-1993."

80. DiNardo and Lemieux, "Diverging Male Wage Inequality in the United States and Canada."

81. Kuhn and Robb, "Unemployment, Skill and Labour Supply"; and "Shifting Skill Demand and the Canada-US Unemployment Gap."

82. John W. Budd, "Union Wage Determination in Canadian and US Manufacturing, 1964-1990: A Comparative Analysis," *Industrial and Labor Relations Review,* Vol. 49, no. 4 (July 1996), pp. 673-89, compares US and Canadian union wage bargaining up to 1990. He finds that during the 1980s, Canadian unions did a better job of maintaining real wages than US unions. Whether this pattern would extend to the 1990s, when Canada in particular experienced a large negative demand shock, is unclear. E. Prasad and A. Thomas, "Labour Market Adjustment in Canada and the United States," *Canadian Public Policy,* Vol. 24 (February 1998), pp. S121-37, present aggregate time-series evidence that suggests that there was a smaller real-wage response to demand shocks in Canada than in the US, but find this smaller wage response had only a limited effect on unemployment persistence.

83. See DiNardo and Lemieux, "Diverging Male Wage Inequality in the United States and Canada." This very useful study covers the period 1981-1988 only.

84. The appropriateness of the wage-inflexibility hypothesis has been examined for other sets of countries by David Card *et al.,* "Changes in the Relative Structure of Wages and Employment: A Comparison of the United States, Canada, and France," NBER working paper no. 5487, (March 1996), and Nickell and Bell, "The Collapse in Demand for the Unskilled and Unemployment Across the OECD." Card *et al.* compare Canada, the US and France; their main finding is that increases in unemployment which, according to the

hypothesis, should have been more concentrated among the unskilled in France than anywhere else, were instead quite evenly distributed there. Nickell and Bell, using summary statistics from a larger number of OECD countries, attribute only a small share of increased unemployment to relative demand shifts between skilled and unskilled workers.

85. W. C. Riddell and A. Sharpe, "The Canada-US Unemployment Rate Gap: An Introduction and Overview," *Canadian Public Policy,* Vol. 24 (February 1998), pp. S1-S35.

86. Edward E. Leamer, "Wage Inequality from International Competition and Technological Change: Theory and Country Experience," *American Economic Review,* Vol. 86, no. 2 (1996), pp. 309-14, explores this hypothesis in the European context for a set of OECD countries by computing the relative exposure of different countries to trade shocks.

87. Card and Riddell, "A Comparative Analysis of Unemployment in Canada and the United States."

88. This possibility is supported by the observation that, in contrast to North America, in countries without unemployment insurance systems, like India, unemployment is higher among educated than uneducated workers. With no real safety net, the unskilled simply cannot afford not to work. It is also supported by Kuhn and Robb ("Shifting Skill Demand and the Canada-US Unemployment Gap") who observe that, at fixed real wages, the labour supply of US men has increased in the past decade and a half.

89. Richard B. Freeman, "Crime and the Job Market," NBER working paper no. 4910, National Bureau on Economic Research, Washington, 1994.

90. Ian Macredie, "The Effects of Survey Instruments on the Canada/US Unemployment Rate Gap," paper presented at the CSLS/CERF Conference on the Canada-US Unemployment Rate Gap, Ottawa, February 9-10, 1996.

91. John Naisbitt, *Megatrends Asia: The Eight Asian Megatrends that are Changing the World* (London, ON: Nicholas Brealey, 1997).

209

Income Redistribution in Canada: Minimum Wages Versus Other Policy Instruments

Nicole M. Fortin and Thomas Lemieux

Introduction

Minimum-wage legislation is one of the oldest policy instrument of government intervention in the labour market. In Canada, the first minimum-wage laws, applicable to women in certain types of employment, were enacted during the 1910s. Six Canadian provinces had implemented such laws by 1920.[1] The scope of minimum-wage legislation gradually expanded over the years to cover young workers and men. By the 1960s, most workers were covered by minimum-wage laws. 211

The original policy objective of minimum-wage legislation was to protect women and children, who were perceived to be the most vulnerable and exploited groups of workers at that time. During the same period, related legislation regarding excessively long hours of work and unhealthy working conditions was introduced. In all cases, the basic goal of the legislation was to impose minimum standards in the conditions of employment.

The fundamental goal of minimum-wage legislation is to guarantee a decent or fair wage for all workers in the sectors covered. This type of legislation may also have other consequences (intended or unintended) for the workings of the labour market. Since Stigler, economists have questioned the principle of minimum-wage legislation because of its potential adverse effect on employment.[2] The textbook minimum-wage theory – in which a minimum wage set above the free market equilibrium for less-skilled labourers moves the economy along the demand curve and thus reduces employment – has long been at the centre of the argument against minimum wages. There is still much debate, however, over the empirical magnitude and importance of the adverse effect of minimum wages on employment. In their influential book, Card and Krueger argue that minimum wages have no adverse effect on employment in the United States.[3] Recent studies for Canada also suggest that minimum wages have, at best, only a small adverse effect on employment.[4]

Minimum-wage legislation may also help reduce poverty and thus serve as a redistributive tool, even if this is not its primary goal. If a large proportion of minimum-wage workers are poor, and raising the minimum wage effectively increases the income of these workers, then a higher minimum wage will help reduce poverty. It is not clear, however, that these conditions prevail in today's labour market.[5] It is often believed, as argued by Gramlich, that minimum-wage workers are mostly secondary earners; i.e., teenagers and wives, from middle- and high-income families.[6] Raising the incomes of these workers is clearly not an effective way to fight poverty. But, according to Benjamin, only 36 percent of minimum-wage workers in Canada, accounting for only 19 percent of hours worked, are teenagers.[7] He also finds that while the poorest families are not headed by minimum-wage earners – rather, they have no earner at all – more than 40 percent of minimum-wage earners come from low-income families.

If minimum wages are used to redistribute income, this raises the question of who pays for the redistribution. As underlined by Freeman, the answer to this question depends on the labour- and product-market conditions in the sectors where minimum-wage earners work.[8] The potential groups of payers are thus the consumers of goods produced by minimum-wage workers, the shareholders in businesses who employ minimum-wage workers, and the low-wage earners themselves who may suffer disemployment effects or longer unemployment spells. The answer may also depend on the other redistributive schemes. As argued by Webb, in the absence of a minimum wage, the community or the state may be partly subsidizing the employers of teenagers and wives who pay them "a wage insufficient to keep them in full efficiency."[9] In that respect, minimum wages may be seen as moving redistribution from the state to the market.

Finally, the minimum wage may be an effective tool to reduce wage inequality. DiNardo, Fortin and Lemieux have shown that the falling real value of the US federal minimum wage during the 1980s has contributed significantly to rising wage inequality there.[10] In the fiery debate on the pros and cons of minimum wages, relatively little emphasis has been placed on the effect of minimum wages on the reduction of wage inequality and, more generally, on the reduction of wage differentials between men and women and between younger and older workers.[11] This singular neglect of the effect of minimum wages on the reduction of inequality is particularly remarkable given that rising wage inequality and changes in the gender-wage gap have attracted much attention in the recent economic literature. The debate on these issues reflects the same concerns about social justice and fairness as were at the heart of the early minimum-wage legislation. Such concerns may explain ongoing public support for these policies.

The first goal of this paper is to investigate the contribution of minimum wages to the reduction of inequality in Canada. For that purpose, we analyze the effect of minimum wages on the distribution of wages using Statistics Canada's 1988 Labour Market Activity Survey (LMAS) and 1995 Survey of Work Arrangements (SWA).

The second goal of the paper is to compare the redistributive impact of minimum wages with that of other policy instruments. We do this by studying the impact of minimum wages on the distribution of family income (based on an income-to-needs ratio) relative to other redistributive programs using Statistics Canada's 1993 Survey of Labour and Income Dynamics (SLID). If minimum wages are to be used as redistributive instruments, they must increase the wages of low-paid workers significantly; in other words, they must have some bite.

The other important queries – who pays and what are the unintended consequences on employment – have already attracted much attention in the literature and are not addressed directly in this paper. These two concerns – who benefits and who bears the cost – are not unrelated. Evaluating the impact of the minimum wage on the distribution of wages may help assess its negative efficiency effects. The more bite the minimum wage has, the more likely it is to affect the employment opportunities of less-skilled workers. If the negative efficiency effects of the minimum wage were found to be important at a given wage level in a particular economy, these effects would have to be weighed against its potentially beneficial redistributive effects.

In addition to the minimum wage, we consider two other redistributive instruments: social assistance (SA) and unemployment insurance (UI). These are the two most important income support programs not directed at the elderly. Note that these redistributive programs may also entail some disemployment effects. A comprehensive comparison of the various programs would have to take these potential disemployment effects into account. This formidable task, however, is beyond the scope of this study. Here, we set a more modest objective of assessing the relative effectiveness of these programs in redistributing income.

Minimum Wages and the Distribution of Wages

Our first objective is to find out which groups of workers are most helped by the minimum wage and whether it has a significant impact on the wage distribution of the groups affected.

nicole m. fortin and thomas lemieux

Data

Using US data, DiNardo, Fortin and Lemieux showed that a sizeable proportion of the workforce (up to 12 percent in 1979, but only 4 percent in 1988) earns the minimum wage, and that high minimum wages have an important impact on the shape of the distribution of wages. In a histogram, the large concentration of workers at the minimum wage translates into a spike at that value. In a smoothed histogram, this spike is smoothed, so that instead of looking like a bell curve, the distribution of wages has its lower tail compressed by the minimum wage. When attempting to reproduce a similar analysis for Canada, we are confronted with two problems. First, there are many effective minimum wages in Canada, which calls for an analysis at the provincial level. Second, large databases containing reliable hourly wage data on which a detailed analysis by province could be based, are not yet available for the 1990s.[12] These problems must be kept in mind when considering the evidence below. In the only other Canadian study of the effect of minimum wages on the distribution of wages to date, Green and Paarsch focus on teenage wage distributions over the 1980s.[13] Shannon focuses on the effect of minimum wages on the gender gap in 1986.[14]

During the 1980s in Canada (and in the United States) minimum wages did not keep pace with inflation or rising average industrial wages, despite frequent nominal increases.[15] While the precise year when the ratio of the minimum wage to the average industrial wage reached its lowest point varies by province, it is generally not until the 1990s that the downward trend in this ratio was stopped or reversed. We use the 1995 SWA and the 1988 LMAS to compare the distribution of hourly wages.[16] The nominal value of minimum wages in the 10 provinces for these years, the average industrial wage and the ratio of the minimum wage to that average are reported in table 1. The table shows that in 1988 the ratio hovered in the low 40-percent range; by 1995, it was over 45 percent in Ontario and Quebec. In figure 1 we indicate the lowest and highest of these provincial minimum-wage values by a vertical line. We do not use the distinction between the adult minimum wage and the youth subminimum since, as reported by Katz and Krueger and Baker, Benjamin and Stanger, the youth subminimum is seldom used.[17]

A graphically clear way to illustrate the impact of minimum wages on the distribution of hourly wages is to picture the distribution using a smoothed histogram whose area is equal to one, called a *kernel density* estimate.[18] The kernel density estimates for men and women for the years 1988 and 1995 are shown in figure 1. The kernel density estimates presented in this paper reflect the distribution of wages per hour worked in the economy rather than the distribution of

214

Table 1
The Minimum Wage Relative to the Average Industrial Wage[1] by Province, 1988, 1993 and 1995

PROVINCE	1988			1993			1995		
	Adult minimum wage	Average industrial wage	Ratio	Adult minimum wage	Average industrial wage	Ratio	Adult minimum wage	Average industrial wage	Ratio
Newfoundland	4.25	9.71	0.44	4.75	11.80	0.40	4.75	12.43	0.38
PEI	4.25	8.17	0.52	4.75	9.89	0.48	4.75	10.37	0.46
Nova Scotia	4.00	10.13	0.39	5.15	11.77	0.44	5.15	11.22	0.46
New Brunswick	4.00	10.01	0.40	5.00	11.89	0.42	5.00	12.11	0.41
Quebec	4.75	11.23	0.42	5.85	13.59	0.43	6.45	14.03	0.46
Ontario	4.75	11.64	0.41	6.35	14.06	0.45	6.85	14.80	0.46
Manitoba	4.70	10.57	0.44	5.00	12.32	0.41	5.25	12.51	0.42
Saskatchewan	4.50	10.38	0.43	5.35	11.70	0.46	5.35	12.74	0.42
Alberta	4.50	10.73	0.42	5.00	12.91	0.39	5.00	12.81	0.39
British Columbia	4.50	12.61	0.36	6.00	14.99	0.40	7.00	16.39	0.43

[1] Average hourly earnings by industry, industrial aggregate excluding education industries, excluding overtime, monthly, not seasonally adjusted, employees paid by the hour, firms of all sizes.

Note: Minimum wages are measured in November of each year.

Source: Labour Canada; CANSIM.

nicole m. fortin and thomas lemieux

Figure 1

The Impact of Minimum Wages on the Distribution of Hourly Wages by Gender, Canada, 1988 and 1995

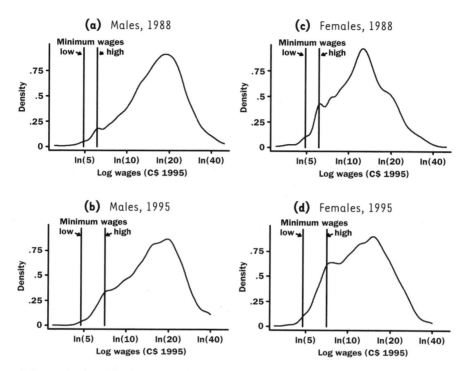

Note: Based on kernel density estimates of real log wages in 1995 dollars.

wages per worker. Rather than focusing only on full-time workers, we include part-time workers in our samples but weight the observations by the weekly hours of work to better reflect the contribution of each worker to the labour market.[19]

We define as minimum-wage workers individuals whose wage is within 25 cents of the provincial minimum wage.[20] Under this definition, minimum-wage workers accounted for 3.5 percent of the hours worked in 1988. For 1995, it is more difficult to identify minimum-wage workers *per se* because of a rounding problem.[21] However, applying a similar definition, the proportion of hours worked by low-wage workers was 5.3 percent in that year.

The Impact of Minimum Wages on the Distribution of Wages

Figure 1 shows that the impact of minimum wages on the shape of the distribution of male and female wages was more important in 1995 than in 1988. In

1988, the distributions exhibit a more or less regular bell shape with small humps around the highest minimum wage. In 1995, the minimum-wage hump has gained more importance, and there is a sizeable increase in the lower part of the distribution in 1995 relative to 1988. The proportion of hours worked by men at a wage between $5.00 and $10.00 increased from 15 percent in 1988 to 22 percent in 1995; among women, that proportion increased from 32 percent to 36 percent. In 1995, the minimum wage seems to push up or compress the bottom end of the female wage distribution. Such an effect would be consistent with the view that increasing the minimum wage may also raise wages above the minimum wage, as argued by Grossman, for example.[22] In the US, Card and Krueger did find these small spillover effects for wages just above the minimum.[23] In Canada, Benjamin found only limited evidence of such spillover effects in 1990. This limited evidence is consistent with our 1988 density estimates.

It is difficult, however, to go beyond this simple visual evidence of the impact of the minimum wage on the wage distribution in 1995. When we simulate what the distribution of male and female wages would have been in the absence of a minimum wage in 1995, we find sizeable changes in the asymmetry (or skewness) of the distributions.[24] This simulation implies, however, almost no change in the standard deviation of wages. These results should be interpreted with caution because there are some difficulties with the SWA data.[25]

Furthermore, there are other factors (e.g., unionization) that work in the other direction and tend to spread out the wage distribution. The changes in distributions between 1988 and 1995, illustrated in figure 1, are still notable given that over the 1980s the distribution of hourly wages in Canada remained remarkably stable.[26] As noted by Picot, changes in earnings inequality over the 1980s were mostly due to changes in hours of work; i.e., more hours worked per week by men and more weeks per year by women among higher earners. He finds that changes in the distribution of hourly wages played a much smaller role. He also finds "a slightly larger share of jobs at the very bottom of the distribution" in 1993 compared with 1986, but notes that different cyclical patterns might have been at work.[27] Our findings suggest that while there is no significant change in wage inequality from 1988 to 1995, as measured by the 90-10 wage differential, for example, there are increases in the proportion of hours worked at lower wages that correspond with the increase in mass at the bottom of the wage distributions.[28]

Figure 2 superimposes the density estimates of the distributions of male wages for 1988 (dotted line) and 1995 (solid line) for each of the six regions considered. Because of the small number of observations available in the SWA, we had to regroup the observations for some provinces for which we

Figure 2

The Impact of Minimum Wages on the Distribution of Male Hourly
Wages by Region, Canada, 1988 and 1995

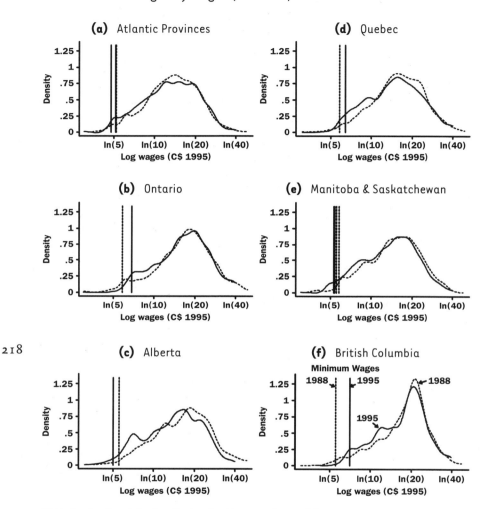

(a) Atlantic Provinces

(b) Ontario

(c) Alberta

(d) Quebec

(e) Manitoba & Saskatchewan

(f) British Columbia

Note: Based on kernel density estimates of real log wages in 1995 dollars.

did not have enough observations to obtain reliable kernel density estimates.
Figure 2 shows even more clearly than did figure 1 the increases in the proportion of hours worked by men at lower wages. There are a few regions: the
Atlantic provinces, Ontario and British Columbia, where minimum wages
appear to act as a wage floor. The figure also shows clear union peaks around
$20.00 in Ontario and British Columbia.

adapting public policy to a labour market in transition

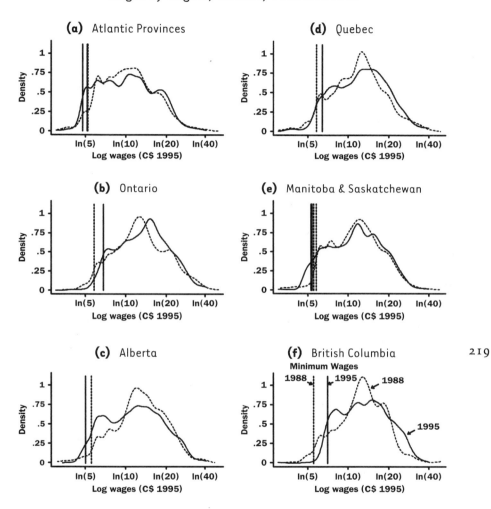

Figure 3

The Impact of Minimum Wages on the Distribution of Female Hourly Wages by Region, Canada, 1988 and 1995

(a) Atlantic Provinces

(d) Quebec

(b) Ontario

(e) Manitoba & Saskatchewan

(c) Alberta

(f) British Columbia

Minimum Wages
1988   1995   1988
1995

Note: Based on kernel density estimates of real log wages in 1995 dollars.

Figure 3 illustrates the results of the same exercise for women. The striking feature in these graphs is the union peak around $12.00 in 1988, which widens in most regions in 1995. Unionized workers make up a substantial proportion of all workers: they represent 34 percent of female workers in 1988 and 39 percent in 1995 (among men, these proportions are 41 percent in 1988 and 43 percent in 1995). This union peak visually masks the importance of the minimum

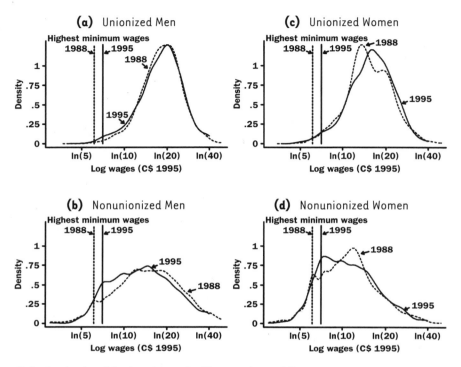

Figure 4
The Impact of Minimum Wages on the Distribution of Hourly Wages of Unionized / Nonunionized Workers by Gender, Canada, 1988 and 1995

Note: Based on kernel density estimates of real log wages in 1995 dollars.

wage as a floor for female wage distributions. For that reason, in figure 4 we present densities estimated separately for unionized and nonunionized workers. Figure 4 shows that in 1995 the mode of the wage distribution among nonunionized women, that is, the wage for which the proportion of hours worked is the highest, was $7.00, the highest minimum wage. For nonunionized men, minimum wages appear to be important as well.

The characteristics of minimum-wage workers go beyond this divide between nonunionized and unionized workers, the latter including almost no minimum-wage workers. Table 2 shows the changing characteristics of low-wage workers over the 1988-95 period. In 1988, low-wage male and female workers were mostly younger (under 24), whereas in 1995 a majority of low-wage female workers were 24 and over. In both years, low-wage workers are underrepresented among university graduates. Minimum-wage workers are mostly concentrated in sales

Table 2

Characteristics of Low-Wage Workers, Canada, 1988 and 1995

| | Percentage of hours worked by low-wage workers | | | |
| | 1988 | | 1995 | |
CHARACTERISTICS	Male	Female	Male	Female
Share of low-wage workers in the workforce	1.6	3.1	3.7	7.1
AGE GROUP				
Younger (≤ 24)	57.5	57.7	59.0	46.8
Older (>24)	42.6	42.2	41.0	53.2
EDUCATION				
8 years or less	15.2	7.0	4.9	7.0
High school and post-secondary	77.6	88.0	88.3	88.7
University degree	7.2	5.0	6.8	4.3
OCCUPATION				
Professionals, managers, & health care workers	19.5	12.4	5.5	5.0
Clerical workers	6.0	20.4	9.0	19.6
Sales persons	12.7	20.6	24.0	24.0
Service workers	25.2	37.2	37.4	39.2
Craft workers	14.1	5.6	18.3	7.8
Labourers	9.4	2.8	9.4	3.5
Primary sector workers	13.2	1.0	4.1	0.9

Note: In 1988, low-wage workers are those whose wage is within $0.25 of provincial minimum wage; in 1995, hourly wages are available only to the dollar, low-wage workers are identified less precisely as mini mum-wage workers. Observations are weighed by the product of the sample weight and the number of hours worked a week.
Source: Authors' calculations from the 1988 LMAS and 1995 SWA.

and service occupations. The growth in low-wage occupations has taken place mostly in service occupations, thus mirroring general economic trends.

Figure 5 illustrates the dramatic decline in the labour market opportunities of younger male and female workers. While in 1988 young men and young women had bell-shaped wage distributions and a substantial proportion had jobs in the $10.00-$20.00-an-hour range, in 1995 that proportion had declined substantially and the mode of both distributions was at the minimum wage. It is interesting to note that the difference in the shapes of the 1988 and 1995 densities for young workers mirrors to some extent the differences in the shapes of the densities of teenage workers who were and were not receiving the minimum wage, as estimated by Green and Paarsch.[29] This lends some support to

Figure 5
The Impact of Minimum Wages on the Distribution of Hourly Wages of Young Workers by Gender, Canada, 1988 and 1995

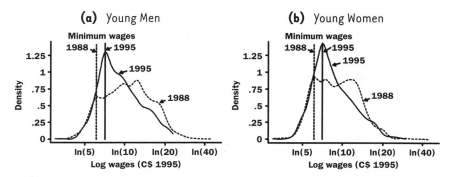

Note: Based on kernel density estimates of real log wages in 1995 dollars for workers aged 24 or younger.

our interpretation that the spikes in figure 5 are, to a large extent, attributable to the higher minimum wage. What is unclear is whether there is a link between the higher minimum wage and the decline in the proportion of hours worked at wages higher than $10.00 an hour from 1988 to 1995.

The decline in labour market opportunities for men has been documented by several authors including Beaudry and Green, and Morissette.[30] They show that the age-earnings profile of recent cohorts of young men has shifted downward relative to the age-earnings profiles of previous cohorts. These studies also suggest that young men who start today at lower wages than their counterparts did in the mid-1970s may also have lower earnings growth thereafter. Card and Lemieux, and Meunier *et al.* show that limited labour market opportunities among young people lead them to stay with their parents well into their mid-20s and delay household formation.[31] Many young people are unable to find permanent, well-paying jobs and settle for minimum-wage jobs.

In summary, this evidence suggests that in 1995 minimum wages played an important role as a wage floor for all women and for young men. As such, it could be argued that it reduced the wage gap between men and women and between the young and the old. Minimum wages and unionization rates were higher in 1995 than they were in 1988. These two institutional factors can be seen as a powerful counterforce against the increasing wage inequality stemming from the increase in low-wage jobs. On the other hand, it could also be argued that the larger role of the minimum wage in 1995 led to larger disemployment effects than it did in 1988.

The Impact of Minimum Wages and Other Redistributive Programs on the Distribution of Family Income

Having provided evidence that minimum wages have some impact on wage distribution in Canada, particularly that of women and young workers, we now want to assess their value as policy instruments for redistributing income. This involves several positive and normative issues. On the positive side, we want to know how big the minimum wage is as a program for redistributing income, and who benefits the most from it. In other words, we want to evaluate the size and the incidence of the minimum wage viewed as a transfer program. We also want to know how the minimum wage fares as a redistribution program relative to other programs in the policy arsenal. We will compare the minimum wage with UI and SA, which are the two largest transfer programs for the non-elderly in Canada.[32] We will also address the normative issue of how good or efficient the minimum wage is as an instrument for redistribution.

Throughout this section, we assume that the minimum wage has no adverse effect on employment. We will thus overstate the redistributive benefits of the minimum wage if it does have such an adverse impact, since some low-wage workers would lose their jobs when the minimum-wage increases. We also assume that the minimum wage has no effect on the wages of workers earning more than the minimum wage (no spillover effects). This assumption probably leads us to understate the redistributive benefits of the minimum wage, since the earnings of low-wage workers earning slightly more than the minimum wage may well increase when the minimum wage increases.

223

In theory, we may either be understating or overstating the redistributive benefits of the minimum wage, depending on the importance of disemployment effects relative to the spillover effects. Since most of the empirical evidence suggests that neither effect is particularly large, we have ignored the distributive impact of disemployment and spillover effects.[33]

Data

Until recently, it would have been difficult to compare the importance and incidence of the minimum wage relative to UI and SA because of limitations in the data. Fortunately, all the necessary information is now available in the first cross-sectional wave (1993) of the SLID. The SLID contains detailed information on all sources of individual and family income, hourly wages, annual hours of work and family composition (see the appendix for more details). We can thus classify individuals by their level of individual or family income and then compare the impact of the minimum wage relative to other transfer programs using the same

nicole m. fortin and thomas lemieux

categories of family income. Using the LMAS, Benjamin was only able to look at the incidence of the minimum wage on the distribution of family earnings (by decile), since this data set does not contain information on sources of income other than earnings.[34] Our study provides the first opportunity to look at the link between minimum-wage earnings and family income in Canada.

The Importance and Incidence of the Minimum Wage

Table 3 presents three measures of the importance of the minimum wage for the country as a whole and for the provinces separately. As before, we define minimum-wage workers as individuals who held at least one wage-and-salary job paying between 25 cents below and 25 cents above the minimum wage in 1993.[35] The first column reports the proportion of wage-and-salary workers who worked at the minimum wage in 1993. This ranges from 4.7 percent in Alberta to 11.5 in Newfoundland. As a general rule, a smaller fraction of individuals tend to earn the minimum wage in the three richer provinces (Ontario, Alberta and British Columbia) than in the other provinces. For the country as a whole, 6 percent of wage-and-salary workers earn the minimum wage. This is comparable to Benjamin's figure, despite important differences between his and our definition of minimum-wage workers.[36] The proportion is smaller than that typically found in the United States.[37]

An alternative measure of the importance of the minimum wage is the proportion of hours worked (by wage-and-salary workers) at the minimum wage. This figure is 3.6 percent in Canada, which is smaller than the proportion of workers who earn the minimum wage (6 percent) and reflects the fact that minimum-wage workers tend to work fewer hours per year than other workers. The minimum wage looks even less important when it is measured as the ratio of the earnings of minimum-wage workers over total earnings (third column), which is 1.5 percent for Canada. This figure is four times smaller than the ratio of minimum-wage workers as a proportion of all workers, because minimum-wage workers work fewer hours and have much lower wages (by definition) than the rest of the workforce.

The basic message of table 3 is that the minimum wage is a small transfer program in Canada.[38] Furthermore, only a fraction of this 1.5 percent of earnings represents a transfer to minimum-wage workers, since most of them would surely have earned something even in the absence of a minimum wage. For example, assume that the minimum wage doubles the average wage of minimum-wage workers and has no disemployment effects. In this case, the minimum wage would effectively transfer 0.75 percent of total earnings to minimum-wage workers.[39]

Table 3

Percentage of Workers, Hours of Work, and Earnings
at the Minimum Wage, Canada, 1993

	% of all workers	% of all hours worked	% of all earnings
Canada	6.0	3.6	1.5
Newfoundland	11.5	6.5	2.6
PEI	7.8	5.3	2.1
Nova Scotia	6.3	4.2	1.6
New Brunswick	7.3	4.0	1.8
Quebec	6.7	4.2	1.7
Ontario	5.0	3.1	1.4
Manitoba	8.3	5.3	2.3
Saskatchewan	9.5	6.2	2.8
Alberta	4.7	2.4	0.9
British Columbia	5.7	3.1	1.3

Note: Minimum-wage workers are those whose wage is
within $0.25 of provincial minimum wage.
Source: Authors' calculations from the 1993 SLID.

Even if the minimum wage is only a small program in aggregate, it could still have a sizable effect on specific groups of workers likely to earn low wages. Tables 4 and 5 present the incidence of minimum-wage employment and earnings and the incidence of total wage-and-salary earnings and employment for men and women, respectively, in 1993. Most noticeable is the fact that minimum-wage employment and earnings are disproportionately concentrated among young workers. Among men, 29.3 percent of minimum-wage workers are teenagers (aged 16-18) and 41.5 percent are young adults (aged 19-23), despite the fact that these two groups represent only 4.5 percent and 11.8 percent of the male workforce, respectively. As mentioned earlier, the age groups used in this paper are not strictly comparable to those used in other studies, where teenagers are defined as workers aged 15-19 and young adults as workers aged 20-24. A back-of-the-envelope calculation suggests that the 15-19 and 20-24 age groups would represent 44.2 and 36.9 percent of minimum-wage workers, respectively, if standard age groupings were available in the SLID.[40]

Women are also more likely to work at the minimum wage (table 5). Sixty-four percent of minimum-wage workers are women, even though women represent only 48 percent of the entire workforce. Perhaps not surprisingly, young

Table 4

Distribution of Male Wage-and-Salary Workers and Male
Minimum-Wage Workers by Age, Education and Family Status, 1993

	MALE POPULATION	Male wage & salary workers			Male minimum-wage workers		
		% of all workers	% of all hours worked	% of all earnings	% of all workers	% of all hours worked	% of all earnings
MALE SHARE	50.0	52.3	57.6	62.8	37.3	37.9	37.8
AGE GROUP							
16 – 18	6.5	4.5	1.5	0.6	29.3	15.5	15.1
19 – 23	10.4	11.8	8.6	4.5	41.5	41.7	41.7
24 – 63	83.1	83.7	90.0	94.9	29.2	42.8	43.2
EDUCATION							
Drop-out	26.8	22.0	20.1	16.4	33.6	31.7	32.2
High school	14.5	15.0	15.8	14.3	15.5	19.6	19.1
Some postsecondary	15.0	15.5	14.0	11.8	35.5	35.2	35.4
College or trade	29.3	32.1	33.3	34.9	10.1	10.2	9.9
University degree	14.4	15.4	16.8	22.6	5.3	3.3	3.4
FAMILY STATUS							
Younger (16-23)	16.9	16.3	10.0	5.1	70.8	57.2	56.8
Living alone	10.4	11.3	15.4	16.1	7.8	10.1	10.2
Head	4.5	6.1	10.0	12.9	2.2	1.2	1.3
Living with parents	52.7	50.2	43.4	41.6	60.4	57.5	57.1
Living with lone parent	15.3	14.6	12.8	11.0	17.9	16.6	17.0
Unidentified	17.1	17.8	17.9	18.5	11.7	14.4	14.4
Older (24-63)							
Living alone	13.5	12.7	12.4	11.5	22.3	23.6	24.8
Spouse without kids	21.2	19.8	19.7	19.8	13.7	11.8	11.7
Spouse with kids	45.5	49.2	50.4	53.6	28.4	35.0	34.3
Lone father	1.8	1.6	1.5	1.5	1.4	0.8	0.4
Unidentified	18.0	16.6	16.0	13.6	34.3	28.7	28.3

Note: Minimum-wage workers are those whose wage is within $0.25 of the provincial minimum wage.
Source: Authors' calculations from the 1993 SLID.

workers represent a smaller fraction of minimum-wage workers among women than among men. Among women, more than half of minimum-wage earnings (57.2 percent) are earned by adults (aged 24-63). Among men, this proportion is lower (43.2 percent). For men and women considered together, slightly more than half of minimum-wage earnings (51.9 percent) are earned by adults, despite the fact that only 38.7 percent of minimum-wage workers are adults.[41] This

Table 5

Distribution of Female Wage-and-Salary Workers and Female Minimum-Wage Workers by Age, Education and Family Status, 1993

	FEMALE POPULATION	Female wage & salary workers			Female minimum-wage workers		
		% of all workers	% of all hours worked	% of all earnings	% of all workers	% of all hours worked	% of all earnings
FEMALE SHARE	50.0	47.7	42.4	37.2	63.7	62.1	62.2
AGE GROUP							
16 – 18	5.9	4.4	1.5	0.7	23.0	13.9	13.8
19 – 23	10.6	12.3	9.3	5.6	32.5	29.1	29.0
24 – 63	83.6	83.3	89.2	93.7	44.5	57.0	57.2
EDUCATION							
Drop-out	24.2	16.1	13.8	10.2	29.0	26.6	26.4
High school	17.3	16.6	16.9	14.9	18.6	20.8	21.1
Some postsecondary	14.8	15.7	14.0	12.2	25.4	21.9	21.9
College or trade	31.3	37.0	38.7	39.9	22.6	28.9	28.9
University degree	12.4	14.7	16.6	22.4	4.5	1.7	1.7
FAMILY STATUS							
Younger (16-23)	16.4	16.7	10.8	6.3	55.5	43.0	42.8
Living alone	10.1	11.6	16.0	17.5	9.2	7.6	7.3
Head	13.0	14.2	18.6	20.8	7.4	6.8	6.8
Living with parents	45.9	45.0	38.6	36.1	47.7	44.4	44.2
Living with lone parent	11.0	11.0	8.6	7.5	12.2	11.2	11.1
Unidentified	20.0	18.2	18.2	18.1	23.0	30.0	30.9
Older (24-63)							
Living alone	12.4	13.1	15.2	16.7	12.1	10.0	10.5
Spouse without kids	21.5	20.1	21.2	21.1	21.2	20.6	20.4
Spouse with kids	43.0	46.0	46.0	42.1	40.6	40.4	40.5
Lone mother	7.3	6.6	6.6	6.8	10.0	11.6	11.5
Unidentified	15.8	14.2	14.2	14.4	16.0	17.4	17.2

Note: Minimum-wage workers are those whose wage is within $0.25 of the provincial minimum wage.
Source: Authors' calculations from the 1993 SLID.

227

reflects the fact that adult minimum-wage earners tend to work more hours than teenagers and young adults.

Minimum-wage workers also tend to be less educated than other wage-and-salary workers. Among men, high-school dropouts represent 33.6 percent of minimum-wage earners but only 22 percent of the whole workforce. In contrast, university graduates represent only 5.3 percent of male minimum-wage workers, even though they represent 15.4 percent of the male workforce. A similar pattern is observed for women (table 5). The differences between the educational groups are even more pronounced when we look at the distribution of hours of work and earnings. Overall, our findings on the distribution of minimum-wage workers by age and education are similar to those reported by Benjamin for 1990.

The last two panels of tables 4 and 5 show a detailed breakdown of the incidence of the minimum wage among youth (aged 16-23) and adults (aged 24-63) by type of family arrangement. The tables indicate that 68 percent of young men and 57 percent of young women live with their parents (in either dual-parent or lone-parent families).[42] Youth living with their parents are overrepresented among minimum-wage workers. This suggests that a substantial fraction of young minimum-wage workers may be living in relatively well-to-do families, even if their own earnings are low.

Among adults, there is a relatively high incidence of minimum-wage workers among men living alone and lone mothers. For example, men living alone represent 12.7 percent of all male workers but 22.3 percent of male minimum-wage workers. Similarly, lone mothers represent 6.6 percent of the female workforce but 10 percent of female minimum-wage workers. The incidence of the minimum wage by family status indicates that a disproportionate share of adult minimum-wage earners are the sole wage earners in the family, while the opposite is true for youth. The earnings of minimum-wage workers are thus more likely to be the only source of family income for adults than for youth. This suggests a stronger connection between the minimum wage and family income for adults than for youth.

We explore the connection between the incidence of the minimum wage and family income in more detail in table 6. More precisely, we compute a family income-to-needs ratio for each individual by dividing total family income by the family equivalence scale.[43] The advantage of using a family income-to-needs ratio is that it is more directly related to the economic well-being of individuals than are other income measures. For instance, many individuals, particularly young people, might live in wealthy families even if their own incomes are low. Thus it is better to look at the income of the whole family than at the income of one member of the family. Furthermore, a family equivalence scale is necessary to take account of the fact that larger families need a higher family income to achieve the same economic well-being than do smaller families. Note that we find qualitatively similar results when we look at the distribution of unadjusted family incomes instead.

We then divide the sample into deciles based on these income-to-needs ratios. The first column of table 6 presents the distribution of minimum-wage

228

Table 6
Distribution of Minimum-Wage Workers and Earnings by Decile of Adjusted Family Income, Canada, 1993

DECILE	Minimum-wage workers			Minimum-wage earnings		
	All minimum-wage workers	Youth living with parents[1]	Youth living with parents/all	All minimum-wage earnings	Youth living with parents[1]	Youth living with parents/all
1st	12.5	6.1	20.4	10.1	4.0	12.2
2nd	13.9	7.7	23.2	13.1	8.5	19.8
3rd	16.7	16.2	40.4	21.3	17.0	24.5
4th	12.0	13.6	47.0	12.2	13.9	34.9
5th	12.2	16.1	54.8	11.3	16.7	45.1
6th	8.4	9.4	46.5	7.8	7.4	29.0
7th	7.9	11.2	58.8	8.5	11.2	40.3
8th	7.4	9.2	51.8	6.0	10.6	54.2
9th	4.4	4.9	47.1	4.6	5.8	38.5
10th	4.7	5.6	49.3	5.1	5.0	29.9
First 5	67.3	59.7	36.9	68.0	60.1	27.1
Last 5	32.7	51.2	32.0	39.9	38.3	38.3

[1] Youth living with their parents are under the age of 24 and live with their parents in a husband/wife/children family or in a lone-parent family.
Note: Family income is adjusted using a family income-to-needs ratio.
Source: Authors' calculations from the 1993 SLID.

workers across deciles. It clearly shows that minimum-wage workers are more concentrated in the bottom than the top end of the distribution. For example, 67.3 percent of minimum-wage workers are in the first 5 deciles of the distribution. Note however, that there are more minimum-wage workers in the second (13.9 percent) and third (16.7 percent) deciles than in the first decile (12.5 percent).[44] This is explained by the fact that the poorest families (first decile) tend to be poor because individuals in these families do not work very much. We discuss this issue in more detail below.

The second column of table 6 shows the same distribution for youth living with their parents (in dual-parent or lone-parent families). As a general rule, young minimum-wage workers living with their parents are less concentrated in the bottom of the distribution than are other minimum-wage workers. This is especially true in the 2 lowest deciles, where the proportion of young minimum-wage workers living with their parents is two times lower than the corresponding proportion among all minimum-wage workers. This pattern

nicole m. fortin and thomas lemieux

can also be seen in the third column. Young workers living with their parents only account for 20 percent of all minimum-wage workers in the first 2 deciles, compared with around 50 percent in middle and upper deciles. Notice, however, that young minimum-wage workers living with their parents are still disproportionally represented in the 5 lowest deciles (bottom of the second column).

The proportion of minimum-wage earnings earned by workers in the 5 lowest deciles (fourth column) is almost identical to the proportion of minimum-wage earners in these deciles. Using earnings accentuates the gap between the first and third deciles of the distribution (10.1 percent and 21.3 percent of all minimum-wage earnings, respectively). This, once again, reflects the fact that individuals in the first decile supply fewer hours (at or above the minimum wage) than do individuals in other deciles. The last two columns show that the earnings of young minimum-wage workers living with their parents are less concentrated in the lowest 5 deciles than are the earnings of all minimum-wage workers.

In summary, minimum-wage workers tend to be concentrated in the lower half of the distribution of adjusted family income. This is true even for youth living with their parents, who disproportionally come from the lower-middle class (deciles 3 to 5). Our results clearly do not support the view that typical minimum-wage workers are teenagers living in upper-class (deciles 9 and 10) or upper-middle-class (deciles 6 to 8) families. This being said, the minimum wage remains a small transfer program, which limits its ability to change the distribution of family income in Canada in a quantitatively important way.[45]

The Minimum Wage Compared with other Redistributive Policies

Broadly speaking, the minimum wage and other programs like SA and UI can achieve some redistributive objectives, even if this is not their primary goal. While the objectives and design features of the programs are clear, their precise redistributive outcomes are not. By definition, minimum-wage laws are designed to increase the wages of workers who would otherwise usually earn less than the minimum wage because they are less skilled, less productive or excluded from higher-wage jobs for other reasons. In contrast, SA provides a basic level of income to families that have few or no other sources of income, and UI provides income support to workers who are temporarily out of work. Since these programs target individuals with low incomes and/or low wages, they should all have some redistributive benefits.

Conceptually, there are several reasons why it is difficult to compare the actual distributional impact of these programs. The first problem is that the programs are much more complex than indicated by the stylized descriptions provided above. For example, not all workers are covered by the minimum wage; eligibility to SA benefits is subject to income and asset tests; and the duration of UI benefits depends on the duration of the previous job and on the state of the local labour market. It is, therefore, difficult to compare the distributional impacts of these programs on the basis of their design features. We will take instead a resolutely empirical approach and present the actual incidence of these programs by decile of adjusted family income.

The second problem is that, unless labour market choices are exogenous, the incentives provided by the various programs will affect the behaviour of workers. This will in turn affect the redistributive benefits of the programs. On the one hand, a higher minimum wage may provide incentives to the workers affected to supply more hours in the labour market (if the labour supply elasticity is positive). The income of these workers might, therefore, increase more than it would have in the absence of this behavioural response. On the other hand, the adverse employment effects (on the employer's side) of the higher minimum wage could reduce the income of minimum-wage workers by reducing their hours of work and worsen their position.

SA perhaps provides even stronger incentives to workers to alter their behaviour. Above a small "disregard" amount, a dollar earned by a SA claimant results in SA benefits being cut by roughly the same amount, which discourages SA claimants from returning to work.

The situation is further complicated by potential interactions between the different programs. For example, the minimum wage will have no effect on the income of individuals who have withdrawn from the labour market to take advantage of SA benefits. Other programs such as workers earnings supplements might mitigate the redistributive impact of the minimum wage. For example, in Canada, some provinces provide an earned income supplement for low-income workers as part of the national Child Tax Benefit Initiative. To the extent that the minimum wage raises the earnings of minimum-wage workers, it will also reduce their supplement. This interaction between the two programs reduces the redistributive benefits of the minimum wage.

It would be a formidable challenge to address the issues of behavioural response and program interaction in a formal analytical framework. We take a more pragmatic approach by first reporting the observed incidence of the various programs by decile of adjusted family income, keeping in mind that this is not a complete representation of the true redistributive benefits of the program in the presence of behavioural responses. In the next section, we will discuss how our conclusions would be affected by introducing behavioural responses and possible interactions among programs.

nicole m. fortin and thomas lemieux

Table 7

Average Minimum-Wage Earnings and Government Transfers
by Decile of Adjusted Family Income, Canada, 1993

	Mininum-wage earnings	Social assistance	Unemploy-ment insurance	All transfers[1]	Taxes on income[2]	Total income
DECILE			($)			
All	163	505	835	2,148	4,878	24,358
1st	165	2,557	538	4,510	283	7,655
2nd	214	1,365	1,098	3,812	1,121	11,914
3rd	347	507	1,133	2,782	1,998	15,140
4th	199	267	1,180	2,501	3,032	18,621
5th	185	182	1,045	2,002	3,897	21,417
6th	127	72	925	1,584	4,470	23,517
7th	139	34	940	1,560	5,374	26,600
8th	97	61	700	1,289	6,330	29,929
9th	75	8	561	923	8,061	35,580
10th	83	2	234	521	14,212	53,199
DISTRIBUTION			(%)			
1st decile	10.1	50.6	6.4	21.0	0.6	
First 5	68.0	96.5	59.8	72.6	21.2	
Last 5	32.0	3.5	40.2	27.4	78.8	

[1] May include child benefits, worker's compensation and GST credits.
[2] Federal and provincial income taxes.
Note: Family income is adjusted using a family income-to-needs ratio.
Source: Authors' calculations from the 1993 SLID.

Table 7 compares the distribution of minimum-wage earnings by decile of adjusted income with the distributions of SA, UI, total government transfers and taxes (provincial and federal). More precisely, we compute a family income-to-needs ratio for each individual, and rank individuals on the basis of this variable. We then compute the mean value of each program variable (mean minimum-wage earnings, mean SA income, etc.) among individuals in each decile. We present the distributions in absolute dollar levels to illustrate the relative importance of the different programs. We also present the proportion of transfers, minimum-wage earnings and taxes that applies to the lowest decile, the 5 lowest deciles, and the 5 highest deciles at the bottom of the table to compare the progressivity of the different programs.

Table 7 reinforces our previous conclusion that the minimum wage is a small transfer program. Average minimum-wage earnings (over all deciles) are $163, compared with $505 for SA, $835 for UI, and $2,148 for total government transfers. These numbers suggest that, as a transfer program, the minimum wage is three times smaller than SA and five times smaller than UI. Furthermore, these figures still overstate the importance of the minimum wage, since most minimum-wage earners would have positive earnings in the absence of a minimum wage. However, as long as this overstatement is relatively the same in all deciles, our analysis of the incidence of the minimum wage by decile will not be affected by this problem.[46]

How does the incidence of the minimum wage by decile of adjusted family income compare with the incidence of other transfer programs? The second column of table 7 shows that SA is much more concentrated at the very bottom of the distribution than are minimum-wage earnings. Individuals in the lowest decile receive 50.6 percent of total SA payments, which amounts to $2,557 per individual in this decile. SA benefits are a negligible source of income for individuals in the 5 highest deciles. The incidence of the various programs is also illustrated in figure 6, which shows that SA is much more directly targeted at the 2 lowest deciles than are other programs. As we will discuss in the next section, however, these results should be interpreted with caution, since SA benefits are mechanically connected to (low) family income.

In contrast, UI income is much more evenly spread across the deciles. In fact, the impact of the minimum wage is more concentrated at the bottom end of the distribution than the impact of UI. Individuals in the lowest decile only get 6.4 percent of UI payments, compared with 10.1 percent of minimum-wage earnings. When we move to the five lowest deciles, these numbers are 59.8 percent and 68 percent, respectively.

The fourth column of table 7 provides the same information for all government transfers considered together; these may include child tax benefits, worker's compensation and GST credits.[47] These transfers are concentrated in the lowest 2 deciles and then decline slowly as we move up in the distribution. Overall, the 5 lowest deciles receive 72.6 percent of transfers compared with 68 percent of minimum-wage earnings. Total transfers are thus only slightly more progressive than the minimum wage when we look at the 5 lowest deciles. They are better targeted at the 2 lowest deciles than the minimum wage because of SA. In the absence of SA, government transfers would be roughly equal to $2,000 per individual for each of the first 5 deciles. The fifth column of table 7 shows that, not surprisingly, the income tax system plays an important redistributive role. Only 21 percent of total income tax is paid for by individuals in the lowest 5 deciles.

Figure 6

Minimum-Wage Earnings and Government Transfers as a Proportion of Total Income, by Decile of Adjusted Family Income, Canada, 1993

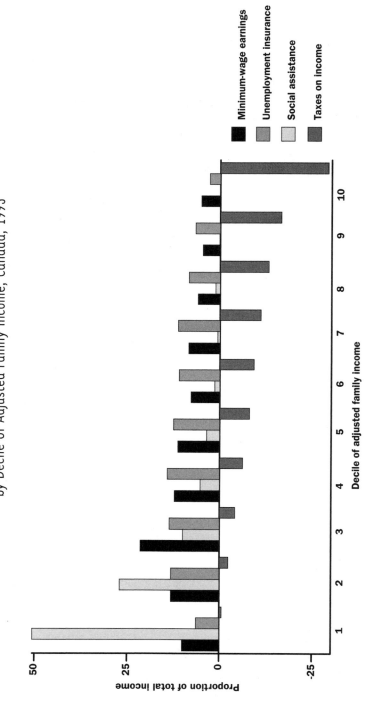

Source: Table 7.

If we consider that the primary goal of redistributive policies is to equalize adjusted family incomes, SA achieves that goal most directly, since it is explicitly targeted at low-income families. In contrast, most other programs are not explicitly targeted at low-income families. The aim of UI is to compensate individuals (not families) for temporary losses of labour income, while minimum-wage policies guarantee a basic wage level to low-wage workers. These two programs nevertheless do redistribute some income across families, since temporary earnings losses and low wages are negatively correlated with the family income-to-needs ratio.

Many authors, including Burkhauser, Couch and Glenn, have argued that the minimum wage is not a good way of redistributing income because of this imperfect connection between low wages and a low income-to-needs ratio.[48] According to our findings, an even stronger argument could be made against UI on these grounds. The alternative to the minimum wage proposed by Burkhauser, Couch and Glenn is an earned income tax credit (EITC), which is now an important redistribution program in the United States. The EITC, like SA, is determined on the basis of family income. Unlike SA, however, the EITC is an earned income supplement that is gradually phased out as earnings increase. It creates less disincentives to work than SA.

Burkhauser, Couch and Glenn find that the EITC is more explicitly targeted at low-income families than the minimum wage. This is not very surprising. As long as the sole goal of redistributive policies is to reduce the dispersion in adjusted family income and the labour market behaviour of individuals is exogenous, SA and EITC are by definition better tools for redistribution than the minimum wage.

Discussion and Normative Implications

The conclusions we have reached up to this point are only valid under the assumptions of no behavioural response and no program interactions. How would these conclusions change if these two assumptions were relaxed? One partial answer to this question can be obtained by ranking individuals by the income-to-needs ratio they should have given individual characteristics. More precisely, we predict the decile (of the income-to-needs ratio) into which an individual is likely to fall on the basis of observed characteristics such as education, age and family status.[49] For example, an individual can fall into the lowest decile either for reasons over which he/she has little control, like poor education or lone parenthood, or for reasons over which he/she has more control, like the decision not to work in order to take advantage of SA. Intuitively, behavioural responses should have less impact on predicted deciles than on actual (or observed) deciles.

Table 8
Average Minimum-Wage Earnings and Government Transfers by Predicted Decile of Adjusted Family Income, Canada, 1993

	Mininum-wage earnings	Social assistance	Unemploy-ment insurance	All transfers[1]	Taxes on income[2]	Total income
DECILE			($)			
All	163	505	835	2,148	4,878	24,358
1st	200	1,014	937	2,953	3,346	19,332
2nd	193	738	933	2,600	3,746	20,529
3rd	186	611	913	2,410	4,016	21,492
4th	179	531	889	2,272	4,281	22,387
5th	172	472	863	2,158	4,546	23,289
6th	164	424	835	2,054	4,832	24,256
7th	155	382	805	1,952	5,162	25,356
8th	144	342	772	1,844	5,568	26,688
9th	131	303	734	1,724	6,114	28,443
10th	113	265	687	1,575	7,011	31,216
DISTRIBUTION			(%)			
1st decile	12.2	20.0	11.2	13.7	6.9	
First 5	56.8	66.2	54.2	57.5	41.0	
Last 5	43.2	33.8	45.8	42.5	59.0	

[1] May include child benefits, worker's compensation and GST credits.
[2] Federal and provincial income taxes.
Note: Individuals are ranked by the income-to-needs ratio they should have given their observed characteristics (i.e., age, education and family status).
Source: Authors' calculations from the 1993 SLID.

Table 8 compares the distribution of minimum-wage earnings by predicted decile of adjusted family income to the distribution of SA, UI, total government transfers and taxes. Generally speaking, using predicted instead of actual income-to-needs ratios smooths out the distribution of the various programs. For example, average SA income in the first predicted decile is only $1,014, compared with $2,557 in the first actual decile. Furthermore, average minimum-wage earnings fall monotonically across predicted deciles, while they reach a peak in the third decile of actual adjusted family income.

Overall, correcting for behavioural response by looking at predicted instead of actual deciles does not qualitatively affect our conclusions. SA remains a more progressive program than the minimum wage or UI, though the difference between these programs is less dramatic here than in table 7. The differences between tables 7 and 8 also reflect, to some extent, the importance of interactions among the different programs. As mentioned earlier, the minimum wage has no effect on the earnings of individuals who have decided to quit the labour market to take advantage of SA benefits. The difference in minimum-wage earnings in the first 2 predicted deciles, relative to the first 2 actual deciles, may thus reflect both the effect of a behavioural response and interactions between the minimum wage and SA.

Up to this point, we have evaluated the incidence of the different redistribution programs across deciles of adjusted family income. This corresponds with a very specific notion of equity, in which the equalization of income-to-needs ratios is the sole criterion used to evaluate the programs. Our findings indicate that SA is the best way to achieve this redistributive objective, since it is explicitly targeted at low-income families. Although this objective is a useful benchmark to start with, we think it ignores other important dimensions of equity. Most importantly, programs such as SA and EITC are solely based on family income, irrespective of the work effort of individuals. Everything else being equal, one individual working 50 hours a year at $100 an hour and another one working 1,000 hours at $5 an hour will get the same amount of SA or EITC. On the other hand, the second individual could benefit substantially from a higher minimum wage. He or she could also receive UI if the 1,000 hours of work were concentrated in the first part of the year.

This simple example illustrates the fact that, relative to SA or the EITC, the minimum wage tends to help low-wage workers who supply a large number of hours to the labour market. In other words, if all individuals worked the same number of hours, the minimum wage might be a much more efficient tool for reducing disparities in adjusted family income. We illustrate this point in tables 9 and 10. In table 9 we present average hourly wages, average hours of work per year and average individual earnings in each decile.[50] We also report the fraction of earnings of minimum-wage workers. The table indicates that individuals in the lowest deciles have low earnings both because of low wages and low hours of work. They are also much more likely to earn the minimum wage.

Next, we compute how much of the wage gap and the hours gap between the different deciles cannot be explained by standard factors (gender, education, experience and province of residence).[51] These two gaps are reported in the last two columns of table 9. They are normalized to have a mean of zero. In other words, average hours plus the hours gap gives the adjusted hours of work in each decile (adjusted for differences in gender, experience, education and province). Adjusted wages are similarly defined. These results suggest that hours play a

Table 9
Average Wages, Hours of Work and Earnings by Decile
of Adjusted Family Income, Canada, 1993

DECILE	Average hourly wage[1] ($)	Average hours of work	Average earnings ($)	Ratio of minimum-wage earnings to total earnings	Hourly wage gap[2] ($)	Hours gap[3]
1st	9.04	262	2,360	0.070	-4.11	-592
2nd	10.46	607	6,318	0.034	-3.27	-249
3rd	11.75	826	9,672	0.036	-2.49	-96
4th	13.38	918	12,274	0.016	-1.32	-85
5th	14.20	1,023	14,500	0.013	-0.27	46
6th	14.74	1,103	16,211	0.008	0.06	137
7th	15.91	1,176	18,657	0.007	1.00	136
8th	17.16	1,240	21,198	0.005	1.88	222
9th	18.61	1,319	24,524	0.003	2.93	227
10th	22.44	1,296	29,027	0.003	5.59	255

[1] Average hourly wages are hours-weighted. The advantage of using this measure is that average earnings are equal to the product of the average hours of work and the hours-weighted average hourly wage.
[2] The difference between the average wage in the decile and the average wage over all deciles that is not explained by differences in gender, education, experience and province of residence.
[3] The difference between the average hours of work in the decile and the average hours of work over all deciles that is not explained by differences in gender, education, experience and province of residence.
Note: Family income is adjusted using a family income-to-needs ratio.
Source: Authors' calculations from the 1993 SLID.

more important role in explaining low family income than wages do. One way to see this is to compute the elasticity of adjusted hours with respect to adjusted wages across the 10 deciles, which gives us a labour supply elasticity of 1.5.[52] This suggest that hours change more quickly across deciles than do wages. Since this elasticity is much larger than standard estimates of the labour supply elasticity discussed by Killingsworth, this suggests that individuals in the lowest deciles work a small amount of hours for reasons other than low wages, gender, experience, education, or province of residence.[53]

In table 10 we simulate what the minimum-wage earnings would be if this hours gap were eliminated. To do this, we make the simplifying assumption that the fraction of earnings at the minimum wage is not affected by changes in hours of work. This means that if closing the hours gap doubles the average hours of work in a decile, it will also double minimum-wage earnings. The results of this simulation are reported in the last two columns of table 10.

Table 10

Distribution of Simulated Minimum-Wage Earnings When the Hours Gap Is Eliminated, by Decile of Adjusted Family Income, Canada, 1993

	Actual		Simulated[1]	
	Minimum-wage earnings	Proportion of total minimum-wage earnings	Minimum-wage earnings	Proportion of total minimum-wage earnings
DECILE	($)	(%)	($)	(%)
1st	165	10.1	538	26.1
2nd	214	13.1	301	14.6
3rd	347	21.3	387	18.8
4th	199	12.2	217	10.5
5th	185	11.3	177	8.6
6th	127	7.8	112	5.4
7th	139	8.5	123	6.0
8th	97	6.0	80	3.9
9th	75	4.6	62	3.0
10th	83	5.1	67	3.2
First 5	222	68.0	324	78.5
Last 5	104	32.0	89	21.5

[1] Simulated minimum-wage earnings are obtained by assuming that the increase in minimum-wage earnings is proportional to the increase in hours due to the elimination of the hours gap.
Note: Family income is adjusted using a family income-to-needs ratio.
Source: Authors' calculations from the 1993 SLID.

These results show that the minimum wage would be much more explicitly targeted at the 2 lowest deciles of the distribution if the hours gap was eliminated. These 2 lowest deciles would account for 26.1 percent and 14.6 percent of all minimum-wage earnings, respectively. Under this scenario, only SA would still be more progressive than the minimum wage. Government transfers as a whole would be substantially less progressive than the minimum wage.

This simulation suggests that the minimum wage would be a more effective redistributive policy instrument if the source of low earnings in the lowest deciles was low wages rather than low hours of work. This is a relevant policy issue since "workfare" provisions for SA claimants have recently been introduced in several Canadian provinces (e.g., Alberta and Ontario) and in the United States. The redistributive impact of the minimum wage will likely increase as a result of these workfare provisions which force individuals in the lowest deciles to supply more hours to the labour market. This suggests that the redistributive role of the minimum wage will probably become more important in the future than it has been in the recent past.

Finally, we want to point out that focusing exclusively on family income-to-needs ratios implies that the sources of income in a given family are irrelevant – for instance, it does not matter if we cut the wages of the wife and the children in half, as long as the wage of the husband is increased accordingly. This would in turn imply that wage discrimination against women is irrelevant as long as their husbands benefit sufficiently from discrimination against women. These examples illustrate that it is probably too narrow an objective to focus redistribution efforts solely on the income-to-needs ratio. We would probably want to give considerable weight to this particular objective, but some attention should also be given to other objectives, such as the reduction of wage inequality *per se*. Similarly, we would probably want to encourage work effort, even if it has some negative effects on the distribution of the income-to-needs ratio. Expanding the set of goals of redistribution policies makes the minimum wage look like a more comprehensive policy instrument.

Conclusion

In this paper, we analyze the effects of minimum wages on the distribution of wages and on the distribution of adjusted family income (income-to-needs ratio) in Canada. We also compare the role of the minimum wage as a redistributive policy with the role of other transfer programs like SA and UI.

We find that the minimum wage has a significant impact on the shape of the bottom end of the wage distribution. This impact is more important in 1995 than in 1988 because the value of the minimum wage relative to average manufacturing wages and the proportion of hours worked at low wages increased during this period. This change is particularly striking for young workers.

We then analyze the link between the minimum wage and the distribution of adjusted family income. We find that individuals in the lower half of the distribution benefit the most from the minimum wage. Individuals in this part of the distribution account for close to 70 percent of the earnings of all minimum-wage workers. In this sense, the minimum wage is almost as progressive as all government transfer programs considered together, since 72 percent of these transfers are received by individuals in the lower half of the distribution. However, other government transfers, especially SA, are more directly targeted at individuals in the two lowest deciles.

We also find that the minimum wage is a small program, since total earnings at the minimum wage only represent a third of total SA payments and a fifth of total UI payments. The small size of the program is the main reason why its redistributive impact is modest relative to other transfer programs. This conclusion is different from that reached by others who attribute the weak link between the minimum wage and family income to the fact that minimum-wage earners are drawn from all family income deciles. This link may be weak compared with an ideal program, but it is not weak compared with the full set of transfer programs that currently exist in Canada.

We conjecture that the role of the minimum wage as a redistributive program will grow substantially in the future for two reasons. First, there have been very substantial cuts to other transfer programs since 1993 as a result of government efforts to eliminate budget deficits. There is every indication, given the growth in the number of low-wage jobs, that the minimum wage will continue to be a more important program than it was in 1993. In addition, workfare is becoming an increasingly important component of SA programs in most provinces. By design, these programs substantially increase the hours of work of individuals at the bottom end of the income distribution. Since many of these individuals are likely to work at the minimum wage, the redistributive impact of the minimum wage could increase substantially in the years to come.

241

Appendix

The 1988 Labour Market Activity Survey (LMAS) and the 1995 Survey of Work Arrangements (SWA)

Our LMAS and SWA samples include all paid employees aged 15 and over (as opposed to those aged 16 and over in the SLID) who report an hourly wage of $1.00 or more. In the 1995 SWA, the hourly wages are top coded at $40.00; in the 1988 LMAS, they are not. Note that we use information on the main job in the 46th week of 1988 (the 3rd week in November) in the LMAS to facilitate comparison with the data from the SWA. We end up with 29,968 observations from the 1988 LMAS and 16,352 from the 1995 SWA. Both the LMAS and SWA ask workers whether they are paid by the hour, so for these workers we should have been able to obtain a relatively exact measure of hourly wage. For the other workers, we use a measure of average hourly earnings. Unfortunately, for workers paid by the hour (66 percent of the sample in 1995, which is up from 59 percent in 1988), the hourly wage has been rounded to the nearest dollar figure in both the master file and the public-use file of the SWA. To make the 1988 and 1995 densities comparable, we also rounded the wages of workers paid by the hour in the 1988 LMAS.

The difference between the densities using actual and rounded hourly wages is illustrated in Figure A-1. In the densities using rounded hourly wages, the minimum-wage spike is a little more distinct, but the general shape of the density remains the same as with actual wages. Note that we use the Consumer Price Index for Canada as a deflator to express 1988 dollars in terms of 1995 dollars.

Figure A1
Density Estimates of Original and Rounded Wages, 1988

(a) Males

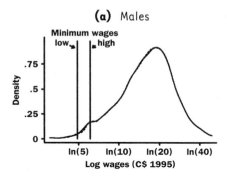

(b) Females

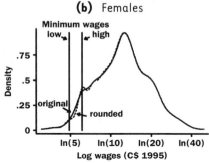

1993 Survey of Labour Income Dynamics (SLID)

Like the LMAS, the 1993 cross-section of the SLID contains detailed information on individuals' hourly wages and annual hours of work (for up to three jobs held in 1993). This information is essential for assessing the importance and the incidence of the minimum wage. Like the Survey of Consumer Finances (SCF), the SLID also contains detailed information on annual income sources, both for individuals and their families. What is unique about the SLID is that the information previously available in the LMAS and the SCF is now available in one survey. For example, using the LMAS Benjamin (1995) was able to look at the incidence of the minimum wage only on the distribution of family earnings, since that data set does not contain information on sources of income other than earnings.

The 1993 cross-section of the SLID contains detailed information on 29,934 individuals living in all 10 provinces. Unlike most other Canadian data sets that contain information on individuals aged 15 and over, only individuals aged 16 or over at the end of 1993 are surveyed in the SLID. Relative to the 1988 LMAS and the 1995 SWA, the SLID might undercount slightly the number of minimum-wage workers because it misses some 15-year-old workers. Since we want to compare the minimum wage with other transfer programs for the non-elderly population, we restrict our analysis to individuals under the age of 64. After discarding observations with missing income (individual or family) or education data, we end up with a sample of 24,065 individuals.

The SLID contains information on the wage both at the beginning and at the end of the job in 1993. Because of missing data on the initial wage, we determine the minimum-wage status by comparing the end-period wage with the minimum wage prevailing at that time in the province of residence. We classify as a minimum-wage worker an individual who has earned the minimum wage in at least one job in 1993. On the other hand, we count as minimum-wage hours and earnings only the hours and earnings on minimum-wage jobs.

Kernel Density Estimation

Kernel density estimates are easily understood by reference to histograms. Histograms represent the frequencies of observations in a number of bins of width h, which determines the coarseness or the smoothness of the histogram. With kernel density estimation, a similar parameter, denoted h, is called the bandwidth. Here, the choice of *bandwidth* is done using the rule of thumb $h = 1.06n^{-1/5}$, which gives the optimal bandwidth for a normal density function. This results in values of $h = 0.075$ in 1988 and $h = 0.08$ in 1995, which imply a little under-smoothing with respect to the optimal bandwidth for the densities under study. In a histogram, the frequency of observations in any given bin can be computed as a sum of weights that give the value one to observations in the bin and zero to observations outside the bin. The sum of the weights may be normalized by dividing it by the number of observations times the binwidth. Instead of using such a rectangular weight function, the kernel density estimates presented here use a bell-shaped Gaussian weight function, and can be characterized as a sum of bumps placed at the observations.

244   Note also that each observation is weighted by the product of the sample weight and the usual hours of work per week. These hours-weighted estimates put more weight on workers who supply a large number of hours to the market bivariate distribution of hours and wages, the hours-weighted distribution of wages corresponds to the marginal distribution of wages of this bivariate distribution.

Notes

1. Edith Lorentsen and Evelyn Woolner, "Fifty Years of Labour Legislation in Canada," Legislation Branch, Labour Canada, September 1950, p. 7.

2. George Stigler, "The Economics of Minimum Wage Legislations," *American Economic Review*, Vol. 46, no. 3 (1946), pp. 358-65.

3. David Card and Alan Krueger, *Myth and Measurement: The New Economics of the Minimum Wage* (Princeton, NJ: Princeton University Press, 1995). The consensus view before Card and Krueger was that the minimum wage had a negative, albeit small, effect on employment. See, for instance, Charles Brown, Curtis Gilroy and Andrew Kohen, "The Effect of the Minimum Wage on Employment and Unemployment," *Journal of Economic Literature*, Vol. 20 (June 1982), pp. 487-528.

4. Michael Baker, Dwayne Benjamin and Shuchita Stanger, "The Highs and Lows of the Minimum Wage Effect: A Time Series-Cross Section Study of the Canadian Law," *Journal of Labor Economics*, Vol. 17 (April 1999), pp. 318-350.

5. See, for example, Richard V. Burkhauser and T. Aldrich Finegan, "The Minimum Wage and the Poor: The End of a Relationship," *Journal of Policy Analysis and Management*, Vol. 8, no.1 (1989), pp. 53-71.

6. Edward M. Gramlich, "Impact of Minimum Wages on Other Wages, Employment, and Family Incomes," *Brookings Papers on Economic Activity*, Vol. 2 (1976), pp. 409-51.

7. Dwayne Benjamin, "Minimum Wages in Canada," in Al Berry (ed.), *Labour Market Policies in Canada and Latin America* (Norwell, MA: Kluwer Academic Publishers, forthcoming).

8. Richard B. Freeman, "The Minimum Wage as a Redistributive Tool," *The Economic Journal*, Vol. 106 (May 1996), pp. 639-49.

9. Sidney Webb, "The Economic Theory of a Legal Minimum Wage," *Journal of Political Economy*, Vol. 20 (December 1912), pp. 973-98.

10. John DiNardo, Nicole M. Fortin and Thomas Lemieux, "Labor Market Institutions and the Distribution of Wages: A Semiparametric Approach," *Econometrica*, Vol. 64 (September 1996), pp. 1001-44.

11. Among the exceptions, see Freeman, "The Minimum Wage as a Redistributive Tool."

12. The problem is that the samples available in the 1993 SLID and the 1995 SWA are two times smaller than in the 1988 LMAS. This is an important limitation for performing a detailed analysis of wage distributions by province.

13. David A. Green and Harry J. Paarsch, "The Effect of the Minimum Wage on the Distribution of Teenage Wages," working paper no. 97-02, Department of Economics, University of British Columbia, 1996.

14. Michael Shannon, "Minimum Wages and the Gender Wage Gap," *Applied Economics*, Vol. 28, no. 12 (1996), pp.1567-76.

15. See figures 1 and 2 in Benjamin, "Minimum Wages in Canada."

16. The details of the sample selection are contained in the appendix.

17. Lawrence Katz and Alan Krueger, "The Effects of Minimum Wages on the Fast Food Industry," *Industrial and Labor Relations Review*, Vol. 46, no. 1 (October 1992), pp. 6-21; Baker, Benjamin and Stanger, "The Highs and Lows of the Minimum Wage Effect."

18. For more on kernel density estimation, see the appendix.

19. As explained in the appendix, each observation is weighted by the product of the sample weight and the usual hours of work per week. Note that, as indicated, the other reported statistics may be based on the same weighting scheme.

20. Given that workers may round up their answers when questioned about their hourly wage, it is usual to consider minimum-wage workers to be individuals whose wage is within a given interval of the actual minimum wage. Note also that few workers earn less than 25 cents below the minimum wage. This may be attributable to noncompliance, noncoverage or reporting errors.

21. Because of a rounding problem in the 1995 SWA, the minimum-wage interval is occasionally larger in 1995. For example, since in Saskatchewan the minimum wage is set at $5.35, we consider workers earning $5.00 in that province as being at the minimum wage (see the appendix).

22. Jean B. Grossman, "The Impact of the Minimum Wage on Other Wages," *Journal of Human Resources*, Vol. 18, no. 3 (1983), pp. 359-78.

23. David Card and Alan Krueger, "Minimum Wages and Employment: A Case Study of the Fast Food Industry in New Jersey and

245

Pennsylvania," *American Economic Review*, Vol. 84, no. 4 (1994), pp. 772-93.

24. We use the rank regressions methodology proposed in Nicole Fortin and Thomas Lemieux, "Rank Regressions, Wage Distributions, and the Gender Gap," *Journal of Human Resources*, Vol. 33, no. 3 (1998), pp. 610-43, to simulate what the distribution of wages would have been in the absence of a minimum wage. The simulation is done by estimating in a flexible fashion the distribution of wages using an ordered probit model, linearizing the kink in the returns to skill functions that can be attributed to the minimum wage and predicting the new probabilities of belonging to each wage interval. An important difficulty in that simulation is that there are many minimum wages in Canada and we have to linearize over a large interval. This simulation implies a change in the coefficient of skewness of 9 percent among men and 42 percent among women.

25. The simulation results are imprecise because provincial samples are small and wages are rounded to the nearest dollar value (see the appendix).

26. We compared the densities of male and female hourly wages for 1981 and 1988 in Canada. Our results (unpublished) indicate no significant changes between the 1981 and 1988 hourly wage distributions, either for men or women, or men and women combined.

27. Garnett Picot, "Working Time, Wages and Earnings Inequality Among Men and Women in Canada, 1981-93" (paper presented at the annual meeting of the Canadian International Labour Network, "Labour Market Institutions and Labour Market Outcomes," Burlington, Ontario, August 1996), p. 29.

28. We find a 1 percent increase in the 90-10 wage differential for men from 1988 to 1995 and less than 1 percent decrease in the same differential for women. These changes are not statistically significant.

29. Green and Paarsch, "The Effect of the Minimum Wage on the Distribution of Teenage Wages."

30. Paul Beaudry and David A. Green, "Cohort Patterns in Canadian Earnings and the Skill-Biased Technical Change Hypothesis," working paper no. 97-03, Department of Economics, University of British Columbia, December 1996; Beaudry and Green, "Employment Outcomes in Canada: A Cohort Analysis," in this volume; René Morissette, "The Declining Labour Market Status of Young Men," in Miles Corak (ed.), *Labour Markets, Social Institutions, and the Future of*

Canada's Children (Ottawa: Statistics Canada, 1998), pp. 31-50.

31. David Card and Thomas Lemieux, "Adapting to Circumstances: The Evolution of Work, School, and Living Arrangements Among North American Youth," in D. G. Blanchflower and R. B. Freeman (eds.), *Youth Employment and Joblessness in Advanced Countries* (Chicago: University of Chicago Press, 2000), pp. 171-213; Dominique Meunier, Johanne Boisjoly, Paul Bernard and Roger T. Michaud, "Eternal Youth? Changes in the Living Arrangements of Young People," in Corak (ed.), *Labour Markets, Social Institutions, and the Future of Canada's Children*, pp. 157-170.

32. Note that unemployment insurance has been renamed employment insurance in 1996.

33. For the United States, see Brown, Kilrowy and Kohen, "The Effect of the Minimum Wage"; and Card and Krueger, "Minimum Wages and Employment." Recent work for Canada also suggest modest disemployment effects (see Baker, Benjamin, and Stanger, "The Highs and Lows of the Minimum Wage Effect"). Finally, Card and Krueger report some small spillover effects of the minimum wage in the fast food industry.

34. Benjamin, "Minimum Wages in Canada," shows that individual earnings are uniformly equal to zero in the lowest decile of the family earnings distribution (nobody works in these families). By definition, there are no minimum-wage workers in this decile. This data limitation in the LMAS understates the distributive role of the minimum wage at the very bottom end of the distribution.

35. We use the plus-or-minus-25-cents window because of possible measurement error (rounding) in wages. When we look at the exact minimum wage, the proportion of minimum-wage workers is systematically larger in provinces where the minimum wage is an exact dollar figure than in provinces where it is not (see the appendix for more detail).

36. Benjamin, "Minimum Wages in Canada," looks at the incidence of minimum wage "jobs" as opposed to minimum-wage workers. He finds that 5.9 percent of jobs are minimum wage jobs. He classifies a job as minimum-wage when it pays below the minimum wage plus 5 cents. We took up to 25 cents above the minimum wage, but unlike him, we do not count jobs that pay less than 25 cents below the minimum wage.

37. For example, Card and Krueger, "Myth and Measurement," find that 7.1 percent of workers were affected by the minimum wage increase of 1990-91 (from $3.35 to $4.25).

38. US studies also tend to find that the minimum wage is only a small transfer program. For example, Card and Krueger, "Myth and Measurement," find the 1990-91 increase in the minimum wage from $3.35 to $4.25 only increased earnings by 0.2 percent. Since, on average, the wages of workers affected by the minimum wage increased by 48 cents (from an average of $3.77 before the increase), a back-of-the-envelope calculation indicates that minimum-wage earnings represented 1.6 percent of total earnings (0.2 percent times 3.77/0.48) in the United States in 1990.

39. This is probably an overestimate of the true transfer. The average minimum wage in Canada was $5.90 dollars in 1993, which means that this calculation assumes that minimum-wage workers would have earned less than $3 in the absence of a minimum wage, which seems implausibly low.

40. These calculations are based on the assumption that the proportion of minimum-wage workers of a certain age is a linear function of age.

41. These proportions are not reported in the tables. They are weighted averages of the proportions for men and women, where the weights are the share of minimum-wage workers who are men and women, separately.

42. These proportions are probably higher, since the public use files of the SLID did not provide enough information to identify the family arrangements of 17.1 percent of young men and 20.0 percent of young women. For example, if a grandparent lives in a family with parents and children under the age of 25, this family is not identified in the SLID.

43. The family equivalence scale is computed by giving a weight of 1 to the first person aged 16 and over in the economic family and a weight of .7 to other individuals aged 16 and over. Each child (aged 15 or under) in the family gets a weight of .6. The equivalence scale is obtained by summing up the weights of all family members.

44. Benjamin, "Minimum Wages in Canada," finds a higher fraction of minimum-wage workers in the second decile of the family earnings distribution (29.5 percent) and a lower fraction (0 percent) in the lowest decile, since nobody works in that decile. Overall, he finds that 58 percent of minimum-wage earners are in the 5 lowest deciles of the family earnings distribution. This is substantially less than our finding that 68 percent of minimum-wage workers are in the 5 lowest deciles of the family income-to-needs ratio. Card and Krueger, "Myth and Measurement," find that 63 percent of US minimum-wage workers are in the lowest five deciles of the distribution of family income.

45. A similar conclusion is reached by Michael T. Shannon and Charles M. Beach, "Distributional Employment Effects of Ontario Minimum-Wage Proposals: A Microdata Approach," *Canadian Public Policy*, Vol. 21 (September 1995), pp. 284-303.

46. A sufficient condition for this to be the case is that (1) minimum-wage workers in each decile earn the same wage in the absence of a minimum wage, and (2) the elasticity of income with respect to the minimum wage (one minus the employment elasticity) is the same in all deciles.

47. We do not look explicitly at child benefits, since they mix national child tax benefits (which are means-tested) with Quebec family allowances (which were universal in 1993).

48. Richard V. Burkhauser, Kenneth A. Couch and Andrew J. Glenn, "Public Policies for the Working Poor: The Earned Income Tax Credit Versus Minimum Wage Legislation," in S. Polachek (ed.), *Research in Labor Economics*, Vol. 15 (Stamfort, CT: JAI Press, 1996), pp. 65-109.

49. We compute the predicted probabilities of falling in each decile by estimating an ordered logit model. The explanatory variables used in the logit model are age, age-squared, dichotomic variables for gender and provinces and a series of dichotomic variables corresponding to the education and family arrangements categories listed in tables 4 and 5.

50. Note that we weight the hourly wage of each individual by his or her hours of work to compute the average hourly wage. The advantage of this hours-weighted average is that average earnings are equal to the product of average hours and hours-weighted average wages. The product of average hours and unweighted average wages is not equal to average earnings unless the covariance between hours and wages is equal to zero.

51. More specifically, we run standard regressions of hours (for all individuals) and wages (for workers only) on a set of decile dummies; a set of province dummies; and a full set of interactions among gender, age categories (10 categories), and education categories (4 categories).

52. The elasticity is estimated by running a regression of log-adjusted hours on log-adjusted wages (by decile). The estimated coefficient is 1.49 with a standard error of 0.33. Similar results are obtained when SA claimants, who have low predicted hours and wages, are excluded from the sample.

53. Mark Killingsworth, *Labor Supply* (Cambridge: Cambridge University Press, 1983).

247

Reforming the Welfare System:
In Search of the Optimal Policy Mix

Guy Lacroix

Introduction

Canada's social assistance programs were established under the Canada Assistance Plan (CAP) of 1966, and aimed at providing financial assistance to all individuals in need. The plan consolidated the existing *ad hoc* programs. In recent years Ontario, Alberta and British Columbia have introduced major changes to their programs. Quebec is also in the process of enacting a major overhaul of its program. These changes parallel those introduced in the US through the Personal Responsibility and Work Opportunity Act of 1996.

In Canada, two factors have led provincial policy makers to advocate changes to their programs. First, federal transfers under CAP were significantly reduced as of 1990, when a 5 percent growth ceiling was imposed on transfers to Ontario, Alberta and British Columbia. Furthermore, cost sharing of welfare expenditures ended in 1995 for the remaining provinces and was replaced by block funding. Carter[1] has estimated that the federal government's share of expenditures on social programs decreased by as much as 33 percent between 1995 and 1998. Second, in addition to these cuts, most provinces have witnessed dramatic increases in their caseloads over the 1980s and 1990s. In the US, similar patterns have been observed over the same period.[2] Not surprisingly, increased caseloads and reduced funding have exerted a tremendous fiscal strain on provincial governments.

Admittedly, the primary goal of all these reforms is to somehow control escalating program costs. In Canada, the empirical evidence that has emerged in the

249

public debates over the need for and directions of reforms has been anecdotal at best. Implicit in most discussions is the assumption that the welfare system is itself responsible for the increase in caseloads. Yet, welfare programs in Canada have been surprisingly little investigated by economists, compared with those in the US and Europe. Thus, much of what we know about incentive effects is borrowed from research focusing on welfare programs that are different in design from ours and/or implemented in different contexts.

Aside from growing caseloads, three other trends are seen as particularly worrisome. First, the proportion of children born in female-headed households has increased steadily over the years. Because the incidence of poverty is generally more severe among these families, this is regarded as particularly socially undesirable. Second, the proportion of able-bodied individuals among welfare claimants has also increased steadily over the years. Finally, the average welfare spell-length increased drastically for some groups following the 1991-92 recession.

Fortunately, research has been done on these topics in Canada in the past few years. The primary purpose of this paper is to report on some of this research as well as relevant research conducted (mainly) in the United States and Europe. Many welfare programs provide training schemes on a voluntary/compulsory basis. Their efficacy in getting individuals off welfare has been the subject of much research in the US and abroad. We will also survey some of the important results of this research.

250   The paper is divided into four main sections. In the next section, we provide background information on the problem. We will look into changes in the composition of caseloads over time as well as their evolution across provinces. We will also examine whether trends in caseloads can be correlated with changes in benefit levels and the business cycle. In the third section, we document the dynamics of welfare participation in Canada. We will focus on spell lengths on and off welfare, exit rates and related distributions. Next we look into the incentive effects of the welfare programs. In so doing, we will separate the effects of the welfare system on participation and the duration of welfare spells. Finally, we concentrate on the efficacy of employment programs.

The relevant literature can be divided into two categories. The first focuses on the evidence that can be gleaned from the many randomized experiments conducted in various US states and in Canada. The second relies on nonexperimental data. In recent years, economists have shown renewed interest in nonexperimental data, primarily because of methodological innovations and also because some issues cannot be properly addressed with experimental data. As we will see, although the two approaches are complementary, results from the experimental

Table 1
Social Assistance Program Expenditures and Caseloads, Selected Provinces, 1981-1995 (millions of 1986 dollars)

	Quebec		Ontario		British Columbia	
	Expenditures	Caseloads	Expenditures	Caseloads	Expenditures	Caseloads
1981	1.58	302,300	1.11	203,100	0.48	66,300
1982	1.61	325,400	1.13	214,900	0.48	75,200
1983	1.82	396,800	1.26	253,100	0.71	127,900
1984	2.09	415,300	1.40	261,500	0.86	146,000
1985	2.20	424,400	1.48	264,900	0.91	153,400
1986	2.28	416,100	1.55	266,400	0.91	147,600
1987	2.16	390,100	1.67	283,400	0.87	142,300
1988	2.20	357,900	1.82	288,200	0.84	138,000
1989	1.95	340,700	1.99	314,400	0.81	133,000
1990	1.97	343,900	2.25	349,200	0.79	125,700
1991	1.86	366,200	2.97	474,900	0.84	144,500
1992	2.18	413,400	4.10	600,800	0.97	167,700
1993	2.48	450,700	4.90	656,900	1.16	193,800
1994	2.66	473,000	5.18	696,800	1.27	210,400
1995	2.76	479,400	5.23	678,400	1.34	221,800

Source: Social Program Information and Analysis Directorate, HRDC.

and nonexperimental studies are relatively similar. In our conclusion we will summarize the main results of the literature and indicate their policy implications.

Time Series Evidence on Caseloads and Program Costs

To better understand what prompted governments to implement or propose changes to their welfare programs, it is useful to first look at some basic statistics on program participation and expenditures over time. Social assistance programs in Canada are mainly administered by provincial and municipal governments and are available to all low-income families and individuals. Benefits are needs-tested, based on household income from all sources and vary according to family composition. Exemptions, tax rates and deductions are determined by the provinces (or municipalities) and vary considerably by province.[3] It is thus conceivable that the dynamics of welfare participation across provinces depict different patterns.

Table 1 reports caseloads and total program expenditures for Quebec, Ontario and British Columbia in millions of 1986 dollars. These provinces show very distinct growth patterns in both expenditures and caseloads. Quebec has always had proportionately more households on welfare than most provinces. For instance, up until 1990 its caseloads were more numerous than Ontario's, although its population amounted to between 75 percent (1981) and 66 percent (1995) of Ontario's. Thus, between 1981 and 1995 total expenditures in Quebec increased by 75 percent and caseloads by as much as 58 percent. Yet much of this growth occurred after the 1992 recession. Indeed, until then, yearly expenditures were relatively stable at approximately $2 billion. Ontario witnessed the most dramatic changes of all. Between 1981 and 1995, program expenditures increased nearly fivefold and caseloads increased over threefold. The figures also indicate that between 1981 and 1988 program expenditures and caseloads increased steadily at a rather low rate. As of 1988, caseloads started increasing rapidly. Between 1989 and 1995 alone, caseloads increased by approximately 115 percent. Much of this increase can presumably be explained by deteriorating labour market conditions after the 1991-92 recession. As we will see later, the increases observed between 1988 and 1991 are highly correlated with the provincial unemployment rate. Finally, British Columbia, much like Quebec, experienced fluctuating caseloads and program expenditures up until 1991. Following 1991, both increased very rapidly in BC.

The numbers in table 1 clearly show that the 1981-82 and 1991-92 recessions had persistent impacts on program expenditures and caseloads. The numbers may be misleading, since both these variables increase naturally with population growth.[4] It is thus preferable to focus on dependency rates, defined as the ratio between caseloads and population under the age of 65. Figures 1a, 1b, and 1c plot the dependency rates for the three provinces between 1981 and 1995 against adult male unemployment rates. Quebec and British Columbia have procyclical dependency rates that depict a very small positive trend (figures 1a and 1c). In contrast, Ontario appears to have gone through a change in regime around 1989-90 (figure 1b).

In recent years, dependency rates have reached unprecedented levels. Different explanations have been proposed to account for this. First, it has been argued that the high levels of unemployment that were reached in the 1991-1992 recession may be partly responsible. Second, it has been argued that the tightening of UI eligibility rules may have diverted a significant proportion of potential UI claimants onto welfare.[5] Finally, changes in welfare benefit levels have also been proposed as a potential explanation for rising dependency rates.

For both Quebec and British Columbia there appears to be a strong correlation between welfare dependency and the rate of unemployment. Hence, when the unemployment rate increases the dependency rate increases, with a certain

Figure 1
Welfare Dependency[1] and Unemployment Rates for Adult Males, Selected Provinces, 1981–1995

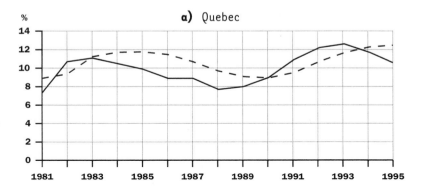

a) Quebec

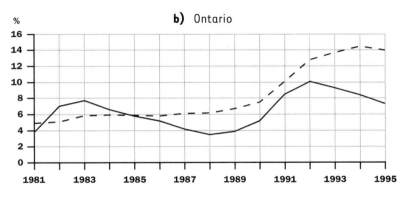

b) Ontario

c) British Columbia

——— Unemployment rate   – – – Dependency rate

[1] Dependency rates are calculated as the ratio between welfare caseloads and the population under the age of 65.
Source: Social Program Information and Analysis Directorate, HRDC.

253

guy lacroix

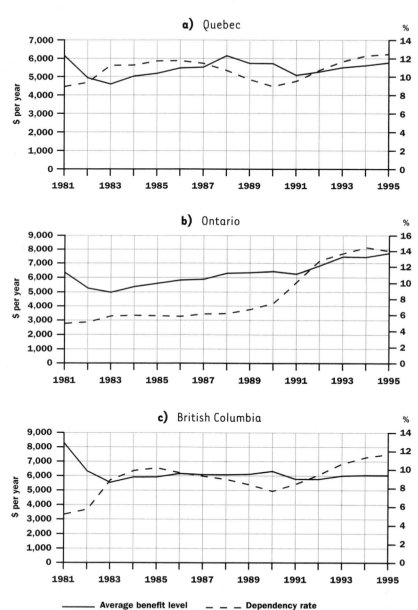

Figure 2
Average Welfare Benefits and Dependency Rates,
Selected Provinces, 1981-1995

a) Quebec

b) Ontario

c) British Columbia

——— Average benefit level — — — Dependency rate

[1] Average benefit levels are calculated using total program expenditures over average yearly caseloads.
Source: Social Program Information and Analysis Directorate, HRDC.

254

adapting public policy to a labour market in transition

lag.[6] Conversely, decreases in the unemployment rate are soon followed by decreases in the dependency rate. Ontario presents a drastically different picture, however. Between 1981 and 1990, the dependency rate increased steadily, albeit at a low rate. During the same period the unemployment rate fluctuated considerably, with a peak in 1983 and a trough in 1988. As of 1990, both variables increased sharply in a parallel fashion.[7] It is clear from these graphs that unemployment and welfare dependency rates are closely linked. Nevertheless, the situation in Ontario between 1981 and 1989 provides an interesting contrast that would be worth investigating. The situation in British Columbia also raises interesting questions. For instance, its unemployment rate following the 1992 recession was much lower than that prevailing in the years following the 1981-82 recession. Yet dependency rates in recent years have reached much higher levels than those observed around 1982.

In figures 2a, 2b, and 2c, average benefit levels are calculated as total program expenditures over average yearly caseloads. This enables us to investigate whether any correlation can be established between the level of benefit provided by provincial welfare programs and dependency rates. This does not take into account the changing composition of caseloads (which may be partly driven by changes in benefits and/or regulations directed at specific groups). The data for Quebec and British Columbia (figures 2a and 2c) show hardly any correlation between the two variables (-0.26 and -0.31, respectively). Data for Ontario (figure 2b) reveal a correlation of over 0.86. Naturally, one cannot conjecture from these figures that changes in the dependency rates are driven by changes in benefit levels. Many factors simultaneously affect entry into and exit from welfare. The increase in real average benefits may simply reflect a compositional effect; for a given caseload, an increase in the proportion of lone mothers will translate into increased program expenditures and an increase in the average level of benefit. Conversely, increased benefits aimed at youths may stimulate entry into welfare, thus increasing dependency rates but decreasing the average level of benefit.

Table 2 provides statistics on the composition of caseloads in Quebec and British Columbia between 1981 and 1995.[8] The first striking feature of these figures is the difference between the proportion of employable beneficiaries in Quebec and British Columbia. In Quebec, the proportion increased very slightly between 1981 and 1995, whereas in BC it nearly doubled. Unfortunately, no data are available beyond 1992 for BC, but one can conjecture that the difference in the proportion of employables has narrowed down in recent years. In fact, while the dramatic increase in BC's proportion of employable beneficiaries (from 38.5 to 56.1 percent) occurred between 1981 and 1985, the increase in Quebec occurred earlier between 1975 and 1979 (from 41.3 to 71.6 percent).

guy lacroix

Table 2
Composition of Welfare Caseloads, Quebec and British Columbia, 1981–1995

	Quebec					British Columbia				
	Emp.[1]	Single	CNC[2]	CWC[3]	SP[4]	Emp.[1]	Single	CNC[2]	CWC[3]	SP[4]
	(as a percentage of total)					(as a percentage of total)				
1981-82	69.5	61.5	5.6	10.6	22.3	38.5	56.6	6.3	7.9	28.4
1982-83	70.9	62.5	5.6	10.5	21.4					
1983-84	73.4	63.6	5.7	11.3	19.4	54.2	61.3	5.6	10.2	23.0
1984-85	73.2	63.3	5.7	11.3	19.7					
1985-86	72.8	63.9	5.7	10.4	20.0	56.1	62.1	5.0	9.2	23.6
1986-87	73.6	63.3	5.8	10.0	20.9					
1987-88	74.1	63.0	6.3	10.1	20.6	52.0	61.0	4.7	8.0	26.3
1988-89	72.7	62.7	6.4	9.7	21.2					
1989-90	72.0	63.3	6.5	9.1	21.1	58.4	61.8	4.5	6.7	27.0
1990-91	73.3	64.8	6.1	8.3	20.8					
1991-92	75.9	65.1	5.7	8.7	20.5	63.8	64.3	4.1	6.7	24.9
1992-93	76.7	65.3	5.5	9.1	20.1					
1993-94	77.6	65.2	5.4	9.6	19.8					
1994-95	78.0	64.4	5.4	10.0	20.1					

[1] Employable
[2] Couples with no children
[3] Couples with children
[4] Single parents

Source: Gouvernement du Québec, Ministère de la sécurité du revenu, *Un parcours vers l'insertion, la formation et l'emploi*; Gouvernement du Québec, Ministère de la sécurité du revenu, *De l'aide sociale à la sécurité du revenu: Rapport statistique 1994-1995*; G. Barret and M.I. Cragg, "An Untold Story: The Characteristics of Welfare Use in British Columbia," *Canadian Journal of Economics*, vol. 31, no. 1 (1998), pp.165-88.

The second striking feature of this table is the distribution of beneficiaries according to household type. The distributions in the two provinces are comparable and are relatively stable over time. For instance, single individuals represent about 63 percent of all beneficiaries at any point in time. Couples without children account for 5.6 percent of the caseloads, on average, and couples with children account for approximately 10 percent of the caseloads in Quebec and 7-8 percent in BC. Finally, the proportion of single parents has also remained fairly stable across time, although it is slightly higher in BC (25 percent) than in Quebec (21 percent).

The Dynamics of Welfare Participation

The previous section focused on the evolution of caseloads and program expenditures over time. Changes in caseloads can arise from changes in entry rates, average spell lengths and/or the repeated use of welfare. It is thus important to characterize these in order to have a better understanding of the utilization of welfare programs.

The most efficient way to analyze welfare spells is to use the so-called conditional exit probabilities. These are simply defined as the probability that a person who has been on welfare for t-1 months leaves the following month (month t). Formally, we write:

$$\lambda(t) = \frac{N(t)}{R(t)}$$

where N(t) is the number of individuals who have exited welfare in month t and R(t) is the population at risk, i.e., the number of individuals who could have exited in month t.[9] It can be shown that the conditional probability of surviving t months on welfare, given that an individual has survived t-1 months, is related to the conditional exit probability as follows:

$$S(t) = \prod_{t_j < t} (1 - \lambda(t_j)), \quad t \geqslant 0$$

The expected duration of welfare spells is related to the survival function as follows:[10]

$$E(t) = \sum_{j=1}^{\infty} S(j)$$

These three concepts – the hazard rate, survival rate and expected duration – are widely used to describe the dynamics of welfare (or UI) participation. Hazard rates can also be used to compute the distribution of completed spells in two different ways, depending upon whether individuals are beginning a spell or are in the midst of a spell.[11]

(1) Individuals beginning a spell [D(t)]:
Assume 100 individuals enter welfare at time t = 1. In order to get the fraction of spells that will last t months, one simply calculates the fraction of individuals who will still be on the program after t-1 months, and multiplies by the probability of exiting after t months. Thus,

$$D(1) = \lambda(1)$$
$$D(2) = \lambda(2)D(1)$$
$$\vdots$$
$$D(t) = \lambda(t)\left\{1 - \sum_{j=1}^{t-1} D(j)\right\}$$

(2) Individuals in the midst of a spell [F(t)]:
Here, we are interested in the distribution of completed spells of 100 individuals drawn at random from the population currently on welfare. This is just the distribution of new spells weighted by the fraction of all persons on the program at a point in time who will be on welfare for exactly t months:[12]

$$F(t) = \frac{tD(t)}{\sum_{j=1}^{\infty} D(j)}$$

Empirical Results: Quebec and British Columbia
In order to implement the above methodology, a large panel data set is necessary. Recently, two studies were conducted in Canada using large administrative data sets.[13] Duclos *et al.*[14] use a random sample of over 95,514 employable individuals in Quebec for the period 1979-93. These individuals experienced 195,273 spells of welfare during that period. Barrett and Cragg[15] use similar data for British Columbia for the period 1980-92. Their sample comprises 87,288 individuals (employable and nonemployable) who experienced 205,926 welfare spells.

Exits from Welfare

Tables 3a and 3b present data on exit rates and on the distribution of completed spells for Quebec and BC.[16] The data are disaggregated by household type and tabulated on the basis of semesters to allow direct comparisons. Looking at exit rates first, a striking feature of the table is that they are systematically lower in Quebec (table 3a) than in British Columbia (table 3b). In the first semester, Quebec's rates are roughly half of BC's. The difference in exit rates tends to decrease more or less with duration depending on household type. In both provinces, though, exit rates decrease with duration. This is an indication that individuals exhibit negative duration dependence, i.e., the probability of their leaving welfare decreases the longer the time they spend on it. This is consistent with results found for women in the US. There are several possible reasons for it, including changing preferences for leisure, depreciating human capital that shifts the wage-offer distribution, or employer screening.[17] Note that the apparent duration dependence may simply be due to unobserved heterogeneity that is not accounted for in these calculations.[18]

We now turn to the completed spell distributions. For each household type, the middle column represents the distribution of 100 new spells. The rightmost column represents the distribution of 100 ongoing spells chosen randomly. These distributions are striking evidence that participation in welfare is highly dynamic. To illustrate, let's focus on single men. The middle column suggests that if 100 single men enter welfare at any point in time, as many as 36.3 in Quebec and 75.1 in British Columbia will exit in one to six months. Of those who remain on welfare, 25 (12) will exit within the next six months in Quebec (BC). Nearly 61 percent of single men in Quebec and over 87 percent in British Columbia will experience spells shorter than a year. Thus, very few individuals will experience very long spells on welfare. Nevertheless, over time, an increasing proportion of those on welfare will experience long spells. In Quebec, only 5.1 percent of all ongoing spells by single men will last between one and six months. Conversely, as much as 42.4 percent of all ongoing spells by single men will last six years or more (table 3a, column 3). In BC, the situation is completely different: at any point in time, as many as 24.6 percent of ongoing spells by single men will last less than six months and only 16.7 percent will last six years or more (table 3b, column 3).

The figures for single parents are worth emphasizing. In Quebec (BC), as many as 42.5 (71.3) out of 100 new spells in this group will last less than a year. Yet in Quebec as many as 63.1 percent of all ongoing spells will last over six years. In British Columbia, 33.6 percent of all spells for single parents will last over six years. The other household types reveal similar patterns, though not as dramatic.

Table 3 (a)

Distribution of Welfare Spells and Exit Rates by Spell Duration, Quebec, 1979-1993

SPELL DURATION (months)	Single men EXIT RATE (%)	Single men Completed spells distribution — Persons beginning a spell	Single men Completed spells distribution — Persons at a point in time	Single women EXIT RATE (%)	Single women Completed spells distribution — Persons beginning a spell	Single women Completed spells distribution — Persons at a point in time	Single parents EXIT RATE (%)	Single parents Completed spells distribution — Persons beginning a spell	Single parents Completed spells distribution — Persons at a point in time	Couples without children EXIT RATE (%)	Couples without children Completed spells distribution — Persons beginning a spell	Couples without children Completed spells distribution — Persons at a point in time	Couples with children EXIT RATE (%)	Couples with children Completed spells distribution — Persons beginning a spell	Couples with children Completed spells distribution — Persons at a point in time
1-6	36.3	36.3	5.1	33.3	33.3	4.3	25.4	25.4	1.9	40.6	40.6	6.2	36.5	36.1	4.8
6-12	38.6	24.6	10.4	34.1	22.7	8.7	22.9	17.1	3.8	38.9	23.1	10.5	35.9	22.9	9.1
12-18	29.5	11.5	8.2	28.1	12.3	7.9	17.1	9.8	3.6	25.8	9.3	7.1	24.9	10.2	6.8
18-24	23.9	6.6	6.5	21.5	6.8	6.1	13.8	6.6	3.4	20.7	5.6	5.9	21.6	6.6	6.2
24-30	20.4	4.3	5.4	19.7	4.9	5.6	12.5	5.1	3.4	17.8	3.8	5.2	17.9	4.3	5.2
30-36	17.6	2.9	4.5	16.4	3.3	4.6	10.7	3.9	3.1	16.2	2.8	4.7	17.1	3.4	4.9
36-42	15.5	2.1	3.9	16.7	2.8	4.6	10.5	3.4	3.2	14.1	2.1	4.1	16.3	2.7	4.6
42-48	13.9	1.6	3.4	13.9	1.9	3.7	9.9	2.8	3.1	15.3	1.9	4.4	13.9	1.9	3.8
48-54	12.3	1.2	2.9	13.1	1.6	3.4	10.8	2.8	3.5	14.9	1.6	4.1	14.2	1.7	3.7
54-60	11.5	1.0	2.7	11.5	1.2	2.9	8.4	1.9	2.7	14.5	1.3	3.8	13.6	1.4	3.5
60-66	9.8	0.8	2.3	12.5	1.1	3.1	8.6	1.8	2.8	14.9	1.2	3.7	11.9	1.0	2.9
66-72	10.2	0.7	2.3	12.3	0.9	2.9	7.4	1.4	2.4	14.3	0.9	3.3	11.8	0.9	2.8
72+		6.4	42.4		7.2	42.2		18.0	63.1		5.8	37.0		6.9	41.7
TOTAL		100.0	100.0		100.0	100.0		100.0	100.0		100.0	100.0		100.0	100.0
EXPECTED SPELL DURATION	21.3 months			23.5 months			40.1 months			19.7 months			22.6 months		

Source: J.-Y. Duclos et al., The Dynamics of Welfare Participation in Quebec, working paper no. 9817, Université Laval, Québec, Qc, 1998.

adapting public policy to a labour market in transition

Table 3 (b)

Distribution of Welfare Spells and Exit Rates by Spell Duration, British Columbia, 1980–1992

SPELL DURATION (months)	Single men EXIT RATE (%)	Single men — Completed spells distribution: Persons beginning a spell	Persons at a point in time	Single women EXIT RATE (%)	Single women — Persons beginning a spell	Persons at a point in time	Single parents EXIT RATE (%)	Single parents — Persons beginning a spell	Persons at a point in time	Couples without children EXIT RATE (%)	Couples without children — Persons beginning a spell	Persons at a point in time	Couples with children EXIT RATE (%)	Couples with children — Persons beginning a spell	Persons at a point in time
1-6	75.1	75.1	24.6	73.8	73.8	20.1	57.2	57.2	9.5	77.8	77.8	26.8	75.9	75.9	24.6
6-12	47.2	11.7	14.6	42.0	11.0	11.6	33.0	14.1	8.3	45.8	10.2	14.5	47.6	11.5	14.8
12-18	35.3	4.7	9.8	30.4	4.6	8.2	23.5	6.7	6.6	36.3	4.4	10.3	34.0	4.3	9.4
18-24	30.1	2.6	7.5	24.4	2.6	6.4	20.2	4.4	6.1	31.0	2.4	7.9	27.0	2.3	6.9
24-30	26.1	1.6	5.9	20.3	1.6	5.1	18.9	3.3	5.8	24.3	1.3	5.5	24.8	1.5	5.8
30-36	21.7	1.0	4.4	18.4	1.2	4.6	16.8	2.4	5.2	19.5	0.8	4.1	21.6	1.0	4.7
36-42	19.8	0.7	3.7	16.8	0.9	4.0	16.0	1.9	4.8	22.7	0.7	4.4	20.3	0.7	4.1
42-48	20.0	0.6	3.5	16.3	0.7	3.8	13.5	1.3	3.9	21.7	0.5	3.9	19.6	0.6	3.6
48-54	17.5	0.4	2.7	12.3	0.5	2.7	16.7	1.4	4.8	22.4	0.4	3.5	17.5	0.4	2.9
54-60	18.1	0.3	2.6	14.4	0.5	3.1	15.9	1.1	4.2	21.0	0.3	2.8	15.4	0.3	2.3
60-66	17.0	0.2	2.2	12.5	0.3	2.5	15.7	0.9	3.9	22.4	0.3	2.6	15.4	0.3	2.3
66-72	14.4	0.2	1.7	11.2	0.3	2.2	15.6	0.7	3.4	9.9	0.1	1.0	19.0	0.3	2.6
72+		1.1	16.7		2.1	25.9		4.3	33.6		0.8	12.7		1.1	16.0
TOTAL		100.0	100.0		100.0	100.0		100.0	100.0		100.0	100.0		100.0	100.0
EXPECTED SPELL DURATION		7.3 months			8.8 months			15.8 months			6.5 months			7.1 months	

Source: Computed by author, based on data provided by G. F. Barret.

261

guy lacroix

Table 4 (a)
Distribution of Off-Welfare Spells and Exit Rates by Spell Duration, Quebec, 1979–1993

SPELL DURATION (months)	Single men			Single women			Single parents			Couples without children			Couples with children		
	EXIT RATE (%)	Completed spells distribution Persons beginning a spell	Persons at a point in time	EXIT RATE (%)	Completed spells distribution Persons beginning a spell	Persons at a point in time	EXIT RATE (%)	Completed spells distribution Persons beginning a spell	Persons at a point in time	EXIT RATE (%)	Completed spells distribution Persons beginning a spell	Persons at a point in time	EXIT RATE (%)	Completed spells distribution Persons beginning a spell	Persons at a point in time
1-6	23.2	23.0	1.4	19.5	19.5	1.0	24.7	24.7	1.7	16.2	16.2	0.8	21.2	21.2	1.3
6-12	10.6	8.5	1.6	7.1	5.7	0.9	13.4	10.1	2.0	8.8	7.4	1.1	11.4	9.0	1.6
12-18	12.1	8.2	2.6	8.0	6.0	1.6	12.5	8.2	2.8	7.9	6.0	1.6	9.5	6.7	2.0
18-24	8.6	5.2	2.3	5.6	3.9	1.4	8.7	5.0	2.3	5.5	3.9	1.4	6.8	4.3	1.8
24-30	6.8	3.7	2.2	4.2	2.8	1.3	7.2	3.7	2.3	5.5	3.6	1.7	5.9	3.5	1.9
30-36	5.5	2.8	2.0	3.6	2.3	1.3	6.5	3.1	2.3	4.7	2.9	1.7	4.9	2.7	1.8
36-42	4.6	2.2	1.8	3.3	2.0	1.3	5.4	2.4	2.1	3.5	2.1	1.4	4.6	2.4	1.9
42-48	4.2	1.9	1.8	2.9	1.7	1.3	4.5	1.9	1.9	2.8	1.6	1.3	4.4	2.2	2.0
48-54	3.7	1.6	1.8	2.2	1.3	1.1	4.5	1.8	2.1	2.8	1.6	1.4	3.7	1.8	1.8
54-60	3.2	1.4	1.7	2.3	1.3	1.2	3.6	1.4	1.8	2.4	1.3	1.3	3.2	1.5	1.7
60-66	3.0	1.2	1.6	2.0	1.1	1.2	3.3	1.2	1.8	2.3	1.2	1.4	3.3	1.5	1.8
66-72	2.7	1.1	1.5	2.0	1.1	1.3	3.3	1.2	1.9	2.3	1.2	1.4	3.0	1.3	1.8
72+		39.1	77.7		51.6	85.1		35.1	74.9		50.9	83.6		41.9	78.7
TOTAL		100.0	100.0		100.0	100.0		100.0	100.0		100.0	100.0		100.0	100.0
EXPECTED SPELL DURATION	79.4 months			118.1 months			64.1 months			103.9 months			76.6 months		

Source: J.-Y. Duclos et al., The Dynamics of Welfare Participation in Quebec, working paper no. 9817, Université Laval, Québec, Qc, 1998.

Table 4 (b)

Distribution of Off-Welfare Spells and Exit Rates by Spell Duration, British Columbia, 1980–1992

SPELL DURATION (months)	Single men			Single women			Single parents			Couples without children			Couples with children		
	EXIT RATE (%)	Completed spells distribution: Persons beginning a spell	Persons at a point in time	EXIT RATE (%)	Completed spells distribution: Persons beginning a spell	Persons at a point in time	EXIT RATE (%)	Completed spells distribution: Persons beginning a spell	Persons at a point in time	EXIT RATE (%)	Completed spells distribution: Persons beginning a spell	Persons at a point in time	EXIT RATE (%)	Completed spells distribution: Persons beginning a spell	Persons at a point in time
1-6	40.2	40.2	1.8	33.7	33.7	1.9	39.9	39.9	2.1	33.9	33.9	1.2	36.3	36.3	1.3
6-12	25.9	15.5	2.4	20.8	13.8	2.6	21.5	12.9	2.5	20.1	13.3	1.6	21.6	13.8	1.8
12-18	14.3	6.3	1.6	12.0	6.3	2.0	11.8	5.6	1.8	11.0	5.8	1.2	11.5	5.7	1.2
18-24	10.9	4.2	1.5	9.2	4.3	1.9	9.1	3.8	1.7	9.7	4.6	1.3	9.6	4.2	1.3
24-30	7.8	2.6	1.2	7.2	3.0	1.7	7.0	2.7	1.5	5.7	2.4	0.9	6.3	2.5	1.0
30-36	6.9	2.1	1.2	5.6	2.2	1.5	5.5	1.9	1.4	5.3	2.1	0.9	5.6	2.1	1.0
36-42	5.1	1.5	1.0	5.1	1.9	1.5	4.6	1.5	1.3	4.2	1.6	0.8	4.5	1.6	0.9
42-48	4.5	1.2	0.9	4.3	1.5	1.4	4.0	1.3	1.2	3.8	1.4	0.8	4.4	1.5	0.9
48-54	3.6	1.0	0.8	3.6	1.2	1.3	4.1	1.3	1.4	2.9	1.0	0.7	3.4	1.1	0.8
54-60	3.1	0.8	0.8	3.0	1.0	1.1	3.8	1.1	1.3	3.1	1.1	0.8	2.7	0.8	0.7
60-66	2.6	0.6	0.7	2.1	0.7	0.9	3.1	0.9	1.2	2.6	0.8	0.7	2.8	0.8	0.7
66-72	2.3	0.6	0.6	2.5	0.8	1.1	3.2	0.9	1.3	2.4	0.9	0.8	0.6	0.6	0.6
72+		23.4	85.5		29.8	81.2		26.3	81.4		31.1	88.4		28.9	87.9
TOTAL		100.0	100.0		100.0	100.0		100.0	100.0		100.0	100.0		100.0	100.0
EXPECTED SPELL DURATION	69.0 months			73.6 months			61.1 months			80.3 months			72.0 months		

Source: Computed by author, based on data provided by G. F. Barret.

263

guy lacroix

Bane and Ellwood[19] report results for single parents in the US using Panel Survey of Income Dynamics (PSID) data from 1968 to 1980. They found that the exit rates exhibit strong duration dependence, and that over 68.3 percent of ongoing spells last more than six years.[20] Their results are quite similar to those found for Quebec by Duclos *et al*. We must thus conclude, as do Bane and Ellwood,[21] that most welfare program resources are spent on individuals experiencing very long spells.

Naturally, the fact that the exit rates differ significantly across provinces has a direct bearing on expected spell duration. The first thing to notice is that spells last much longer in Quebec than they do in British Columbia. However, in both provinces the expected spell duration is relatively constant across demographic groups, except for single parents. Their average spell is roughly twice as long as that of the other demographic groups. The expected spell duration for single parents in Quebec is similar to that reported by Bane and Ellwood[22] for the US (54 months).

Off-Welfare Spells

The distributions that were computed to characterize spell lengths can also be used to characterize off-welfare spells. Essentially, we focus on elapsed time between two spells of welfare. These distributions are particularly well suited to our needs given that many off-welfare spells are right-censored.[23]

The information in table 4 is organized as in table 3. There are a few results in table 4 that are worth highlighting. First, there appears to be pronounced negative duration dependence in both Quebec and British Columbia; the longer individuals remain off welfare, the less likely they are to return. This is true for all demographic groups, as shown by the rapidly decreasing hazard rates. On the other hand, the exit rates of off-welfare spells in British Columbia are greater than those in Quebec. This implies that the average off-welfare spell is shorter in British Columbia. Indeed, single men in Quebec will stay off welfare for an average of 79 months before returning, while those in British Columbia will remain off welfare for an average of only 69 months. The difference between single women and couples without children is even more pronounced. In contrast, single parents in both provinces will remain off welfare for approximately the same length of time, 60 months, and will return to welfare faster than any other group.

From tables 3 and 4, one must conclude that the dynamics of welfare participation in the two provinces differ considerably; welfare spells are much longer in Quebec, but return rates are much lower. Ideally, these two dimensions of welfare dynamics should be integrated into a single measure of welfare dependency. But there are many ways to define an index of welfare dependency.[24]

Table 5

Welfare Dependency Index by Household Type,
Quebec and British Columbia

	Quebec	British Columbia
Single men	21.2	9.6
Single women	16.6	10.7
Single parent	38.5	20.5
Couples without children	15.9	7.5
Couples with children	22.8	9

Note: Calculations by authors based on data from tables 3 and 4.

The one used in this paper is simple to compute and has a neat intuitive interpretation. Let DW_i be the average welfare spell length of household type i. Further, let DOW_i be the average duration off welfare of the same household type. Thus, $DT_i = DW_i + DOW_i$ is the total duration of a complete cycle (on-welfare-off-welfare). Thus, welfare dependency can be defined as:

$$d_i = DW_i \times \frac{1}{DT_i}$$

The welfare dependency index d_i corresponds with the fraction of a cycle that is spent on welfare. If the cycle is repeated continuously, d_i measures the average time over a cycle that is spent on welfare. The second term on the right-hand side of the equation is the frequency with which household type i starts a new cycle. For example, if $DT_i = 100$, $1/DT_i = 0.01$, thus, this household has one chance out of a hundred to start a new cycle each month. The index is such that a household that has long but infrequent spells may show less dependency than another household that has short but frequent spells.

We computed the index for each household type, and for both provinces, on the basis of the expected spell duration reported in tables 3 and 4. The results presented in table 5 are interesting. For instance, despite the fact that Quebec households stay off welfare longer, each household type in Quebec depicts more welfare dependency than its counterpart in BC. Also, single women in Quebec show less welfare dependency than single men, despite the fact that their spells last longer, on average. There are no significant differences between single men and single women in British Columbia. In both provinces single parents rely most on welfare, by far. The dependency index for single parents is twice as large as that for any other demographic group in both provinces. This is because they have longer welfare spells and shorter stays off welfare.

The policy implications of these results are quite clear. First, welfare programs should target services to entrants who have returned to the program within a year or so of leaving. To the extent that these individuals have already made an attempt at economic independence, targeted intervention to help them try again may be useful. Second, if postprogram assistance is provided to reduce recidivism, the crucial period is the first six months. This is especially true in British Columbia, where short-term recidivism is more prevalent.[25]

Incentive Effects of Welfare Programs

The previous section focused on the dynamics of welfare participation in Quebec and British Columbia. The analysis was based entirely on nonparametric estimations of hazard rates using large administrative files in both provinces. These estimations are very useful to characterize the dynamics of welfare participation. Our goal now is to investigate the extent to which welfare participation is related to program parameters.

Incentive Effects in the United States

The incentive effects of the US welfare program, which is essentially limited to single parents, have recently been surveyed in an important paper by Moffitt.[26] The literature reviewed in that paper shows unequivocally that the main policy variables have the expected impact on labour supply and welfare participation. More recent research reinforces these findings. For instance, Fitzgerald,[27] using the 1984-85 panels of the Survey of Income and Program Participation (SIPP), finds that benefits and local unemployment rates substantially reduce the exit rates from welfare. Blank and Ruggles[28] use the 1986-87 panels of SIPP and conclude that higher benefits reduce exit rates and increase recidivism, while higher local unemployment rates also tend to lower exit rates. Finally, Keane and Moffitt[29] also use the 1984 SIPP panel and find that higher benefits increase participation. Interestingly, their study also indicates that lower tax-back rates increase labour supply but that the overall effect on caseloads is positive. This is primarily due to the so-called "break-even problem," according to which lower tax rates raise the break-even level and thus draw some individuals onto the rolls.[30]

The literature on the US program Aid to Families with Dependent Children (AFDC) has convinced many that being on welfare is clearly the result of a decision process. In fact, the bulk of the empirical literature supports that claim. Yet Moffitt warns that the elasticities typically found in the literature cannot explain the long-term trends, or indeed any recent trends in welfare caseloads. While the program parameters undoubtedly affect the decision to participate and to remain on welfare, other unaccounted for factors may be just as important in explaining the growth in caseloads over the years.

Incentive Effects in Canada

The welfare system in Canada is generally regarded as being poorly designed.[31] Its main features are such that, once on the rolls, individuals have very little incentive to leave. Indeed, high tax-back rates, (relatively) high benefit levels, few proactive measures, etc., are all conducive to long welfare spells. Fortunately, research on the incentive effects of the welfare system in Canada has increased significantly in recent years. The research can be classified into three broad categories, according to the nature of the data used and the measure of welfare participation. The first category uses yearly data on the proportion of provincial populations on welfare over time. These have fluctuated considerably in the past decade. Differences in provincial programs are used to explain the variations in these dependency rates. The second category uses survey data to study the incidence of welfare, i.e., the probability that an individual will receive welfare payments in a given year. Differences in provincial program parameters are studied and the impact of these differences on the probability of receiving welfare payments estimated. Finally, the third category uses administrative data to study the dynamics of participation in a given province. In this type of study, variations in program parameters over time are studied and the impact of these variations on exit and return rates estimated. In what follows, we will summarize the main findings of the literature for each category separately.

Studies of Dependency Rates

The starting point of most studies focusing on dependency rates is the apparent structural increase that follows major economic downturns. Indeed, as shown in figure 1, dependency rates in all three provinces usually decrease following a recession, but not to their previous levels. Researchers have thus tried to determine whether the positive trend in dependency rates may be partly explained by changes in program parameters.

Naturally, the main difficulty in relating changes in the dependency rates to program parameters is that the latter may be highly correlated with business cycles. Fortunately, provincial jurisdictions have made important changes to their programs at different times over the past 15 years. Brown[32] thus uses data for Ontario, Alberta and British Columbia over 1981-93 to study, separately, the relationships between dependency rates and unemployment rates, and dependency rates and benefit levels. His results show that in Ontario increases in welfare benefits account for 16 percent of the increase in caseloads. The results for the other provinces are not as clear. He also finds that the unemployment rate has a similar impact on caseloads.

Brown provides some evidence that benefit levels to some extent explain the observed trend in caseloads. Yet this leaves out the potentially important relationship between UI eligibility rules and welfare caseloads. The tightening of the eligibility rules may directly affect provincial caseloads. Fortin[33] uses data on all 10 provinces for the period 1975-93 and includes a measure of UI availability. His results show that spillover effects from UI restrictions are responsible for 33 percent of increased welfare usage while increased benefits account for approximately 17 percent.[34]

Two studies have investigated the relation between dependency rates and benefits more recently. Both studies include measures of UI availability and minimum-wage rates. Stark[35] uses data for nine provinces (PEI was excluded) for 1982-96. His specification includes relative benefits, i.e., benefits/minimum wage earnings, as well as dummy variables for the province and the year. His results show that there is a positive and highly significant relationship between relative benefits and dependency rates. Fortin and Crémieux[36] provide a very detailed analysis of the relationship between welfare caseloads and UI eligibility rules and benefits. They use data for Quebec, Ontario, Alberta and British Columbia for 1977-96. Their results are similar to those of Fortin in that as much as 25 percent of the observed increase in caseloads is attributable to more stringent UI availability restrictions. Furthermore, the 25 percent increase in welfare benefits in Ontario between 1985 and 1994 is found to be responsible for 22 percent of the increase in the province's caseloads in the early 1990s.

Studies of Take-Up Rates

The principal studies of take-up rates in Canada are Allen,[37] Charette and Meng,[38] Dooley[39] and Christofides et al.[40] They all use survey data on welfare claimants and nonclaimants to analyze the participation decision.[41]

Allen uses data from the 1986 Canadian census to study the impact of provincial benefit levels, liquid assets exemptions, earnings exemption and tax-back rates on the participation decision. Among other things, his results show that the decision to participate in welfare is affected by these variables as expected *a priori*. Charette and Meng use data from the 1989 Labour Market Activity Study (LMAS) much for the same purpose as does Allen. The results of Charette and Meng indicate that benefit levels, earned income exemptions and tax-back rates all affect the participation decision. These results are consistent with the notion that welfare participation is an economic decision based on labour supply considerations. Christofides *et al.* use the same data as Charrette and Meng to study the decision to either work or claim welfare benefits. Although these decisions are not statistically independent, Christofides *et al.* find that welfare parameters (benefit levels, tax-back rates, etc.) have no impact on the decision to participate in welfare. The authors note that the absence of any relationship may be attributable to the fact that changes in welfare program parameters may affect participation over time, and cross-sectional data may be unable to uncover such a relationship.

Dooley uses data from the Survey of Consumer Finances between 1973-91 to conduct an analysis similar to Charette and Meng[42]. Dooley conjectures that more liberal provinces may provide more generous welfare benefits and attach less stigma to being on welfare. If this is true, one should observe a positive association between benefit levels and the participation decision. Using a time series of cross-sections provides a richer variation in provincial program parameters and enables him to include provincial dummy variables. These dummy variables, or so-called "provincial fixed-effects," are expected to capture components of the provincial programs not accounted for in the other variables. Overall, Dooley's results are consistent with those of Allen and Charette and Meng. If anything, these studies find the impact of benefits on welfare participation to be larger than do studies using cross-section data. On the other hand, Dooley finds the tax-back rates have no impact on participation, as did Christofides *et al.* [43]

Studies of Spell Duration
The literature on spell duration is almost nonexistent in Canada due to the lack of appropriate panel data. Nevertheless, a number of studies were conducted recently using administrative data. Barrett[44] uses data for British Columbia for the period 1980-92 and both Fortin and Lacroix, and Fortin *et al.*[45] use data for Quebec for the period 1979-93. Dooley and Stewart[46] use similar administrative data for Ontario for the period 1983-94. All three studies focus on approximately the same period. The main difference between these studies is that both Barrett and Fortin and Lacroix study spell duration for various demographic groups, whereas Dooley and Stewart concentrate on lone parents.

All three studies use exactly the same econometric framework: the semiparametric proportional-hazard model. They seek to explain the duration of observed welfare spells by looking at changes in program parameters, individual characteristics and macroeconomic variables (unemployment rates, minimum-wage rates, etc.). The main benefit of using such long time frames is that most policy

Table 6
Impact of Selected Policy Variables on Welfare Spell Duration by Age, Gender and Family Status

	Quebec Benefits	Quebec Min. wage	Quebec Unemp. rate	Ontario Benefits	Ontario Min. wage	Ontario Unemp. rate	BC Benefits	BC Min. wage	BC Unemp. rate
WOMEN									
18-24	**pos**	neg	**pos**	n.a.	n.a.	n.a.	**pos**	**neg**	**pos**
25-30	**pos**	**neg**	pos						
30-45	**pos**	pos	neg						
MEN									
18-24	**pos**	**neg**	**pos**	n.a.	n.a.	n.a.	**pos**	**neg**	**pos**
25-30	**pos**	**neg**	**pos**						
30-45	**pos**	neg	**pos**						
LONE PARENTS									
18-30	**pos**	**pos**	**pos**	**pos**	**neg**	**pos**	**pos**	pos/neg	pos
30+	**pos**	neg	**pos**						

n.a. not available
Note: Bold characters indicate that the variable had a significant impact at conventional levels (5%).

adapting public policy to a labour market in transition

variables have changed considerably at one time or another, which facilitates identification of their mean impact on spell durations.

The main qualitative findings of these studies are reported in table 6. Generally, the results are consistent with the view that exits from welfare are at least partially determined by financial considerations. Increases in benefits translate into longer spell durations. This result is statistically significant for every household type in the table. The impact of the minimum-wage rate is not so clear cut. Some groups are adversely affected while others are not. For instance, single women and men in Quebec and British Columbia leave welfare sooner when the minimum wage increases. On the other hand, lone parents' spell duration increases or decreases with the minimum-wage rate depending on the province of residence. Finally, whenever the unemployment rate increases, all groups see their welfare spells extended.

The literature on the incentive effects of welfare programs in Canada, although in its infancy, indicates that decisions to participate in and remain on welfare are sensitive to program parameters. At the moment we know too little to make any statement about the extent to which changes in provincial caseloads are determined by program parameters. Nevertheless, all the studies conducted so far indicate that program parameters do matter.

The Impact of Government-Sponsored Training Programs

Most provincial welfare programs provide various job-search assistance and skill-enhancing programs that aim to increase self-sufficiency. The unemployment insurance program provides similar assistance. In the US, programs such as these have been much researched in recent years. As mentioned earlier, the literature can be divided into two broad categories: experimental and nonexperimental (econometric).[47] This section will briefly review the main lessons that can be drawn from this literature. Evidence from European countries, whose institutions perhaps have more in common with Canadian institutions, will also be underlined.

Experimental Evaluations
For the past 15 years, many US states have implemented small-scale experiments in order to evaluate the potential impact of specific provisions of their assistance programs.[48] These experiments are conducted within either of two frameworks: (1) individuals on welfare across the state are randomly assigned to an experimental or control group; or (2) assistance programs are modified only in a certain number of sites (cities, counties, etc.) and all the participants are subjected to the new rules in the "saturated sites." The impact of the new program is then

assessed by comparing the behaviour of the control and experimental groups (in 1), or by comparing the behavioural responses between the saturated sites and other similar sites (in 2).[49]

Recent evaluations of these experiments can be summarized as follows:

(1) Programs that provide intensive support and on-the-job training generate the most significant increases in income. These increases are still noticeable several years after program completion.

(2) Job-search assistance generates smaller but persistent gains. These programs cost less and appear to be most efficient for individuals who have had little contact with the labour market (individuals with long spells, lone parents, etc.).

(3) The increases in income following participation in these programs are sufficiently modest that most participants still qualify for benefits. Consequently, the programs do not yield substantial savings on total program costs.[50]

One of the most ambitious experiments was conducted in the state of Washington in 1988. The Family Independence Program (FIP), a five-year experiment, provided parents with the opportunity to acquire job skills through education, training and employment. Large bonuses were paid for full-time and part-time work. Child-care and other support services were available to participants. The program was also intended to change the image of and attitudes toward welfare by providing a more supportive and less stigmatizing environment than that provided under the AFDC. Independent evaluations of the FIP were recently conducted by Long and Wissoker[51] and Leigh.[52] Surprisingly, both conclude that the FIP appears to have had little effect on employment and earnings and has resulted in increased welfare use and average benefits. The most puzzling question is why the program's success in significantly increasing employment and training investment is not reflected in subsequent labour market opportunities and reduced welfare dependency? The studies suggest a variety of reasons for this failure. Among them are the following:

(1) The positive incentives were not matched with any program requirements. The lack of obligation probably allowed many participants to make no effort to reduce their participation in welfare.

(2) Frequent staff contacts were envisioned at the outset. However, cost neutrality (with respect to AFDC) made follow-through impossible. The program was thus scaled back and many of the changes envisioned by the FIP were never implemented.

(3) Leigh claims that features of the FIP that increased the attractiveness of welfare tended to be dominant over program features designed to facilitate the transition to self-sufficiency.[53]

A novel experiment is currently under way in two Canadian provinces, New Brunswick and British Columbia. The Self-Sufficiency Project (SSP) is a large-scale demonstration project designed to determine whether making work pay more than welfare can help interested single parents choose work over income assistance.[54] The main features of the SSP program are: (1) a substantial financial incentive for working relative to not working;[55] (2) a relatively low marginal tax rate on earnings; and (3) a requirement to work a minimum of 30 hours per week.

The minimum work hours requirement aims at preventing workers from reducing their work hours in response to the program. To qualify for SSP, single parents had to be on welfare for at least 12 out of the 13 months prior to November 1992. This requirement was intended to prevent individuals from applying for welfare simply to gain eligibility for SSP and to focus program resources on long-term recipients.

Individuals were randomly selected from the administrative records in both provinces. The first cohort includes over 2,122 individuals, of whom 1,056 are in the control group and 1,066 are in the program group. Recently, Card and Robins[56] presented the results obtained from observing the first cohort over 18 months of program eligibility. Their results provide convincing evidence that financial incentives do increase labour market attachment and significantly reduce welfare participation. For instance, the proportion of recipients in the program group working full-time is about twice as high as that in the control group. But the average wage of the full-time workers is only $1.00 to $3.00 per hour above the minimum wage. It is thus likely that many will return to welfare when the supplement ends, unless significant wage progression occurs.

Card and Robins report that the average welfare and SSP payment for the program group is higher than the average welfare payment for the control group for the first 23 months of the experiment. They also report that the percentage of people receiving either welfare or SSP in the program group is consistently higher than the percentage on welfare in the control group. This implies that a "sizeable percentage of people receive supplement payments under SSP, but would have moved off welfare even in the absence of the program."[57]

These findings are consistent with those reported earlier on the impact of program parameters. Individuals do appear to be sensitive to financial incentives. However, it is not clear to what extent the behaviour of the program group is affected by the fact that the supplement is temporary (three years). If individuals are forward-looking, their behaviour may be significantly affected by the finite duration of the program.[58] To that effect, many researchers have recently questioned the relevance of using random experiments to study long-run

273

program impacts. They advocate using nonexperimental methods to avoid some of the caveats associated with such experiments.

Nonexperimental Evaluations

Recently, a number of studies have advocated using nonexperimental methods to assess the impact of training programs. One obvious reason to use nonexperimental methods is that there are many large data sets (administrative files or survey data) that contain much information on program participants and nonparticipants. The main problem with such data is to control for selectivity into the programs.[59] Experiments avoid this problem of selectivity by randomly assigning individuals into the control or the experimental groups. Hence, a simple comparison of the employment rates of the trainee and control groups will yield an unbiased estimate of the effects of training on the probability of employment.

Ham and LaLonde[60] have shown that comparisons between the employment and unemployment spells of trainee and control groups may very well yield significantly biased estimates of the effect of training. The reason is simply that random assignment does not guarantee that the trainee and control groups experiencing employment and unemployment spells are random subsets of the experimental sample. Thus formal statistical models must be used to adequately assess the impact of training programs on the duration of future employment and unemployment spells.

Ham and LaLonde use data from the National Supported Work (NSW) demonstration project to model the work histories of trainees and control groups. This program provided work experience to a random sample of eligible women in the AFDC program. Gritz[61] uses data from the National Longitudinal Survey on Youth (NLSY) to study the work histories of a sample of men and women. Unlike in Ham and LaLonde, participation in training programs had to be modelled explicitly to account for selectivity bias. Bonnal et al.[62] use nonexperimental data collected in France by l'Institut Nationale de la Statistique et des Études Économiques (l'INSEE) from 1986 to 1988. The paper uses an approach that is similar to although more complex than Gritz's, and focuses on the impact of French youth training programs on the labour market trajectories of unemployed individuals. Finally, Cockx and Ridder[63] use administrative data on welfare recipients in Belgium to model program effects on spell duration.

All these papers aim at modelling the changes in labour market participation following participation in a training program. All, except for Ham and LaLonde, must explicitly account for the nonrandom assignment into training programs. The results of Ham and LaLonde are somewhat encouraging. They show that NSW raised women's employment rates essentially by helping those who had found a job to remain employed longer. In contrast, the three other studies report rather disappointing results. For instance, Gritz[64] finds that, while private training programs increase the duration of women's future employment spells, they have no impact on men's future employment spells. Furthermore, his results indicate that "participation in government-sponsored training programs actually deteriorates the labour market circumstances of individuals, though this result is based upon a relatively small number of government trainees."[65] Bonnal et al. and Cockx and Ridder use much larger data sets and basically come to the same conclusion. Bonnal et al. find that in France subsidized, on-the-job training has a positive impact on the future employment spells of those who are poorly educated, while it has no impact on the employment spells of those who are more educated. Community work is found to have no effect on future transitions for the least educated, and even to have a negative impact on those with a vocational diploma. Cockx and Ridder and Bonnal et al. also report considerable selectivity in the training programs. In Belgium social employment, when properly modelled, is found to increase welfare dependency.

There is some evidence that some programs in Canada do have a positive impact in helping participants off the UI or welfare rolls. Recently, Park et al.[66] studied the impact of UI training programs. They used administrative data coupled with survey data collected from January 1988 to June 1991. With a sample of 2,450 trainees and 927 nontrainees, they compared trainee and nontrainee incomes in the post-training period. They used a difference-in-difference estimator to account for selectivity into the training programs. Overall, they found that programs such as Fee Payer (where the training is paid for by a third party or by the trainee), Job Entry (which promotes the re-entry of women who have been absent from the labour market for at least three years or youths who are no longer required to attend school) and Skill Shortages have a significant impact on the post-training income of trainees.

In Quebec, employability programs aimed at welfare participants were evaluated using a similar approach.[67] A random sample of over 5,000 trainees and nontrainees was chosen from the administrative files. The groups were chosen to have similar profiles in terms of duration on welfare and socio-demographic characteristics. They were interviewed 6 and 18 months after the training period. A comparison of the employment rates and incomes of the two groups in the post-training period shows that classroom training has a significant impact on the employment rates of lone mothers, but not those of single individuals. Furthermore, subsidized employment seems to have a significant impact on various household types.[68]

Finally, Fortin *et al.* [69] have studied the impact of UI and welfare training programs on the labour market transitions of welfare claimants in Quebec. They use administrative data to study the programs' impact on the duration of welfare, employment and unemployment spells. To account for selectivity biases, they use a difference-in-difference estimator similar to that used by Park *et al.* The results of Fortin *et al.* show that all training programs have substantial impacts on the durations of employment, unemployment and/or welfare spells. In particular, they have found that participation in an EI training program translated into longer employment spells for men, and shorter unemployment spells for both men and women. Participation in welfare training programs, on the other hand, does not benefit men. Indeed, they have found that male participants had longer welfare spells and shorter employment spells. Women participants were found to have shorter employment spells. Finally, the Job Entry program was found to benefit both men and women and was associated with longer employment spells and shorter welfare spells.

Conclusion

As is the case in many countries, program expenditures and caseloads of welfare programs in Canada have continued to rise over the past few decades. In recent years, these increases have been greater, placing a fiscal strain on all levels of government. One of the more troubling aspects of increasing caseloads is that the proportion of able-bodied recipients has dramatically increased in the past 15 years or so. This is a symptom that we should definitely worry about.

In this paper we reviewed studies of the dynamics of welfare participation by able-bodied recipients in two Canadian provinces, Quebec and British Columbia. The evidence indicates that there are significant flows into and out of welfare programs in both provinces. To a certain extent, it can be argued that the welfare system is doing what it is intended to do, that is, provide temporary relief to needy individuals. On the other hand, a close look at the data also reveals that a disproportionate share of program expenditures is devoted to long-term recipients. These recipients can be found in all household categories, but they are more likely to be single parents.

A comparison of the dynamics of welfare participation in Quebec and British Columbia raises an interesting puzzle: How is it that two provinces that fall under the same UI program and have relatively similar welfare programs[70] can generate such different welfare dynamics? We showed that the average spell length in Quebec is much longer than that in British Columbia. On the other hand, time spent off welfare is much shorter in British Columbia. Solving

276

this puzzle would certainly aid the formulation of adequate policy recommendations. Otherwise, it seems that policies should focus on long-term recipients and provide adequate help for repeat users.

The paper also reviewed the literature on the incentive effects of welfare programs in Canada and elsewhere. It generally found that individuals respond to financial incentives in their decisions to take up and to remain on welfare. We currently know too little about the incentive effects in Canada to make any strong statements about the extent to which changes in caseloads are driven by policy variables. It has been suggested that the unprecedented welfare dependency rates observed in recent years may be explained by the changes made to the UI program. We cited empirical evidence that supports this claim. Research on the interaction between UI and welfare is badly needed in Canada to formulate appropriate policy measures.

Finally, we briefly reviewed the literature on training programs. The emerging consensus in the United States is that few programs have a significant impact on the outcomes of participants, however measured. On the other hand, programs that are well targeted usually perform much better and do make a difference. The results of studies conducted in Europe are usually in line with those conducted in the US. In Canada, too little research has been carried out to warrant any strong statements. It is nevertheless likely that Canadian programs aimed at the disadvantaged will produce similar results.

277

Notes

* The author wishes to thank the editors of the current volume as well as Alice Nakamura for very useful comments.

1. G. Carter, "Federal Restraints on the Growth of Transfer Payments to the Provinces since 1986-87," *Canadian Tax Journal*, Vol. 42, no. 6 (1994), pp. 1504-32.

2. R. Moffitt, "Incentive Effects of the US Welfare System: A Review," *Journal of Economic Literature*, Vol. 30 (March 1992), pp. 1-61.

3. For a detailed comparison of the US and Canadian systems, see R.M. Blank and M.J. Hanratty, "Responding to Need: A Comparison of Social Safety Nets in Canada and the United States," in D. Card and R. B. Freeman (eds.), *Small Differences that Matter* (Chicago: University Press, 1993), pp. 191-232.

4. It has been argued that increased immigration may be partly responsible for such trends. It is true that the proportion of immigrants on welfare in Quebec increased steadily between 1981 and 1995 (from 4.5 percent to 14.1 percent). See Gouvernement du Québec, *Un parcours vers l'insertion, la formation et l'emploi* (Quebec City, QC: Ministère de la sécurité du revenu du Québec, 1996), p. 20. Yet Duclos *et al.* have found that immigrants in Quebec have shorter spells on welfare (see J-Y. Duclos, B. Fortin, G. Lacroix and H. Roberge, *La dynamique de la participation à l'aide sociale au Québec: 1979-1993*, Rapport préparé pour le compte du Ministère de la sécurité sociale du Québec, 1996). Baker and Benjamin have shown that immigrants in Canada usually have lower take-up rates (see M. Baker and D. Benjamin, "The Receipt of Transfer Payments by Immigrants in Canada," *Journal of Human Resources*, Vol. 30, no. 4 [1995], pp. 650-75).

5. For instance, the proportion of unemployed individuals in Quebec who benefit from the UI program fell from 80 percent in January 1993 to less than 58 percent in June 1996. Also, the dependency rate increased from 9.2 percent to 12.4 percent between 1990 and 1995. It has been estimated that over one quarter of this increase is attributable to changes made to the program (see P. Fortin and F. Séguin, *Pour un régime équilibré axé sur l'emploi*, Rapport de deux membres du Comité externe de réforme de la sécurité du revenu du Québec, 1996). Browning *et al.* also provide evidence that the changes to the UI program contained in Bill C-113, which made voluntary quits ineligible to benefits, resulted in significant increases in welfare participation (see M. Browning, S.R.G. Jones and P. Kuhn, *Studies on the Interactions of UI and Welfare Using COEP Data Set* (Ottawa: Human Resources Development Canada, 1995).

6. The contemporaneous correlations for Quebec and BC are 0.57 and 0.45, respectively. When the dependency rates are lagged one year, their correlation coefficients are 0.91 and 0.61, respectively.

7. The correlation coefficient for the whole period is 0.72 (both contemporaneous and lagged). For the years between 1998 and 1995, the coefficient is 0.86, while for the years between 1981 and 1988 it is -0.09.

8. The figures for Quebec are for the month of March each year. The figures for BC are yearly averages of monthly caseloads.

9. Censored observations must be accounted for in the risk set.

10. Notice that the sum is taken over infinity. Naturally, we cannot compute a survival probability for durations that last longer than those observed in the data. In what follows, we will assume that $S(t \mid t>t\_max) = S(t\_max)$. In other words, the survival probabilities for durations that last longer than the longest observed duration are assumed constant and equal to the survival probability of the longest observed duration. This assumption was first made by R.D. Gill "Censoring and Stochastic Integrals," *Mathematical Centre Tracts*, Mathematisch Centrum, Amsterdam, 1980, p. 124. The Monte Carlo experiments by J.P. Klein, "Small-Sample Moments of Some Estimators of the Variance of the Kaplan-Meier and Nelson-Aalen Estimators," *Scandinavian Journal of Statistics*, Vol. 18, no. 4 (1991), pp. 333-340, showed that this assumption was best at predicting mean duration. We make the same assumption for the Quebec and BC data to allow direct comparisons.

11. Formal derivation of these distributions can be found in M.J. Bane and D.T. Ellwood, "Slipping Into and Out of Poverty: The Dynamics of Spells," *Journal of Human Resources*, Vol. 21, no. 1 (1986), pp. 1-23.

12. To be valid, this definition requires that we assume a no-growth steady state.

13. Similar work is currently being conducted for Ontario by M.D.Dooley, "The Evolution of Welfare Participation Among Canadian Lone Mothers from 1973-1991," *Canadian Journal of*

Economics, Vol. 32, no. 3 (1999), pp. 589-612, and for Newfoundland by G. Lacroix, "The Dynamics of Welfare Participation in Newfoundland," report prepared for the Applied Research Branch, Human Resources Development Canada, Ottawa, Ont., 1999.

14. J.-Y. Duclos, B. Fortin, G. Lacroix and H. Roberge, "The Dynamics of Welfare Participation in Québec," working paper no. 9817, Université Laval, Québec City, QC, 1998.

15. G. Barrett and M.I. Cragg, "An Untold Story: The Characteristics of Welfare Use in British Columbia," Canadian Journal of Economics, Vol. 31, no.1 (1998), pp. 165-88.

16. Gary Barrett kindly provided detailed data for the British Columbia tables. Note that the tables focus on employable individuals to allow comparisons with Quebec.

17. For further discussion, see T. MaCurdy, "A Synthesis of the Behavioral Aspects of Welfare Dependency and an Assessment of the Findings," working paper no. E-89-11, Hoover Institution, Stanford University, Stanford, Calif., 1989.

18. Indeed, if exit from welfare is partly determined by motivation, then more motivated individuals will leave on average earlier than less motivated individuals. Consequently, the proportion of less motivated individuals will increase with duration. Thus, the composition of the welfare population will change with duration, which will lead to decreasing hazard rates. Therefore, duration dependence may simply reflect a compositional change in the population rather than a genuine behavioural component.

19. M.J. Bane and D.T. Ellwood, The Dynamics of Dependence: The Routes to Self-Sufficiency, report prepared for the US Department of Health and Human Services, 1983.

20. Welch has recently found that the average spell duration in the US has been significantly underestimated in previous research (see S.M. Welch, "Nonparametric Estimates of the Duration of Welfare Spells," Economics Letters, Vol. 69, no. 2 [1998], pp. 217-21).

21. Duclos et al., "The Dynamics of Welfare Participation in Quebec"; M.J. Bane and D.T. Ellwood, Welfare Realities: From Rhetoric to Reform (Cambridge: Harvard University Press, 1994); and Bane and Ellwood, The Dynamics of Dependence.

22. Bane and Ellwood, The Dynamics of Dependence.

23. To briefly explain the concept of right censored, suppose you observe people on welfare between January 1998 and December 1998. Those who are on welfare in December 1998 are right-censored. We know their spell will probably go on for a few more months, but we do not know how many. For a more detailed analysis of welfare returns in British Columbia, see R. Bruce et al., "Those Returning to Income Assistance," Canadian Journal of Economics, Vol. 29, special issue, Part I (1996), pp. S33-S38.

24. See, for example, T. MaCurdy, "Measures of Welfare Dependency: An Evaluation," working paper no. E-89-10, Hoover Institution, Stanford University, Stanford, CA, 1989.

25. For similar policy recommendations concerning the US, see R. M. Blank and P. Ruggles, "Short-Term Recidivism among Public-Assistance Recipients," American Economic Review, Vol. 84, no. 2 (1994), pp. 49-53; and Bruce et al., "Those Returning to Income Assistance," for similar findings in British Columbia.

26. Moffitt, "Incentive Effects of the US Welfare System."

27. J.M. Fitzgerald, "Local Labor Markets and Local Area Effects on Welfare Duration," Journal of Policy Analysis and Management, Vol. 14, no. 1 (1995), pp. 43-67.

28. R.M. Blank and P. Ruggles, "When Do Women Use AFDC and Food Stamps? The Dynamics of Eligibility vs. Participation," NBER working paper no. 4429, Cambridge, MA, 1993.

29. M. Keane and R. Moffitt, "A Structural Model of Multiple Welfare Program Participation and Labor Supply," discussion paper no. 1080-96, Institute for Research on Poverty, Wisconsin University, 1996.

30. These two terms can be explained as follows. Welfare claimants may be allowed to work and thus earn income. The tax-back rate is the amount by which welfare benefits are reduced for each dollar of earned income. The tax-back rate is often 100% (sometimes more); thus each dollar earned reduces benefits by a dollar. The break-even level is the level of earned income above which an individual is no longer eligible for welfare benefits. Thus,

Let G = welfare benefits
t = the tax-back rate
the break-even level of income is G/t. Hence, whenever t decreases, welfare claimants tend to work more. The impact on total caseloads

is unclear, since now more people qualify for welfare benefits since (G/t) has increased.

31. OCDE, *Études économiques de l'OCDE: Canada* (Paris: OCDE, 1994).

32. D.M. Brown, "Welfare Caseload Trends in Canada," in *Helping the Poor* (Toronto: C.D. Howe Institute, 1995), pp. 37-90.

33. P. Fortin, "The Future of Social Assistance in Canada," Department of Economics, Université du Québec à Montréal, Montreal, QC, 1995, mimeographed.

34. See endnote 6.

35. A.A. Stark, "An Examination of the Growth of Social Assistance Receipt in Canada," Department of Economics, University of British Columbia, Vancouver, BC, 1997, mimeographed.

36. P. Fortin and P.-Y. Crémieux, "The Determinants of Social Assistance Rates: Evidence from a Panel of Canadian Provinces, 1987-1996," Department of Economics, Université du Québec à Montréal, Montreal, QC, 1998, mimeographed.

37. D.W. Allen, "Welfare and the Family: The Canadian Experience," *Journal of Labor Economics*, Vol. 11, no. 1, Part 2 (January 1993), pp. S201-23.

38. M.F. Charette and R. Meng, "The Determinants of Welfare Participation of Female Heads of Household in Canada," *Canadian Journal of Economics*, Vol. 27, no. 2 (1994), pp. 290-306.

39. Dooley, "The Evolution of Welfare Participation."

40. L.N. Christofides, T. Stengos and R. Swidinsky, "Welfare Participation and Labour Market Behaviour in Canada," *Canadian Journal of Economics*, Vol. 30, no. 3 (1998), pp. 595-621.

41. An important issue that has not been dealt with in Canada concerns so-called incomplete participation in welfare programs. Indeed, the extent to which individuals who are eligible for welfare benefits do not claim them has not been well documented in Canada. For evidence in the US, see Blank and Ruggles, "When Do Women Use AFDC and Food Stamps? The Dynamics of Eligibility vs. Participation." For a recent analysis in Britain, see J.-Y. Duclos, "Estimating and Testing a Model of Welfare Participation: The Case of Supplementary Benefits in Britain," *Economica*, Vol. 64 (February 1997), pp. 81-100.

42. Dooley, "The Evolution of Welfare Participation"; Charette and Meng, "The Determinants of Welfare Participation."

43. Dooley, "The Evolution of Welfare Participation"; Allen, "Welfare and the Family"; Charette and Meng, "The Determinants of Welfare Participation"; Christofides *et al.*, "Welfare Participation and Labour Market Behaviour in Canada."

44. G. Barrett, "The Duration of Welfare Spells and State Dependence: Evidence from British Columbia," Department of Economics, University of British Columbia, Vancouver, BC, 1996, mimeographed.

45. B. Fortin and G. Lacroix, "Welfare Benefits, Minimum Wage Rate and the Duration of Welfare Spells: Evidence from a Natural Experiment in Canada," working paper no. 9708, Department of Economics, Université Laval, 1997; B. Fortin, G. Lacroix and J.-F. Thibault, "The Interaction of UI and Welfare, and the Dynamics of Welfare Participation of Single Parents," *Canadian Public Policy*, Vol. 25, supplement 1 (November 1999), pp. 115-132.

46. M. Dooley and J. Stewart, "The Duration of Spells on Welfare and Off-Welfare Among Lone Mothers in Ontario," *Canadian Public Policy*, Vol. 25, supplement 1 (November 1999), pp. 47-72.

47. For a discussion of the pros and cons of each method, see G. Burtless, "The Case for Randomized Field Trials in Economic and Policy Research," *Journal of Economic Perspective*, Vol. 9, no. 2 (1995), pp. 63-84; and J.J. Heckman and J.A. Smith, "Assessing the Case for Social Experiments," *Journal of Economic Perspective*, Vol. 9, no. 2 (1995), pp. 85-110.

48. A very detailed and comprehensive account of these experiments is provided by J.M. Gueron and E. Pauly, *From Welfare to Work* (New York, NY: Russell Sage Foundation, 1991). For recent comprehensive surveys of US studies, see also R.J. LaLonde, "The Promise of the Public Sector-Sponsored Training Programs," *Journal of Economic Perspectives*, Vol. 9, no. 2 (1995), pp. 149-68; and D. Friedlander, D.H. Greenberg and P.K. Robbins, "Evaluating Government Training Programs for the Economically Disadvantaged," *Journal of Economic Literature*, Vol. 35, no. 4 (1997), pp. 1809-55.

49. Homogeneity of saturated and nonsaturated sites is sometimes achieved through regression analysis.

50. Bell and Orr recently evaluated seven experiments that were conducted in different states under the AFDC Homemaker-Home Health Aide Demonstration Project (see S.H. Bell and L.L. Orr, "Is Subsidized Employment Cost Effective for Welfare Recipients?" *Journal of Human Resources*, Vol. 29, no. 1 [1994], pp. 42-61). Individuals were trained for four to eight weeks to provide care for chronically ill patients. Then they were integrated into a subsidized job that could last up to 12 months. From a strict cost-benefit point of view, only two of the experiments paid their way. Unfortunately, the authors could not establish why these two experiments were successful.

51. S.K. Long and D.A. Wissoker, "Welfare Reform at Three Years," *Journal of Human Resources*, Vol. 30, no. 4 (1995), pp. 766-90.

52. D.E. Leigh, "Can a Voluntary Workfare Program Change the Behavior of Welfare Recipients? New Evidence from Washington State's Family Independence Program," *Journal of Policy and Analysis Management*, Vol. 14, no. 4 (1995), pp. 567-89.

53. Moffitt shows that the long-run caseload effects of programs emphasizing employment and training are difficult to predict *a priori* (See R. Moffitt, "The Effect of Employment and Training Programs on Entry and Exit from the Welfare Caseload," *Journal of Policy Analysis and Management*, Vol. 15, no. 1 [1996], pp. 32-50).

54. For a detailed description of the experiment see S. Lui-Gurr, S.C. Vernon and T. Mijanovich, *Making Work Pay Better Than Welfare: An Early Look at the Self-Sufficiency Project* (Vancouver: Social Research and Demonstration Corporation, 1994).

55. The program is run in British Columbia and New Brunswick and provides earnings supplements equal to half the difference between a participant's gross labour income earnings and a break-even level equal to $37,000 in BC and $30,000 in New Brunswick. Unearned income, other family members' incomes or family size do not affect the supplement.

56. D. Card and P.K. Robins, "Do Financial Incentives Encourage Welfare Recipients to Work? Initial 18-Months Findings from the Self Sufficiency Project," working paper no. R-96-9E, Applied Research Branch, Human Resources Development Canada, Ottawa, ON.

57. Card and Robins, "Do Financial Incentives Encourage Welfare Recipients to Work," p. 10.

58. Card and Robins, "Do Financial Incentives Encourage Welfare Recipients to Work?"

acknowledge that the temporary nature of the program may affect somewhat the behavioural response of participants.

59. Selectivity bias is a fundamental problem in the evaluation literature and is well known to economists. Those who participate in training programs have unobservable characteristics that are systematically different from those of individuals who do not participate, for example, motivation to work. If there is selectivity bias, the analyst will attribute impacts to the programs that are in fact due to individual motivation.

60. J.C. Ham and R.J. LaLonde, "The Effect of Sample Selection and Initial Conditions in Duration Models: Evidence from Experimental Data on Training," *Econometrica*, Vol. 64, no. 1 (1996), pp. 175-205.

61. R.M. Gritz, "The Impact of Training on the Frequency and the Duration of Employment," *Journal of Econometrics*, Vol. 57 (May-June 1993), pp. 21-51.

62. L. Bonnal, D. Fougère and A. Sérandon, "Evaluating the Impact of French Employment Policies on Individual Labour Market Histories," *Review of Economic Studies*, Vol. 64, no. 4 (1997), pp. 683-713.

63. B. Cockx and G. Ridder, "Social Employment of Welfare Recipients in Belgium: An Evaluation," Université Catholique de Louvain, Belgium, 1996, mimeographed.

64. Gritz, "The Impact of Training on the Frequency and the Duration of Employment."

65. Gritz, "The Impact of Training on the Frequency and the Duration of Employment," p. 49.

66. N. Park, B. Power, W.C. Riddell and G. Wong, "An Assessment of the Impact of Government-Sponsored Training," *Canadian Journal of Economics*, Vol. 29, special issue, Part I (April 1996), pp. S93-98.

67. See F. Tarte and A. Boisvert, *Relance auprès des prestataires de la sécurité du revenu ayant participé à un programme de développement de l'employabilité ou d'intégration en emploi*, Direction de l'évaluation et de la statistique, Ministère de la sécurité du revenu du Québec, 1994.

68. Recently, though, Warburton and Frketich warned that the subsidized employment programs may very well have sizeable displacement effects (see W.P. Warburton and C.L. Frketich, "Toward More Complete Cost Benefit Analysis of Wage Subsidy Programs,"

Canadian Journal of Economics, Vol. 29, special issue, Part I [1996], pp. S90-S92).

69. B. Fortin, D. Fougère and G. Lacroix, "The Impact of Government-Sponsored Training Programs on Labour Market Transitions," report prepared for Applied Research Branch, Human Resources Development Canada, 1999.

70. Boychuk provides an interesting taxonomy of the provincial welfare programs (see G. Boychuck, "Reforming the Canadian Social Assistance Complex: The Provincial Welfare States and Canadian Federalism," in D.M. Brown and J.W. Rose [eds.], Canada: The State of the Federation [Kingston, ON: The Institute of Intergovernmental Relations, 1995], pp. 115-42). The Quebec program is classified as a "market-family enforcement" regime (along with Saskatchewan's and Alberta's), whereas the British Columbia program is classified as a "market performance" regime (along with New Brunswick's and Nova Scotia's). Both are considered to promote labour market participation, but through different routes. The market family enforcement regime ensures that assistance is relatively unattractive, whereas the market performance regime uses positive employment and incentive schemes.

Public Pension Programs and Labour Force Attachment

Michael Baker and Dwayne Benjamin

Introduction

The perilous state of the finances of Canada's public pension programs has been the subject of much discussion. Most of the concern is rooted in disturbing demographic trends: the number of potential pension recipients is growing faster than the number of potential pension contributors. In a pay-as-you-go system, unless benefit or contribution rates are changed, the pension budget cannot balance. These trends motivated the recent changes to the Canada Pension Plan (CPP) with the enactment of Bill C-2 in December 1997. The most significant aspect of this legislation was the accelerated increase in contribution rates to 9.9 percent of earnings, almost double the old rate of 5.85 percent. Of course, demographic trends do not translate directly into the balance sheet of the CPP – they are mediated through the labour market. Furthermore, the links between the labour market and public pensions run in two directions. First, individuals' labour force status largely determines whether they are contributors or beneficiaries. Changes in the structure of the labour force, especially the participation or retirement decisions of older workers, will clearly affect the ratio of contributors to beneficiaries. Trends in wage growth will also affect the level of contributions per contributor and the level of benefits for pension recipients, since these benefits are tied to past earnings. Second, the labour force status of an individual may itself depend on the parameters of the public pension program. Most obviously, the decision to retire may be responsive to incentives provided by the terms of old age pension plans. The level of benefits

285

or any earnings tests (the clawback of benefits associated with labour market earnings) might also affect whether older people work after formal retirement.

To what extent can the labour force status of older workers be taken as given by policy makers, i.e., what is the relative balance of the two-way links between pensions and retirement? Obviously, an important question for policy makers is whether changes in the parameters of the CPP/QPP can affect the labour force attachment of older Canadians. The debate surrounding previous reforms suggests that many believed the answer was "yes." For example, some suggested that the introduction of early retirement provisions to the plans over the 1980s would encourage older Canadians to withdraw from the labour force. This would lead the economy to downsize through attrition, much as firms (and universities) are trying to do today. Furthermore, it was believed (and still is, to some extent) that these older workers are "clogging up" the labour market for larger, younger cohorts of workers. Against this background, it is important to note that public finance concerns dictate the opposite requirement – encouraging older workers to keep working, perhaps by increasing the retirement age to 67, as proposed in Canada, or to 70, as proposed in the United States. In either case, the critical question is whether shifting the policy lever of CPP/QPP pension parameters could promote either of these ends by affecting the labour force attachment decisions of Canadians.

In this paper we explore this question, summarizing recent evidence on the links between labour force activity and public pensions. We begin with an overview of the basic trends in working patterns and the financial state of the CPP/QPP programs. In the main part of the paper we summarize recent attempts to estimate the impact of changes in public pensions, such as early retirement provisions and retirement (earnings) tests, drawing on evidence from Canada and the United States. This evidence suggests that pension programs are only weakly connected to labour force behaviour, at least in the short run. If the CPP/QPP can be characterized as an out-of-control freight train, then changes to pension parameters of a similar order to those made in the past may be viewed as placing pennies on the track. In fact, there may be no way to change retirement behaviour through changes in public pension parameters, at least to the extent required by the state of the public coffers. This leaves the alternatives that are (to many) unattractive: significant increases in contribution rates (the path adopted in Bill C-2) or major decreases in the level of benefits to correct the budget imbalance. Unfortunately, we know very little about the labour market effects of these types of policy changes, though given the magnitude of changes typically considered, it is unlikely that they will be entirely neutral.

It is important to note that the CPP/QPP is only one of three programs that can be thought of as a package of social security programs directed toward the elderly.[1] Indeed, the interlinkages among the programs can have unintended effects on labour market incentives.[2] Some of the key features of these programs are presented in table 1. We highlight the policy parameters most likely to affect labour market attachment (at least in the short run): (1) the level of benefits; (2) the age of eligibility; and (3) any clawback of benefits for postretirement labour market earnings. This list does not exhaust the possibilities. For example, the level of benefits paid by the CPP/QPP is based on past employment status and earnings levels, and may affect work decisions throughout the life cycle. Also, the effects of the income and payroll taxes necessary to finance these programs are ignored.

The Old Age Security (OAS) is the foundation of income support for the elderly, providing, as of January 1999, a monthly check of $410.82 to all individuals, regardless of their work history. Eligibility depends entirely on age, and there were 3.7 million beneficiaries in 1998 receiving a total of $17.7 billion in benefits. Since 1989 the universality of the OAS benefit has been eroded, and it is now tied to income (not just earnings). A steep 15 percent clawback, in addition to income taxes, reduces the potential importance of this program to higher income Canadians. The Guaranteed Income Supplement (GIS) is a supplement to the OAS, providing additional benefits to lower income individuals. There is a heavy 50 percent clawback rate on the GIS for income in excess of the OAS benefit, but the base level is sufficiently high that 1.4 million elderly people were still eligible to collect at least some GIS payments, with total benefits paid in 1998 totalling $4.8 billion. In principle, the clawback of either OAS or GIS might affect the labour force decisions of the elderly. These incentive effects have been largely unexplored.[3]

CPP/QPP benefits are tied to individual labour market histories by both the number of years and level of contributions. Pension receipt can be initiated at age 65 at full entitlement, or at any other age between 60 and 70 at an actuarially adjusted rate. For example, the adjustment for early retirement (60-64) is a reduction in benefits of 6 percent per year.[4] Early retirement provisions were introduced into the QPP in 1984 and into the CPP in 1987. By December 1998, 62 percent of new retirees (CPP recipients) were between 60-64 years old (*versus* zero in 1986), highlighting the popularity of this option.

Unlike the US Social Security system, the CPP/QPP does not have an earnings test whereby benefits are reduced if an individual works too much after retirement. There is a requirement that an individual should have "substantially

287

Table 1
Old Age Security in Canada and the United States, 1999

PROGRAM	Individual eligibility	Individual maximum monthly benefits	Reductions
CANADA			
Old Age Security (OAS)	Age 65 + Universal demogrant	$410.82	Reduced by $0.15 for every dollar of income over $53,215 (zero at $85,893)
Guaranteed Income Supplement (GIS)	Age 65 + Income less than $11,736. Means tested	$488.23	Reduced by $0.50 for every dollar of non-OAS income.
Canada/Quebec Pension Plan (CPP/QPP)	Age 65+ (normal) Age 60-64 (early retirement) Benefits and eligibility based on earnings history	$751.67 (retirement at age 65) Reduced by 1/2% per month for age less than 65/increased symmetrically if retiring after age 65.	No earnings test. Earnings test to determine eligibility for early retirement, but not thereafter.
US			
Social Security	Age 65+ (normal)[1] Age 62-64 (early retirement) Benefits and eligibility based on earnings history	$1373 (retirement at age 65) Reduced by 5/9% per month for age less than 65	Earnings test: Reduced by $0.33 for each dollar of earnings over $15,500 per year for age 65+. Reduced by $0.50 for each dollar of earnings over $9,600 per year for age 62-64.

[1] The normal retirement age is set to rise in the US beginning in 2000. By 2022, the normal retirement age will be 67.
Source: Human Resources Development Canada web site, "www.hrdc-drhc.gc.ca," February 1999; United States Social Security Administration web site, "www.ssa.gov," February 1999.

ceased working" to be eligible for early retirement, but this is a weak test: it is a one-time only test and is not relevant after eligibility has been established.[5] Those who wish to can simultaneously work and collect CPP benefits. Retirement tests – which are designed to align two distinct notions of retirement: the collection of a pension and the cessation of work – have long been viewed as taxes on work and as potentially detrimental to the welfare of the elderly.

The maximum retirement benefit under the CPP was $752 per month in 1999, though the average retirement payment (in December 1998) was $408. The total benefits paid out under the CPP in 1997 were $23.8 billion (including disability insurance payments).

As a point of comparison, the US Social Security program is also sketched in table 1. There are a few important differences between the Canadian system and US Social Security. First, the US system is tailored to individuals with previous earnings and is a pension program more than an income support program. Second, the early retirement provisions are less flexible and the actuarial reduction of benefits slightly steeper. Also, the retirement age is gradually being increased from 65 to 67 over the next 25 years. Third, there are significant earnings tests, especially on early retirees, although the implicit tax rates have been reduced in recent years. Note also that Social Security benefits are only reduced for employment income, not other pension or investment income as is the case for OAS and GIS benefits in Canada. Finally, at least at the maximum rates, the US program is more generous (10 percent at a 0.75 exchange rate) than the entire Canadian system. This generosity does not, however, come cheaply. Both the CPP/QPP and Social Security are financed by payroll and specific income taxes. As of 1999, the combined employer/employee contribution rate is 12.4 percent in the United States (not including Medicaid), but only 7 percent for the CPP/QPP, though this rate will rise to 9.9 percent by 2003. The OAS and GIS, in contrast, are financed out of general tax revenues.

The CPP/QPP was designed as a pay-as-you-go pension plan, so in principle current benefits should be covered by current contributions. However, in practice, there is also a buffer fund (the CPP Account) that contains approximately two years worth of benefits and generates interest income for the plan. In recent years, the balance in the CPP fund has been declining, not growing. In 1996-97, for example, the balance declined by over $1 billion to approximately $37.8 billion. Before the enactment of Bill C-2, even incorporating planned increases in the contribution rates, actuaries estimated that the CPP account would be fully depleted by 2015. The recent changes, particularly the increase in contribution rates to a steady-state level of 9.9 percent, are expected to restore financial sustainability to the CPP.[6] As is usually the case with these actuarial calculations, however, the results can be sensitive to the assumed interest rates or rates of return. One of the other significant changes to the CPP is a redirection of investment strategies, whereby savings in the CPP Account will be invested in higher yielding securities instead of government debt. The assumed real rate of return in recent projections is 3.85 percent. This may turn out to be an optimistic projection, and the ultimate success of the reformed CPP will hinge to some extent on the long-run performance of the securities market. Turning to the United States, the Social Security trust fund holds only 17 months worth of benefits, but current contributions exceed benefits. This positive balance in net contributions is expected to persist until early into the

Figure 1

CPP/QPP Benefits and Contributions Per Capita, Canada, 1971-1998

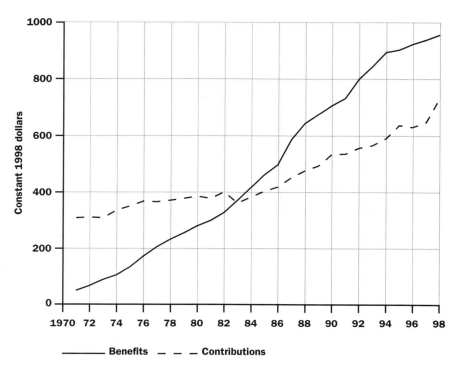

Source: Statistics Canada, cat. no. STC 13-001; CANSIM.

next century, so the projected exhaustion of the Social Security trust fund will occur sometime in 2032.

The problems that plague the CPP/QPP are easily identified in trends in benefits and contributions. Figure 1 shows the level of real benefits and contributions per capita since 1971. As recently as 1982 contributions exceeded benefits. However, since 1971, real benefits (per capita) have increased almost 20-fold, while real contributions have barely doubled. The current gap between annual benefits and contributions is around $225 per person, yielding an annual CPP/QPP deficit of $5.5 billion. However, the immediate impact of the increase in contribution rates is also apparent in figure 1, with the sharp increase in contributions between 1997 and 1998. The current deficit is noticeably lower than the $300 per person that existed in 1997.

The overall deterioration of CPP/QPP finances over the past decades is the result of several factors. First, as figure 2 illustrates, benefit levels cannot be supported by current contribution levels. At present, each contributor puts

adapting public policy to a labour market in transition

Figure 2

CPP/QPP Contributions and Benefits per Contributor and Beneficiary,
Canada, 1971–1996

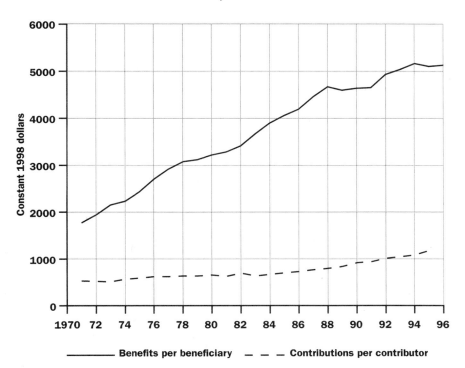

Benefits per beneficiary — — — **Contributions per contributor**

Source: Statistics Canada, cat. no. STC 13-001; CANSIM; Health and Welfare Canada, *Statistical Bulletin, Canada Pension Plan* (Ottawa: 1969-79); Health and Welfare Canada, *Monthly Statistics, Income Security Programs* (Ottawa: 1980-98); Human Resources Development Canada, *Canada Pension Plan, Contributors* (Ottawa: 1994, 1996 and 1997); Régime des Rentes du Québec, *Bulletin Statistique* (Quebec City: 1997).

around $1,000 into the pot, while beneficiaries draw over $5,000. Benefit levels (per beneficiary) have tripled since 1971, while contribution levels (per contributor) have only doubled. Viewed from another angle, the CPP/QPP deficit has widened *despite* the fact that the CPP/QPP tax has more than doubled in real terms. In the early 1970s average benefits were low because the full provisions of the pension plans had not yet been implemented, and many of the retirees had made limited contributions to the plans.[7] The long-run secular increase in average benefits reflects rising real wages, as well as the fact that today's retirees have contributed to the plans for most of their working lives.

Figure 3 demonstrates that the most dramatic changes have occurred in the numbers of retirement beneficiaries and contributors. It is these variables that will be affected directly by demographic shifts and changes in labour

michael baker and dwayne benjamin

Figure 3
Number of CPP/QPP Beneficiaries and Contributors Per Capita, Canada, 1971-1996

(a) Retirement Beneficiaries

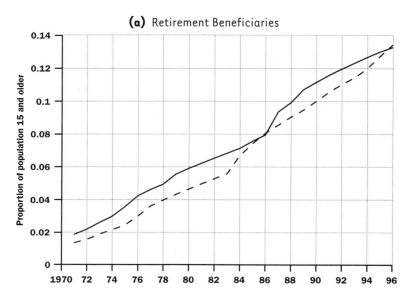

(b) Contributors

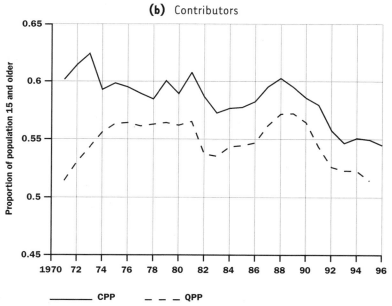

——— CPP   — — — QPP

Source: Statistics Canada, CANSIM; contributors and beneficiaries, administrative data as reported in the sources to Figure 2.

adapting public policy to a labour market in transition

force behaviour. In the top panel, the number of retirement beneficiaries is plotted. There are a couple of points worth noting. First, in both jurisdictions, the number of retirees per capita has gone up by a factor of six since 1971. Second, the introduction of early retirement provisions had a profound impact on the number of beneficiaries. This can be seen in the relative shift of the QPP profile around 1984 as early retirement was introduced into this plan, and the corresponding shift in the CPP profile in 1987 when a similar reform was made to the CPP. It is in the 1984-1987 window that the two profiles meet. In previous years, the number of CPP retirees exceeded the number of QPP retirees.[8] In the bottom panel, the figure shows that the number of contributors per capita is declining, and certainly not keeping pace with the number of beneficiaries. As a result, the number of contributors per retirement beneficiary has fallen from over 30 in 1971 to 4 today. This ratio is still slightly higher than that in the United States, where there are 3.3 Social Security contributors per beneficiary. In summary, fewer contributors are paying more taxes to support more retirees, who are collecting higher benefits.

What lies ahead? To some extent the number of beneficiaries and contributors is a simple function of the age structure of the population. In figure 4 we plot the frequency distribution of population by age in Canada in 1998. The number of individuals aged 60 years and over indicates the number of potential retirees. In five years, when the next cohort (those currently aged 55-59) begins retiring, the number of retirees per capita will rise, since this is a larger cohort than the current cohort aged 60-64. This pattern continues as the baby boom cohorts reach age 60. It is only when those currently aged 30-34 reach the age of 60 that the number of potential new retirees will be fewer than their predecessors. While demographic structure is an important determinant of the number of beneficiaries and retirees, it is not the only one. Labour force status is an another factor, and labour force participation rates have changed significantly over the past 20 years. Some of these changes have accentuated the adverse effect of demographics on CPP/QPP finances.

Figures 5 and 6 show retirement "hazards" for men and women in Canada in 1970, 1980 and 1990. These plots are based on age-employment profiles, and use cross-section differences in labour force status by age to impute the probability of transition from employment to nonemployment. The top panel shows the transition from working at least one week in the reference year to not working at all. There is a noticeable spike at age 66. This probably reflects retirement at age 65, as age is recorded in the census six months after the reference year. More Canadian men retire at age 65 than any other single age. Around 30 percent of those who are working at age 65 cease to work by age 66.

293

michael baker and dwayne benjamin

Figure 4

Population Distribution by Age and Gender, Canada, 1997

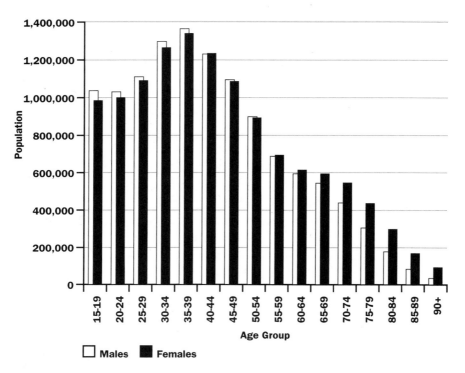

Source: Statistics Canada, CANSIM (Matrix 6213).

The probability of retiring after age 65 appears to be falling slightly over the period, while the probability of retiring before age 65 appears to be rising. In the second panel, we can see that the spike at age 65 is even sharper when we restrict our attention to movement out of full-year, full-time work. As well, we can see a slight increase in the probability of this transition at younger ages. As suggested by the differences between the top and bottom panels, some men move into part-year or part-time work. However, calculations from the censuses suggest that the number of men in this age interval who are engaged in part-time work is declining over time. Retirement tends to be complete. In figure 6, comparable hazards are reported for women. As with men, there is a pronounced spike at age 65 and an increase in the hazard over time among those under 65.

Figure 7 shows the employment-population ratios for various age groups, based on Labour Force Survey (LFS) data. For men, employment rates have been falling for all age groups, but especially those aged 60-64. Therefore, we can see an increase in early retirement relative to the standard retirement age of 65.

Figure 5
Male Employment/Nonemployment Transition Hazards by Age, 1970, 1980 and 1990

(a) Exiting Employment

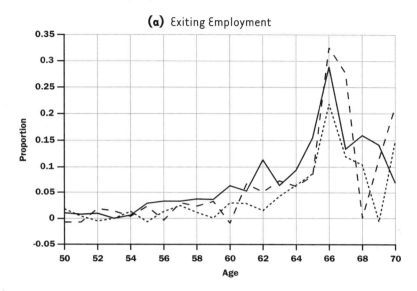

(b) Exiting FYFT Employment

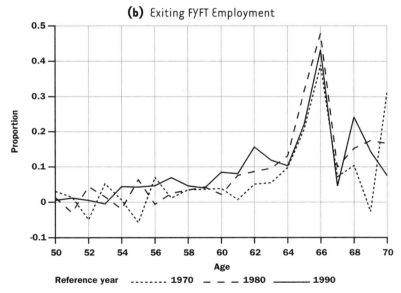

Reference year .... 1970 — — — 1980 ———— 1990

Note: Each panel shows the "pseudo hazard" or implied "exit rate" out of employment in the reference year by age. This is calculated from the cross-sectional age-to-age difference in the proportion of men working. The top panel reports the probability of "exiting" any type of work during the reference year, while the bottom panel reports the probability of "exiting" full-year, full-time work (FYFT) in the reference year.

Source: Statistics Canada, Census of Canada, 1971, 1981, and 1991, Public Use Microdata Files, Individual Files.

michael baker and dwayne benjamin

Figure 6
Female Employment/Nonemployment Transition Hazards by Age, 1970, 1980 and 1990

(a) Exiting Employment

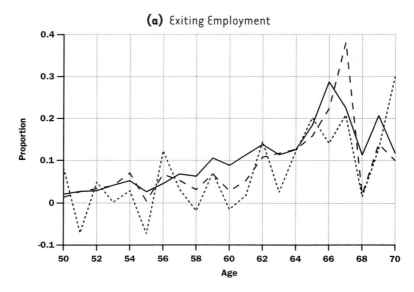

(b) Exiting FYFT Employment

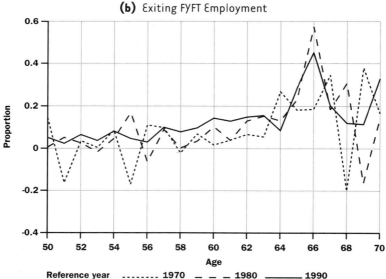

Reference year .... 1970 _ _ _ 1980 _____ 1990

Note: Each panel shows the "pseudo hazard" or implied "exit rate" out of employment in the reference year by age. This is calculated from the cross-sectional age-to-age difference in the proportion of women working. The top panel reports the probability of "exiting" any type of work during the reference year, while the bottom panel reports the probability of "exiting" full-year, full-time (FYFT) work in the reference year.
Source: Statistics Canada, Census of Canada, 1971, 1981, and 1991, Public Use Microdata Files, Individual Files.

adapting public policy to a labour market in transition

Notice that the trend toward early retirement has been essentially constant over the 25-year period. It is clear that even if the age distribution of the population was stationary, the number of retirees would have risen relative to the number of contributors (at least among men). An obvious question is how much of this behaviour can be explained by the structure of social security programs.

The bottom panel displays the same information for women. There is no discernible downward trend in employment rates here. Secular increases in female participation outweigh any tendency toward earlier retirement. This trend has had a positive effect on the contributor-beneficiary ratio: increases in female participation have attenuated the sharp decline in the ratio that resulted from the decline in male participation. Note, however, that female participation rates have levelled off since 1990. Thus, it is not clear the CPP/QPP will benefit from changes in the labour market activity of women in the future. This will depend in the end on whether women are paying actuarially fair CPP/QPP premiums.

The preceding discussion illustrates the ways in which labour force attachment has implications for the state of CPP/QPP finances. The next question, which is more difficult to answer, is to what extent do the links run the other way? Does the structure of the CPP/QPP affect labour force attachment, for example, by determining the retirement age? Can the parameters of the plans be set to compensate for the effects of demographic shifts or influence labour market participation trends?

The Effects of the CPP/QPP on Retirement Behaviour

How would changes in key CPP/QPP parameters, such as the age of retirement or the level of benefits, affect the labour market behaviour of older workers? Answering this question demands robust evidence of the effects of public pensions on labour supply and retirement decisions. At first glance, based on a number of pieces of evidence, the answer appears to be obvious.

First, retirement rates and pension wealth have been increasing in tandem since the inception of the CPP/QPP. Figure 2 shows, for example, that benefits per CPP/QPP recipient have been increasing steadily in real terms, while figures 3 and 7 show the corresponding increases in the number of CPP/QPP beneficiaries and decreases in employment rates, respectively. The accumulation of the pension wealth necessary to generate these benefits indicates that Canadians are now better able to afford to retire earlier.

Second, in US data we find that retirement ages bear a striking correspondence to pension rules. In the Social Security program, early retirement is permitted

Figure 7
Employment/Population Ratios by Age and Gender, Canada, 1971–1995

(a) Males

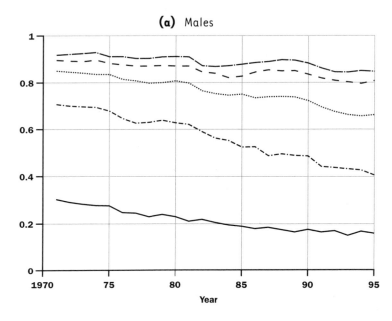

(b) Females

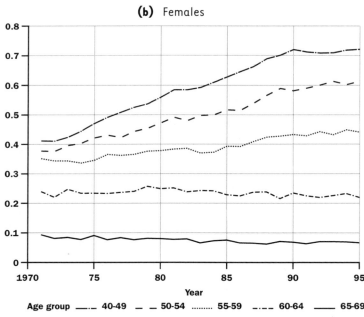

Age group ——·— 40-49 — — 50-54 ········· 55-59 —··— 60-64 —— 65-69

Source: Statistics Canada, Labour Force Survey, 1971-95.

adapting public policy to a labour market in transition

starting at age 62 (*versus* 60 in Canada). The retirement hazard of American males displays a spike at age 62, in addition to the usual spike at 65. It seems unlikely that this is a coincidence: there is no such spike in Canada where there is nothing special about age 62 in the public pension plan.

As it turns out, however, the links between public pensions and labour force behaviour are not as easy to establish as this casual evidence suggests. In this section of the paper we explore the main avenues through which the CPP/QPP can affect labour supply and retirement. We begin with a brief review of the economic theory linking pensions to labour supply. In addition to the correlations noted previously, this is the source of most of the evidence. We then discuss the practical difficulties in constructing an empirical case that the CPP/QPP matters for retirement.

We define retirement as the initiation of receipt of a public pension, rather than withdrawal from the labour force. The first set of questions, then, concerns the determinants of the age of retirement or, more narrowly, the role of public pensions in this decision. Second, we examine the nature or intensity of retirement. For most people, initiation of the CPP/QPP and (virtually) complete and permanent withdrawal from the labour force are the same thing. In principle, however, individuals can work after they "retire," and public pension plans can affect this decision as well. One of the most important ways that they affect the postretirement labour supply is through earnings tests, which remain an important feature of US Social Security, but are effectively absent from the CPP.

The objective is to determine whether public pension plan parameters matter in these decisions. Of course, they may not. A recent Statistics Canada monograph summarizes the reasons given by respondents in the 1994 General Social Survey (GSS) to the question of why they retired.[9] Twenty-five percent of men reported that they retired for health reasons, while a further 10 percent had lost their jobs and had become unemployed. Sixteen percent more retired because of mandatory retirement. Such men may not have been responding to the incentives of the CPP. On the other hand, 24 percent retired "by choice," and another 11 percent because the "person feels old enough." Clearly, some men retire "voluntarily," especially in the case of early retirement, and the CPP provisions may affect the attractiveness of that option.

Theory

If public pensions are administered as intended, it is difficult to explain why they would affect the age of retirement. To focus the discussion, consider an individual at age 59 who has worked since the age of 24 and will qualify for the maximum pension at the official retirement age of 65. For the time being, ignore the issues of private pensions, savings, potential wage growth and mandatory retirement, and focus on the marginal incentives provided by the CPP. From the perspective of age 59, the individual can compare the relative pension benefits at each of the possible retirement ages, ranging from 60 through 70 (for example). If he or she retires before age 65, the pension is reduced, while if retirement is delayed until age 66 or later, the pension is higher. The adjustment in benefits is one-half percent for each month by which the retirement age differs from age 65. If this adjustment is actuarially fair, so that the expected net present value of pension benefits (accounting for mortality, etc.) is the same whatever age of retirement is chosen, the CPP/QPP provides no incentive to retire at any particular age.

One obvious way the CPP/QPP can affect retirement incentives, therefore, is if the early-retirement adjustments are actuarially unfair; that is, the expected net present value of benefits varies with the age of retirement. In an earlier paper, we show that the expected present value of benefits is higher at age 60 and declines thereafter.[10] In other words, there is a slight subsidy to early retirement. This subsidy increases the opportunity cost of working past age 60 and might encourage early retirement. Also, actuarial adjustments are based on averages (e.g., mortality rates) over the population. Not surprisingly, therefore, the implicit subsidies to early retirement will vary across individuals. One way in which this subsidy varies is by potential income levels. For example, the actuarial reductions in CPP/QPP benefits for early retirement are partly offset by higher GIS benefits at age 65 for low-income individuals. Thus, a reduction in monthly benefits of $1 for early retirement generates $0.50 of additional monthly GIS benefits for these pensioners. In this case, the subsidy to early retirement is much higher. Individual preferences also play a role in the retirement decision. If the discount rate for someone is higher than the actuarial rate, then they will view early retirement as relatively attractive. In the same way, if individuals have private information about life expectancy, then the expected present value of pension benefits may vary systematically by age.

The assumption implicit in the calculation of the actuarial adjustment and in the present value of lifetime pension benefits is that a dollar today and a dollar tomorrow can be compared on the basis of the market (real) rate of interest. There are a number of reasons why this may not be true for elderly workers. First, if there are liquidity or borrowing constraints, then pension benefits cannot be freely transferred across time at the market rate of interest. In fact, one cannot go to the bank and borrow against future CPP/QPP or private pension wealth, so liquidity constraints in this respect may be plausible.

The existence of more general borrowing constraints will also increase the relative value of a dollar today. Second, individuals' preferences over time may be such that the value of income today exceeds the value of income tomorrow by more than the market discount rate. If individuals are risk-averse, precautionary motives may lead them to prefer to take the money now, rather than wait. On average, then, the current actuarial adjustment to the CPP/QPP for early retirement may still provide incentives for early retirement, and these incentives will probably vary systematically among individuals.

There are a number of other ways in which the public pension scheme may affect the retirement age. Clearly, the level of benefits and pension wealth may provide a pure income effect, encouraging earlier retirement. An unanticipated increase in benefits would lead to less work, while a decrease in benefits would reduce the affordability of retirement. As well, many pensioners are not in the position of our notional retiree. For example, they may not have accumulated their full entitlement to pension benefits. Similarly, since pension benefits are linked to earnings in the last three years of work (four years in 1998 and five years thereafter), there may be an incentive to keep working in order to increase the basis upon which pension benefits are calculated. Because benefits are linked to earnings, not wages, a gradual shift to part-time work would adversely affect pension benefits. For this reason, individuals would want to leave employment all at once, rather than gradually.[11]

Rules governing the level of benefits may also affect labour market attachment after initiation of the public pension. The level of benefits will affect the affordability of retirement through a pure income effect, much as it affects the retirement age. Unanticipated increases or decreases in CPP/QPP or other old age security benefits will potentially affect contemporaneous labour supply decisions of the elderly. Earnings tests will also affect the attractiveness of work. In the United States (and in Canada until the mid-1970s) pension benefits are subject to an earnings test. If labour market earnings exceed some threshold, pension benefits are reduced according to a formula (see table 1). These earnings tests have been viewed as taxes on work and thus as undesirable. Certainly, earnings tests lead to strong predictions about labour market behaviour. Individuals should work up to the exemption level. Above the exemption level, earnings are taxed, and net wages lower. On the margin, we should see "bunching" of individuals at the exemption level.

There might also be more complicated interactions between the retirement programs, other non-age-related government programs and the labour supply. For example, in the calculation of Employment Insurance (EI) benefits, CPP/QPP benefits and employment earnings are treated similarly. Essentially, this means that it is difficult to collect CPP and EI simultaneously. For some individuals, early retirement provisions may be more attractive than maintaining attachment to the labour force and eligibility for EI. For those with higher earnings, it may be more attractive to maintain the option of collecting EI benefits than to initiate early CPP benefits. Some of these possibilities are explored by Green and Riddell, who investigate the effects of UI benefit disentitlement on individuals aged 66-70 in 1996.[12] There may also be interactions between the CPP/QPP and Workers' Compensation, since Workers' Compensation benefits are also reduced by the amount of CPP benefits received. Why suffer a permanent actuarial reduction in CPP benefits by initiating early retirement if these early benfits are fully taxed away? Clearly, accounting for these possible interactions is important in assessing the full impact of public pensions on retirement decisions.

Evidence

A useful place to start a discussion of the evidence of the impact of public pensions on retirement decisions is the retirement hazards in the United States. As noted previously, there is a significant spike in the hazard at age 62, corresponding with the early retirement provisions of the US Social Security program. Similarly, trends in retirement behaviour correspond with trends in the generosity of public pensions. This would seem to suggest that public pension plans "matter" and provide *prima facie* evidence that retirement ages are certainly affected. Researchers, however, disagree on this point. For example, Christopher Ruhm argues that: "[t]he sharp reduction in the labour supply of 62-year-olds highlights the importance of the early retirement provisions of Social Security."[13] In contrast, Franco Peracchi and Finnis Welch "are not convinced that wealth effects as they are ordinarily defined, specifically those that afford increased postretirement consumption through Social Security and private pensions, can be assigned a major role in explaining trends in labour supply behaviour of older men."[14]

On one side of the debate is the argument that it is no coincidence that the minimum age for receipt of Social Security benefits corresponds with the significant popularity of age 62 as the age to retire. Michael Hurd carefully argues this point in his survey.[15] He also reviews the cross-section evidence he and Michael Boskin provided earlier when they showed that individual retirement at age 62 is positively related to individual social security wealth.[16] How can this cross-section evidence be used to explain the trend toward early retirement? One possibility would be an increased sensitivity to social security wealth (i.e., an increase in the income effect in the demand for leisure). An alternative to this change in preferences would be increased social security wealth in the face of borrowing constraints. James Kahn emphasizes these borrowing or liquidity constraints by showing that it is individuals with little wealth, whose liquidity is most likely to be constrained, who are most likely to take early retirement at age 62.[17] Finally, Christopher Ruhm explores the trend in the numbers of those retiring at age 62.[18] He argues that the increase in the spike cannot be explained by changes in individuals' observable characteristics (such as education), which leaves increases in Social Security wealth as the most important component of the explanation. Despite the simple theory, this evidence points to the importance of the Social Security retirement age in retirement decisions.

The opposing arguments are presented in studies which find little correlation between the modification of Social Security parameters and retirement behaviour. For example, Alan Krueger and Jorn-Steffen Pischke examine the retirement behaviour of the so-called "notch" generation.[19] The 1977 revisions to Social Security eliminated double indexation, which permanently lowered the Social Security wealth of one birth cohort relative to previous cohorts. If Social Security wealth is an important determinant of retirement patterns, one would expect the notch cohort to exhibit different behaviour. The authors, however, can find virtually no effect of these revisions. Franco Peracchi and Finis Welch acknowledge the growing spike in the retirement hazard at age 62, but point out that its emergence lags the introduction of early retirement in 1963, and it has continued to grow despite reforms that have made such behaviour less attractive.[20] Instead, they emphasize that individual characteristics associated with poor labour market outcomes are becoming increasingly important predictors of retirement. It is these characteristics – education, race, region of residence and recent unemployment experience – that are simultaneously correlated with low wages and low wealth. Thus, some of the apparent wealth effect may be a labour supply response. Furthermore, trends in labour force participation of less-skilled older workers mirror those of their younger counterparts. Thus, changes in worker characteristics or the labour market might account for a considerable portion of the retirement trends. In the Canadian context, Lars Osberg also highlights the importance to retirement behaviour of poor labour market opportunities, concluding that retirement might be better described as a form of constrained labour supply behaviour.[21]

Why is it so difficult to establish a robust connection between social security and retirement behaviour? The main problem is the lack of credible, independent variation in program parameters that could be traced through to labour supply behaviour. For example, correlations between secular trends in social security wealth and retirement behaviour may reflect an income effect, or alternatively the reverse causality: social security generosity levels are adjusted

michael baker and dwayne benjamin

upwards as the constituency of social security recipients grows. Equally plausible, the trends could be entirely independent, with increases in retirement rates reflecting secular increases in private wealth, and social security benefits reflecting the same underlying trend. It is difficult with time-series data alone (or pooled cross-sections) to disentangle these effects. It is also problematic to use cross-section variation to identify the effects of a national program like social security – everybody faces (approximately) the same program parameters at some point. Previous researchers have tried to exploit cross-sectional differences in accumulated social security wealth to identify the links between pensions and retirement. Unfortunately, individual social security wealth is related to individual wages, non-public-pension wealth, labour force history, and attitudes toward work, and these other factors confound the estimation of a pure social security effect.

One of the advantages of studying public pensions in Canada is that we have two jurisdictions (CPP and QPP). While most of the program parameters are the same, there have been discrete changes in the programs that occurred at different times. This allows the researcher to exploit cross-jurisdictional variations in the programs in order to estimate the effect of program changes. In a few previous papers we use differences in the timing of these changes to estimate the effect of the CPP/QPP on the labour market decisions of older men.

In one study, we examine the effect of the introduction of early retirement in Canada.[22] Early retirement provisions were introduced to the QPP in 1984 and to the CPP in 1987. We therefore have control groups for each policy change. By comparing the changes in behaviour in the jurisdiction that experienced the policy change with the changes in the other jurisdiction, we can control for common trends in the two labour markets. Also, by comparing the response of the affected age groups (in this case 60-64) with other age groups (like the 50-54 age group), we can also control for different business-cycle effects in the two jurisdictions.

Our basic findings can be seen in figure 3 (and loosely in figure 7).[23] First, in figure 3, it is apparent that in 1984 the number of retirement beneficiaries in Quebec increased relative to the rest of Canada. Similarly, in 1987, the number of beneficiaries increased in the rest of Canada relative to Quebec. This graph provides relatively convincing evidence that the early retirement provisions induced more Canadians to opt for early retirement and start to receive their public pension. We would thus expect a corresponding drop in the labour force attachment in Quebec relative to the rest of Canada that coincides with the retirement patterns observed in figure 3. In figure 7 we show national, rather than jurisdiction specific, trends in employment. However, there appears to have been no sudden drop in employment rates among those aged 60-64 in the 1980s. In fact, the 1980s seem to be just another segment of the secular trend from 1970 to 1995. When we separate the figures for Quebec and the rest of Canada (not shown), in fact, a parallel emerges: there is a secular decline in the labour force attachment of those aged 60-64. In particular, there is no evidence of jurisdiction-specific effects with the introduction of early retirement provisions, as was apparent in figure 3. We conclude that while the introduction of early retirement provisions had a significant effect on the collection of CPP/QPP benefits, it had no effect on labour force behaviour. Why might this be so? One possibility is that the CPP retirement test is so weak that individuals began collecting CPP and kept on working. This does not appear to be the case, as the vast majority of CPP/QPP recipients "substantially cease working" altogether. The answer seems to be that those who began collecting CPP/QPP had a low attachment to the labour market anyway, much as suggested by Peracchi and Welch.[24]

The whole point of this "difference of differences" approach is that we have a control group with which we can construct a counterfactual picture of what they would have done if the policy had not changed. More people did indeed withdraw from the labour force when early retirement provisions were introduced in Quebec in 1984. However, the same also happened in Ontario, where people were unaffected by the QPP changes and early retirement was not yet permitted. A similar pattern can be observed following the introduction of early retirement into the CPP in 1987. Again, more individuals withdrew from the labour force, but this also occurred in Quebec, where early retirement provisions had already been in place for a few years. The introduction of early retirement thus appears to have significantly increased the take-up rates of CPP/QPP benefits, without affecting labour force behaviour.

In the end, it appears that the secular trends in retirement behaviour were driven by more fundamental factors than early retirement provisions of the public pension scheme. However, this need not imply that early retirement provisions *never* matter. It appears that a spike in the retirement hazard at age 60 is emerging in Canada when one looks at more recent data. This suggests that whatever effect early retirement has on behaviour (if any) has taken a while to work its way into individual labour supply decisions. This also suggests that similar changes to the CPP or QPP might have only long-run effects on behaviour, and would not be useful tools for short-run tinkering, which was certainly one of the motivations for the 1984/87 changes.

In another paper we explore another episode where the CPP and QPP diverged and examine the effects of the removal of the retirement test from the CPP/QPP.[25] This earnings tax was removed, first from the CPP in 1975, and then from the QPP

michael baker and dwayne benjamin

in 1977. Standard economic theory makes specific predictions regarding the responses to this reform. For some workers, there is a labour-supply-reducing income effect, as they are allowed to keep all of their CPP benefits and continue working, whereas before they received no CPP benefits. For those near the exemption level, there would be potentially offsetting income and substitution effects: the income effect would be the same as for other workers, while the substitution effect would lead to more hours worked as the "tax on work" was eliminated.

We find very little effect of the policy change on the labour supply of those men who were working. As with the introduction of early retirement, Canadians were apparently enthusiastic about collecting the extra government check that was made available to them. However, even focusing on those workers likely to be most affected by the tax decrease – those near the exemption – we find no evidence of a labour supply response. However, we still observe sizable changes in retirement behaviour, even if it is not in accordance with the simple labour supply model. We find that fewer people retired in the conventional sense of withdrawing from the labour force. It seems that the earnings test made employment less attractive than retirement, and that its elimination resulted in fewer individuals quitting work. This type of behaviour is consistent with a labour supply model with fixed costs. These fixed costs help explain the nonmarginal nature of the retirement decision; i.e., complete withdrawal from work as opposed to smaller changes in hours worked. If this interpretation is correct, then the introduction of high implicit taxes on earnings through the public pension scheme might reduce the number of people working.

In summary, this evidence suggests that retirement behaviour depends largely on factors other than the public pension plans. Certainly, it seems unlikely that changes in the retirement age, for example, which are similar to the introduction of early retirement, would lead to substantially different retirement patterns. While the reintroduction of a retirement test might have a larger impact, this reform would presumably discourage labour participation, which is not consistent with the objective of promoting greater self-reliance among the elderly or the trend in Social Security reforms. Of course, previous changes to the pension plans have had significant public finance implications, and increases in the retirement age or similar decreases in benefits might yet contribute to solving budgetary problems.

The Effects of Private Pensions

The preceding evidence suggests that public pensions may have limited short-run effects on retirement behaviour. In particular, there is no evidence that the introduction of early retirement provisions encouraged anyone to retire from their jobs, but only to initiate their CPP/QPP benefits sooner. How general is this result? To what extent might private pensions offset or reinforce the responses to CPP/QPP program parameters? Are private pensions responsible for the secular decline in the labour force attachment of older workers? Are there features of private pension plans that encourage individuals to retire at particular ages? These questions constitute an entire research agenda. Unfortunately, very little evidence exists that enables us to resolve these issues, if for no other reason that there are few data sets with the variables necessary for an adequate treatment of these. Even when firm-specific data are available, there is always a concern about whether results can be generalized.

There is a more fundamental problem. Pensions are little more than private savings. As such, savings and pensions are properly viewed as a joint-decision variable, along with labour supply. Even late in one's life cycle, current pension wealth is inextricably linked to past and future labour supply decisions, and is as much a residual of intertemporal consumption-leisure decisions as a determinant of current labour supply. More concretely, most people accumulate a private pension specifically *so that they can retire*. Individuals can choose their retirement age from age 20, and select a package of wage and pension benefits and other savings instruments accordingly. It thus makes no sense to view pensions as a purely independent feature of the budget constraint. Someone who wishes to retire at age 55 will choose a pension plan that allows them to do so. Of course, to some extent this problem also affects analysis of the CPP – the program parameters may reflect aggregate preferences toward retirement – but in this case individuals have no control over the features of the plan as they do with a private plan. Similarly, unanticipated changes in the program can still have pure policy effects (as would be the case with unexpected changes in private pension plans). For now, however, we put off this issue and briefly explore how private pensions might affect retirement decisions, in particular as they interact with the CPP/QPP.

In 1997 only 34 percent of the labour force was in a private pension plan. Most of these individuals – 87 percent – belonged to a defined benefit plan. It makes sense, therefore, to consider the retirement incentives provided by this type of plan. For most plan members, 65 is the normal age of retirement, though 60 is the age for 16 percent of public sector workers and 3 percent of private sector workers.[26] Almost all of these plans permit early retirement with an actuarial reduction in benefits. In 1988, over half of plan members were also eligible for special retirement, where early retirement was accompanied by a subsidy.

The theoretical effects on retirement age of these features of private plans are similar to those of the public plans described earlier. In the absence of liquidity constraints, if early retirement reductions in benefits are actuarially fair, then the permission of early retirement should have no effect on the retirement age. Obviously, if there is a large subsidy to early retirement, we would expect this to have important incentive effects on retirement, especially if the subsidies are unanticipated. Most firms have *de facto* retirement tests, in that individuals must leave the firm, though of course, they can work elsewhere. Unfortunately, beyond anecdotal evidence from specific firms, there is little data on the relative importance of these subsidies.

Can private pensions explain the retirement trends documented in figure 7? Two types of evidence are relevant for this question. First, there has been very little change in the incidence of private pensions over the past 25 years. In 1970, 34 percent of the labour force was covered by a pension plan. This number has fluctuated over time, but is still at 34 percent of the labour force. Of course, this lack of change in aggregate pension coverage probably understates the coverage of potential retirees, since current retirees were more likely to have been covered by pensions than those who began working before World War II.

More telling evidence is provided by Christopher Ruhm.[27] He notes that most researchers find that for workers with a long attachment to a firm, the actuarial value of pension wealth is maximized when they are in their early sixties. This would seem to suggest that private pensions encourage some degree of early retirement. Ruhm also notes, however, that this calculation is not relevant for workers who have not been attached to the firm for their entire careers. For most employees, possible incentives for early retirement are offset by the high returns to accrual of pension benefits. Individuals who joined firms later in their careers have a greater incentive to remain with the firm, both to increase their years of service and to increase the final earnings base upon which pension benefits are calculated.[28]

Ruhm also examines the impact of private pension coverage on retirement age using data from the Retirement History Survey (RHS) of the US Social Security Administration. He finds that private pensions actually increase the labour market attachment of men in their late fifties and very early sixties. For men aged 62-64, there was no correlation between pension coverage and labour force attachment, while for men over 65, coverage by private pensions was positively related with retirement. These results, and the corroborating evidence for workers with lower tenure, suggest that the pension accrual considerations are important in retirement decisions and that these considerations may dominate subsidies for early retirement. Apparently, private pensions play a complicated role in retirement decisions and, moreover, their effects vary across different groups in the labour force. More conclusively, however, there does not appear to be evidence that the aggregate trends can be causally linked to an increase in the prevalence of private pensions.

Other Linkages with the Labour Market

The discussion to this point suggests that public pensions have little effect on labour force behaviour, at least in the short run. Underlying retirement trends are (apparently) driven largely by changing preferences and accumulations of private wealth. Individual retirement decisions are also based on labour market opportunities, which may be quite poor for some older workers, as well as factors like health. Are the labour market consequences of the CPP/QPP, therefore, restricted to potentially long-run labour supply decisions? Are the links between the labour market and public pensions unidirectional, running only from the labour market to pension benefits and contributions? Should labour economists be concerned about the CPP/QPP, or should it remain the domain of public finance economists?

There are at least two ways in which CPP/QPP policy still matters for labour economists. The first relates to intergenerational equity. As Philip Oreopoulos notes, almost all of the proposed reforms to the CPP/QPP, including the recent increase in premiums, involve net transfers from the younger to the older generations.[29] This means that there may be important cohort wealth effects on the labour supply patterns of the young compared with those of the old. This will be compounded if (when) the benefits of new retirees are cut. Based on previous discussions, benefits are most likely to be cut through an increase in the normal retirement age, that is, the age of eligibility for full benefits. Peter Diamond discusses the political attractiveness of this type of benefit reduction.[30] As noted already, such a cut would not likely have a significant immediate effect on the retirement plans of the elderly. Also, in our examination of the removal of the retirement test, we saw little response to the lump sum transfer of CPP/QPP benefits to those who were working above the break-even point.[31] If short-run income effects were important, we would have expected a reduction of labour supply for this group. Most studies of retirement behaviour, however, suggest that wealth is an important contributor to early retirement, controlling for wages and labour market opportunities. If pure income effects dominated, permanent reductions in lifetime wealth would likely increase the attachment of workers to the labour market over their lifetimes, including during their early retirement years. If liquidity constraints are important, then individuals will make even greater demands to access their public pension wealth.

309

michael baker and dwayne benjamin

The second and more immediately important factor is taxes. Throughout our discussion we have focused on the impact of public pension benefits on the labour supply of the old, ignoring the impact of pension contributions on the young. These contributions are best thought of as taxes and cannot properly be viewed as savings, since the actuarial value of contributions far exceeds the benefits, as Oreopoulos noted. The increase in the contribution rate to 9.9 percent of pensionable earnings represents a doubling of the individual and payroll taxes associated with social security. While there may be sound fiscal reasons for this reform, one cannot assume that a tax increase of this magnitude will have no effect on the labour market.

We know very little about the effects of either income or payroll taxes on labour supply in Canada, although there have been recent advances in our knowledge in the area of payroll taxes. Jonathan Kesselman reviews some of the arguments in favour of using payroll taxes as the tax mechanism to finance public pensions.[32] As recent results show, the incidence of payroll taxes falls almost entirely on workers in the form of lower wages.[33] While Kesselman correctly notes that payroll taxes are probably the best tax mechanism for financing social security, there can be no escaping the possible impact of this tax increase on the labour market. Furthermore, some studies suggest that there may be short-run adjustment costs on the employment side as a result of payroll taxes, until the incidence is fully borne by workers. Then again, if the margin of adjustment is new (young) hirees, the distributional impact of the increase in contribution rates may occur among younger cohorts. None of this is to deny the need or desirability of these types of reforms, but rather to point out the positive (*versus* normative) potential impact of these changes on the labour market.

Conclusions

There have been dramatic changes in the labour market behaviour of older workers in Canada over the past 20 years. For example, in 1970 roughly 70 percent of men aged 60-64 worked in an average week, while by 1995 the proportion had fallen to 40 percent. While the trends among women are less dramatic, we have not seen the sharp increase in employment among those aged 60 and above which is a defining characteristic of younger women. These trends, together with the demographic shifts caused by the baby boom and decisions about contribution and benefit rates made in the late 1960s, have led to the CPP/QPP fiscal crisis that now dominates the discussion of social security in Canada.

Recent attempts to correct the fiscal balance have involved large increases in contribution rates. In this paper we ask whether policy makers can influence retirement rates, which in turn might have a positive effect on public finances. More precisely, we examine this policy option within the context of the public pension plans. Based on current evidence, it appears that the possibilities are very limited. For example, there is little consistent evidence that changing the official retirement age or the initial age of retirement strongly influences people's labour supply choices, at least within the time-frame in which a response would be needed to have a positive impact on plan deficits. While increasing the retirement age might ultimately have a positive impact on the bottom line, this is more likely to be a result of the effective reduction in benefits that this reform represents. To the extent that the actuarial adjustments, whereby those who initiate early pensions collect (in present value terms) more benefits, are unfair, then a delayed retirement age might also help. We presented evidence that when offered the chance to initiate early retirement benefits, retired Canadians have tended to take it. Delaying their benefits will not affect the retirement decision, but it might reduce the total value of benefits collected. There is further evidence that earnings tests have a greater effect on labour market behaviour, but it seems unlikely that the reintroduction of these tests to the CPP/QPP is consistent with current objectives.

These perhaps pessimistic conclusions must be tempered by the fact that we know relatively little about the relationship between retirement and public pensions in Canada, and even less about the relationship between retirement and private pensions. In many countries, research programs are underway to examine the consequences of an aging population. These countries face many of the same demographic shifts and fiscal challenges as Canada does. Clearly, there is a need to initiate a complementary research program in Canada to better understand how labour market behaviour is related to those aspects of public and private pension plans that are unique to this country.

311

michael baker and dwayne benjamin

Notes

We thank John Burbidge, France St-Hilaire, Craig Riddell and conference participants for useful comments and Mary Grant for excellent research assistance.

1. See John Burbidge, *Social Security in Canada*, Canadian Tax Paper no. 79 (Toronto: Canadian Tax Foundation, 1987), especially chap. 2, for a comprehensive summary of the motivation for and development of the public provision of old age security and pension programs in Canada.

2. For example, in Michael Baker and Dwayne Benjamin, "Early Retirement Provisions and the Labor Force Behavior of Older Men: Evidence from Canada," *Journal of Labor Economics*, Vol. 17, no. 4 (October 1999), pp. 724-756, we show how actuarial adjustments to the CPP/QPP for early retirement can be undone by offsetting changes to the level of GIS that an individual can collect.

3. Michael Baker provides an analysis of the incentive effects of the Spouse's Allowance component of the GIS in "The Retirement Behavior of Married Couples: Evidence from the Spouse's Allowance," NBER working paper no. w7138 (May 1999). Jonathan Gruber provides simulations that highlight the interaction of the different incentives in all three components of Canada's income security system in Jonathan Gruber, "Social Security and Retirement in Canada," in Jonathan Gruber and David A. Wise (eds.), *Social Security and Retirement Around the World* (Chicago, IL: University of Chicago Press, 1999), pp. 73-100.

4. Therefore, individuals applying at age 62 would receive 82 percent (100-[3x6]) of their full pension entitlement.

5. To have "substantially ceased working," CPP applicants must show that their earnings in the month prior to application are below what their monthly CPP benefits would be.

6. In fact, the new contribution rates are close to the 10 to 10.5 percent rates suggested by Tamim Bayoumi as the long-run, budget-balancing contribution rate. See Tamim Bayoumi, "Aging Population and Canadian Public Pension Plans," International Monetary Fund Working Paper, WP/94/89 (1994).

7. The provisions of both the CPP and QPP were phased in gradually over a 10-year transition period from 1966 to 1976.

8. Figure 3 shows only regular retirement beneficiaries and excludes Disability Insurance (DI) beneficiaries. Coinciding with the introduction of early retirement in the CPP in 1987, the CPP increased the level of DI benefits, bringing them into line with the QPP. This increase in DI benefits has also been linked to an increase in DI receipts, with its own adverse consequences for the CPP budget. See Jonathan Gruber, "Disability Insurance Benefits and Labor Supply," NBER working paper no. 5866 (December 1996), for more details.

9. Manon Monette, *Canada's Changing Retirement Patterns: Findings from the General Social Survey* (Ottawa: Statistics Canada, Housing, Family and Social Statistics Division, 1996).

10. Baker and Benjamin, "Early Retirement Provisions and the Labor Force Behavior of Older Men."

11. Michael Hurd discusses this and other features of the labour market that lead to sudden rather than gradual withdrawals from employment. See Michael Hurd, "The Effect of Labor Market Rigidities on the Labor Force Behavior of Older Workers," in David A. Wise (ed.), *Advances in the Economics of Aging* (Chicago, IL: University of Chicago Press, 1996), pp. 11-58.

12. David Green and W. Craig Riddell, "The Economic Effects of Unemployment Insurance in Canada: An Empirical Analysis of UI Disentitlement," *Journal of Labor Economics*, Vol. 11, no. 1, Part 2 (January 1993), pp. s96-147.

13. Christopher Ruhm, "Secular Changes in the Work and Retirement Patterns of Older Men," *Journal of Human Resources*, Vol. 30, no. 2 (Spring 1995), p. 381.

14. Franco Peracchi and Finis Welch, "Trends in Labor Force Transitions of Older Men and Women," *Journal of Labor Economics*, Vol. 12, no. 2 (April 1994), p. 238.

15. Michael Hurd, "Research on the Elderly: Economic Status, Retirement, and Consumption and Saving," *Journal of Economic Literature*, Vol. 28, no. 2 (June 1990), pp. 565-637.

16. Michael Hurd and Michael J. Boskin, "The Effect of Social Security on Retirement in the Early 1970s," *Quarterly Journal of Economics*, Vol. 99, no. 4 (November 1984), pp. 767-90.

17. James Kahn, "Social Security, Liquidity, and Early Retirement," *Journal of Public Economics*, Vol. 35, no. 1 (February 1988), pp. 97-117.

18. Christopher J. Ruhm, "Secular Changes in the Work and Retirement Patterns of Older Men," *Journal of Human Resources*, Vol. 30, no. 2 (Spring 1995), pp. 362-85.

19. Alan Krueger and Jorn-Steffen Pischke, "The Effect of Social Security on Labor Supply: A Cohort Analysis of the Notch Generation," *Journal of Labor Economics*, Vol. 10, no. 4 (October 1992), pp. 412-37.

20. Peracchi and Welch, "Trends in Labor Force Transitions of Older Men and Women."

21. Lars Osberg, "Is it Retirement or Unemployment? Induced 'Retirement' and Constrained Labour Supply among Older Workers," *Applied Economics*, Vol. 25, no. 4 (April 1993), pp. 505-19.

22. Baker and Benjamin, "Early Retirement Provisions and the Labor Force Behavior of Older Men"; and Michael Baker and Dwayne Benjamin, "Working Time Over the Life-Cycle: Do Public Pensions Matter?" in S. Houseman and A. Nakamura (eds.), *Working Time in Comparative Perspective Volume II: Studies of Working Time over the Life Cycle and Nonstandard Work* (Kalamazoo, MI: Upjohn Institute for Employment Research, forthcoming, 2001).

23. For a more formal analysis, see Baker and Benjamin, "Early Retirement Provisions and the Labor Force Behavior of Older Men."

24. Peracchi and Welch, "Trends in Labor Force Transitions of Older Men and Women."

25. Michael Baker and Dwayne Benjamin, "How Do Retirement Tests Affect the Labor Supply of Older Men?" *Journal of Public Economics*, Vol. 71 (January 1999), pp. 27-51.

26. The figures reported in this paragraph are drawn from Statistics Canada, *Pensions in Canada*, various issues, Cat. no. 74-401.

27. Christopher J. Ruhm, "Do Pensions Increase the Labor Supply of Older Men?" *Journal of Public Economics*, Vol. 59, no. 2 (February 1996), pp. 157-75.

28. Similar pension accrual effects have been noted in the Canadian context, for example by Morley Gunderson and James Pesando, "Retirement Incentives Contained in Occupational Pension Plans and Their Implications for the Mandatory Retirement Debate," *Canadian Journal of Economics*, Vol. 21, no. 2 (May 1988), pp. 244-64; and Morley Gunderson and James Pesando, "Does Pension Wealth Peak at the Age of Early Retirement?" *Industrial Relations*, Vol. 30, no. 1 (winter 1991), pp. 79-95.

29. Philip Oreopoulos, "Bad Tasting Medicine: Removing Intergenerational Inequity from the CPP," *Choices*, Vol. 2, no. 7 (November 1996), pp. 1-22.

30. Peter Diamond, "Public Provision of Pensions: The Doug Purvis Memorial Lecture," *Canadian Public Policy*, Vol. 22, no. 1 (March 1996), pp. 1-6.

31. Baker and Benjamin, "How Do Retirement Tests Affect the Labour Supply of Older Men?"

32. Jonathan Kesselman, "Payroll Taxes in the Finance of Social Security," *Canadian Public Policy*, Vol. 22, no. 2 (June 1996), pp. 162-79.

33. See Charles Beach, Zhengxi Lin and Garnett Picot, "The Employer Payroll Tax in Canada and its Effect on the Demand for Labour," unpublished paper, Queen's University, 1995; Zhengxi Lin, Garnett Picot and Charles Beach, "The Evolution of Payroll Taxes in Canada: 1961-1993," Statistics Canada, Analytic Studies Branch, Research Paper no. 90 (1996); and Jonathan Gruber, "The Incidence of Payroll Taxation: Evidence from Chile," *Journal of Labor Economics*, Vol. 15, no. 3, Part 2 (July 1997), pp. S72-101.

313

Michael Baker is Associate Professor in the Department of Economics and a Research Associate of the Institute for Policy Analysis, both at the University of Toronto, and a Faculty Research Fellow of the National Bureau of Economic Research (NBER) in Cambridge, MA. In his research, he investigates the effects of a wide range of labour market policies and institutions. Most recently, he has examined the impact of Ontario's pay equity laws and the incentive effects of Canada's income security programs for seniors. Current research focuses on recent provincial welfare reforms, as well as the relationship between health and labour market participation.

Paul Beaudry is currently Professor of Economics at the University of British Columbia. He has previously held faculty positions at Boston University and the University of Montreal. Professor Beaudry is also an Associate of the Canadian Institute of Advanced Research (CIAR), a Faculty Research Fellow of the National Bureau of Economic Research (NBER) and an Associate Researcher at Centre interuniversitaire de recherche en analyse des organisations (CIRANO). Professor Beaudry's main research interests are in the areas of macroeconomics, income distribution and labour economics.

Dwayne Benjamin received his Ph.D. from Princeton University in 1989, before joining the University of Toronto, where he is currently Professor of Economics.

In 1996-97 he taught at the Woodrow Wilson School, Princeton University, and he has also been a visiting scholar at the Australian National University (ANU). His research focuses on a variety of labour market issues in Canada and the US, as well as developing countries. In a Canadian context, he has explored questions pertaining to immigration, minimum wages, and continues to investigate issues related to aging. For developing countries, his main interests concern the connections between labour market institutions and household welfare. His current projects focus on the impact on households of economic transition in China, including the consequences of institutional reform for the elderly.

Jean-Michel Cousineau is a labour economist, and is currently Professor at the School of Industrial Relations and Research Fellow at the Centre de recherche et développement en économique (CRDE), at the University of Montreal. His current research interests include the economics of poverty and social indicators.

Nicole M. Fortin is Associate Professor of Economics at the University of British Columbia and Research Associate at the Centre de recherche et développement en économique (CRDE) at the University of Montreal, and at the Centre interuniversitaire de recherche en analyse des organisations (CIRANO). She is a specialist in non-parametric analysis in labour economics and her recent research has focused on gender and policy issues.

David A. Green is Associate Professor of Economics at the University of British Columbia. He completed his undergraduate work at Queen's University and his Ph.D. at Stanford University. His main research areas of interest are wage and earnings inequality, the impact of social programs on the labour market, and the interaction of technology and the labour market.

Morley Gunderson holds the Canadian Imperial Bank of Commerce Chair in Youth Employment at the University of Toronto, where he is Professor at the Centre for Industrial Relations (Director from 1985-97) and the Department of Economics. He is also a Research Associate of the Institute of Policy Analysis, the Centre for International Studies, and the Institute for Human Development, Life Course as well as an Adjunct Scientist at the Institute for Work and Health. His current research interests include: youth employment, voluntary activity, gender discrimination, the aging workforce, pensions and mandatory retirement, public sector wages, immigration, childcare arrangements and labour market behaviour, workers' compensation, and the impact of globalization on the employment relationship and labour policy.

Peter Kuhn is Professor of Economics at the University of California, Santa Barbara. He received his Ph.D. from Harvard University in 1983. Since then he has taught at the University of Western Ontario and McMaster University. He has been a visiting Professor at Princeton University, University College London, the London School of Economics, the University of Munich, and the Australian National University (ANU). Kuhn has published empirical and theoretical papers on several aspects of labour economics, including trade unionism, discrimination, immigration, displaced workers, unemployment, employment contracts, and comparative labour markets. His current research interests include the effects of information technology on labour markets and the role of non-cognitive skills in wage determination.

Guy Lacroix has a Ph.D. in economics from Laval University and has completed postdoctoral studies at Princeton University. He is currently Professor in the Department of Economics at Laval University. Guy Lacroix specializes in labour economics, applied econometrics, and health economics. His research focuses on the interaction of income security policies (in particular welfare and unemployment insurance programs) and individuals' labour market behaviour, as well as the impact of training programs on the labour market transitions of disadvantaged individuals.

Thomas Lemieux is Professor of Economics at the University of British Columbia and Research Associate at the National Bureau of Economic Research (NBER), the Centre de recherche et développement en économique (CRDE) at the University of Montreal, and the Centre interuniversitaire de recherche en analyse des organisations (CIRANO). He is a specialist in labour economics and has conducted extensive research on the determinants of the structure of wages in OECD countries.

W. Craig Riddell is Professor in the Department of Economics at the University of British Columbia and an Associate of the Canadian Institute for Advanced Research (CIAR). His research interests are in labour economics, labour relations and public policy. His current research focuses on unemployment and labour market dynamics, the role of human capital in economic growth, experimental and nonexperimental approaches to the evaluation of social programs, unionization and collective bargaining, gender differences in labour market behaviour and outcomes, unemployment insurance and social assistance, and education and training. Professor Riddell is former Head of the Department of Economics at UBC, former Academic Co-Chair of the Canadian Employment

Research Forum (CERF), and Past-President of the Canadian Economics Association.

France St-Hilaire is Vice-President, Research at the Institute for Research on Public Policy (IRPP). She joined IRPP as a research director in 1992. She currently oversees the Institute's research agenda and coordinates ongoing projects on human capital and labour market policy. France St-Hilaire is the author of a number of monographs and articles in the areas of public finance, social policy and fiscal federalism. She holds a graduate degree in economics from the University of Montreal. Prior to joining IRPP, she worked as a researcher at the Institute for Policy Analysis of the University of Toronto and in the Department of Economics of the University of Western Ontario.

Arthur Sweetman is currently an Assistant Professor in the School of Policy Studies at Queen's University. He studies economic issues related to labour markets and health, and has done or is doing research on the economics of education, government programs for the disabled, immigration, unemployment insurance (employment insurance), unions, discrimination, displaced workers and microfinance. He is an academic member of the Western Research Network on Education and Training (WRNET), a SSHRC sponsored initiative that is studying the connections between education and work.

François Vaillancourt holds a Ph.D. from Queen's University (1978) and is currently Professor of Economics and Research Fellow at the Centre de recherche et développement en économique (CRDE) at the University of Montreal, and Fellow at the C.D. Howe Institute. He teaches, conducts research and has published extensively in the areas of public finance and the economics of language. He has conducted research and acted as a consultant for organizations such as the Canadian Tax Foundation, the Conseil de la langue française, the Department of Finance, the Economic Council of Canada, Statistics Canada and the World Bank.

MEMBER OF THE SCABRINI GROUP

Quebec, Canada
2000